Dolly & Zane Grey

WESTERN LITERATURE SERIES

Dol...

Zane Grey

LETTERS FROM A MARRIAGE

EDITED AND WITH COMMENTARY BY

Candace C. Kant

UNIVERSITY OF NEVADA PRESS

RENO & LAS VEGAS

Western Literature Series
University of Nevada Press, Reno, Nevada 89557 USA
Copyright © 2008 by University of Nevada Press
All rights reserved
Manufactured in the United States of America
Design by Kathleen Szawiola

Library of Congress Cataloging-in-Publication Data
Grey, Zane, 1872–1939.
[Correspondence. Selections]
Dolly and Zane Grey : letters from a marriage / edited and with
commentary by Candace C. Kant.
p. cm. — (Western literature series)
Includes bibliographical references and index.
ISBN 978-0-87417-749-7 (hardcover : alk. paper)
1. Grey, Zane, 1872–1939—Correspondence.
2. Authors, American—20th century—Correspondence.
3. West (U.S.)—In literature. I. Grey, Lina Elise, d. 1957.
II. Kant, Candace C., 1949– III. Title.
PS3513.R6545Z485 2008
813'.52—dc22
[B]   2007040972

The paper used in this book is a recycled stock made from 50
percent post-consumer waste materials and meets the requirements
of American National Standard for Information Sciences—
Permanence of Paper for Printed Library Materials, ANSI/NISO
Z39.48–1992 (R2002). Binding materials were selected for strength
and durability.

FIRST PRINTING
17   16   15   14   13   12   11   10   09   08
5   4   3   2   1

For Doc and Dolly

"Would'st have a bell of deep and perfect sound,
So perfect that the metal melts in air
And is all music? Seek thou, then with care
The fairest virgin in thy land around."
So Chinese priests of making gongs expound,
That all their folk may hasten, glad, to prayer.
"When thou has found the woman pure and fair
In the hot metal then must she be drowned."

To me, a poet, came a maiden bright,
Who looked not back, who would become a part
Of all my music, die that she might give
My song new harmonies: In the fierce light
And flaming of the furnace of my heart
Her girlhood perished that my songs might live.

Inscribed by hand in Zane Grey's Journal,
November 4, 1909

CONTENTS

CONTENTS

ILLUSTRATIONS

(following page 202)

Lina Elise Grey, "Dolly," 1890s
Pearl Zane Grey, University of Pennsylvania, late 1890s
Dolly, Lackawaxen
Zane Grey, Lackawaxen, circa 1910
Dolly, circa 1906
Zane Grey, late 1890s
Dolly, circa 1906
Dolly with a bass, Delaware River close to Lackawaxen
Dolly, Lackawaxen, circa 1906
Dolly and Zane, Lackawaxen, 1906
Dolly and Zane, Lackawaxen, 1906
Lillian Wilhelm, circa 1908
Lillian Wilhelm, Lillian's sister, Claire, and Zane Grey, circa 1915
Lillian Wilhelm, Zane Grey, and Claire Wilhelm, Grand Canyon,
    circa 1915
Elma Swartz and Lillian Wilhelm, Lackawaxen, circa 1912
Elma Swartz, Claire Wilhelm, and Lillian Wilhelm, Lackawaxen,
    circa 1912
Lillian Wilhelm, Claire Wilhelm, and Elma Swartz, Delaware River at
    Lackawaxen, circa 1912
Elma Swartz, Lackawaxen, 1912
Lillian Wilhelm, Claire Wilhelm, Elma Swartz, and Emmeline Jones,
    Lackawaxen, 1916
Emmeline Jones, Elma Swartz, Lillian Wilhelm, and Dorothy
    Ackerman, Lackawaxen, 1916
Dorothy Ackerman, Long Key, Florida, 1916

PREFACE

ALMOST AS MANY WORDS have been written about Zane Grey as he wrote himself. There are literary analyses of his work, anecdotal tales of his adventures, magazine articles about various aspects of his life from his birthplace to the fishing spots he frequented, catalogs of his many books and articles and of the films made from his work, and several biographical treatments, including a recent excellent biography by Tom Pauly, *Zane Grey: His Life, His Adventures, His Women.* This book falls into none of those categories. Instead, it focuses on the private side of the man who was Zane Grey and the startling relationship he had with his wife, Dolly. Perhaps outwardly conventional, their marriage was strikingly unconventional when revealed—as it is—in their letters. Moreover, for the first time this work brings Dolly Grey, who is usually only addressed peripherally, into the center of the picture and gives her equal billing with her famous husband. Of the two, Dolly has perhaps the more complicated and appealing personality.

The practice of writing letters and conducting a relationship through the written word was not unusual when they met in 1900, before the age of telephones and instantaneous electronic mail. The post was delivered twice a day, and most young couples, particularly in an urban setting, would have communicated through that method. After the Greys had married and were apart for months on end, the relationship was continued through writing, their primary means of communication. Even after the rise of telephones and other means of conversing, such as radios, the habit of writing was so ingrained in both of them that they continued this form of discourse. Indeed, in the thirties, when Zane was most often in the South Seas, letters were the most inexpensive way to impart information, a concern during the Depression years. Both Zane and Dolly were exceptionally skillful with the written word, and their letters are the most eloquent expression of their feelings and the facts of their lives.

These letters were saved by Dolly, then by her children, though some are clearly missing. I came to know Loren Grey, their youngest son and former president of Zane Grey, Inc., while working on an earlier book, *Zane Grey's Arizona.* He made his parents' letters available to me. In editing the letters, I have refrained from inserting my voice, only adding what is necessary to clarify and connect, letting the letters tell Dolly and Zane's story in their own words. Where there was duplication, I selected the most informative letter to include. I shortened some letters that were very long by incising material that in my opinion did not contribute any new information or was extraneous to the story. To give flavor to the tale, I did leave in material about the historical context, especially that which revealed everyday living, where it was possible to do so without unnecessarily lengthening an already lengthy manuscript. To further flesh out the tale when the story called for it, business letters and letters from other sources were included. Flourishes in the letters, which were written by hand, are indicated by long dashes (————). Loren Grey also made available to me a diary that Dolly kept, some of which had been published previously in Frank Gruber's biography, *Zane Grey.*

These letters and diary reveal much about Zane and Dolly's relationship and their lives. They make it clear that Zane was intimately involved with other women from the early years of the marriage until the end of his life and that Dolly knew all about it. This aspect of their marriage—that is, Zane and Dolly's efforts to cloak his other relationships with respectability—has been available to other researchers but has not been revealed until recently, with Tom Pauly's biography. It is as if there was a conspiracy of silence, perpetuating that silence originally developed by Zane and Dolly to hide the clay feet of a man who became almost legendary. Now the family wishes the truth to be known. There is an unexplored depth to the relationship that offers a valuable lesson in love, commitment, and lasting marriage and an insight into the toll that genius takes—a lesson that is relevant to modern life.

ACKNOWLEDGMENTS

MANY PEOPLE have contributed to this work, and I thank them. Loren Grey's constant helpfulness was indispensable. He and Zane Grey, Inc., made the letters available, but Loren did more than that. He shared his memories, sometimes pleasant and sometimes painful, with me, and he gave me insights into his father's and mother's personalities as well as the family dynamics at work. Bonnie, Loren's beloved wife, bubbled with enthusiasm over the manuscript, boosting my confidence. I am so sorry she and Loren are not here to see the book published. The College of Southern Nevada graciously awarded me a sabbatical to complete the manuscript, and many of my colleagues voiced encouragement. Alan Balboni, especially, has always given me constructive criticism when necessary and motivating words when those were needed. Michael Green said the right word to the right person at the right time. Joan McGee proofread the entire manuscript and spotted errors I had missed. Joanne O'Hare at the University of Nevada Press has been steadfast in her commitment to this project. But my greatest debt is to my family. Charles, my son, has given me incentive, as he has out-published me in a very demanding field but still takes interest in my work. Caren, my daughter, has urged me to complete this project and to put things in perspective. My granddaughter, Sophia, is my inspiration. My husband, Jim, has put up with this project for a very long time with patience, forbearance, encouragement, and interest. To all of these individuals, my deepest, heartfelt thanks.

Dolly & Zane Grey

Introduction

I T   I S   I M P O S S I B L E   to estimate the impact that Zane Grey had on the reading and movie-viewing public in the early years of the twentieth century without resorting to anecdote. His first successful novel, *Heritage of the Desert* (1910), sold over eight hundred thousand copies. His second, *Riders of the Purple Sage* (1912), sold over one million copies in its first year of publication, making Zane Grey an author of national and even international reputation. His literary output was overwhelming by any measure. By his death in 1939, his writing filled over ninety-six volumes, including western romances, short stories, baseball tales, fishing adventure sagas, one novel set in Tahiti, and another set in Australia. His books were on best-seller lists in hardbound editions beginning in 1915 with *The Lone Star Ranger,* again in 1917 with *Wildfire,* and then every year thereafter from 1917 to 1924.[1] Zane Grey became the name for a huge enterprise based on his writing, including magazine serials, hardbound books, international editions, movie versions, stage versions, comic strips, children's books, and eventually a corporate structure. The public demand for his work was immeasurable. His wife Dolly once wrote, "You, the man, must live up to the name you have created. You can't quit. You can't be anything but great. You dare not. In that sense, you don't even belong to yourself, but to the millions to whom you stand for an ideal."[2]

As usual she was right, at least in part, for he had not created that name alone. Dolly Grey guided, directed, and managed Zane Grey's career just as surely as if she were his business partner rather than his wife. Her role has been neglected by others who examined his life, because it was not a public role. He supplied the imagination, the ability to transform the emotions he felt into the western romances he wrote, and the name. She supplied the expertise in editing and the business acumen, for she managed all affairs with editors, publishers, and Hollywood producers and directors.

Together they created an image that defined their outward lives. Grey's books were promoted as reading material appropriate for all ages, from young readers to the aged, acceptable both in schools and in libraries. Should there be anything in his personal life that contradicted that image, the marketability of his work would suffer. And there was something in his personal life that threatened his success: his numerous affairs with other women.

In two senses Grey's life was itself a fiction. Outwardly, he lived a conventional married life with Dolly and their three children. But this was a facade that concealed his many dalliances with young women, which both Zane and Dolly took great pains to hide. Ironically, this hidden life also contained elements of fantasy. In it he lived and relived the romantic plots he created, casting himself as the romantic hero, wooing and winning the young and beautiful heroine. In a letter to Robert Hobart Davis, Zane's friend and literary agent, Dolly referred in an oblique way to this trait, writing, "the man has always lived in a land of make-believe, and has clothed all his own affairs in the shining garments of romance, and it is as if these were rent and torn and smirched."[3] While she was referring to Zane's reaction to John O'Hara's *Appointment at Samarra,* her words speak volumes about Zane's mind.

Much of Zane and Dolly's married life was spent apart. In the early years, he traveled in the West three to four months out of the year then spent the coldest months of the winter in Long Key, Florida, or in California, usually with feminine companions, leaving Dolly behind. Later, in the twenties, he discovered the South Seas and fished there for as much as six months at a time, spending more time in Oregon in the summers, again without his wife. The two maintained their relationship through letters, thousands of letters, written over a span of thirty-nine years, from the time they met in

1990 until Zane's death in 1939. These letters run the gamut of emotions, from mushy love letters to bitter documents full of animosity, from reports of business matters to reproaches regarding failures and mistakes.

The letters reveal that their marriage was anything but ordinary. Indeed, throughout the thirty-four-year marriage Dolly was far from the only woman in Zane's life. What is even more startling is that she was completely aware of it and, in order to conceal the truth from the public, became an unwilling accomplice. She knew of this part of his nature from the years of their courtship and at least initially hoped that he would leave that behind him as marriage provided for his emotional and physical needs. That was not to be, and Dolly had to adjust to the reality of what her relationship to her husband was. She endured years of bitter loneliness, and for a time the marriage was in great peril, but divorce was unthinkable to women of her class and station in that time period, particularly those with children. In 1911 she wrote in her diary, "Marriage is for children. They are the closest bond between husband and wife, a bond which should hold when all other things fail."[4]

After the move to California in 1918, she emerged from her ordeal with resignation to his habits and determination to be everything else to her husband, if not his only lover. She came to look upon her earlier self as a "fearful prude" and wrote in her diary that it was "only the California atmosphere, or perhaps I should say the western environment, that finally released me after the age of thirty."[5] Not only did she accept his habits, she collaborated in hiding them from the public, actively protecting him from the consequences of his actions, which often were naive, thoughtless, and irresponsible. The women were referred to as secretaries (who did little typing), nieces (of which he had none), or literary assistants (whom he did not need, since he had Dolly). Chaperones were along to prevent talk, and Dolly even hosted the women in her own home, her presence assuring the appearance of propriety. Instead of dwelling on the failings of her marriage, she concentrated on building a financial empire based on his work. Money earned from his writing was divided in half. He used his portion for yachts and fishing. She put hers in real-estate and stock-market investments, eventually becoming the president of a bank.

In the relaxed atmosphere of Southern California, with the presence of the film industry and the increasing availability and acceptability of divorce in the twenties, Dolly still did not leave her philandering husband. This might be attributed to her affinity for his great wealth, but according to the divorces granted in those days, she would have received a large portion of the wealth earned and rights to that yet to be earned, so that reason does not stand the test. It might be said that she had become accustomed to the lifestyle, with a house in Catalina and another in Altadena, servants, luxury cars, and the respect and privilege afforded to her as Mrs. Zane Grey. But her letters suggest that all that meant only additional worries for her. What does stand out is her unwavering belief in his genius, steadfast commitment to him, understanding of the demons that plagued him, and a genuine affection. On their twenty-ninth anniversary she wrote,

> I wonder if anyone has had as varied and eventful a life as I have during twenty-nine years. After all, despite the fact that I dare not mention all this passage of time to Z.G., I think it is quite an achievement to be "Happy Though Married" for such a long time. But it has always been my claim that friendship and understanding and a working together are the bases for lasting marriages. I will not say that the modern method of on again off again may not be better. Perhaps I should not compare them at all. Perhaps what they do now with short marriages and easy divorces are a product of the times and a necessity of the times. However, even the people of our generation are getting their divorces just the same. But somehow I have the feeling that Doc and I will stick it out to the end, even though I would never seek to hold him if he desired any other arrangement.[6]

The portrait of Zane that emerges from his letters is not always a flattering one, and his fans may well be dismayed. It should be remembered, however, that he was a product of his times, and in that era the peccadillos of men, particularly wealthy men, were winked at by society. Indeed, Dolly looked realistically at the environment into which Zane had been born, and she once remarked about his family that "they have always believed that a man can do anything, but that a woman should be above reproach."[7] Zane could hardly have helped having this point of view himself.

In the early years of his marriage, Zane earnestly tried not to give in to temptation, but he usually failed. In a letter written in 1906, shortly after his marriage, he tells Dolly of his struggles,

> I have tried to stop profanity. The old words fly to my lips. I have tried to kill the deadly sweetness of conscious power over women. A pair of dark blue eyes makes me a tiger. I loved my sweetheart in honest ways more than any other: I love, I love my wife, yet such iron I am that there is no change.

He tried to hide his dalliances from her, but she always knew.

When the money began pouring in after the publication of *Heritage of the Desert* in 1910 and he was able to indulge his desires, he made no further attempt to shield her from his nature, doing exactly what he wanted, at a cost to all those around him. Nevertheless, it would be an error to conclude that he was heartless. He sincerely loved his wife and deeply regretted causing her pain, but he equally sincerely felt that the emotions aroused in him by his flirtations were necessary to his writing and were poured into his work. Holding her to a higher standard than he set for himself, he believed her jealousy was a base emotion that she should be able to rise above, seeing his true nature. And with a twisted perception of reality, he denied any immorality. Writing to his friend Alvah James, he said,

> When I read some of your letter to Dolly, she asked; "What does he mean by moral?" So far as I am concerned I can remember only a couple or at most a very few times when I might have been called immoral. And even then considering my simplicity, my intensity, my sincerity, I doubt that it could have been called so. Every emotion I ever had has gone into my books.[8]

When he was honest with himself, which happened most often in the midst of one of his black moods or when he awoke in the middle of the night, he bitterly reproached himself for his failings, particularly for having hurt Dolly. This happened more often as he grew older. Writing to James in 1936, he stated, "No doubt you sacrificed yourself for your family. I never did that, I sacrificed everybody." Self-doubt and periodic bouts of depression, which he called his black moods, tortured him. For all his pursuits—fishing, baseball, women, writing—the prize always eluded him. Never trusting those around him, convinced that he was surrounded by conspiracies, he never allowed anyone except Dolly to be truly emotionally close to him. Perhaps that was a result of the hidden portion of his life, which made him suspicious and untrusting. Although surrounded by an entourage at all times, he was always lonely. In all of the letters over thirty-nine years, he only once stated that he felt really happy.[9]

As to the exact nature of his relationships with the other women, it is impossible to say. Ambiguity will always remain, because the letters written to them and by them were destroyed after his death.[10] Those few letters that exist do not deal with any matters of substance or emotion. We have only what Dolly and Zane said in regards to those relationships in their letters to each other. Yet that is enough to conclude that these affairs were both emotional and physical and were sufficiently threatening that both Zane and Dolly made every attempt to cloak them with a respectability they did not have.

Grey developed deep, involved relationships with each woman that were not just sexual in nature, but emotional and intellectual as well. He remained involved with the women for long periods of time, in Mildred Smith's case for over fifteen years. And for Zane the women were a part of his work, or so he thought. They aroused in him the emotions that he then channeled into his writing, and they served as prototypes for his heroines, sometimes directly, like Lillian Wilhelm for Mescal in *Heritage of the Desert* and Bernice Campbell for Martha Ann Dixon in *Wyoming*, for example, but more frequently, as composites of the women he had known. Dolly once wrote with great insight, "A genius needs to be fed by many personalties which he mashes and grinds up as a mill does, in order to get the finished product."[11]

Dolly was talented, capable, well educated in her own right, and ambitious, but she was willing to play a secondary, supportive role. She has appeared superhumanly tolerant, patient, and long suffering, sacrificing her immediate needs for a larger vision. In reality she has been defined by men, reduced to the supporting role while Zane has been the star. Now her voice, clear and articulate, reveals that she was not the long-suffering, self-sacrificing victim, although she did like to paint herself that way to her husband. She had a voice and a will of her own. She was accomplished, confident, comfortable with publishers, movie-studio heads, and bank presidents. She was the one solid, steadying influence for her children and her famous husband. She was his Northern Star. They completed each other. Zane Grey would never have been the success he was if there had been no Dolly. This is their story.

1900–1912

CHAPTER 1

The Brown-Eyed Rose and
the Black-Eyed Devil

LACKAWAXEN VILLAGE lies on a peninsula of meadow framed by the blue water of the Delaware River and the ripples of Lackawaxen Creek. The river boasts trout, smallmouth bass, and walleye, and, in the late spring, shad.[1] On either side are hills thick with forest and alive with wildlife of all varieties. The region still attracts sportsmen who seek a primitive environment, but in 1900 it boasted a large hotel, the Delaware House, built in 1852. Situated on Pennsylvania's northeastern border with New York State, it was less than a hundred miles from New York City as the crow flies, only three hours away by the Erie Railroad, and was a popular resort for jaded New Yorkers fleeing the heat and noise of the city.

Zane Grey, a young dentist from New York City, was there for fishing and canoeing in the summer of 1900 with his brother, R.C.[2] Seventeen-year-old Lina Roth, or Dolly as her family called her, was there in the company of her mother and two girlfriends, recovering from the death of her father. One afternoon late in August, Dolly and her friends were enjoying the cool breeze on the bank of the river. So intent were they on their conversation that they failed to notice the approach of a canoe until it touched the shore. In it were Zane and R.C., equipped with cameras, photographing the young women.[3]

Dolly found the older man intriguing (he was twenty-eight). Zane, or Doc as he was called, was admired by many women. In fact much of his practice consisted of young ladies who enjoyed the attentions of a handsome dentist. He was of medium stature with thick black hair, heavy brows, and a brooding demeanor. His semiprofessional baseball career and his fishing, canoeing, and hiking gave him an athletic build. His moody dark eyes drew Dolly almost as much as the literary ambitions he confided to her. He was an irrepressible flirt, she instantly knew, and much of what he said could not be taken seriously, but he seemed fascinated by her mind, a trait not commonly found in men of that era. For Dolly was an intellectual and had ambitions. She was to enter Hunter College that fall to study English literature and planned to continue on to Columbia University and eventually to teach. She was familiar with the music of the great composers, loved great literature, and was fluent in German.

She was also good humored, with an air of confidence and satisfaction that intrigued Zane. Strikingly handsome, she was not tall or slender, but curvaceous. Her long hair was the color of chestnuts with golden highlights, and she wore it up to enhance her delicately shaped and finely balanced features. She too was athletic, enjoying long hikes and playing basketball, but had a quiet, poised, introspective nature and even in a crowd was remarkable for her serenity.

Zane returned to New York only a few days after they met, and Dolly, still in Lackawaxen, wrote a flirtatious and frivolous letter to him almost immediately.

> Is it vain of me to tell you this? No, because we love each other. I wouldn't tell anybody else.
>
> Last night we had a moonlight sail which was perfectly delicious.
>
> The only thing on such occasions is that I miss you so much, always wishing you were with me.[4]

In the city they met around her schedule of studies and his practice. He escorted her to dinner and shows, called on her at home, and took her for walks. She told him of her college adventures. They communicated by letter, making arrangements to meet, giving reasons why they could not, or simply talking. By December he pressed her about her feelings toward him. She coyly replied,

DECEMBER 13, 1900

I hardly know what to say about it. I didn't like it for it frightened me a little. I will, however, be perfectly honest with you, and try to tell you how I feel, as well as I can. Sunday, when you came I did have a more or less indifferent feeling, and it has been so all this week. Tomorrow it might be different again. I can't tell. There was one time when I thought I almost loved you, and that feeling may come again.

It is hard to explain, but I think it is because I go to college, and see so much of other girls, and enjoy myself with them, that I feel indifferent at times. Besides, I am too young to think of such things. Before I met you, I never thought of love, and if I did, I thought of it as something in the far future. I expected to love someone sometime, and knew that when I did, it would be with my whole heart and soul. Whether I ever will love you in that way I can not tell, and you will have to have a great deal of patience with me. Perhaps if you don't say anything or write anything to me about it for awhile it will be better . . .

Yours,

Lina R.

Arguments and misunderstandings occurred. Both had other companions and commitments, and there were conflicting demands of school, family, and work. What made it more difficult was that Dolly's mother did not like Zane. In her eyes he had little to offer her daughter. A dentist who frittered his time away with baseball and fishing was not destined for success, and his admiration of women hinted of trouble. His background, in her eyes, was unexceptional, not just because Ohio was regarded by New Yorkers as a primitive backwoods, but also because of the Greys' financial losses in the 1890s. Even the Zanes of Revolutionary War fame, for whom Zanesville was named, failed to impress her. Finally, there was the eleven-year age difference. Dolly was just too young to become serious about an older man.

Her mother's disapproval sometimes made it difficult for Dolly to invite Zane to her home. At those times Dolly came to his office or they met somewhere else. Central Park was their favorite place, for there they could stroll about, occasionally finding themselves secluded from others who also enjoyed the park. Dolly and her family traveled to Lackawaxen each summer for a few weeks, and often those visits coincided with Zane's presence there.

Mrs. Roth's opposition may have strengthened Zane and Dolly's attraction for each other, but Zane resented her disapproval and her efforts to prevent Dolly from becoming more attached to him. Dolly's mother encouraged her daughter to entertain other suitors, making Zane jealous, even though he condescendingly dismissed Dolly's feelings about his other girlfriends. First at Hunter College, then at Columbia, Dolly met many young men and was surrounded by a lively group of friends who were warmly welcomed to her mother's apartment, making Zane quite upset.

JANUARY 5, 1902

Dear Dolly,

I am not writing this note to apologize. I don't intend to do that. I am tired of being two-faced with that fellow and I refuse to be so any longer.

I wish to say how utterly absurd you are when you reproach me as you did today about my going with other girls and your being jealous. Why, you can't understand what jealousy is! You might feel it in some childish fashion, but a woman's jealousy you cannot appreciate, let alone feel.

Jealousy is a horrible thing. It sent me away from you today when I was perfectly happy. It changed that sweet feeling of love into something terrible. Tonight I am miserable. I feel like I wanted to go and get drunk; to disgrace myself; to do something awful.

You had the nerve to tell me to my face that he doesn't care for you? Do you mean to tell me that he would not care for a woman that made me, even me, love her? There is a great deal of egotism in that remark but it is expressive of what I feel. Which is; that if I love you, men who have not had the advantages I have had to know women, simply could not help it.

I am tired of trying to see you alone and be like other lovers are, you are not like any other girl. If you were, I would not have this feeling tonight which unnerves me and brings up all that is worst in my nature.

If I could see you alone even occasionally and you would care for me as you did for fifteen minutes today, I would be happy and contented and the time might come when I could accomplish something and you would be proud of me. As it is, what chance have I to show you the best that is in me? I haven't any chance.

You blame me for so much that is your fault. I want to know positively if you are ever going to be like other women? Are you always going to be about fifteen years old? Are you always going to put someone before me? If you are I would like to know it now and perhaps I might save myself a great deal of unhappiness.

When I think of the places I might go; of the girls I might go to see and all that, I get angry with myself. You have spoiled that. Even when I do go I would rather have you. It would be all right if we could be like other people. But I am not happy at all. I feel like a thief or a convict when I am in your house. I have been made to feel that you cannot go anyplace with me; that I am up alone with you for a few minutes only because it can't be helped, etc., etc. I say, I am tired of it.

I suppose you don't believe that I know any nice girls, girls just as nice as you are, who are just as well brought up and whose mothers are quite as particular as yours, who treat me differently. Well, I do.

Can't you understand that I love you and you are all the world to me? I don't care for anybody else. I want you.

Now if you will please sit down and write me your ideas upon this you would save a great deal of unhappiness for both of us, especially if you will do as any girl would who loved a man.

Yours

Pearl

On another evening when he arrived at her home to find another young man present, he wrote,

Dolly,

I was brutal to you today, but I could not help it. I was suffering for myself and I had to be brutal to resist your sweet pleading. When it was all over I cried like a baby or a fool. I had not intended writing you but I have thought that perhaps it would be best if I did. You were so shocked, so surprised that you seemed to think it was a jest. I said that I refused to accept the place you offer me and I meant it. I could not be satisfied to be considered last in everything. You always say you consider me first but when it comes to the test, you do not.

I never dreamed that I could love anyone as well as I have you. To be in your presence was a delight to me. When you touched me I would thrill with joy, and when you kissed me I became a madman almost. I was proud of you, of your beauty, of your wit and cleverness, of everything that was yours. I gloried in the fact that I had such a singular nature that I had given no other woman anything of love or passion, and I would have shown it a thousand times more had you allowed me. I remained in New York despite all the wishes of my folk at home. I told my mother and brothers all about you, something heretofore unheard of in me, and I have given up all the girls I ever knew for you. I thought of you all the time. This is the simple, entire truth. You have just told me that I was tired of you. So much for your understanding me. When we parted at Lackawaxen my heart was heavy and I had a foreboding of evil as I feared those were the last of our happy days. We might have known that it could not last.

When I was last up to see you I knew that my worst fears were realized. I found that I could not see you when I wished, not to say anything of being alone with you. Your old interests and attractions came back with a rush as soon as you returned to the city, and it was simply impossible that I could be first in your thoughts. I could not hope to influence you against all these things, especially your own desire for them. Do you think I could stand somewhere in the background and see all of this? To note your acceptance of attentions from other men, and I don't mean everyday platonic friendship, to hear you say you could not see me when I wished, and to have that old feeling of uncertainty come back. I might have been able to stand that before the trip to

Lackawaxen, but after your kisses, your promises, your sweet forgetfulness of self, I could never do it. I tell you I came down to earth with a dull thud last Wednesday night when I came to see you. I had been in the clouds.

I have been a better man in every way since I have known you and that is something a woman's influence never did for me before. Now that it is gone what do you suppose will become of me?

If you wish your letters and pictures, especially those pictures you have not seen, I will send them or destroy them as you wish. That is all, Dolly. You are free.

Dolly did not disagree with her mother that she was superior in breeding, background, and education to Zane, but she thought he could overcome his deficiencies with her help. Zane admitted his shortcomings, but that did not prevent explosive reactions when he thought his dignity had been assaulted.

NOVEMBER 2, 1903

I have never, in our acquaintance, been as angry as I am now. Red said my face was white as a sheet. I haven't looked at it, but I believe him. Why you wish to humiliate me before my brother and Ellie is incomprehensible to me. I positively deny your insinuation that I have no refinement. I may have abrupt mannerisms but, at least, I am not the cad you make me out.

If your Grandmother took offense at my silly attempt at facetiousness she is a fussy old fool. I meant nothing but fun. I simply tried to say something pleasant. Usually I am so serious that I offend people on that score. Now that I have made an ass out of myself trying to be funny I'll know better in the future. When I see your grandmother again, and I hope I won't, I will not speak to her at all. When you sat back there, with that amused smirk on your face and told Red and Ellie that, I simply—well, all I will say is that you don't let the grass grow under your feet in that path you are walking which leads to where I shall want nothing whatever to do with you.

A woman who ought to know me well, and who could make that mistake, does not think very much of her own side of the question. Several times you corrected me, or reproved me, in the presence of others, and whether or not I was guilty has nothing to do with it. I should not advise you to attempt it in the future. If people misunderstand me I cannot help that: If they think I am a boor because I try to be pleasant that is no fault of mine. I want you to distinctly understand even if I do make grammatical mistakes and errors of etiquette, that I think I am far removed from any men I ever met at your house or your friends.

I have told you a thousand times to be careful in what you said to me, for I cannot help my nature. You seem to try with all your might to make me angry with you, to stand in your own light. For once I read in your eyes what you think of me, and it made me wild. I have no vocabulary to tell you what I feel, and I shall try no further. Suffice it to add that when I have told you nearly all about myself, of my early life and its trials, of my weakness, or the struggle I have made to be something, and especially when I have cared so much and am caring more all the time, to find that I have been in an unsympathetic, insipid, unfeeling school, I am disgusted. All the influence you ever had, and it had been wonderful, would not amount to a hill of pins at this moment. I can't strike a woman, I can't do anything. But I'll not have you trample on my pride again.

Dolly apologized, and he responded,

NOVEMBER 4, 1903

My Dear Dolly,

Your letter rec'd. I have forgiven you. What you said did not make me love you any the less. I care just as much as ever. Only it hurt terribly. I couldn't see why a woman who seems to want a man to become what you have tried to help me to be will say such things, especially when they are not absolutely or wholly true. I think the great trouble is that I have asked you so much, and looked to you so much that you lost sight of the fact that I am as proud as the devil. That was a simple little thing you said, but it made me crazy, and no one saying it, besides you, could have made me so angry.

Well, it's past. Please do not make yourself ill on my account. That's what you always do, make yourself ill so I have no chance to do anything but forgive you. If you wish I should like to see you tomorrow at lunchtime.

Yours

Pearl

Zane was bored with dentistry and wanted to write. Dolly thought he had a talent for writing if it could be developed, disciplined, and channeled. Her studies gave her the knowledge and background he did not have, and she encouraged him to begin. Never doing anything halfway, Zane began a novel about the heroic actions of his great-great-grandmother, Elizabeth Zane, during the American Revolution. He called it *Betty Zane*. With the zeal of the novice he wrote feverishly through the winter of 1901–2, alternating between elation and despair and often turning to Dolly for help.

He asked her advice on literary matters and wanted her encouragement, but writing took a toll on his emotions. One moment he was happy, full of confidence; the next, plunged into deepest despair, convinced that life was pointless and all effort futile. What surrounded him registered acutely on his senses, giving him a talent for description, but at a price. Lack of self-esteem, a feeling that his early years had been wasted, and the impossibly high standards he set for himself brought periodic bouts of torturous depression. When these moods beset him, Dolly responded with insight, understanding, and practical advice.

OCTOBER 20, 1901

Tuesday Eve

Dear Pearl,

I can't tell you how sorry—that's not the right word—I feel for you when you feel the way you did for the last few days, and yet I can understand it perfectly. A nature like yours is one which fluctuates from the heights to the depths, and I know that to you the depths are very deep and dark. It is part of that emotional make-up which gives you the power to write. And, Pearl, you know that I believe you have that power. That you unfortunately twisted and distorted that thoughtless remark of mine was probably due to your state of mind. At any rate, I know you did not feel so about it on Sunday. It was only after you became discouraged that you misconstrued it. You say that I don't believe in your views about women, etc. There you are mistaken. I don't think you can find anyone who believes in you more thoroughly than I do. That I fight against your opinions at first is natural, for they are disillusionment and often pain, but in nine cases out of ten, I have had to admit to myself that you

were right. And I have come to believe that you are right in most of your judg-
ments about human nature, even though I still maintain that you look too
much on the dark side. It seems to me that life would be too bitter for me if I
let the evil overshadow the good the way you do. In every person in this world
there is some good if we only try to seek it out.

Take yourself for instance. Don't be offended at this, please, or take it in
the wrong way. You yourself are not perfect and have certain faults which may
seem as heinous to certain persons as their characteristics seem to you. But do
you think that if I allowed your faults to look larger to me than your better
qualities, I would care for you as I do? And the same way you towards me. I
have also some very grave faults but instead of magnifying them you choose
to magnify my good qualities. I will not ask you to make any effort in that
direction towards other people but don't think that everybody is bad and out
of gear. When I find out things are very bad I feel awful for awhile but I
rebound from it. My nature is elastic. I may be an awful fool, but I am happier
and will not miss so much of what is really good by looking too much on the
dark side.

You have often told me that you have found some good in every woman.
Why not then in every man? I have found, at least with the men with whom I
come in contact, that I can trust them in some things much better than
women. For instance, I find that a woman will pick her best friend to pieces,
and I have not found a man who does that. I suppose you will laugh and say I
have had no experience with men. True enough, but I am glad to say that in
the few men I have been well acquainted with I have found good qualities as
well as bad. Human nature at its best is weak and does not combat evil—
cannot combat it very well.

Pearl, write as you feel and see, but have you ever seen anyone who is
absolutely bad? I don't think so. I grant you that there is much wickedness but
it is not all wickedness and you know it as well as I do, and you'll see it if you
let yourself.

Now, these are all very high principles, and I don't live up to them by any
means for I am only human. But even in trying we get a clearer, broader view,
and even if we don't succeed the trial will do us good.

Don't be discouraged. I am sure I am not wrong when I say you will do something great someday. But make your aim the highest, if you fall short of that the first or second time, your effort will at least help you to attain your goal. Goodnight, I have such a headache that I've been wanting to scream all evening. But I've forgotten it temporarily in writing to you. It's back now.

Your Dolly

Not all of Dolly's suggestions were welcome, even though Zane recognized her wisdom pertaining to literary matters. Once, after a chance comment she made about his writing, he responded,

OCTOBER 19, 1903

My Dear Dolly,

I am sorry to tell you that I am now in the midst of the worst "horrors" I ever had in my life. I tell you, simply because if you do not see me soon, or hear from me, you always get disturbed. I do not think I could explain to you, either. I think I have realized more than ever before what utter impossibility it is for me to become a writer. What I have written would not have interested you at all were it not that you were interested in the man who wrote it. You said, "If you happened to pick up a book with what I had written, unknown to you, you would not read it." That is the best criticism you ever made me; and, it just about killed me. I have never realized in the slightest how much I looked up to you, how much inspiration and help I really got from you, how much hope for the future I had until I knew what you really thought.

I could not, if I tried, find words in which to explain my misery for two days. As you have so often said of my reasoning power, "I am a rudderless boat upon a sea shore." You have time and time again, unconsciously put aside my opinions with contempt. It is not that you are not right, for I feel this too, it is simply that I am a poor sentimental fool. You would have been kinder if you had told me sooner.

Last night I took out my MSS and tried to destroy it. I couldn't because I felt the act would be murdering someone. I will try again, and also to give up this poor dream of becoming a writer. You will say—but not to me because I don't want to hear it—that I am very foolish and absurd and all that.

I can't help that. I have only just learned that I must unlearn all I've known, even my simplest thoughts, before I could ever become what the world calls a great writer.

Most horrible of all is the feeling that I have lost something. I do not want to be a great writer any more. I wanted to write what I saw was the truth; truth about women, and men. Not what I thought, but what I know. And you have taught me that what I think and know could never be accepted by the world.

I know what you think of me. You believe that I am gifted with a quick and facile imagination, that I have fire and all that, but you believe that I am narrowminded, that I do not know men and women, nor human nature. You think that with time and study I would get over my narrowness, and grow to love men, and look for the good in them.

My powers of observation are pretty keen, and I never saw any good in any men yet. And I've looked pretty hard for it. But I can see their greed, and selfishness, and rottenness.

In other words, a man cannot tell what he knows about such things as long as the other people don't know it too.

And I would never be content simply to echo other men's sentiments. One thing I know, and that is that I do not believe any man ever lived who had had just such experience as I have had. I never knew of one, nor heard of one. It is next to impossible to write without getting your own experience and personality.

Perhaps such men as Longfellow and Emerson and Hawthorne were ideal men. I believe they were. But what chance have I to meet such men?

The men I have known have either been men who professed Christianity, believed they were good, and at the same time were hypocrites, stole their friends' wives, and daughters, and money, or they have been men utterly worthless as far as the custom of the world goes, and therefore useless from my point of view.

To sum it all up I have been chasing a phantom. It has been hard for me to tell you this, because I know you will be sorry.

I know you are the sweetest and best little girl that ever lived, and I love you a million times more than I ever did anything else, but I am outside of all this, and you can't help me.

I cannot help but thank you because you have helped me, yet I wish to God you had never encouraged me at all.

Yours

Pearl

Most of her advice was practical, encouraging, carefully phrased, and well received, and her influence clearly shaped his writing.

The novel was finished in the spring of 1902 and sent to numerous publishers, but it was returned with letters of rejection. Dolly was firm in her reassurances, hastening to add that difficulty in getting a first work published was no reflection on the merit of the work but only what a beginning writer must expect. She could tell him of dozens of well-known authors who could not get their early work accepted. What was important was that he continue to write, experimenting with different forms, different styles.

Accordingly, Zane wrote about what he knew best, the outdoor life, and in the spring of 1902, *Recreation* magazine accepted one of his short pieces, "A Day on the Delaware." The following year, *Field and Stream* printed "Camping Out" in its February issue. He was paid ten dollars for each, confirmation he could write material that sold but hardly the breakthrough he needed.[5] What he wanted was a published work to show, something he could refer to in correspondence, something that would establish him as a writer and make editors willing to look at his other efforts. What was needed was the publication of *Betty Zane.*

Arrangements were made with Charles Francis Press, and the book was printed in December. It was illustrated by Zane, who also designed the cover. Reputedly financed by a "wealthy patient," rumors persist that the wealthy patient was Dolly, and he presented a copy to her for Christmas 1903.[6]

Regardless of who paid the printing bill, it was Dolly who encouraged him to make this effort and helped him along the way. He asked her opinion; she gave him assurance. He lacked technical knowledge of grammar and syntax; she possessed it. She rewrote his manuscript in her flowing handwriting and edited it for language and style. The book was truly a shared project, and the result a shared triumph. Zane realized that his efforts would never have occurred if it were not for Dolly and that future accomplishments would only happen if Dolly were beside him to help him. He found, almost to his surprise, that he depended on her and that their tumultuous friendship had developed into something extraordinary.

JANUARY 1902

My dear, selfish old sweetheart,

I just wanted to remind you that if I do not see you soon I won't care much what happens. I want to see you all the time.

We came very near having a scrap the other day, do you know that? And you said I was cranky. I am going to be so nice to you this year that you will be miserable unless I am with you. I am going to love you so much that you will forget your name, and when to eat and sleep. I am going to be so proud of you (and show it too) that all your girlfriends will be crazy jealous. And I am going to try to be so nice to your mama that she will want to cut you out. If I can succeed in these resolutions I will be revenged for your unkindness Tuesday. And I am pretty likely to succeed when I once make up my mind.

Well, goodnight, my dear, brown-eyed rose,

Yours

Pearl

Sometimes this new relationship was uncomfortable, especially to a man who had always been somewhat detached from the women he knew. Once he presented Dolly with a bill.

ZANE GREY, D.D.S.

100 WEST SEVENTY-FOURTH STREET

NEW YORK CITY

JAN. 29, 1902

Miss Lina E. Roth (Del. To Dr. Grey)

Services $86,000,000

18 months torture, unrest, dissatisfaction, trouble, hard work

for loss of many nights sleep

for loss of peace of mind

for loss of heart

for loss of ability to admire any other girl

for inclination to depreciate myself

for a constancy I never dreamed I possessed

for the sweet, blind, tumultuous feeling that allows no rest

In consideration of the fact that I must be paid at once, if you have not the money I will accept your soul—no less.

But his admiration for her grew.

MARCH 6, 1902

My Darling Dolly,

I too enjoyed that walk through the park in all that fearful blizzard. It was fearfully cold, and we never noticed it. I suppose it was the "Divine Spark" that kept us warm. I don't think I ever saw you when you looked so pretty. Your face was glowing: It was red and covered with snow. Your hair was powdered with white flakes, and your eyes were bright. You certainly made a picture I am not likely to forget in a hurry.

My dear, it is very easy to explain what you feel. When you are alone with me you are just your natural self, as nature made the woman. The feelings you have then are the true ones, and the ones that are most likely to govern your life, because life is always influenced most by those feelings which are the strongest. When you are with me you are content because you love.

When you are not with me everything is different. You go back, as it were, to your old life, which is still the same as it was before you knew me. There are a thousand things that will come up everyday to make you unhappy. You must try and understand that the greater part, at least nine tenths of your life, is lived apart from me and every little detail of your everyday life, every word almost, antagonizes your love for me, with the results that you see me, and then you just forget it all. Which is, after all, the best proof in the world that as long as you love me and we are together you will be content whatever happens.

Yours

Pearl

Four years after their first meeting, Dolly wrote,

AUGUST 28, 1904

My Dear Baby Doodle Bugs,

In my letter this morning I completely overlooked the fact that this is our fourth anniversary, and that after thinking about it half the night. Do you think we ought to congratulate each other on the fact that we met four years ago today? Think how much has happened since then, and what we have grown to be to each other. Not merely lovers, but companions, friends, mentally and physically, if I might so state it. And it has been the sweetest thing in my life, although it frightens me occasionally to think how absolutely my happiness depends on you and you alone. I thought I loved you as much as it was possible for me to love, before this summer, but it has grown so much deeper in the last two months that no comparison is possible. And oh, how I want you now. I long for you so that it has made me sick, almost.

Goodbye, my old black eyed devil. Don't forget your Dolly, and that she's pining away for you. With all my love,

As ever,

Dolly

And he answered,

AUGUST 30, 1904

Monday Eve

My dear Solace

I remembered the 28th and the things it connotes. I am, however, rather of the opinion that we should erect a monument to that date, and inscribe it,

"Doc's Waterloo."

For surely twas that. Reckoned by the last two weeks I think I am fortunate that I am alive and well.

I have found two young ladies, who, when I approached them, puffed up like toads, and said, "No second fiddle for me, I guess." I don't understand them.

Well, with love

Doc

Marriage was the inevitable next step, but it was a complicated one. Entwined in the decision was Zane's wish to abandon dentistry and concentrate on writing. The seclusion of Lackawaxen was, he thought, a perfect setting for a home with Dolly and a place for him to write. With help from Reba and Dolly, he purchased three acres of land on the south side of Lackawaxen Creek where it joined the Delaware River. On the property were a farmhouse and a barn.[7]

Yet he hesitated. He enjoyed the company of women and drew them to him almost unconsciously. He would not have been human had he not responded. He did not know if he was capable of giving the single-hearted devotion she craved, and if he could, would it destroy him as a writer? But if she were willing to dare it, he would try.

SEPTEMBER 27, 1904

Monday Evening

My dear Dolly,

I saw the places where we first saw each other, and in my mood of today they were regarded as never before. It all came back, and with it the three years and more following, what they have been to me, and what they will become for me.

For I can feel myself slipping, slipping as once you said you were. And, Dolly, I felt today as if it would be good and best and happy for me to slip until I was safely in your arms for all my life.

No doubt I shall catch my foot on a stone, or a projecting ledge, or a root—something which will check that downward—nay upward fall, for a moment, but inevitably I am lost. And I am glad of it.

You, with your singularly even and lofty nature, can never understand what I have been, and what it means to me to utterly change my nature. But I am going to do it—for you; for you because you have helped me to see what I can do, what may be possible for me, what life means. I do not expect to attain this completely for years, still I am confident that I shall. I will.

I made up my mind today. I didn't load myself with too much. This is how wise I was. I did not say I shall never look into another woman's eyes again, or run from any pretty girl, or tease you any more.

But I said I would study and read and write all that I could. I do not look for any reward. I cannot help being ambitious; I want a name; I'd like a little of the flesh pots of Egypt, and I'd like to have a few nice things, but if these never come, I shall never be a sour-complexioned old grouch. I shall have you, and any man ought to be content with so much of this world's blessings, and knowledge, and love.

I must be a strange man. Any man, except me, would faint at the thought of winning a woman of your attainments, because the past would be sure to cast a shade which would envelope both in darkness and cold. I mean that a man who had a long string of murders in his past would be afraid to marry a woman, unless she had no mind, or unless he intended to murder her also.

But I have not the slightest fear. What I shall be for you will make up all that I may have lost. . . . You shall let me teach you all I know, and teach me all you know. You shall help me write literature, not thoughtless, careless books, but throbbing, red-blooded histories of life. You shall share it all some-day. First I'll atone to you for all I've done, and love you because you have made me want to do that; then I'll atone to you for all the wrongs I've done other women, and love you for all that I have lost in losing them.

Yours

Pearl

Dolly had long ago committed herself to him.

JANUARY 3, 1904

Tuesday Eve

Dear Doodle-bug,

Had you received my letter when you wrote yours? I passed in the L last night and saw you sitting at your table writing.

Have you recovered from your feeling of Sunday? It worries me terribly to see you so, but in one say I think it's good for you. It seems to me no more than natural that a man constituted as you are, in whom changes are working as they are in you, should have those occasional mental and moral upheavals. Your life and thoughts in the past have been wrong to a great extent. I think this is greatly due to environment, for you have great and good instincts, and natural qualities.

It must be a fight of these against wrong habits that have been formed. It may be a hard fight, but I am sure of the outcome. I have every confidence and all faith in you. I say this, not because I love you, but looking at things in calmness. I am out of myself tonight, or am I perhaps my right self? This morning I tried to get away from my love for you, to have a look at it. It seemed strange to me in that mood, that I should think of and want all the time, just one man in this great universe of people, that my happiness, my future, my life should be entirely dependent on him alone. The force of that feeling is what drives me wild, crazy sometimes. I never cease for one instant, wanting to be with you. All my desire, all my strength is merged in that one feeling. You don't realize it, or you'd be afraid.

Ever your Dolly

Just before Christmas 1904, he took Dolly to Ohio to meet his mother and father. Though she wanted to stay longer, she quickly returned to New York to be with her mother. A letter from Zane followed her.

DECEMBER 24, 1904

I could not go to bed tonight without getting rid of some of the feelings I have. We had a splendid dinner and were all cheerful and happy. I am thankful for many things. I can keep my mother from that horror, worry, and give her a comfortable home in which to end her days. We all have something to look forward to which is, Oh! so different from former Christmases.

I took a long tramp in the snow and darkness after dinner and was thankful when I came in for the comfort here, and I did not forget to think for and pity the homeless on this cold winter night. I was thankful for all, but most thankful for you, my Dolly. I can't easily describe the feeling, unless you allow me poetic license, and you do rarely, but as I think you'd rather hear it so than not at all, why here goes:

I am thankful for that companionship you give me and the sweetness and content I get from it. I am thankful for your good health and sound body, and sounder mind, and for the freshness and originality of your personality. I am thankful for your passionate love which makes you nearer me and for your restless jealousy—which gives me unholy joy.

But most of all, when I am lost in those dark moods, those depths that stretch gloomy and gray before me like a somber forest deep showing no road nor way to the light; when that old depression weighs down on me, and I walk the streets sick, miserable, for no reason at all except that I long for God only knows what, long for something with a power which makes wealth, within me which I think might move the world and then sicken to know that perhaps all that shall live of me to remind may be some empty words inscribed on a cold stone thus: "After life's fitful fever he sleeps well!"

When I am lost in the darkness of the present and future which is sadder and wilder than any Dante ever traversed; when I am lost utterly, I see you! My North Star, the wanderer's true guide, and I do not lose hope. Before I knew you I had no Northern Star! My dear, this is more than love.

Pearl

1905-1906

CHAPTER 2

The Eternal Feminine

A MORE PASSIONATE DECLARATION of love would be hard to find, and Dolly and Zane began to plan marriage in earnest. This was to be a complete commitment not just to each other, but also to a literary life. Zane would close his dental office and move to Lackawaxen, where he would work on his second novel. Dolly would complete her studies at Columbia. She was in her last semester there, but had difficulty concentrating on her classes. Her mind was filled with happy fantasies of marriage, but doubt crept in. When they first met she was one of many women in his life, and he was one of many men in hers. She had eliminated her other suitors, but despite his protestations she was not sure if he had as well. She had no desire to be one of many, and her suspicions and occasional unpleasant knowledge of other girlfriends brought worry, sleeplessness, arguments, and illness. She knew that he relied on her for advice and encouragement, and she felt she must always demonstrate faith and trust.

DECEMBER 25, 1904

Dear Pearl,

Your letter was my best Christmas present. I cannot attempt to tell you how much it meant to me. It gave me the same feeling as I had when you put "Betty Zane" into my hands last Christmas—it made me cry. Oh, Pearl, I hope I'll always be to you what that letter expressed. Sometimes I fear I'm not worthy to hold so high a place in your life, for after all I'm only a woman and dependent for love, life even, on you. But strange to say, rather than be your ideal, I'd be your wife for an ideal cannot participate in all the everyday sweetness of such a relation. Can I be both? When I think of my petty jealousy and selfishness (for so I must call it) I am afraid. I realize that I have failed you lately—that I have fallen below your standard. I can only plead illness as my excuse. What right have I to be dissatisfied that I cannot have you right away? The thought that you care for me above all other women ought to be enough. . . .

Ever your

Dolly

But she could not deny her feelings.

JANUARY 15, 1905

Dear Doodles,

. . . . I went with Mrs. Isler to see Lohengrin last night.[1] It is a beautiful opera. I analyzed my feelings very particularly and found nothing of what you claim music arouses in people. Perhaps I did long for you a little more, but the place caused that as much as anything. In one way it taught me a lesson. The story, briefly, is this: Elsa of Brabant has been accused of murdering her brother. She calls for a knight she has seen in her dreams to come and fight for her, and Lohengrin appears, vanquishes her foe, etc. He falls in love with her and they are married, but he tells her that she must never ask where he came from or who he is. But she, incited by Ortrud, cannot conceal her curiosity and anxiety, does ask him, and he has to leave her. That's where my lesson comes in. It's always the "eternal feminine" the world over. A woman is a woman and as such has faults that are hard to overcome. She may trust a man fully, but yet worry and fuss and feel unhappy in spite of it. I guess that's my case. But I've made up my mind that I'm a fool and I will stop it. Only you must have patience. The thought, which will come once in a while, that I might lose you, or that either of us might die before I get you, sets me crazy. In one way, I cannot understand it. What is there in being married that makes such an enormous difference in my mind? If I had to die tomorrow, I could die in peace if I were married to you, and in torture if I weren't, and I'd feel the same about you. Why is it?

However, Doodles, I don't want to frighten you. I haven't the slightest wish to, or intention of, dying, and I hope you haven't either.

Dolly

Zane did not understand how Dolly felt about his friendships with other women. It never occurred to him that he should give them up or that in continuing his association with them he was in the wrong. He even told her about them. After one such evening, he wrote,

FEBRUARY 18, 1905

My Dear Dolly,

I slept heavy and dull last night so this morning I feel wretched. It does seem so absurd and foolish for us to have the feelings we have. I was not angry with you last night, but I was with myself. If I would not allow you to persuade me to do things my better judgment tells me are wrong, we'd get along better.

I can see absolutely no reason for the failure of the evening for us, and yet it was a failure. The fact is that you and I are not nearly so intellectual, and sensible, and such good students of psychology as we think we are. We are a couple of chumps, that's all. Which is the bigger chump I can't say.

We were annoyed last evening because your mother insulted me. Well, I ought to be used to it, and I promise you I'll never notice it again. I also apologize for the way I talked about what is not my business, does not concern us, and might not influence our association together in the least.

I understand your rather emotional mood, feel sorry for you, and wanted to comfort you. But on account of the feelings aroused in me by the preceding incident I couldn't.

In conclusion, I realize I have been wrong to talk to you of all those things pertaining to our future. You won't believe it, still I know it is wrong, because it rouses feelings in you which might well be left slumbering at the present time. Again I have made you my confidante, and let you into my secrets, and told you a great deal about other women with whom I have been, and am associated. I could just as well, perhaps better, have kept all this to myself. It seems my weakness is a reluctant fear of hurting you. Well, I shall change a little in the future, and see if I can't paddle this canoe a little straighter and smoother. It would be an eternal shame if through some carelessness or foolishness we'd have a smash up now.

I care more (when I'm serious I never say love, but of course I mean I love you more) than I used to and I think I know more.

Yours

Pearl

Dolly increasingly submerged her identity and ambition into his, developing her role as literary collaborator, nudging him away from themes and styles she thought unappealing and toward what would gain the results they wanted: sale of his work to publishers and purchase of his stories by readers. Profitability measured success or failure, and when she questioned whether a work would sell, she condemned that piece to a rewrite or a quick demise. Popular fiction was not held in high regard by either of them, but they saw it as an avenue to establishing his name as a writer. Once recognized, he could write what he wanted—a psychological novel. In fact he had already started it. Calling it *Shores of Lethe* or *Mel Iden,* he had worked on it sporadically since the previous year. The dental office was closed for good in April 1905 and Zane moved to Lackawaxen. His mother and sister came to New York in March to help with the packing, then they went to Lackawaxen to advise him on the improvements needed to make the farmhouse livable and to help unpack. Notes and letters flew between Zane and Dolly almost every day.

1905

Dear Doodles,

I dreamt last night that a man I know very slightly was very violently in love with me. When I showed my preference for you he said he was going to kill you. Isn't that pleasant? You see, I can have romantic dreams too.

MAY 3, 1905

Dear Pearl,

I believe I must be crazy or something. I just realized this morning what a process your letters always went through. When I receive them I read them at least three times with various emotions. Then they travel around with me all day long, being read at intervals. Before I go to sleep at night I read them once or twice more, put them under the pillow, and read them again in the morning before I put them away. Then I usually take out all the recent ones about once a week and read them. Don't you think there must be something the matter with me?

Love, from your

Dolly

MAY 4, 1905

Dear Doodles,

At this particular minute I am so crazy, wild, to have you that I don't know what to do. I get these feelings every once in a while and they're almost unbearable in their intensity. If I could only see you and hold on to you for a few minutes. Unfortunately over a hundred miles intervene and it is the consciousness of that which drives me wild. However, it can't be helped and it is profitable for neither of us for me to write about it. . . .

Your lonely,

Dolly

I'm hoping for a letter tomorrow.

Zane's father passed away suddenly in July, leaving Zane and his brothers responsible for their mother and sister.[2] Zane had never been as close to his father as he was to his mother, sister, and brothers, particularly R.C., and his father often seemed a stern and remote figure. Still, he was saddened by his death. After the funeral the family gathered to discuss what to do. They agreed that Mrs. Gray and Ida would move to Lackawaxen and live in the farmhouse they had helped clean and furnish that summer until a separate house could be built for them nearby. Other changes were in the works. R.C., Zane's younger brother, proposed to Rebecca Smith (called simply Reba), daughter of a well-to-do family from Blair, Pennsylvania, and the wedding date was set for September.[3] Much excitement surrounded the event.

SEPTEMBER 7, 1905

Most Charming of Maidens!

Your letter came at noon. Reddy, who arrived last night at one-thirty, said the same things of N.Y. as you did. I guess I'm pretty well satisfied to stay here for awhile.

Mother and Ida are crazy about the stuff Red brought home. He gave me two dandy books and Mother a canary bird, and underclothes at $5 per suit, besides lots of other things from Reba.

Reba gave Red a ring, and say! Dolly, I wish you could see it. Two large diamonds and a ruby. It cost $750.00 if it cost a dollar.

Red and Reba will spend a little time here after they get spliced.

Betty had her kittens, three black and one Stubbs. I don't know who to blame for the others. You ought to have seen Stubbs when he saw that canary-bird. He was in my arms and he growled, but I didn't think much about it. I let him down and by Jiminy! He jumped ten feet right upon the cage and if Red hadn't grabbed him he'd have torn the cage to pieces. I licked him like the dickens and he never batted an eye. Oh, he's a wonder.

Remember to think about me and take care of your health.

I finished chapter 4 last night.

Yours devotedly,

Pearl

R.C. and Reba planned to live in Lackawaxen in the summers and New York in the colder months, and they purchased two acres adjoining Zane's land for their home. When they built their house, they built another for Mrs. Gray and Ida, with some financial help from Zane. Zane was working on another novel, *The Last Trail*, with Dolly's assistance. She read each chapter after it was completed and gave advice. Rapid progress was made without the demands of a dental practice and with plenty of time to concentrate. Zane was delighted at the ease with which the words came to him.

SEPTEMBER 13, 1905

My dearest Dumpsky,

Not that I have the dumps here, however. The day has been pleasanter, and my back has been better, so I'm fairly satisfied. I'd like to see you and—

!!!!——————I slipped there and nearly fell off. I've got chapter 7 coming in great shape. Hope you are well and love me lots for I love you heaps.

Yours

Pearl

If this letter isn't silly enough for you let me know.

SEPTEMBER 14, 1905

My dear Boy,

Your letter wasn't silly, but a dear. Only I fail to understand such hiero-glyphics as ——————. What can you possibly mean? Perhaps in the long while that we have been parted you have bent your energies to acquiring some new language. Otherwise I don't understand what an author needs with such signs.

You must be working faster than a steam engine to have already begun chapter seven! I am very anxious indeed to read of the course of Miss Helen's lovemaking. I suppose like the proverbial course of true love it is far from smooth. Make it as rough and exciting as possible for that stimulates interest and makes people rejoice so much more when they get together.

Yesterday I took a walk and passed Teacher's College, and I was surprised at the feeling I had. I didn't care even to look at it. I was thoroughly sick and tired of it, and very thankful I wasn't going to return. When I analyzed that feeling I felt that it was due more to the people that were there, the sort of a strained social atmosphere that prevails. It is all so refined. There are numbers and num-bers of old maid school teachers all working hard and without doubt very praiseworthy, but narrow in mind and narrow in morals. They are too old, most of them, and too set in their ways to be broadened by the splendid education which they can get there. They get the formal part of it and miss the spirit of the thing, and that, to my mind, is what counts. Before examination time they were always like walking encyclopedias, and after examinations they didn't understand why I got higher marks than they did. In reality, I probably knew less than they did. But I didn't mean this to degenerate to a panegyric on myself. Only I'm glad I'm out of it. I want now to live and love and be loved and what I learn hence forward I will learn from the point of view of life. All our knowledge counts for nothing if we cannot ultimately apply it to our daily lives.

I had a very nice little note from Janey today inviting Mama and myself to come over Sunday afternoon.[4] She writes that she saw Rome on Sunday for the last time and she says "Don't let us talk very much about it, Doll," in her letter. I think that is dead game and I admire her a great deal for it. Of course, Janey is young and she'll get over it easily, but I know she cared a great deal for Rome. She is now looking for a position as a stenographer. She'll get along because she's bright and has a pretty good education.

If I should lose my Doodles, I'd slink into a corner and lie down and die right then and there. I'd never care to look at anyone again. But that is anticlimax because I couldn't do much looking after I died. Well—sufficient unto the day is the evil thereof.

Goodbye, now. Don't stop writing to me, and I'm living in anticipation of the 23rd or thereabouts.

Your own,

Dolly

R.C. and Reba were married on September 25. R.C.'s plunge into matrimony, jumping the gun on his older brother as he did, prompted Zane to think seriously of doing the same and to write at length to convince Dolly that he was trying to make himself worthy of her.

OCTOBER 1905

Dear Northstar,

Several times today I have wondered how it is possible that you do not become disgusted with me when I get such spells as I had yesterday. I tell you, Dolly, while psychological introspection has been good for me, it has taken away much of the "old boy's" assurance, and satisfaction, if such may be that I ever felt the latter. I am becoming slowly acquainted with the bundle of faults which go to make up the frail individual on whom you have cast your hopes. And I shudder! Not for your hopes, but for mine.

Just what is the matter with me I cannot exactly determine. I think I am occupied too egotistically with myself, with thoughts of the future, with longings for fame, with worry for the slow advancement of my progress, with a thousand things which should, of course, be prudentally [sic] thought of in the conception of work, but left absolutely out of the details.

This, I am sure, has taken the place of my old other. If worry and anxiety about one's work, if the poorly suppressed eagerness, and unsatisfied longing for results, even if bad in their effects, really contributed anything good toward the result, then I wouldn't care a rap, but it's exactly the opposite effect all this strained, cloudy, fiery inner atmosphere has upon my efforts.

And I'm going to correct it all. I think when I tell you that, while I actually tremble at the enormity of the obstacle before me I am going to surmount it, you will think more of me than if I talk and whine all the time about what I'd like and make no effort to attain it.

But I realize I have other sides of my character to revolutionize, and one especially which will make the present task look easy. I am hoping, by forgetting the great defect in my character, the poison at the roots, as it were, and devoting myself entirely to the others I shall, when I succeed in rooting them out, find the great one in a condition of retreat and unable to stand a sudden mad onslaught, with the help of my right-hand general, who will then be on the field. More than this no mortal, burdened, restricted by nature as I am, ever undertook. I am sure of your help and consideration. . . .

Yours

Pearl

A month before they were to marry, he wrote an even more revealing and amazing letter, one that left no doubt as to his nature, clearly indicating the role he expected to play in marriage and the one he expected her to play as well.

OCTOBER 16, 1905

Dearest,

When I append that—no, not append, but begin with such weakness you may be sure Wetzel's Waterloo is sneaking stealthily along his trail.

From your letter—"see what you can do, and justify my belief in you." What kind of poetry is that? My dear, dear child, hope all you can for me, believe all you hope, but don't think a Zane can ever be a Smith, a Jones, or Brown or any other name that spells a different species.

I am myself—groping still in the dark, rising with your gracious help, broadening, perhaps, loving you surely better than ever, learning more the ways of life, understanding better the faults of men, softening under some wonderful process, out of the narrow rut of selfish thoughts, yet still myself.

I can see now where once I was blind. Any selfish pride of conquest is slowly giving into a lust for knowledge, to understand the multiplicity and complexity of a woman's moods, to dive into her heart, searching for secrets, yet ever with that still——-music of humanity ringing in my ears.

My blood is red, I know, pure, I hope and believe, but as it was born of woman so it will never be free of that softness—that woman charm. I am come to the point where I intend to marry a woman—is not that an awful, a terrible thing for me? I mean—unworthiness.

Outside of my present situation I know the longest day of my life and all its days I shall never lose the spirit of my interest in women. I shall always want to see them, study them, interest them. I never grow tired of women. Even my development has added tenfold to this fateful thing. Every woman raises my antagonism, excites my instinct of wonder and fear, and pity. Where I once wanted to break a girl's heart—with that horrible cruelty of the young and ignorant—now I want to help, cheer, uplift, develop, broaden, show things, and at the bottom still a little of that old fateful vanity.

Am I wrong? Am I only a monster? I love you truly, if such a man can love truly. I know I can quake your heart with a look, but I fear you sometimes with a trembling soul. I fear your strength. You are tearing my heart out by the roots, cutting, sculpting, remodeling my character at the expense of blood and flesh and old fixed institutions of hard set bones.

Many times this last three weeks I have, with outward coldness, regarded you with burning passion and exultant pride. Mine! All Mine! That sensitive soul, that delicate brain, that mysterious womanhood. And passion folded his tent like the Arab and slunk away into the dark.

My dear baby—my grand woman, my sister, friend, companion, teacher, sweetheart—if you couldn't love and understand without sorrow, regret and that other, beyond feeling, if you cannot be content as my wife, as the mother of my children, someday, as the guide to that work I want to do and let the rest go, do not [illegible] for you shall be wrecked over the shoals of your own sensitiveness.

{ 40 }

After all, be sensible. I am myself to you—and you can sum me up. What am I to any other woman? What have I been? A mystery—a stumbling block—a different man—a study—a source of vanity, interest, sentiment, love, and passion, a little something over which she fights her heart, soul, nature, understanding, and in the end has no regrets.

If I loved Nell, Kate, Maud, Alice, Laura, Edith, Daisy, Mabel, Emily, Madge, Betty—named in the order girls have earnestly influenced me—what is that to you? I put you far away from these as something to keep and to cherish.

I shall not write such a letter to you again, and it is doubtful if I ever again tell you so much. I feel better now. I seem to have unburdened my burden. I could be happy with 16 women dying of slow torture around me, if only you'd be like you used to be before the devil awoke in you. The conclusion I draw from my feelings over this is that I shall simply grow out of the detestableness, if so be it is that—of my nature. Because I am changing. I do not imagine I shall ever change altogether, but if "along the trail" I lose the vanity and pride will it not be well?

I have paid no attention to unity, logic, reasoning, or anything else in this epistle. I just "write what is written."

Yours

Pearl

Dolly should have had no doubts about his nature and what marriage to him would mean. He could not have made the situation clearer. We do not know how she replied because no answer to this letter is extant, but there was no change in their plans. Less than two weeks later he wrote,

OCTOBER 28, 1905

Darlingest Darling,

Oh! Dear! How I would love to see you, grab you, hug you, kiss you!—!! ————————and Oh! Peaches and Cream!!! I don't really care about breathing the breath of life unless you are somewhere near. I can't eat without you; I can't sleep without, Heavens! I mean without kissing you goodnight; I can't do anything unless you are around. This is a vile, flat, stale, unprofitless world without my doodle-dumpkins. Oh! Say, Dolly, I can't write such stuff as you write. It positively gives me a pain.

Now here's something. I'll see you this week, probably Saturday, and that knowledge ought to make you feel a little better if you love me so blamed much. I wrote you yesterday that I was coming down soon. I'll bet $2 you behave when I get there.

But seriously, I do need to see you. I can't talk to anyone but you. Perhaps, you'd rather I had the crazy feelings you have, and if you do you're foolish. My need of you is greater than yours of me, in spite of all your protestations. You fill up a great void in my mind: all that longing and vain reaching out for God knows what is the better for you. This is a rotten pen. I have the darndest time with pens.

I may not write so often this week, but you'll hear again from me before I come down. Now, be good little Penelope—

Yours

Pearl

Zane and Dolly were married at noon on a golden November day in Dolly's mother's apartment in New York City.[5] The wedding was as brief as the courtship had been long.[6] Only family and close friends were included, because Zane insisted on privacy. He even asked his new brother-in-law, Jack (Julius) to guard the door lest any girlfriends cause a disruption.[7] Dolly asked her friend Ellie to come to lunch, and surprised her with a wedding at which she was the maid of honor. Dolly's grandmother, her uncle Theodore, R.C. and Reba, Ida (who wore a violently purple bolero suit), Jack, Mrs. Roth, and the preacher were the only guests. Dolly's dress was an ordinary suit, light gray in color, with a long gray pleated skirt and a white lace blouse. The coat was long, tight, with leg-of-mutton sleeves, a tight-fitting waist, and padded bust, giving her the desired hourglass figure. It was, according to her, the nicest thing she ever had. The short ceremony was performed by a Universalist minister. After the vows were said, the upstairs neighbor, Mrs. Isler, hosted a luncheon. Mrs. Roth later sent announcements to her circle of friends. After the wedding luncheon, Dolly and Zane left for Lackawaxen, accompanied by Ida (much to Dolly's mother's disgust). They walked to the Hudson River and crossed by ferry then boarded the Erie for the three-and-a-half hour journey. Firelight welcomed them home as Ellsworth, Zane's older brother, and Zane's mother had started a fire. Following long established Pike County tradition, the community converged on the house at ten and showered congratulations and good-natured ribaldry at the couple, who watched from the porch.

1907–1910

CHAPTER 3

The Hermits of Cottage Point

OUTSIDE THE RIVER FROZE and chilly winds brought snow, but Zane and Dolly hardly noticed. The frigid temperatures were braved when wood was chopped or water hauled from the icy river, but inside the old farmhouse they were warm and dry, and for the first time totally alone. R.C. and Reba spent the winter in the city, so their only neighbors were Zane's mother and Ida, who rarely dared the cold to cross the space that separated their houses.

Zane worked on *The Last Trail,* handing each chapter to Dolly as it was finished. She scribbled notes in the margins, corrected grammar, polished, then carefully rewrote each chapter in her own flowing script, more handsome and legible than his. This remained the pattern of their collaboration throughout their marriage.

They had delayed their wedding trip waiting for a small inheritance Dolly was to receive from her grandfather's estate. With great expectation she prepared for the first truly long journey of her life. On the first day of the new year, 1906, Dolly wrote in her journal,

> Today Pearl went to New York to buy the tickets for California. In about a
> week we'll be "over the hills and far away." What a new experience that will be
> for me, who has done absolutely no traveling. Of course, there was work and
> preparation, so that kept me so busy all day that I scarcely had time to miss

Z.G. In the evening I read Balzac. His toils are upon me and I can feel his fascination, but it extends no further than my imagination.

Surprisingly, Zane did not share her enthusiasm. His diary entry for the day they left, January 11, reads,

Tonight I leave for California with my wife. I don't really want to go; I don't seem to have the right feeling. I'd rather stay home. I wonder if that is only transitory, or a fixed unchangeable narrowmindedness. What will be the result of this trip? Shall I come back with a wider knowledge, a deeper insight, a greater breadth, or shall I simply be the same? I say—No! But then, I've said no to many things. There is something wrong with me, with my mind, with my soul. Perhaps I shall solve the problem this time.

They boarded the train in New York City and within twenty-four hours reached Chicago. With only five minutes to spare, they ran to catch the California Limited and on January 15, arrived at the Grand Canyon and registered at El Tovar Lodge. It was quite new, built in 1904 and noted for its luxurious accommodations, but no advertising brochure had prepared Zane or Dolly for their first glimpse of the canyon. Covered with clouds when they arrived in the morning, by evening it was gilded by the sunset, and Dolly wrote in her journal, "It is a second inferno, stupendous, awe-inspiring, glowing with fiery colors."[1]

Of course they took the trip to the bottom of the canyon. Led by two guides, the group rode on horses and mules along a steep narrow path covered with ice at the top, with the canyon wall rising perpendicular on one side and nothing but empty space on the other. Dolly was the only woman in the group, and her mount displayed more spirit than she cared for on that slick and narrow trail. As the party inched downward, the ice disappeared and the weather warmed, so that by the time they were halfway to the bottom of the canyon the weather was summerlike, with "a gurgling stream and green cottonwoods and willows." After a picnic beside the Colorado River, the horses carried the sightseers back up the narrow trail, returning them, weary and sore, to the hotel, a hot bath, and a warm dinner. Two days were required to recuperate from the jaunt.

Several days later Zane and Dolly arrived in Los Angeles and boarded a train for San Diego and the Coronado Hotel to enjoy seventeen acres of carpet and newly installed electric lights. The hotel gardens alone could have absorbed many days, but the main attractions were the ocean and Pacific fishing. The morning after their arrival, Zane bought tackle in San Diego. In the afternoon they cast their lines from the pier, and after some hours of trying, Zane caught a shark.

He bought more tackle the next day and explored the town with Dolly. The following day, January 24, he went on an all-day deep-sea-fishing excursion leaving Dolly behind. Several days later they explored Tijuana, Mexico, then quickly returned for more fishing. Dolly had never been on a boat on the ocean and was somewhat fearful of doing so, but Zane wanted her to try. Her first ocean voyage was not pleasant; as she later wrote,

> How I hated going out in the small boats that tossed around on that blue, blue sea. Maybe it was this day that I had lobster—very delicious—for luncheon, and later had to disgorge the crustacean to its native element. The water was so clear that I could see it go down, piece by piece to unplumbed depths! My god, I've become realistic and I was such a sentimentalist in those days.[2]

After that, and because Zane could not get bait, they left Coronado for Los Angeles and Catalina Island. Another ten days were spent exploring parts of California they had not yet seen: Los Angeles, Santa Barbara, and finally San Francisco, just two months before it was destroyed by earthquake and fire. After only one day in San Francisco, they took the train to Salt Lake City, following the route of the first transcontinental railroad, then boarded the Denver and Rio Grande for Colorado Springs. The scenery was lost on both of them, however, because the train was so crowded that no Pullman berths were available and they had to spend the night huddled in their chairs. By the time they reached the Broadmoor at Colorado Springs, all they wanted was to rest and be ready to catch the train to Chicago. Pike's Peak was glimpsed only from a distance. They arrived in Chicago on Monday, February 19, waited three hours, then climbed onto the Erie, which took them, exhausted, to Lackawaxen.

They remained at home for the rest of the year, settling into the pattern of writing, editing, and rewriting. Occasional short trips to New York City took them away from home. As the weather warmed, Zane completed *The Last Trail* and sent it to try its luck with the publishing world. From time to time he personally delivered the manuscript to an editor, while Dolly visited her mother and grandmother. Frequently these short trips combined business, duty, and pleasure. Sometimes, but not often, Zane went to the city alone, and when he was away for several days he wrote.

Dearest Mushy,

If it's a bad day here tomorrow I'll be home as soon as I can get there, but if it's pleasant I'll stay a day longer.

I purchased a suit and two hats. I got to thinking that as you love me so much and think me so handsome it is certainly my duty to look right.

I took Mr. Murphy to lunch and we arranged for him to come up about the 12th of October. There is an excursion down from L then for $2.50, and I may come down and fetch him back. Mr. Murphy wants to introduce me to some of his literary friends, and I told him we'd be pleased.[3] Was that come ill or ell faut? He will come down this winter for a spell, and fuss round some. I just hope none of your young female relatives hint that I'm no good.

I am anxious to get back the same as I always am when I get away. I don't appreciate you half as much when I'm away. But then you're so mushy all the time; you never say a real idea any more; you just look at me, and then with a whoop and a m-m-m-doo-dle!!! you grab me, and yell "He's mine! He's mine!" Like some wild girl. Now the way you won such a nice husband was by saying fine and intellectual things and looking pale and interesting. I've been gold bricked, that's all.

Well, that's enough nonsense. I am dissatisfied with my efforts towards work these last two weeks. It seems slow steady sure is not my way. I must fire up and go off, or else loaf.

Yours

Pearl

Occasionally, it was Dolly who visited her family in the city.

My dear Dolly,

Snow, snow, endless snow! 12 inches in drifts and 3 feet on the level. All day the white drifting clouds have swirled down, and if it continues all night the hermit of Cottage Point will find a spotless tomb.

Your letter was perused with much pleasure, since it is long ago that I have felt your charm from afar, and with some doubt. Modesty of the type shown presages some Olympian event. I shall try to chasten your mounting spirit when next I see you.

Beware of the emulations of men would be an aphorism in my Pilgrim's Script, if I were every guilty of such muddleheadedness.

Regarding the laundry, I may say what trivial things sometimes the affairs of states, and keep blushing brides from a husband's yearning arms. For inconceivable as it may seem to you—because of your rare modesty—I have missed you like hell. I never needed so many things done in my life, and I have sworn bloody words. But I found the Huyler's candy, and confiscated the box. Repentance waits on me, however, because I have a pain, and the night is long, cold dark, and inevitable.

The snow is seeping, seeping against the windows. All is quiet. I feel lonely and sad without you, yet were you here quite likely I would be cold. I cannot help it. I can see your dear old brown head on the pillow, and hear your restless murmurings. I'd rather you were safe with me, than in that relentless city,

Always

Pearl

The couple welcomed friends who traveled the three hours to visit them, and they displayed the charms of their rustic life. One of Zane's close friends was Alvah James, a sportsman known for articles he wrote based on an expedition up the Amazon River, across the Andes, and to the Pacific. Zane had met him through the Campfire Club, an organization founded in 1897 to promote wilderness skills among eastern sportsmen, which he joined in 1900.[4] He, Dolly, and James often enjoyed evenings at the theater while in the city, and James made several trips to Lackawaxen to test the fishing. On one of these occasions Zane arranged for feminine companionship for his friend, and much to Zane's dismay, James decided to marry her.[5] Other friends were Robert H. Davis, editor of *Munsey's Magazine,* George Shields of *Recreation* magazine, John P. Burkhard and Eltinge F. Warner of *Field and Stream,* all members of the Campfire Club, and Dan Murphy of the United Literary Press.

Perhaps Zane was more occupied with exploring the rivers and woods with his guests than laboring indoors at the writing table, or maybe it was the charms of his young wife, but no writing was done that summer. An attempt to return to the "Mel Iden" manuscript sputtered and died, and the dry spell lingered into the fall and winter. Zane's outlook reflected the short, dark, dreary days, and when he felt like that, no writing was possible. To avoid Dolly's questions, he went alone to New York more often, finding diversion with Dolly's cousin, Lillian Wilhelm.

Lillian was an artist. One year older than Dolly, her childhood had been as sheltered and privileged as Dolly's, and a talent for drawing and painting was nurtured with everything wealthy parents could provide. She attended the Art Student's League, the National Academy, the Leonia School of Art in New Jersey, and finally, Columbia University. She introduced her cousin's husband to her bohemian world. Conversation with her circle jumped quickly from point to point, always returning to Lillian's opinion of this new book, or a play that just opened, or an artist known to the insiders of the art scene. She was not beautiful by ordinary standards: her allure came from her long black hair, flashing eyes, lively wit, and stinging tongue. Zane found her amusing, her company beguiling, and her friends exciting. Perhaps it was not Lillian who attracted him, but the aura that surrounded her, affecting everyone in sight, making ordinary women appear drab.

Dolly became aware that again she was not the only woman in her husband's life. A letter written in an unfamiliar feminine hand, a picture, a lingering glance from a Delaware House guest, told her Zane had returned to his old ways. When he came home from Delaware House late at night whistling, she knew what he was up to—the whistle gave him away.[6] Maybe it was the stifling atmosphere of Lackawaxen in the winter, trapped in the cottage, that made Zane like this. So when Zane and R.C. wanted to go on a fishing trip, Dolly eagerly approved.

Early in the year the brothers left for Tampico, on the east coast of Mexico, to fish for tarpon. On the way there, the ship's captain announced that there was yellow fever in Mexico, and fearing contagion, the brothers changed their plans and left the ship. They settled at Long Key off the coast of Florida, a resort and tropical fishing center. Its "long white winding lonely shore of coral sand, and the green surf, and the blue Gulf Stream" satisfied Zane's desire for warmth and beauty, and fishing gave him time to reflect. He returned home ready to go back to work.

Zane had exhausted family legends as a source for his stories. He wanted new material, and on a trip to New York City shortly after his return from Long Key, he found it. He and Alvah James attended a dinner and lecture of the Campfire Club, where they met Buffalo Jones, a flamboyant character and rich source of stories. Jones had been, at one time or another, a homesteader, farmer, game warden, real-estate salesman, mayor, legislator, and big-game hunter. His sobriquet came not so much from the role he played in the slaughter of the buffalo in the 1870s as from his later attempts to save them. Fearing their extinction, he said, and regretting his part in their demise, or perhaps only seeing another angle, he gathered surviving animals into a herd in the 1880s and 1890s and in 1906 drove them to Arizona, creating a reserve in the lonely stretches north of the Grand Canyon, the Arizona Strip.

Jones now needed more money. To raise funds he toured eastern cities presenting lectures on the necessity of saving the buffalo, describing his preserve, and embellishing his speech with accounts of crossbreeding Black Galloway cattle with buffalo, creating a hybrid, the Cattalo. This alone sparked skeptical laughter, but then Jones further challenged credulity with tales of his own adventures, including capturing mountain lions with a lasso and transporting them alive, on horseback, to zoos. The eastern sportsmen frankly didn't believe him and loudly told him so. Zane, however, was curious about the man and struck by the literary potential of his story. He asked for an introduction.

Zane returned to Lackawaxen bursting with excitement and full of plans for an expedition to Arizona. He would capture proof on film of Buffalo Jones's boasts and in the process acquire material for a book. He would be gone several months. Dolly could not go: it would be a strictly masculine undertaking. He would travel into areas still perilous, with tough westerners who might tolerate an easterner in their company but never a woman. There would be no luxury resorts, no trains, no roads. The only way to get to the land he wanted to see was by horseback. It would be expensive, taking most of what was left of his savings and her inheritance, but he would have material for countless articles and maybe a book.

He expected enthusiastic approval and support from Dolly, but he was disappointed. She begged him not to go and would not be drawn into his excitement. But he was relentless. He countered every argument with one of his own. She did not wish to be separated from him for months; he felt his freedom was necessary if he was to be a writer. In the desert there would be no distractions. She would be unable to help him with his writing; he argued that she could edit and polish after he had written, but the initial spark was his alone. He wanted to look outside himself for inspiration; she wanted him to look inward and write about what he knew best. She objected to the expense; he answered that he must go.

But as the train took him away late in March he had second thoughts, mixed with regrets about his behavior that winter.

SUNDAY

Dear Dolly,

You would probably throw a terribly passionate fit if you read this letter before I go away, but I shall see that you do not. The truth of the matter is, that I am conscious I am no longer sufficient to myself, or to lapse into mushy talk, I miss my girl, or my wife, or my companion, whatever you choose to call yourself. It is no use denying it, and I am conscious of a little humiliation that I've come to that.

I do not want to go away at all. I am afraid if I go I shall stay a month or two. But I do not see how I can avoid going. What I mean is that perhaps I will do well to go and for that reason should not overlook the chance. On the other hand I could stay home and not miss the trip. Surely I would see some great sights and live awhile in the mountains where it is really wild and have a breath of real freedom, but I don't need it. I could get along without it.

This will actually be our first separation, and I am sure it will do you some good. Actually you are incapable of concentrated effort when I am around. Plan out your system for purpose and work and stick to it.

Barring some unfortunate event I shall come back soon, and better for my work. I am in earnest about this work. But I am groping. I am discouraged because of my insufficient training, not because of my gifts. It is a terrible handicap. If a man can't feel that a word, or an action or a plan or deed is wrong what is he to do? He can't write good books, that's certain. I am trying not to be in a hurry, yet I know how little time is left to me.

So I am writing to tell you that I missed you, missed your talk, and your nagging, and your dear old fat warm self in bed, and your coaxing for kisses, and your worship of this poor piece of clay, and all that is you. Which is as much as a declaration of love.

So I am telling you that I have learned to love you in a different way. You fill, or about fill my life. I am quite sure if Helen herself should come back from the shadows and unveil herself to me, that while I might, I suppose I would, rave over her beauty and perhaps yield to it, but she could never hold me, nor any other woman. You see, I cannot wash out that taint in me. It tinges the blood. Perhaps if you would let out the blood that would be a cure. But you know the surgeon's knife kills sometimes.

The truth is I am not so much concerned about my vile nature as I was. To see you getting fat and rosy and happy is a sort of material contradiction to my rottenness. I see myself reflected rather gloriously in your light.

But I am concerned about a name, about a picture, and those things which before marriage did not bother me. My dear, I have caught the can't of this world. I am getting sophisticated. And just when I have evolved out of Mr. Gardiner's psychology and that the best story is an unsophisticated one. If I lose that old free spirit, that daring, that thing which is myself, you will cry your eyes out, for I will be but a pale corpse beside the old flesh and blood man.

More seriously, the portent of this letter is something rather hard for me to confess. You know that I cannot tell all I feel, and that a burst of eloquence on my part is apt to be impulsive. I suppose I do not know the real meaning of love. I am rather indifferent to that which is borne me, and rather careful my own stays locked in my heart, so it can't get away.

Well, then say I love you in my own way. That I delight to tease you, torture you, be indifferent to you, keep you always mine, far from other people,
and hurt you terribly. Say that I miss you, that I am lost without you, that I rely
on you, that I think you ought to watch me flirt with a woman and laugh, that
you must be sweet, clean, good, loving always, that you are apart from other
women because you're mine, that I made you so, like the sculptor who made
a statue, and when the time came touched it to life, and gave up himself.

And when all is said, and you are railing, I think it would be wise for you to
look out upon life at the other women you know. Someday I believe you will
get what you want, and I hope it will be four kids and a better husband, or I
should say, a husband changed for the better.

Yours

Pearl

Zane and Jones were to meet at the Grand Canyon, where they would
organize the expedition and acquire what was needed: horses, dogs, food,
supplies. The plan was to follow the trail into the canyon, using the same
path Zane and Dolly had explored fourteen months before. They would
then cross the Colorado River at Bass's Ferry and climb out of the canyon
on the north side. Weather did not cooperate, however, and the plans were
changed. When a late snow delayed their departure, Zane used the time to
write to Dolly.

MARCH 29, 1907

El Tovar

Grand Canyon

My dearest, sweet doodlekins, honey-baby wife, Dolly!

Is that any better? Your letter (no. 4) made me nearly cry. It was a beautiful
letter. I can't answer it now. Indeed, it seems that few letters I've written you
have been trivial. I have written without putting my mind seriously upon the
letter and you. Please remember this—if I could meet your demands, letter
writing and otherwise, I don't despair of ultimately doing so. My mind needs
rest. Perhaps, rest from worry more than from serious thought.

What a mixture of woman and baby you are! How passionately tenacious
you are! Well, I love you for that, so you need not fear on account of it.

. . . . Luck has been against me from the start. I would not be surprised if I did not get to go after all. But I hate to give up after my trouble and expense. The only thing that bothers me is your distress and loneliness. My dear, honestly I am surprised. I didn't think you loved me so much, and in a way, while it makes me proud, I feel sad about it. If you cannot get along without me I shall come back, that's all.

There is one thing that will please you. I have arranged a trip for you and me for the first time we can spare, perhaps in a year or so. Mr. Rust knows of a canyon where no man, except prehistoric, besides himself has ever put a foot.[7] He reached it after a long, though not hard, climb over the Marble Walls below. This is a most beautiful place. There are great cottonwood trees, grass, and flowers, a grand spring and stream, and deer and beaver. No one suspects this. No one has ever seen it save him. From here the canyon looks like a dark thread.

Well, you and I are going to camp in that canyon alone for two or three months. Mr. Rust will get some men to carry our outfit on their backs—a burro can't go—and we will stay there, and invite our souls.

Think of it! All alone amid the silence and grandeur of the canyon, far from the fretting world, noise, and distraction. Mr. Rust said the peace and contentment of the place startled him, and he's a Mormon, of not vivid impressional faculties, I imagine. How does the idea strike you? Anyway, we are going to take the trip.

I hope I can write you some decent letters from Avalon. I'll try. Please explain things to Red, and tell him I'll answer his letter soon. In fact, tell all the folks and give my love.

As for you, old sweetheart, I'm afraid I can't get along without you as well as I thought I could.

Yours always

Pearl

Zane and Jones took the train to Los Angeles planning to spend several weeks there waiting for the weather to clear, after which they would return to Flagstaff. By the time he reached California Zane regretted the whole enterprise. Dolly was right, the trip was a waste of time and money, and

Jones was not the interesting character he had appeared in New York. Against the California backdrop he seemed simply a fussy old man with annoying habits.

Hotel Lankershim

7th and Broadway

Los Angeles

EASTER SUNDAY 1907

Dear Dolly,

It seems strange to be here in this hotel alive, and I wish I wasn't.

The weather here is delightfully warm. Pasadena was ablaze with flowers. I got in about 9:30 and must wait until tomorrow morning to go to Catalina. Somehow, I don't feel happy or even enthusiastic. I am afraid this trip started wrong, and will be a failure.

Col. Jones is such a selfish, forgetful old fool! He doesn't know where he is half the time. At Las Vegas I had a nice time and got some good material, but so far the rest of the trip has been to kill time. Perhaps tomorrow I will cheer up. I know I am lonesome and rather blue. For instance, all day yesterday Jones rode in a day coach while I went in a Pullman. He's horribly stingy. It was all I could do to get him in a 25 cent bus to come here, and then I had to pay the cabby. So you see I haven't had much company. I wish I had you instead of him. To hell with trains and wild trips! I want, and ought, to write out of my mind and heart.

I'm getting blamed particular about you. I guess I love you very much after all. If it was all a lie, I could forget it all, darling, but being true, 'tis hard to confess.

I don't know how long I'll stay in Catalina, or when I'll get back to the canyon. It may be ten days or two weeks. Anyway, if the trip must be put off and off I'll quit and come home. But if we can get started soon, I'll go through with it. I am certain that it will be a wonderful experience.

I have seen two pretty women, and hated the sight of both. I don't know why. I'm sure they never noticed me. One, in fact, never saw me. She was on the train. She glanced over me just casually. She was pretty self conscious and ordinary. She walked with a little swing of her body and affected to see no one. I seemed to look through both of them. I tell you, Dolly, it will take a Venus, or a good intelligent woman to interest me anymore, in this mood anyway.

Yours, with love

Pearl

When Zane and Jones returned to Arizona, several letters from Dolly were waiting for him.

APRIL 1907

My dear little lonely wife,

I arrived at six pm in a blinding blizzard. The hotel is crowded and me in my tough clothes! Dear, your two letters broke me all up. I am about sick and wish I were home with you.

We have had pretty hard luck in the way of dogs. Colonel Jones is getting them. I'll write to you tomorrow about our plans and I do hope you will get the letter. If you don't I'm afraid you will have a fit.

My dear, I'm much surprised at the tone of your letters and very sorry. If I thought you meant all you wrote, I'd give up my trip. Your letters were splendid, but they made me unhappy. I know I shall come back to loving you more than ever, and I shall be much better every way. I have already got enough material to compensate me for the trouble and expense, and I expect a great deal more.

You must not tell me that you sit around so miserable. I can't stand when you said you were becoming what men call "a shape." I certainly felt a thrill of glad possession. My dear, you are a little goose. You don't know how much you are to me. And I'm not going to spoil everything by letting you get tired of me. Dolly, trust me for one thing, won't you? And that is the fostering and care of your love. You think I don't look after it, but you're dead wrong. I know just how to manage that. The process may be a little painful at times, but it keeps your love sweet and fresh and growing.

I am worried now because you'll about die when I go across the Canyon and you can't hear from me. For 2 cents I'd back out.

Will you promise me when you are getting blue, to think of these words: "Pearl is coming home to me sometime soon, and every day he is gone will make the meeting sweeter. I must think of how good it will be to see him after this our first separation, and how good will be the kisses, and the old familiar intimacy once more."

My dear, you are hard on me. If I let myself go now, with the emotion that I feel, you would be amazed. I am fighting my battle almost alone, Dolly. You don't help me as you used to. You lean on me. I loved you because I thought I could lean on you, and so help myself out, but alas! But I'm afraid I love you more because you do depend so much on me. It makes us equal. It brings me nearer your level. It gives me a little self respect.

I'm going to try to delude myself into thinking you will be not so blue after you get this, and cheer up, and be happy. Tomorrow I shall write you again. I'll close now.

Goodnight now, Dolly. Remember you are in my room, with all that is dear to me, and you are my wife. I don't see how you can be miserable.

Always yours

Pearl

The weather cleared and preparations moved rapidly. Jones and his men handled most of it, so there was not much for Zane to do but wander around Flagstaff, still a frontier town. One day he stumbled onto a trial of an accused cattle thief, Jim Emmett, a Mormon polygamous patriarch who owned the ranch at Lee's Ferry. Upon Emmett's acquittal Zane suggested they travel together to Lee's Ferry, where Grey's party could cross the Colorado and make its way to Jones's ranch.[8] After four days at Lee's Ferry, Grey and his group, which now included Jones, Emmett, one of Emmett's sons, Dave Rust, and a hired man, left for the buffalo preserve and the North Rim. Grey sent a note to Dolly.

APRIL 12, 1907

Friday

Dear Sweetheart Dolly,

We get away right after noon today. I am writing you a little consolation note, but I haven't any news. I hear the Little Colorado is coming up, and we'll have trouble there. You know the old boy has got the river game all right.

You ought to see this crowd of Mormons I'm going with. If they aren't a tough bunch I never saw one. They all pack guns. But they're nice fellows. I shall try to capture you a centipede and a tarantula to bring home to you so you can send them to some of my lady friends.

I expect a wonderful trip. The waiting so long has about made me quit. But it's over now.

Mr. Woolley wants me to go to Kanab to study the Mormons. He had two families and 15 handsome unmarried girls. I guess I won't go. I really would be afraid of so many.

One strange thing about me is this. I may do mean things and cut up some over other women where you are or when you can know of it, but I don't when I am away from you. I've discovered that. Isn't it funny? I thank the Lord I'm so much of a man. And I believe if some peach would bewitch me for a little when I was away I'd be fool enough to tell you. I don't believe you appreciate me; and I think you believe I am worse than I am. Well, this is not when I meant to write.

Goodbye, Dolly, for a time. Be good and careful and happy, not real happy, but enough to scare away the blues. I honestly love you, more than ever I knew. This separation has proved it to me.

Expect to hear from me about May 15th or June 1. And write me to El Tovar. Give my love to mother and Red and all.

Goodbye with kisses

And things

Pearl

Tonight I'll see the stars shine over the desert!

One day's ride brought them to Jones's ranch, where Grant Wallace, a scientist from California, joined them. They then set out for House Rock Valley, thirty miles away, the location of Jones's buffalo preserve. From there they rode over the crest of Buckskin Mountain to Oak Spring Canyon, where Zane had his first taste of hunting mountain lions. One evening the Stewart brothers of Fredonia joined them and told them of a wild stallion, called White King, that had for years evaded capture in the vicinity of Kanab Canyon, Utah. Kanab Canyon was not far away, so they decided to try to capture the horse themselves, to no avail.

The group returned to the Siwash, on the northern rim of the Grand Canyon, where they stalked cougars with the help of the dogs. Zane barely escaped being mauled by one lion, quickly shooting it. Another was treed, chained, and captured. A third, called Old Sultan by Zane, plunged over the canyon's edge to escape the hunters and fell to his death.

When it was over, Zane's companions accompanied him to the bottom of the canyon, where they hailed the keeper of Bass's Ferry. Jones bid him farewell, and Zane boarded the raft to cross the river and return to El Tovar. From there he wired Dolly, "Trip great success. Got all I want. Home Friday. Zane."[9]

He initially wanted to use the material for a series of magazine articles. They could then be bound as a book featuring the exploits of Buffalo Jones. The book would include the Arizona adventure as well as Jones's earlier feats of hunting musk ox in the Yukon and gathering the remaining buffalo in North America into a last herd. His own adventures would be woven into the stories.

He wrote through the summer and fall. The warmth outside tantalized him, but he continued to work. Putting aside the magazine articles, he concentrated on a book in which he tried to convey the frenzy of the hunt, honing his dialogue to short, clipped exclamations of surprise or command, and using his talent to draw word pictures of the Arizona deserts and forests. He wrote and rewrote, searching for the right words.

Dolly read each draft, making suggestions, editing, and shaping his writing so that it reached a level far superior to his earlier efforts. He wrote ten hours a day, and she wrote to Murphy that she was "wildly enthusiastic (for me)" over some of his work.[10]

Early in 1908 Zane wrote Jones that the book was finished, and Jones came to Lackawaxen to read it. He was enthusiastic and wanted to go to the biggest and most prestigious publisher in New York, Harper's, but Zane hesitated. Harper's had rejected all three of his earlier books, and while he knew that this one was better, he had no reason to believe it would be well received there. Jones, however, knew Ripley Hitchcock, the editor, and felt they would at least be able to talk to him. Once in his office, they would persuade him to read the story. They also counted on the fact that western stories were now considered serious adult fiction since the publication of Owen Wister's *The Virginian* in 1903. And the motion picture, *The Great Train Robbery*, had thrilled audiences. Zane's book, with the title *Last of the Plainsmen*, reminiscent of Cooper's classic Leatherstocking Tales, would appeal to the same market.

Jones and Zane were heartily welcomed by Hitchcock and invited into his private office. Jones came quickly to the point: he and Mr. Grey had a story they wanted him to read. When Hitchcock seemed receptive, Zane outlined the theme and content of the book, with Jones adding his comments. After hearing them out, Hitchcock agreed that the market was right for western fiction and their novel sounded as if it were Harper's material, but, he cautioned, the manuscript must be read before a decision could be made. He assured them he would give it his personal attention, but his associates must read it also. Rising, he shook their hands, thanked them for bringing their work to Harper's, and promised to contact them as soon as a decision was made.

Jones had no doubt Harper's would publish the story, and as there were pressing matters at his ranch, he left. Zane returned to Cottage Point. Having submitted manuscripts before only to have them rejected, he was cautious, but this manuscript had had the best reception of any of his works, including the personal touch of a friend of the editor, so he and Dolly were hopeful.

A letter arrived from Hitchcock on February 8 that informed him his manuscript had been rejected.[11] He saw Hitchcock in his office on February 14, when he went to retrieve the manuscript. Hitchcock said his work was "vain, fine, personal, and overwritten, and too full of adjectives." He said he had failed in the long story and saw nothing in it which led him to believe he could handle the short story. But he asked him to return, to keep in touch with him, to bring him his other manuscripts.

When Zane left Harper's he felt like a "squeezed orange."[12] As he wrote in his diary, "when I got up town the little hope these strings he fastened to me were broken by a rather clear enlightenment as to the kind of man Mr. H—is,—which characterization needs no place in my notebook."

Two weeks later, on February 29, Zane met with the editor and manager of the Outing Publishing Company, Mr. Bray. Outing accepted *Last of the Plainsmen* and indicated a publishing date of May.

It was important for Zane to keep writing, and magazine articles were one way to refine his technique. His previous year's hunt gave him material for two magazine pieces.[13] Another trip to Arizona might provide more stories that would appeal to magazine editors. Zane sent letters to his former companions, arranging a hunt for the spring.

This time Dolly helped with the preparations. She was well aware that not too far away in New York City were attractions that might take him further away from her than even a trip to the West. While he was writing, he had little time and no patience for city life and its distractions. And she saw the usefulness of these experiences.

Zane and Dolly traveled together to New York, then he boarded the train for Kansas City to visit a former girlfriend, now married, with whom he had corresponded. From there he would go to Salt Lake City, then to Las Vegas and overland east, entering the Arizona Strip from the north instead of through Flagstaff and Lee's Ferry. Dolly stayed in the city for a month. From Kansas City he wrote:

MARCH 19, 1908

Dear Flopper:

Well, how are they coming, without your affinity?

Arrived in K.C. yesterday morning at nine o'clock, and after some annoyance found accommodations at this hotel. This town is a big one, and very hustling. But all towns are N.G. after the little old New York.

I found Mrs. N. before noon, in a very pretty house in the suburbs. I did not know her at first. She was very slight and pale, white even. I spent the day and evening with her, her husband and relatives. They are all plain, nice, unpretentious, well-to-do western people. I had an hour or so with Mr. N. and a couple of hours with Mrs. N., and find a rather interesting situation which I have hardly understood to my satisfaction. Mrs. N. is unhappy about something, and is failing. But she is a good, square, true, honest, little woman, I am glad to repeat that, and that some of my first impressions must be reorganized. I think Mr. N. either has consumption or is drinking himself to death. I can't figure which, but fancy the latter. Whatever it is, it is the cause of Mrs. N.'s condition. He is an easy going, careless, indifferent sort of southerner, a big hearted fellow and manly, too, but I imagine a little weak. As far as I could tell they care a great deal for each other.

Mr. N. left last night for Las Vegas and expects to be back in a few days. I shall stay here a couple of days and then go on. I want to see the stockyards, and several other interesting places, and also talk over my visit to Las Vegas. I am sure they both want me to come, as well as the hands, and I expect I shall be royally entertained.

They expect to get another ranch in the foothills, with incidentally, a trout stream running by the door. Mrs. N. expects other of her friends to visit her at the same time. I am rather relieved, for in a way, I had fancied a strained sort of condition to face, with another crazy woman in love with love, or me, and that is far out of consideration. It seems either I have changed, or Mrs. N., or both, for there was not at all any of that sentimental raillery which so often consume the time of a lady and gentleman. I feel genuine sympathy for her, and believe it will grow. While I might, I say so, be pleased to have Mrs. N. like me, admire me, and find me more interesting than other men, I could not hurt her, or make her unhappy for an hour. If this sort of mind-state in me is consistent, and I find it in relation to any eighteen year old peach I happen to run across, well, it's off! The fire's out! I'm a dead man.

You may smile in derision at such a suggestion, and well you may, because I certainly hope I haven't got to that just yet. It seems to me I'd come crawling back to my D. like a poor, miserable, crippled dog, and I'd never stray again.

By this time I hope you have become somewhat reconciled to the loss of the sun, the earth, and the other things symbolic of your Doodles. And I hope you will be able to observe some of the lesser spheres, even some of the satellites. But you need not attach any of them to your system. I prefer to have the path around you clear for my own whirling.

Be careful in N.Y. Look out for handsome villains! Look out for trolley cars! Don't catch cold. Ride as seldom as possible in the subway. And think of your wandering, disconsolate, Indian.

Doc

He wrote again from Las Vegas.

SUNDAY EVE

Dearest Dolly,

Just arrived, tired out and sleepy. I'll get this note off and go to bed. I found your letters, and a telegram from Rome, saying Jones was down with grippe in Garden City. I'll have to think what is best to do.

Your letter was very sweet and nice. I'll read it again before I go to bed. You never in your life said anything sweeter than that about the hole in the pillow made by my head. No matter how much kicking I do, my head has to lie beside yours, eh?

. . . You were the finest and bravest kid that ever was when I left. I forgot to tell you in my K.C. letters, but you were simply a thoroughbred. Don't tell me such things do not count, for they do, and in a woman's favor.

Goodnight, with love. I'll write tomorrow.

Yours

Doc

By the first of April he was back in Arizona, on the edge of the desert and ready to hunt mountain lions, but there was a delay. Permission from the authorities to hunt had not yet been received. To pass the time, he, Jones, and others stopped at Lee's Ferry and Tuba City, crossed the Colorado River to House Rock Valley, Kanab, and Fredonia, and rode back to the canyon's North Rim, taking two weeks. Cheerful letters from Dolly reached him in Kanab, but they increased his dismay about the progress of the hunt.

Kanab, Utah

APRIL 14, 1908

Dear Little Girl,

I am sick, crippled, and underweight, a little over 119 pounds. I walked nearly all the way across the desert. The hunt is still in doubt. Frank and Jim might go with Jones. Everyone out here hates him, and I've learned to do the same. Jones used to shoot his dogs with bird shot whenever they chased anything but lions or bears—he used to kick them, too.

I may try to hunt with Jim a little while, but everything depends on my getting to the canyon before long.

I have not written a note in my book, and don't expect to. My impressions have been mild enough for that matter.

I would like to be with you and the cats, and I hope to God I get my old spirit back.

Do not expect letters from me, for you will only be disappointed. This is a nice letter, is it not? Well, I can't write when I am crying, and that's what I'm doing now.

I can say one thing. I know I love you with all that is best and truest in me. How sad it is that what is worse and most false in me dominates my life! Perhaps, someday. But I am always hoping and longing for the unattainable.

It will sadden you to learn that I don't care in the least about my stories, whether they are accepted or not. That feeling has grown for weeks. I'd forgotten them till you wrote about *Everybody's*. I hope you find the little house alright and that you can manage to exist until I come back.

I cannot write anymore. I laugh at your expression of loneliness. God! If you only knew what loneliness and homesickness meant.

Goodbye, and try not to be cast down. That's idle, I know, but still, try.

Yours with love,

Pearl

P.S. I don't think I have the blues, but you may allow for physical exhaustion and disappointment after disappointment in interpreting the feelings beneath this letter.

He was close to giving up and going home, but by the next day permits had arrived and the hunt was on.[14] Zane, Jones, Emmett, Jim Owens, and an unidentified Navajo left Kanab on April 16 and worked their way across the desert into the highest elevations. Powell's Plateau on the North Rim was broached four days later, after a crossing of seventy miles.

If the number captured is the measure, the hunt was a success. Six cougars were treed by the dogs, roped by Jones, who climbed the trees to reach them, dragged to the ground by the rest of the party, muzzled, bound to poles, and carried back to camp. Four others died: one of thirst while being carried to the camp; another killed by the dogs, defenseless because it was tied; two more leaping into the canyon to their deaths, evading their pursuers. Zane participated in the hunt but also photographed the lions and their captors. He left the canyon in the middle of May, using the same route out as the year before, and was home in time to see the issues of *Everybody's* and *Field and Stream* with his articles.

All summer and fall he remained at Cottage Point, using the material from the trip for stories.[15] With four books in print, one more scheduled for release, and a steady income from magazine articles, his writing career seemed on firm ground, and they began to think of a family. Dolly had always wanted a large family, but he had not been quite so eager. Their first three years of marriage had been too unsettled, and to add the responsibility of children seemed risky, perhaps unfair. But he thought this second western adventure would be his final one, time to settle down. Early in 1909 Dolly knew that by their fourth anniversary she would be a mother.

This did not stop them from embarking on a fishing trip to Cuba, Yucatan, and Mexico. Dolly accompanied him on this trip but returned home early, as morning sickness made traveling miserable.[16] Zane continued on the trip. Cuba he found to be "hot, moist, sticky, dirty, and unwholesome."[17] Yucatan was better because there were fewer tourists, but Mexico was the most enjoyable.

Zane had visited Tampico in 1900 before he met Dolly. That time he had traveled by train through the village of Cardenas on the way to the coast. The tracks ran parallel to the Panuco River for part of the time and crossed other streams. Gazing out the window of the train, Zane had glimpsed waterfalls in the distance but could find no one who knew anything about the river or the falls, other than their names. This time Tampico was crowded and the fishing not enjoyable, so he wanted to explore that river. Since his companions were not interested, he persuaded an American he met in Tampico, George Allen, to go with him. They found a lightweight boat and hired a local man, Pepe, as help. They got on the train at Tampico, with the boat loaded as freight, and rode as far as the village of Valles and the Santa Rosa River. They walked upstream to Mica Falls, then, after one night's rest, began their voyage downriver. They encountered oppressive heat and an exotic jungle environment. The river had many species of fish, and along the banks were cypress, bamboo, and cepia trees that were home to yellow and red parrots, parakeets, and other birds. They spotted iguanas, javelinas, jaguars, crocodiles, huge snakes, and wild boars. Ants, mosquitoes, and ticks plagued them. They eventually reached the village of Tamaulipas, and then Panuco. From there they made their way to Tamos and caught the train back to Tampico.[18]

On his way back to Cottage Point, Zane stopped at Long Key for the first time during fishing season. He was curious about what drew anglers there over and over, eventually forming the Long Key Club in 1906. Zane had not been there long when he noticed the peculiar habits of several of the regulars.

> . . . the chief of this brigade, would carry a camp chair out on the beach, and a rod big enough to catch tarpon, and a tin can and a hammer, and a mysterious article about the size of a pancake, only much thicker and heavier. This he would hold on his knees and crack something on it with his hammer. Then, as a small boy throws an apple from a pointed springy stick, Fisherman would swing his big rod and cast bait and sinker far out into a foot of shallow water. This done, he would recline in the camp chair, the rod over his knees, the line between his fingers, and there he would stay! I used to wonder if he was watching the incoming tide. Much as I studied him that first visit of mine at Long Key, I never saw him get even a bite.[19]

The fish being hunted was the bonefish, the most wily and elusive fish of all. Zane was an immediate convert to the quest.

Vacation over, he returned to work harder at his writing, for now he had to support wife and child. He could boast success, for many of his stories had been published. *The Last Trail* was released in January, and he sold several more articles to magazines.[20] Several manuscripts were rejected, one called *Call of the County* and another titled *Old Walls,* and two stories written for *The Youth's Companion* were turned down. In July he decided to rest from study and writing until autumn.

Their son was born in a hospital in New York, as Lackawaxen had no facilities or even a doctor. A month after the birth he wrote,

The night my baby was born, Oct. 1, I lived through new pain. I lay on my back, under the operating room, and listened. I would not close my ears to any sound. Barred from her room by doctors, men who want to be unhampered by emotions, I suffered in ignorance. Every moan, every cry, every sigh, every breath pierced the walls as if they had not been there and cut into my soul . . . the evil that men do is enough; the creating of a pure child in a pure woman should be apart from pain, and its deliverance should not be in agony.

My baby wailed as he came into the world, a long low sad little wail, stranger than any sound, suggestive of life to be. When I saw him first I thought of wonderful incomprehensible things: he looked thousands of years old and wise and sad as all the ages.

Tonight, a month later, I saw him in his mother's arms, a bright eyed little being, a perfect little animal who used his eyes, his lips, his fingers, with no perception of intelligence but with some instinct. And as I watch him change every day, grow every day, so I change and grow.[21]

They named him Romer Zane, after Zane and his brother.

Dolly and son stayed in New York for some time, but after a month Zane returned to Cottage Point to work on a new novel that he called *Mescal*.[22] This story used the North Rim for its setting and the characters were westerners, but the heart of the plot was a love story between an ailing easterner, Jack Hare, and an Indian woman, Mescal. Mescal was an exotic dark-haired beauty, both primitive and innocent, reminiscent of Lillian Wilhelm. Jim Emmett was in the story as August Naab, patriarch of the family that rescues Hare. Dave Rust was also in the story.

The manuscript was handed to Dolly for editing, and copies were sent to Street and Smith, publishers of *Popular* magazine, and to Ripley Hitchcock of Harper's. Zane turned to other projects, writing four short stories between January 22 and January 29.[23] He seemed more comfortable with his writing, and this appeared to bear fruit.[24]

Nevertheless, relations with publishing houses continued to be frustrating. Zane regularly made the rounds with his manuscripts. In his diary on February 23, he wrote,

I do not like the inside workings of a publishing house. I am beginning to see, to learn things I never dreamed of before. The men connected with publishing houses have their interests the same as any other men. Mr. B—is smug, dry, practical. His idea of literature is a good story that has commercial value. He cares absolutely nothing about being true to human life. In fact, he does not know what that is . . . he makes light of deeper purpose in literature. I believe he thinks he has discovered a number of young writers, and imagines he controls them, or directs their efforts, and takes complacent credit for it.

Mr. H—is the literary shark, the sophisticated, conventional, cultured moss-back! But he is keen to discover a good writer, a good book, and to go to his employers, "I have nursed, directed, advised this young writer up to his present acceptability. I have made him." To the young writer he is patronizing, suave, condescending, superior. He expects to be looked up to. He will likely suggest changes in everything the young writer does, not because the work needs it, but because he must be felt. I suppose he has to fight to hold his job in the same way I have to fight to find a publisher. Still it's the most damnable attitude I've yet had to stand.

Most surprising, on March 2 he met with Hitchcock, who received him enthusiastically. Hitchcock wanted *Mescal,* retitled *Heritage of the Desert,* and his future work and handed him a contract, which Zane immediately signed. In his diary he wrote,

How strange that he, who so tortured me, should be the one to encourage me! He expressed a specific and personal interest in me and my future, and wants to form a kind of partnership with me, in which I am to profit by his knowledge and suggestions. Well, it's his business to discover writers, and I'm willing and ready to be discovered. He is very smooth, perhaps deep, I won't go so far as to say hypocritical. But I'll meet him halfway, and be earnest and sincere in my work to do as he wants. Then we'll see. Whatever he means I am indebted to him. I am grateful. For now my real work begins.[25]

CHAPTER 4

Marriage Is for Children

F ULL REALIZATION of Harper's acceptance did not dawn on either Zane or Dolly for almost a month. In April Zane met with Hitchcock again to discuss a variety of matters related to the publication of *Heritage of the Desert*, as well as his juvenile book, and his new affiliation with the publishing house. While there he wrote excitedly to Dolly.

Grand Hotel
New York

Dear Little Lonely Mama!

Now, how's that?

I've got good new and bad. Take the bad first! I lost your frat pin. On the square now. I haven't seen it since I've been here, and I'm very sorry for it had so many associations.

I'm to sign the contract with Harper's Friday. That's settled. But I must do some new stunts to the MS.

Mr. Hitchcock will report on the juvenile Friday. He wants a baseball story for next spring. It must be finished in January.

I've a good deal to tell you about my last interview with him. Lots of significant, simply dazzling things. I'm up in the air, and also scared half out of my wits. But you must wait till I see you.

Mr. Warner tried to cut me down again in price, and I up and told him I couldn't let him have the jungle stuff. I can get $500 for it from Recreation. I'll do enough for Warner to pay you bills (notice!) And then cut him out. Oh! I'm getting pretty fair, thank you!

I'll try not to forget the oranges, etc.

With Love to you and Baby,

Doc

P.S. I'm almost persuaded that you didn't do so badly after all when you married me.

He stayed in the city for several days to get the first copies of *Field and Stream* (with "A Trout Fisherman's Inferno") and to talk to the editors there about another article. Zane's name was featured so often in sporting magazines that he had gained a reputation as an authority, and the editors accorded him due respect. At the back of his mind, however, doubt still lurked about his ability.

Something really vital and wonderful has happened—Harper Brother's acceptance of my desert romance. I do not seem to realize it. I can scarcely say that I am elated. I am glad, of course, but the wild joy I thought I'd feel is not manifest. A panicky feeling seems to be the strongest, a fear that I may not reach up to Mr. Hitchcock's estimate of me. He praised my work and pointed out my faults. Still I am too flowery, too self conscious, stilted, strained. I must ease up in my terse work. More restraint. The strangeness and aloofness of my feeling for my characters must be remedied. I must put in the little significant touches that will make the story rise up stirring and warm with life.

This acceptance marks the great change, focus point, perspective—whatever it is—of my literary labors. Again I don't seem to realize, but I know this realization will come. What I needed most, and have been striving for, is now an assured fact. Rise to meet it I will.[1]

For the rest of April and until October he worked at Cottage Point. Breaking from previous practice, he and Dolly did not encourage visitors and politely refused invitations. His wife and son were all the company he had, and Halley's comet in May was all the excitement he wanted.

Four juvenile novels were the product of this summer of sustained writing. As always, he wrote the first draft and Dolly corrected grammar, tightened construction, then rewrote each chapter in her own hand. By September she was exhausted. She, the baby (now almost a year old), and her mother went to Larchmont, New York, on Long Island Sound for the sea air. Zane stayed at Cottage Point.

Heritage of the Desert was published September 8, and sales were better than for all of his earlier books together. His second juvenile, *The Young Forester*, hit bookstores in October. Royalty checks would not begin to arrive for some time, but their financial prospects were considerably brighter, and he and Dolly wanted to give themselves some of the comforts of life they thought they had earned.

Winter brought the most severe hardships Cottage Point had to offer. Bitterly cold winds from the rivers pierced the flimsy walls of the cottage, making it impossible to warm entire rooms with the only source of heat available, a wood fire, and the fuel for that had to be chopped and hauled to the house. There was no running water; icy water was carried from the river for drinking or bathing. The healthy young couple were not unduly bothered by the cold and the primitive conditions, but there was now a child who might be harmed by rigors that only inconvenienced adults. In Lackawaxen there were no hospitals and no doctors within easy reach. With this in mind and with the prospect of some money, they decided to spend the coldest months in Atlantic City, where the amenities of life were within reach of even a limited income.

Zane and Dolly rented a house there to be shared with the baby, R.C. and Reba, and Zane's mother and sister.[2] Toward the end of November all seven arrived. With so many crowded into one small house there was an appalling lack of privacy, and because the royalty checks had not yet arrived, money was scarce. Then, in February, everyone became ill, and with physical discomfort came irritability and short tempers.[3]

Zane began to think longingly of the western desert. He wrote to David Dexter Rust, who had accompanied him on the last trip, to make arrangements.[4] He wanted to see the Navajo Natural Bridge which Rust had mentioned in an earlier letter, as well as to hunt, visit Kanab and Fredonia again, and see Thunder River. The correspondence continued through the winter and into the spring of 1911, the only pause occurring at the end of January when Zane and R.C. went to Long Key for two weeks of fishing. *Heritage* was in high demand at bookstores, and Zane planned his next novel to capitalize on its success. He would use the same setting and some of the same themes. In particular the Mormons would be more heavily dramatized, along with the western landscape. He wanted more information on Mormons, and Dave Rust, who was prominent in that community, was ideal as the one to help him gain acceptance into insular Mormon towns. Zane wanted to observe polygamy, the most controversial and provocative element of Mormon history, firsthand, as it was practiced.[5] Details of the trip, including financial arrangements, were discussed in detail during the cold, miserable winter months.

When the weather warmed, Zane and Dolly returned to Cottage Point, but after the comforts of the city the lack of modern conveniences seemed more of a burden than before. Dolly wrote in her diary,

March 25, 1911

Today the sun was warm and the birds were busy. When the weather is nice here, one could not want a pleasanter or more beautiful place to stay in. Yet some change is inevitable. We cannot, in fairness to ourselves, live such isolated lives, to say nothing of the primitive conditions we undergo. Before the baby came these things seemed easy to me, but somehow my point of view has changed. Here one is out of communication with reliable physicians, schools, even what up to the time of my marriage I had considered necessities and not luxuries of life, and with no social existence whatever, it seems hardly right that we should stay. Lackawaxen had been a stage in our development without doubt, but I think the time for that is past.

Some of her diary entries allow a glimpse into the couple's life at Cottage Point.

March 24

Today and this evening baby is so sweet that the joy in him is an ache. Each day he learns a new word: yesterday it was "sweetheart," and today "unky" only he says "un-ee." . . . what an unspeakable wonder and joy the possession of a child is.

Marriage is for children. They are the closest bond between husband and wife, a bond which should hold when all other things fail.

April 2, 1911

When he awakes in the morning now, he always sits up to see if we are awake. If not (or if he thinks we're not) he lies down again and his eyes move around and he says a soft word or two. Then at the first movement from us he's up and peeping at us, and smiling and greeting us.

He is just at the imitative age. Today he saw his father unhooking my dress. He watched very attentively, and then when Doc had finished he walked up to me and went through the same motion at the back of my skirt.

It seemed to Dolly that Zane's success at writing, his apparent victory over his attraction to women, and his ability to hold the demons of depression at bay were due in large part to his child. She wrote,

When, as a girl, I thought of marriage, I always wanted a large family. But in the first years when we traveled and especially when Doc persuaded me that my energies would be more profitably employed in helping him, I evaded the issue. Doc did not care for children, or he thought he didn't, and we had been married over three years when I persuaded him that we ought to have one. Now that we both know, we are convinced of our mistake in not having the babies immediately. For there is nothing that counts beside them. And I am firmly convinced that the great change in Doc is due entirely to the baby. One of the greatest pleasures in my life is to see their love for each other.[6]

Family life was confining, however, and Zane was eager for his trip west. He planned to leave April 10 and spent all of March and the first part of April preparing. Charles McLean, editor of *Popular* magazine, was to go along to see the Arizona Strip. Zane wanted Rust to meet him at Flagstaff, but Rust wrote that the boat at Lee's Ferry had sunk. Rust also cautioned that there was too much snow on the North Rim for good hunting so early in April. Nevertheless, Zane had already bought his tickets and planned to arrive in

Flagstaff April 14 and take McLean to Tuba City, Oraibi Pueblo, and finally to El Tovar, where they would wait for Rust.

After the prolonged period of togetherness parting was difficult. Zane wrote Dolly from New York,

> Dear Dolly,
>
> I saw you standing on the land leading to John Smith's, and I felt such a rush of remorse that if I could I would have gotten off the train. This will tell you something of the condition of my mind.
>
> Yours
>
> Zane

And Dolly, with resignation, wrote in her diary,

> April, 11, 1911
>
> It was a wrench for Doc to leave yesterday. He told me it was very difficult, and I think if I'd asked him not to go, he would have been glad to remain at home. But I think it's better that he should go. Doc needs broadening and to develop his power of observation in regard to people. I'm hoping that Mr. MacLean, editor of Popular magazine, will do him much good. He seems so eminently sane and well balanced, with keen judgement. Indeed, the very fact of his holding the position he does argues that.

After he left Dolly went to New York City, keeping busy to avoid loneliness. Born into a three-generation native New York family, Dolly relished her time in the city. She wrote,

> The minute I get to the city, I feel it grasping me. I hurry and rush, dodging here and there, calculating every minute, trying to get the most of the short time I have. I always feel perfectly sure of myself, perfectly at home. The noise and rush and bustle affect me not in the least. And every time I go there, I find something new and wonderful. The Hudson River tunnel opened November 10th, for passengers, and I happened to cross to the Erie Station that day homeward bound. Later, from Atlantic City, I went through the new Pennsylvania Station. And so it goes, always something new and great and wonderful.

And by way of contrast, here we are, living in the most primitive fashion in a backwoods community.[7]

As the days wore on she occupied herself with the practical aspects of living in the country.

April 21, 1911

Several days have slipped by, raced by, rather, and I have been very busy. Perhaps the latter statement should come first, for it's a relation of cause and effect. For four days I did every bit of the work in the house, and that means something in a place like this. To pump water and shovel coal and haul them up and down stairs are muscular tasks. But they make me delight in the strength of my body. Nevertheless, I was not accustomed to all the work, and at evening I was tired out. Two mornings my stove was out which ought to have been heartbreaking, but wasn't. Somehow, being all alone with baby, and shifting for both of us, made me have that primitive sort of feeling in which I joy.[8]

Keeping busy was the antidote to loneliness.

But while Dolly was occupied at Cottage Point, Zane faced delays, setbacks, and frustration. Rust was not in Flagstaff, and Zane assumed he was unable to cross the Colorado River because of the high waters of spring snowmelt. Instead, he hired a Flagstaff man, Al Doyle, as guide and took McLean to Tuba City, Oraibi, Red Lake, Marsh Pass, and Navajo Mountain on a twenty-day tour. In Tuba City, a tiny reservation hamlet seventy-five miles northeast of Flagstaff, Zane heard that parties were crossing the river at Lee's Ferry. Rust simply had not come and sent no word of explanation. On the second of May Zane wired Dolly that he was coming home. What Mormons he encountered on his tour of the reservation would suffice for the time being, and the impressions gathered on his previous trips would serve as the basis for his next novel, augmented perhaps by his disappointment with Rust. The hunting trip was canceled; Zane caught the next train east from El Tovar, missed his connection in Chicago by one minute, but arrived home May 6. Dolly commented,

I think I shall always remember today as a peculiarly vividly happy day. It was not alone that Doc came home, but all the little things conspired to make it so. The weather itself was perfect and we were outdoors all day. Life seems so full and sweet and comforting somehow. Perhaps it was just my own inner satisfaction, but somehow I loved everybody today. . . . A few days like this in a lifetime balance a great deal.[9]

Good news awaited Zane. The first royalty check from *Heritage,* for over a thousand dollars, had arrived. He immediately started the new novel, translating the failure of the trip and his disappointment with Rust into a harsh depiction of the Mormons.

This was a story of Mormons and the man called Lassiter who stalked them, seeking revenge. For the protagonist he created Jane Withersteen, strong, independent, wealthy but persecuted by fellow Mormons for refusing to marry Elder Tull and for befriending Gentiles, non-Mormons. There were also Vern Venters, Jane's loyal herder forced into hiding by the Mormon hierarchy; the bandit Oldring; and Oldring's lieutenant, the masked rider. There were magnificent horses, evil bishops, orphaned children, wild rides through the sage, gunfights, and finally escape for Lassiter and Jane to a secluded canyon sealed forever from the world. He called it *Riders of the Purple Sage.*

It was finished by September, and Dolly thought it the best so far. A rest was earned, so Zane rented a campsite at York Lake for a month for himself, Dolly and the baby, R.C., Reba, and Ida. The vacation ended early.

We had rented a camp for a month. I wasn't happy then by any means, tho I would have felt the same anywhere else. That was a miserably funny experience. The first night Rome and Reba and Ida discovered they had company in their beds. The two former took to a tent and Ida made tracks for home. We were more fortunate in that way—but the weather was very rainy and disagreeable and Doc was crazy because Reba continually prevented his fishing with Rome. As for me—well I had many ills, imaginary and otherwise. I was really and honestly exceedingly nervous, especially about Romer, and whenever he'd go near any dangerous place I'd scream. Rome and Doc evidently thought this was affectation and treated me accordingly. Then I'd cry my eyes out—But why dwell on these unpleasant themes. Suffice it to say that after a week Doc broke up the party. We went home and Rome and Reba betook themselves to a smaller camp on the lake.[10]

Dolly's anxiety was not without cause. She was again pregnant. The baby was due in April, but there was the winter to be faced before then. Cottage Point in winter seemed especially forbidding for a pregnant woman and a child, and New Jersey had not been satisfactory the previous winter, so Zane rented an apartment in New York, close to doctors, hospitals, publishers, and all the diversions the city had to offer. He went to the city to make arrangements and wrote her the results.[11]

OCTOBER 13, 1911

Dearest Dolly,

Well, 'tis did! I signed the lease. Enclosed find plan, with measurements pretty close to accurate. Now you can begin to pack in earnest, and when I get home we'll decide on when to move. To tell the honest truth, I'm both scared and tickled to death. You've got to have some decent furniture in those front rooms. Gee! Well, go ahead and plan. My part is easy. I've got to touch Rome or somebody for some coin, and then work like hell, and I'm grimly settled in mind as to the latter. I hope and believe we'll have a fine winter and a beautiful apartment.

Now, for less interesting matters. I'll probably take your charming relative to a moving-picture show tonight.[12] Tomorrow I'm going to the ball game. I had to buy a ticket from a speculator, $5. There were no single tickets mailed, so I hope to get that $2 back.

Possibly I may be home Sunday. But don't expect me 'til I come, and if I do come I'm going away on Monday. I expect to spend a few days with Anna Wood and her mother. Anna left the hospital too soon, and knocked herself out. So they are going to the country, probably Milford, where she can rest and have better air. She looks terribly fragile to me, a great deal more than when I saw her at the hospital. Then she was the color of chalk. Mrs. W. is all in, too, and they both were very grateful for my offer to spend a few days with them. I would have liked to ask your advice about this—whether it's all right or not, but, well, anyway, I hope you'll not be displeased. So look for me Sunday, and if I don't come I'll write you.

With much love to you and baby,

Yours,

Doc

Please tear up this epistle.

That Zane was with Lillian was disturbing, and his concern for the health of another woman and decision to spend time with her rather than his pregnant wife hurt deeply, but Dolly decided it was no doubt harmless. He had not attempted to hide his actions and since Romer's birth had shown no inclination for his earlier pursuits. She packed and worked on his manuscript, getting it ready for the publishers. Early in November the move was made, and it was another domestic disaster.

> Doc forthwith rented an apartment (157 St. and Broadway, far beyond what we could afford) but high and full of sunshine and air. (I suppose rent is a small thing compared with health.) We packed up most of our belongings and under the generalship of Lew shipped them to N.Y.[13] Then came all the trouble. The furniture did not arrive and Lew and Doc fussed and scolded. Finally it came piecemeal, and on the fourth of November, Romer baby, Lily and I took possession of our new home. It took some time to get settled, and longer to get the furniture mended. Doc had been here a week when we arrived.[14]

Ida, Ellsworth, and Zane's mother had also intended to spend the winter in the city but decided against it. Ida, however, did stay several weeks, as did R.C. and Reba before going to Reba's family in Pennsylvania.

Zane took the finished manuscript of *Riders of the Purple Sage* to Ripley Hitchcock at Harper's and another copy to his friend, Bob Davis, editor of *Munsey's* magazine. Within a few days he heard from Davis: the company liked the story but was afraid of offending Mormon subscribers. At Davis's suggestion, Zane took it to Street and Smith, publishers of *Popular* magazine, with a letter from Davis promoting the book. It was rejected there, too. Then Harper's asked him to come to their offices.

It was not quite a replay of the last interview. Hitchcock warmly praised the book but, like Davis, thought the unflattering portrait of Mormon men intent on enhancing their power through polygamy and oppression might be just too ugly for readers, Mormon and non-Mormon, who found attacks on any religion repugnant. However, in fairness he would hand the manuscript to others for opinions and base his decision on theirs.

Several weeks later Harper's again asked him to meet with them. The consensus was negative. Grey later related his next step.

> Finally, in desperation, I went to Mr. Duneka, then vice president of Harper's, and asked him frankly if he had read "Riders of the Purple Sage." He answered as frankly that he had not; but that some of the readers considered it to "bludgy," whatever that meant. Then I told Mr. Duneka, with more force than frankness, what writing meant to me, what I was going to do, and I asked him if it would not be fair, considering my first book was successful, for him to have faith in me to the extent of reading "Riders of the Purple Sage." He was kind and sympathetic, and promised to do so, though he manifestly had no illusions about the book. When I saw him next, his wife had read it, and so had he. Suffice it to add that my romance of the purple sage was published.[15]

Riders was released in January 1912 and had better sales than anyone expected. Zane went to Long Key with R.C. and Reba in late January and on to Flagstaff, Kayenta, then southern Arizona, leaving pregnant Dolly in the apartment in New York. Upon his return he began a new story using an idea suggested by Bob Davis. Calling it *The Light of Western Stars,* he used southern Arizona and northern Mexico for the setting rather than the Arizona Strip. He worked on it in March and April, finishing it the day after the birth of his daughter, Betty Zane.[16]

This pregnancy was a difficult one for Dolly, and in the last few weeks of it she was confined to her bed. The success of *Riders* meant more luxuries were affordable, so a nursemaid, Mrs. Koch, called "Cookie," was added to the household. Cookie proved her worth immediately, for after the birth Dolly developed a blood clot and was confined to bed for sometime, warned not to move lest the clot move to her heart, causing death. She tried to edit the new manuscript but could not concentrate. From her bed she could see into the old Trinity cemetery and one day watched the funeral procession of Col. Astor, who had perished with the *Titanic*. When she was better the family returned to Cottage Point, but Dolly was still restricted from much activity for the summer.

Through the summer Zane revised *The Light of Western Stars* as suggested by Hitchcock, finishing it in September.[17] He immediately began another novel, again placed in the southern deserts, called *Desert Gold*.[18] Other than one brief visit to southern Arizona he had little firsthand material, so he planned a trip in the late summer, but it had to be postponed. Dolly was still not well enough to be left. Instead he wrote the new novel and prepared *Western Stars* for serialization.

Riders was in its sixth printing by August, and the royalties were pouring in. Zane could now afford interests that he had dropped in leaner days, such as photography. He bought cameras and roamed Lackawaxen taking pictures. He particularly liked to photograph beautiful women against scenic backdrops, and he invited Lillian to pose and to bring her cousin Elma, noted for her beauty. Dolly wrote in her diary,

October 18, 1912

Today, what happened today? I've been alone most of the time with my children. It's been a wonderful autumn day with the gold lights over everything and an intense blue sky. But many of the leaves are down and the sadness of desolation is there.

Friday night Lillian Wilhelm and her cousin Elma Swartz came up to Hobarts. Doc brought them in for a minute. I was curious to see Elma, for I had heard of her beauty. I think I was disappointed, tho' I didn't see her fairly. But something refined, something childish, in her manner, pleased me. All day yesterday Doc spent with them, mostly taking pictures, he said. Today they were at it again, only that they drove down to the brook. At six Doc stopped in for a minute, changed his clothes and went on up with them. But to go back, Elma disappointed me a little more this morning. Both girls had their hair tied up under unbecoming scarfs and I believe Elma's hair is her crowning beauty. But she seemed to have powder on her face. It's strange how that spoils things for me. I love natural beauty, more in a woman than anywhere else, and anything that creates the least artificiality spoils it for me. It makes me feel contemptuous. That is wrong, but I can't help it.

Poor vain Lillian! She is so absolutely obsessed with her looks that she's painful and silly. It's partly Doc's fault, too, greatly, perhaps. He's flattered her til she thinks she's a beauty. When I remonstrate with him, he says, "But what harm is there; it makes her happy." Of course there is harm, but the argument rather stumps me.

I hear my husband. Goodnight.[19]

Chilly winds off the rivers marked the end of pleasant days, and Dolly prepared the cottage to be closed. Zane went to the city to find an apartment for the family, and Dolly followed later. Through November and December Zane worked on *Desert Gold*, finishing it just before midnight on New Year's Eve. Then,

As the old year died, we opened the window, and knelt there far above the city, while the wonderful New Year sound came to us. I can hardly explain the great and terrible, yet beautiful emotion it aroused in me. It seemed the cry of all humanity's sorrow and agony, joy and elation blended in it, all the emotion that flesh is heir to.[20]

1913–1918

PART TWO ■ MIDDLETOWN

CHAPTER 5

The Great Bitterness

M IDDLETOWN was a prosperous inland community with a popula-
tion of twenty thousand or so. It was the hub of Orange County in
southeastern New York State, lying somewhat between the rustic isolation of
Lackawaxen and the metropolis of New York City. Middletown offered the
comforts of city life, electric lights, telephones, running water, but without
the congestion and problems of a larger city. Still essentially rural, it was
surrounded by farms, and the one main street on any given day held more
horses and carriages than automobiles. Off the main street were residential
areas where stately Victorian homes rested comfortably on wide lawns under
sheltering trees.

R.C. and Reba had made it their home for several winters, and Zane and
Dolly thought it might be ideal for them as well. In January 1913 they
bought a large, old-fashioned house on South Street.[1] It was built of wood
painted white, with two stories and an attic, bay windows on the ground
floor, many rooms, and a spacious front porch. The wide lawn had maple
trees in front of the house and cherry and other fruit trees in the back. Hildred Smith, a friend of Dolly's, lived next door with her family. Several
blocks up Zane rented a house for his mother, Ida, and Lew, and a number
of miles out R.C. bought a place. Middletown would be their home in cold
weather, and they could return to Lackawaxen when the weather warmed.

The move was in March, but Zane was in Long Key, and from there he traveled west through Louisiana, Texas, and finally to Arizona. He was gone almost four months, longer than he had ever been away before, and what was worse, this time he took Lillian and Elma with him. Dolly wanted to go but was bluntly told she was not wanted.

The great bitterness, the great hardening came when my husband announced to me that he would take his latest—what shall I call her—inamorata? and her cousin (also my cousin) on a long and unusual trip through the south and southwest with him. It began with the statement that I was unable to go with him now, and therefore the other arrangements. The bottom fell out of the world for me then. Stupidly I said, "but I will go with you" to be told "but I don't want you." Those words burned themselves on my brain.

For awhile I thought the thing would be impossible; that the parents, the relatives of the girl would never consent. But somehow he carried it through. Even, he forced me to appear in public with them, to show my friendliness. Oh, the agony I suffered. Somehow, it is always I who feel the shame, the embarrassment when I am in the company of these friends of my husband. I have never noticed any of it in them. It is because I am a hypocrite, because I am forced to be friendly when I do not feel so. I know them; their relation to him. I have prayed him to keep them away from me and my life. But no, I am necessary to the scheme. I am part of the wherewithal. This summer he had them in the country for several months. They came to see me frequently— kissed me even. And I? Yes? I did the best I could. Why? Is it cowardice? Why do I put up with these things?

Part of the answer, I suppose, is that I care for my husband, that he cannot help these things. They are terrible obsessions with him. He lives in a world of emotion. The girls are not at all what they seem to him. Each one he in turn endows with certain characteristics. When the last one loomed on the horizon, two, L.N. and A.M. went into discard. This new one is more attractive than any for a long while and the stronger hold on his imagination. He has made her his stenographer.

Oh, why write all this miserable stuff. After all, to be absolutely fair, I would have to get on all sides of the question, take up all points of view, and that is impossible. A mere statement of cold fact makes a bad case for my husband.

But he can't be looked at from that angle. Doc is a dreamer, a smiler, an intense egotist. In the same breath he can tell me that it's agony for him to leave me and the children and then that he can't keep from the things in N.Y. Very frankly he tells me that when he's miserable or sick or needs help, he comes home, but his good times he likes with the others. He has spent thousands of dollars on them in the last year, and we certainly can't afford that.

I am getting deeper and deeper, and I feel it's all wrong what I'm writing. If anyone should read this ever, it wouldn't be fair to Doc. After all, he can't help it, he was born so, and for better or worse I must stick to him.[2]

Zane had not hidden his flings from her before they were married, and from their earliest days together there had always been other women in the background. For Dolly's sake he had halfheartedly tried to avoid temptation. Not long after they were married he wrote, "I have tried to kill the deadly sweetness of conscious power over women. A pair of dark blue eyes makes of me a tiger."[3] When he failed at that, he tried to hide his dalliances from her, apologizing when she stumbled onto things that hurt her.[4] Now the success of *Riders of the Purple Sage* proved he was not like others, thus did not need to confine himself by the narrow codes of conduct of ordinary men. All pretense of hiding the women in his life from Dolly was gone. He must be free to experience, to indulge that part of himself that craved the company of beautiful young women. It was through them, he thought, that he gained the passion that was translated into his stories.

I walk miles with my camera. I like to climb the mountains with a girl, and picture her on mossy stones, or lichen-covered cliffs, or rugged trunk or twisted pine or oak. I talk a little and listen much and feel greatly. And my feeling ranges from the wonder of a boy, and the fear of a man who may have a daughter some day, to the keen wild importunities of a lover alone for the first time in the woods with his sweetheart. I feel all the phases of the sex sense in man. I love youth and beauty free and wild in the mountain tops. The flush of cheek, the waving of hair, the action, the reality, the charm—these I feel with all the power there is in me.

Then there is more, infinitely more. The wonder of it all will never cease to hold me. The thousand changes of mood, of feeling! To walk alone in solitude under the pines with a girl with all life before her or a woman already beginning to look backward! That is what I hold as a wonderful privilege of life. I speak a foolish word perhaps or move a thoughtless hand, but it is what I learn, see, feel that counts.

This girl, or that woman, is nothing to me, nothing perhaps beyond the hour or the time. It is only what she represents. I do not deny the sweetness of clasped hands or the fragrance of wind-blown hair. But these things, the physical and the sensual, are not in any sense as memorable as the spiritual. I walk the mountain tops in dreams. If I am with a girl she is actual and has her part. If I am alone then I walk with phantoms—Hetty Sorel—Maud—Lucy—Cosette, or Milady—Guinevere, the duchess in the Man who Laughs—or I walk with women who have passed out of my life. And I know how sad it is. For they cannot come back; I cannot go to them. Friendship, love are in their graves. How the years fly! I am all men for all women, and myself, too, in these dreams.

But hours with a woman on a mountain top are rich with the secrets of human life. Every step, every word, every glance has its story. Apart from charm each has its revelation. For a lonely walk in a lonely forest is not conducive to the manners of the busy world. It is a unique situation for a woman and a rare actress is she who is not natural while wading through deep grass and over broken stones. Perhaps that part of the experience is really new, for as a rule women are unused to wild mountains. But the flame gathering in the eye, and the fire shooting through the clasped hands—these are not new to a woman. Every leaf of the trees whispers her betrayal. There are women and women, not all, perhaps, would let her hand lie in a man's in a lonely mountain top. But these are not many, and I have never met one.[5]

Dolly was his wife, separate from the others, cherished as above all of that, and there was no mistaking his very real affection and emotional need for her and for his children. She was the one he turned to when he needed help, when he was sick and discouraged, and she was his partner in the business of writing.

He left in the middle of February, and Dolly moved the family to Middletown. She saw him to the train station in New York, then she immediately met with Ripley Hitchcock to negotiate producing *Riders* as a stage play.

Wednesday

FEBRUARY 18, 1913

My dear Husband,

This is my first letter to you. Whether it will be the last is still a matter of conjecture on my part. But I simply cannot resist telling you of our interview this morning.

By way of introduction let me tell you something that I know will please you. I wept and sniffled after I left you this morning. I never thought I would! But I did. However, I won't anymore.

We proceeded to Harpers and for one hour and a half I perspired and was miserable under Mr. Hitchcock's fishy eye. First he proceeded to reduce poor Mr. Van Brunt to putty. You know his manner. He said the rottenest things in the most impersonal manner. Wounded the poor man to the very soul, and gave the impression that to even think of dramatizing a book was a high crime. Then he wanted Mr. Van B. to pay about $1000 for the mere privilege of being allowed to dramatize the book. And all this as smoothly as if he were conferring a benefit. Indeed, he kept telling me he wanted to protect my interests. At first I kept mum, but finally I got mad, and told him very politely and sweetly that all I wanted was a fair proposition. Then he called me Portia and addressed me thus for the rest of the conversation. Then he wanted to know what I considered fair, and I said certainly not one half to Harper's. I thought one third to each party would be right. To this both consented, Mr. Van B. as meekly as a lamb. Then Mr. H. kept insisting on the option being paid down. I knew that would be impossible and queer the play, so I suggested that Mr. Van Brunt go ahead independently and without any contract that would bind up the book. For this suggestion I was again called Portia and received a lopsided smile. Mr. Van Brunt agreed to this (very meekly again and rather to my surprise) and so the matter stands. . . . also note this, he didn't get the best of your wife. I got what you wanted.

Well, before I started this letter I was so tired I fell asleep sitting up in my chair. Now I'm wide awake. I stayed out almost all day. Discovered the cutest little lunchroom (very small) and had a bite there. Then I went to a moving picture show (across from Macy's) and enjoyed that. You probably won't like this, but I knew I'd have the dumps if I went home, and this will probably be my last day out. Besides, you are doing exactly what you please, so why shouldn't I? Why should I be tied down and cooped up all the time. I've a life to live too, and I'm eleven years younger than you.

Well, that's a bad topic. My thoughts are my own.

With love,

Dolly

Zane did not write as often as he promised or as frequently as he had in the past when unaccompanied by girlfriends, and when he did write, the letter was addressed to Mrs. Lina E. Grey. Dolly's response was sharp.

MARCH 11, 1913

Dear Doc,

Yours just received. It had the same effect on me that a red rag does on a bull. In the first place, why "Mrs. Lina E. Grey," since your friends are there? Before that it was "Mrs. Zane Grey" and if I'm no longer that, I'd like to know. You know, that's the way divorced ladies are named. Perhaps you have divorced me in the interval?

You talk as if you were cruelly and forcibly separated from your beloved wife and children. And in the next breath you tell me what a glorious time you're having. Those things don't go together. You chose, so I know you're not suffering or missing us very badly, or you wouldn't be away from us. As a matter of fact, you don't deserve to hear one word about us, but as always, I'm "soft" and "easy" and without any moral backbone.

Another thing. You say your friends are having such a fine time. Why on earth shouldn't they? I never heard of anyone who had such a "Cinch." To express it vulgarly, it's "easy money" for them.

I thought you went to Florida to fish. Why don't you?

The children are both fine, and *well taken care of.* At least I am good enough for that. Some day you can stay home and take care of them. And I'll go off and have a good time.

I was poison when I started this letter, but writing about the children has taken it out of me. Nevertheless, I'll send it. It may be salutary. However, don't let it spoil your good time. Life is very short. I'm looking around myself, to see where I can discover some happiness. I think it will have to be in my children. What I need is to _____, never mind. I don't know what it is.

Oh my God, I'm too young and full of life to have to settle down and find my only happiness in my children. I need more. If only I could—but I can't. I'm younger now than I was ten years ago.

Goodbye

Dolly

By the first of April, he was in Arizona and wrote that Dolly could write him at Flagstaff.

APRIL 11, 1913

Dear Doc,

Your epistle reached me just after I mailed a letter to you at Long Key. It wasn't a very pleasant one, so be rejoiced that you missed it.

Romer and I in the pouring rain trudged out to the farm this morning to get some eggs and to see Uncle Rome, who the youngster worships. He wants to be Uncle Rome's boy now, and live with him. He's the most wonderful child that ever was. It's useless to try to tell you all the bright and funny things he says because he says them all the time. If you think what you're missing is worth what you're getting, or to be mentioned in the same breath with it, you're to be pitied.

Also, if you're as homesick as your letters would indicate, you'd have been home long before this. Your sense of duty towards your companions is certainly strong. You never manifested it toward your wife and family.

Why don't you stay in Texas and southern Arizona to get your material? What's your idea in going to Flagstaff? Just to drag those girls over country you've been over twice before? You want new material.

The book comes out on the 17th, Mr. H. wrote me. I'm sorry you want me to send it, for the idea of your seeing it first when you're with those people

and reading it in their society makes me sick. But I'll send it. Don't let them touch it or goodbye. You see, I'm jealous, which ought to make you happy.
  Love from the kids.

Goodbye

Dolly

Zane, Lillian, Elma, and George Morgan (a cook), left Flagstaff for the Navajo reservation with Al Doyle as their guide. Their first stop was Tuba City, then they went over Marsh Pass to Kayenta Trading Post, owned by John and Louisa Wetherill. Zane wanted to spend a month on the reservation gathering material. The Wetherills interested him, living as they did in one of the remotest places in the United States, and the life of a trader to the Indians was just what he wanted for his books. The Wetherills were honest and friends of the Navajos, but many traders were not. There was, he thought, great drama in this.

Zane also wanted to see Rainbow Bridge, which he had heard of first in 1911. This was a natural bridge deep in Indian country. Called Nonnezosche by the Navajos, it was first publicized by Dr. Byron Cummings of the University of Utah after he reached it in 1909. John Wetherill had escorted the group and was the first to see the Rainbow Bridge, but Nasja Begay, a Paiute, had led them there. Zane tried to persuade Wetherill to take him there in 1911, to no avail. It was a long and arduous journey over land that must be crossed on foot in places, and Wetherill was reluctant to take visitors there. This time he convinced him.

Leaving Elma, Lillian, the cook, and the wagons at Kayenta, a small group consisting of only Doyle, Wetherill, Joe Lee (a Mormon cowboy), Nasja Begay, and Zane left for Monument Valley. Skirting Navajo Mountain on the east and north, they crossed the Bald Rocks, which Zane renamed the Glass Rocks, wound through a narrow canyon for twenty-two miles, and came at last to Nonnezosche.[6] They stayed only a day at the bridge then started back following the Navajo Trail to Marsh Pass, where Elma and Lillian waited with the wagons. Wetherill and Nasja Begay returned to Kayenta; Zane and companions traveled to Red Lake then Tuba City and northwest to the splendor of El Tovar and the Grand Canyon. After enjoying the

Grand Canyon for a week, the party left early in June for New York City, and Zane then returned alone to Middletown.

Dolly's welcome lacked warmth, and her coldness made him uncomfortable. In that chilly atmosphere Zane was unable to write, so he went to Lackawaxen, leaving her in Middletown. She joined him in midsummer, and R.C. and Reba came for several weeks as well. Zane wrote in the mornings then spent the rest of his time and took all his meals up the river, where he had installed Elma and Lillian in a bungalow. In August he took Elma and Lillian to the seashore for a few weeks before they went back to New York. Dolly and the children moved to Middletown the first of September for the beginning of school. Zane stayed at Cottage Point to write.

He wrote several stories that summer and fall based on material from this trip. He began two short serials, *The Last of the Duanes* and *Lone Star Ranger,* using the Texas Rangers as characters, and started a new novel, *Wildfire,* setting it in Monument Valley. *Desert Gold* was released April 17 while he was in Arizona after appearing in serial form in the March issues of *Popular* magazine, and it sold well. *The Light of Western Stars* was run as a serial in *Munsey's* from January of 1913 through the May issue and was scheduled for a January 1914 release with Harper's. Several other short pieces were also successful: *Field and Stream* ran "Amberjack of Sombrero Reef" in February and "Following the Elusive Tuna" in September.

Both children contracted whooping cough in October, and Zane went to Middletown to be with them. He stayed through November and December but left in late December to join Elma and Lillian for the New Year's revels in New York City. Shortly afterward he took Elma to Long Key and stayed four months. For much of the time Dolly had no address for him, and at the end of April she moved herself and the children to Cottage Point for the summer with help from R.C., Reba, her brother, Jack, and his wife, Mary.

APRIL 29, 1914

Dear Doc,

You beg me to write you, and give me no address to which to write. So I don't know when or where this will reach you.

Have been so terribly busy that I didn't know where to begin or end. It's after one every night when I get to bed. Today we got off all the freight, fishes all included. Julie of course did the packing. I don't know what I would have done without him.

You ought to see Betty. It's a sin and a crime that you are missing her now. She says everything. Her latest, "Sit down, you're rocking the boat," and is the sweetest darling that ever happened. Whenever she sees me she runs to me with open arms.

Romer is fine, but following in father's footsteps. He will climb almost to the tops of trees.

Au Revoir. If this ever reaches you, kindly send me your address.

Your

Wife

JUNE 2, 1914

Dear Doc,

Just a line or two more. Haven't sent this before as I don't know what address. May take a chance.

Julie, Mary, Romer, and Reba and Rome left yesterday a.m. (The two latter with two dogs, two cats, Amelia and other baggage by auto) for Lackawaxen. Julie is to oversee the moving.

Tomorrow I go. Meanwhile I'm canning cherries like mad. They're fine this year, biggest I ever saw. I'm awfully under the weather and nearly dead, but I'll get over it. There isn't much rest in sight. Company every minute all summer and that means cook and work. But I'm going on a violent spree last two weeks in August if I can possibly arrange it.

Goodbye. I hope to hear from you occasionally. All I've had is two skimpy notes. I was going to send you a kiss, but I won't. It might be a drag on the market.

Dolly

Zane left Florida in mid-May and stayed in Middletown through June, only visiting Dolly in Lackawaxen occasionally.

The estrangement in their marriage began to touch business affairs, particularly in regard to Zane's interest in the motion-picture industry. Since the first commercially successful film, *The Great Train Robbery,* had been made nine years earlier, the industry had matured considerably, and Zane thought his stories would film well because of their action and dramatic settings. He was well aware that motion pictures offered lucrative rewards and a wider audience for his work. There had already been several overtures from film companies, but he would not be available to discuss it, as he planned another long trip with Elma and Lillian. Before, he would have left the details to Dolly; now he entrusted Bob Davis to negotiate.[7] Grey had earlier given Davis the drama rights to *The Light of Western Stars* in consideration and appreciation of the idea for the book, but these applied only to its production as a stage play.[8] Handing him the right to negotiate all motion-picture and dramatic business with not just *The Light of Western Stars*, but also *Desert Gold, The Last of the Duanes, Lone Star Ranger, Betty Zane, Spirit of the Border,* and *The Last Trail,* along with the responsibility to transact all business and collect all money that accrued, especially as Dolly had done this in the past, indicated the degree to which the marriage was threatened.

Leaving Middletown in June, Zane reached Gallup, New Mexico, by the nineteenth. From Gallup he and his party, which included Elma and Lillian, crossed the northwest corner of Arizona. They spent three weeks looking around the Navajo reservation and the Hopi pueblos. When they reached Tuba City, he hired a car and driver and they traveled in relative comfort to Flagstaff, arriving July 22 but going almost immediately to the Grand Canyon.

After only a few days they boarded the train for California, as Zane wanted to try the fishing there. He had fished at Catalina Island on his wedding trip in 1906. Since then the island had developed a respectful reputation among fishermen and a very exclusive organization, the Tuna Club, was founded in 1912, with membership limited to men who had caught a tuna weighing over one hundred pounds. Zane's interest was piqued. At first he ventured as far as Avalon Bay in a rowboat, fishing for halibut and white sea bass, but before long he was going after the big fish.

In the previous eight months, since the New Year, Zane had been home only four weeks, and then his stay was interrupted. Away from Dolly he convinced himself that she was not so badly hurt, even that she was better off for his absence. Neither of them was happy in the tense atmosphere that came from his determination to live life on his own terms, but he could not avoid knowing that his actions affected his children.

Dear Doc,

Romer made me promise to write you and tell you he couldn't wait for you to get home. All of a sudden, as I was undressing him this evening, without a word being said about you, he burst out crying for you. "I want my Dad, I want my Dad, and I can't wait till he gets home. I can't wait." And he kept it up for at least half an hour till I was almost crazy. I asked him why he wanted you. "I want a man," he said. "I want my Dad. I like grouse meat and my Dad never sends me any," he said once. "What's my Dad doing? Why doesn't he come home?" He has those spells every once in a while now.

It is hellishly lonely here, especially evenings after the children are asleep. I'm glad Romer left me a dog. When I'm lonely I'm always frightened to death, and the dog is at least a protection, and a little company.

With Love

Dolly

For the first time since he left she had signed her letter with love. Within the month he was home and for a time put the needs of Dolly and the children ahead of his infatuation with Elma. Dolly was happy but feared he would leave again, so she learned silence. He stayed all of September and October at Cottage Point with them, and when the weather turned cold they returned to Middletown.

With few distractions his writing went well. *The Last of the Duanes* was serialized in the September edition of *Argosy*, and Harper's asked him to combine it with *Lone Star Ranger*, which had been in *Cavalier All Story Weekly* the previous spring, making a longer work that would be published early in January 1915. In California he had started a sequel to *Riders*, called *The Desert Crucible*, and he continued work on it after his return.[9] The story was drafted by the end of October, and Dolly began her work on it as usual. He immediately began another novel, *The Border Legion*. This one was set in the Alder Creek area of Idaho during the 1860s gold rush. It was finished by the end of February, and after five months of sustained effort, Zane went to Long Key, taking Elma and Lillian with him.

All winter he tried to develop an understanding with Dolly. He reassured her that their marriage was very special to him and that no other woman would ever share her status, but he said she must see that what he found with Elma and the others—Lillian's younger sister, Claire, Mildred Smith, Dorothy Ackerman—was necessary to his nature. In some later day, when his passion had cooled, his restless wandering would be over and he would be the husband she wanted. But for now she must accept both sides of his nature and come to know these girls, because in knowing them and seeing how they affected him, she would understand.

Maybe she understood in part, but mostly she feared that tears or anger would drive him away forever. Desertion and divorce were not unheard of, but the worst of social stigma clung to anyone so unfortunate. While she might have the fortitude to withstand the pity of friends and family and the contempt of society, she could not subject her children to that, and the truth was, she still loved him and trusted in his genius. So she tolerated his double life and even helped him construct a facade for the world, especially for his readers, that these women were only his secretaries and bore no other relationship to him. In return he would try to keep his other life separate from her and the children. Arrangements of this nature were not unusual among the wealthy of this time or those with an artistic bent.

Zane left Florida in March and moved into Cottage Point. Elma, Lillian, and Claire stayed in a cottage on the property, but Zane made sure they returned to New York before Dolly arrived.

APRIL 23, 1915

Dear Dolly,

Yours received. I'm awfully sorry you've been up against it, and I am mad, too. I wrote you a cross letter about the shades. I'm sorry, but I'm mad, too, about that.

I'm overjoyed at the prospect of your coming. The girls have worked like Trojans. And they've got their bellies full, and will be glad to go home Saturday. But then I'll be lonesome. And I can't leave this stuff here.

But don't you ever do things just to please me. As if you would! I'll look out for stuff, and keep you posted. Write soon. Love to the kiddies.

Ever

Doc

Zane's effort was productive. He finished the revisions of *The Desert Crucible* and renamed it *The Rainbow Trail.* Harper's contracted to publish it in August. He continued to work on *Wildfire,* the Monument Valley story started the year before.

In early spring Dolly discovered she was pregnant again and told Zane the news early in the summer. The baby was due in November, and Zane was delighted but saw no reason to change his plans. He would leave in July for California to stalk the big fish in the Pacific, particularly broadbill swordfish, and again visit Arizona. Long before the birth he would be home. Elma and Lillian were to go along and were preparing in New York.

Zane and entourage left in mid-July, traveling by train across the Midwest.

JULY 23, 1915

En Route

Dear Dolly,

It's some morning, my dear. Bright, fresh, cool, and the country is beautiful. So far things have gone fine. My proteges are quite well! Ha! Ha! But really, things are fine.

I hope you are being good, true, and patient Penelope. You must be sure to mend all my clothes while I'm away working hard.

Tell Romer boy that I'm on the Great Plains now where the Indians used to chase buffalo. Tell Betty not to forget her Dad. Those kids of mine!

I hope you are having nice weather and compensation for the last few weeks at Lackawaxen.

I thank you, Dolly. I'll never forget how fine you were. You made the hit of your life with me.

With love to you and the youngsters.

Doc

Alone and pregnant, her husband reveling in California with her rivals, bitterness crept into her letters, but Zane attributed it to pregnancy.

AUGUST 31, 1915

Dearest Magic Wife,

Those pictures of my baby and my boy gave me an awful kink. Why, it seems to me that even if I were one of those fellows who pay attention to other women, you would forgive me for their sake! How's that, honey?

I read your letter backwards and when I got to the part where hell commenced, I quit. So I really got a fine letter from you!

You ask "What are husbands for?" Damn if I know. They're no good, that's sure. Now that exogamy stuff women have been pulling off since the beginning of time doesn't affect me. And of late years I'm gradually inclining to the belief that I'll end a pretty good sort.

Rome wrote me a long letter, a sad one, which I don't care to discuss here. But I will say that he said you had been fine to him. I'm sorry that mail arrived that hurt your feelings. I can't always play safe, though I rack my brain to see and forestall.

Your letters about the forthcoming event in November have filled me with dread. Why need you be that way? You are young, strong. You've had two babies. Why can't you see that you have 1000 chances in 1 to go through. I have no fear, yet you make me fear. Never again, Dolly! You've got me buffaloed.

All the same, now I know how sweet babies are, I'm quaking in anticipation of the next one—no, I mean the next twins!

Miss Ackerman wrote me that she had met Jack London, and that he claimed to know me. She confessed to a pride in being able to say that she had visited me. I wonder why he said he knew me. He never met me, or ever saw me to my knowledge. Guess I'm getting to be some guy.

I seem to have been gone a very long time, yet its only six weeks. In less time than that I ought to be home.

Keep plugging along, Dolly, and keep telling Romer what I want him to know and do. Give my baby a hug and tell her not to forget her Daddy. Me!

With a daughter! Oh, Lord! Isn't life strange, and beautiful, and sweet, despite the hell?

Adios, Dolly. Don't forget me, and that I don't forget you.

Ever yours

Doc

The fishing was excellent. He caught fifteen swordfish, the most caught by one angler that summer. The next nearest caught nine. Zane's catch included the biggest taken that year. The rivalry and jealousy among the fishermen was intense, but Zane not only held his own but felt he had "skinned them to a frazzle."[10] He left Catalina early in August for Los Angeles, Grand Canyon, Flagstaff, Holbrook, and Greer to search for material and do some hunting and was home by September.

They remained at Cottage Point until late October then returned to Middletown. Though she was used to such moves, this time it was hard on Dolly and brought morbid thoughts.[11]

October 23, 1915

I am in the midst of packing to go back to Middletown day after tomorrow, and I am praying that my event may be delayed until I get safely settled there. Really, the baby ought not to come until after November 6th, but with the excitement and unusual demands upon me, I'm not so sure. I feel so heavy and not well. However, it won't help to worry and I shall not do so. I wouldn't mind very much if it came up here, but Doc would be terribly upset, because there are no good doctors within call. However, I have full confidence in Mrs. Koch, unless something unusual or complicating happens.

I wonder if to all women before they have a child death comes so near. That is, in their minds. I have no fears, but I feel the possibility. I would like to talk to Doc about it, and plan a few things in such an event, but he won't hear of it at all. Thinks I'm trying to frighten him. Well, I must pack, and at least be ready in case of emergency.

The baby was born November 20, a full month after the move and one day before their tenth anniversary.

There are not many details that I remember except that I paced around a good deal and that periodically Dr. Preston would say to me, "You poor woman, I feel so sorry for you," which speech would always infuriate me, even though I liked Dr. Preston very much. Finally after four, five, or six hours of this business (and Loren was really the fastest one to come), Dr. Preston asked "Cookie" to bring up a table leaf which he insisted that I lie upon. It was rather narrow and, needless to say, hard, and I did not see why this should be inflicted upon me in addition to the other agonies, but so it was. Also, a departure from the other births was that Doc was permitted to witness this one.

I suppose every woman practically goes though the same spasms on such occasions, although we all think we are individual as we do in the other things of life. I know that with every one, I would beg to be given something to dull the pain, and it seems to me that in every birth I have heard of since, the woman would do the same thing. As a matter of fact, I had nothing whatsoever, either with Loren or Betty, but he arrived just the same, and I think he was rather blue, for they turned him upside down and slapped him. He was the heaviest, too, of the three, weighing about nine pounds. I think it was about two-thirty in the afternoon when all was over. Loren was a beautiful baby, or so everyone said, and he continued to be an adorable one.[12]

It was another son, and, after some talk of naming him Zane, it was decided that there were already too many Zanes in the family, causing confusion. He was named Loren. He was the only one of the three not born in New York City, and his was the only birth Zane witnessed.

.

1916

CHAPTER 6

Tempests and Storms

Z ANE STAYED WITH DOLLY in Middletown through the rest of
November and December. The time was spent writing, and with Lillian and Elma in New York, there were few distractions. Dolly was restricted to bed rest, and the household centered on her and the new baby. But cold weather depressed him, and the writing stopped. Confined to the house by snow and ice, he was restless and got on Dolly's nerves, and this made the baby cry. In late January he left wife and children behind in the Middletown winter for the balmy tropics at Long Key, taking Lillian and Elma with him. In warm weather, with his girlfriends, his mood lifted.

Long Key, Florida
JANUARY 23, 1916

Dear Dolly,

You can have the $478 for writing me a nice letter. You may be sure I was relieved. I guess "you-all" will be O.K. soon. When you once get up I hope you take care of yourself and the youngsters. I am always so different about the children and you when I am away. The dynamics being absent, I presume I am able to love my family!

Your "purge of loneliness" was great! You know darn well that you're glad I'm gone for a while. Cheer up and do things! You are a wonderful girl and for Heaven's sake, deserve it!

I am beginning to feel well and happy and I'll be both and do some good work if all goes along safely at home.

Love to you, Loren (how's that fat chunk of a pig anyhow), Betty, Romer—etc.

Faithfully,

Zane

Dolly, in freezing Middletown with a new baby, was miserable, for in addition to Elma and Lillian, another very young woman, Emmeline, had caught his eye, and she was with him in Florida. Dolly, now thirty-two and a mother of three, felt old and unwanted.

Long Key, Florida

JANUARY 24, 1916

Dear Dolly,

I'm indeed glad you are up, and more than pleased to know you mean to work some. I shall work, or else I shall die. And life is pretty nice now. I don't want to give it up yet.

You can bet I'm glad to have Mrs. Koch at home. Every time I lie out in the hammock under the palms in the glorious climate I have a pang to think you and the kids are not here. But, Dolly, it's not possible to have you here. You must not stay long away from them and they couldn't come here. So I've got somehow to enjoy it all—and profit by it—without shame. I hate the cold. And I love the sun. Perhaps I exaggerate the risk and the discomfort for my youngsters.

Your remarks about Emmeline were somewhat sad. Has youth slipped away from you? I think not. And your life has been crowned by success. You have made a man out of me. You have three wonderful children. We have reasonable prospects. I have one bad—or one disquieting habit—and otherwise all seems well. So worth living for.

I would not laugh at you—for that—never. I understand that at least. Perhaps I am thick-headed. There is no reason for you to be very unhappy. The children are beautiful—and all satisfying. Only I can't stand them long at a time. It disrupts me—separates me from my mind.

I am so tired here always. The climate is enervating but I don't care. It's worth it. Love to all.

Ever

Doc

There was nothing for her in Middletown, so she took an apartment in New York for a month and for several weeks did not write to him. She was back in Middletown by the end of February, waiting for his return, when she became ill. She feared it was diphtheria, and knowing his mortal dread of illness wrote him to stay longer even after she knew she was no longer contagious. But he was tired of his companions, tired of the eternally glorious weather, and anxious to get home.

MARCH 3, 1916

Dear Sick A Bed Lady!

I don't think you innocuous or "safe" by a D.S. I think you are mortally afraid of Buck Duane, otherwise yours truly. That's all.

Sorry you aren't well yet. But you'll be O.K. soon. If you get sick again I'll—I'll beat you. It is hot here lately. I'll be glad to be on the way home.

Say, a swell Palm Beach lady—or visitor from there—one of the swell N.Y. contingent—got a little romantic over me—and you should have heard the yell from my adoring satellites. Adoring satellites is fine!

Goodbye, Honey, till Wednesday when I hope to see you again. With love to you all.

Doc

It's nice to go away, if only to go home!

At home in Middletown, he reopened the motion-picture business, personally talking to agents of the studios. He met with no success and finally decided that this was not for him. Writing to Davis, his agent, he said, "I have tried in every way to do something with these moving-picture people. I am not equal to the task. It is a sort of lamb and wolf affair."[1] Both Davis and Dolly discouraged him from dealing personally with the studios and the publishers, with Davis finally bluntly telling him, "And now, old sport,

forgive me for everything I have ever said to you—with the provision that I
am permitted to reiterate the simple, plain, unvarnished statement that you
are a damn bad business man."[2] He further stated,

> I have told you several times: you are a rotten business man, and I reiterate it
> here. The position you occupy in American fiction is a high one and you have
> earned it by sheer ability, plus courage. I still insist that if I could handle you for
> the next five years, the Grey family would have a winter and a summer home,
> built of fireproof material, a retinue of servants, automobiles, boats, and flying
> machines. You never should be permitted to talk to anybody on a business
> proposition, and every time you go roaming around New York to have a com-
> mercial jag, you set yourself back from ten to twenty-five thousand dollars per
> annum. If I could hurt your feelings often enough to keep you out of New
> York, except to visit a few friends, there is nothing I wouldn't say.[3]

Davis almost immediately had two offers for *Riders of the Purple Sage*, one
from a motion-picture broker for $1,000, another from the Fox studios that
offered $1,000 for *The Lost Trail* and $1,500 for *Riders*.[4]

While Zane was away, Dolly could deceive herself about the other women.
She did not have to be in their company or be pleasant to them. But when
he came home, all that changed. There were times that he needed her to
be seen with his inamorata as if nothing were amiss, to quell gossip. As an
author whose books appealed to readers of all ages, he had to have an
unblemished reputation, a public persona beyond reproach. And as three
of his girlfriends were related to Dolly in some fashion, it was logical that
Dolly would be present, making it difficult for her to avoid them.[5] Dolly
wanted herself and the children kept separate and apart from his affairs,
but Zane was sometimes thoughtless.

MAY 22, 1916

Dear Doc,

I'm shaking with fury and if I don't get rid of it, my day will be ruined. Now
let me begin by saying this is not Lil's fault. And this is for you alone. Don't
read it aloud.

Last night Lil met Claire at the train and persuaded me to stay the night with her. All the family—Elma's too, were there. Never mind about that. This morning I went to that place with Lil. A few minutes ago I left her and the last thing she said was "won't you give me a picture of the children? I have none and everyone else, not even related to them has. Elma has them all over her room, the ones at the tea-table."

At that I got so sick and dizzy that I couldn't see. How dare you give her that set of my children and without asking me. I had the pictures made only for you and for Romer because I cared more for you than for anyone. Not even to my own mother or to your mother did I give one. And now I find that you gave one to someone. It's intolerable. That's one of the little things that spoils the flavor of life. How could you do such a thing! You know how unbearably such a thing would hurt me. I'm crying as I write this, in a public parlor.

I won't mention this when I get home and you need not. Perhaps by that time I will have gotten over it. But that is one of the things that will leave a scar. Is it worth your while to wound me so? You knew what such a thing would do to me, else you would have told me.

Dolly

Dolly and Zane went to Lackawaxen in the spring, followed by Zane's female entourage not long afterward. There was little humor in the situation, at least for Dolly, but Zane's attempt to juggle moods and settle spats bordered on the ludicrous.

June 1, 1916

After taking Elma to the train, Doc came back (with Emmeline), fire in his eye, his face white. "I've had another run-in with Emmeline," he said. "She roasted my friends again, and me, and made me so furious that I told her if she didn't treat me decently she could go home." "What did she say?" I asked. "Oh, she said they (Dot and Mildred) were common and vulgar, etc., and as a matter of fact the one that is rottenest and most selfish—Elma—she has conceived a violent admiration for. Damn them all, tall and thin, short and fat." And I had to laugh![6]

Then Lackawaxen was quiet. Elma went to New York; Zane went to California with R.C. and Reba, taking Lillian, Claire, Mildred Smith, and Mildred Fergerson.[7] Elma was to follow. Dolly was left with the children and Emmeline, who was evidently too young to take. The parting was emotional.

JULY 21, 1916

Dear Doc,

There's only a ripple of yesterday's storm today. It was an awful cataclysm for me and I suffered agonies but my soul is purged. I haven't discovered yet if my heart is broken. I'm still numb from the pain. You, who should understand so much, fail so entirely. Especially when it comes to the higher, more subtle shades of emotion and feeling you simply go rough shod over my soul.

Hastily,

Dolly

And Zane replied.

Dear Dolly,

We arrived last night. Had a fine swift trip with only a few hours of heat and dust. I am well, but not yet mentally O.K. Your last "drive" almost put me out. It seemed so unfortunate after all that long time which you know I said was "too good to be true." I am sorry I did not know how you really would feel, for I would have altogether changed my plans.

Expect to go to Avalon this week. Write me there. With love to you and the youngsters.

Ever

Doc

Three young children required a lot of attention, as did the business of publishing, so Dolly stayed very busy when he was gone. They had decided to build an addition to Cottage Point, and Dolly supervised the planning and the work that went on through the summer. Much of the time she was consumed with fear, as polio raged across the country, striking children and adults from all walks of life.

AUGUST 18, 1916

Dear Doc,

Don't send the children any more post cards and tell Reba not to, as I can't let them have them, and I burn all that come. I just read this evening that there were paralysis cases in Los Angeles and California, Arizona, and all along the line, in fact, and I'm not taking any more chances than necessary. Of letters, I burn the outside envelopes and of course I don't let the children handle anything. I never was so terrified in my life, and I wish all the time that you were here. Why should all the responsibility rest on me? If anything happens you will be sure to blame me for that is your way.

Please, you who haven't any cares or worries and have nothing to think of but your enjoyment, please send me some cheerful letters. Tell me nothing can or will happen. But oh, it strikes the rich and the sanitary and the careful people, just as it does the poor, dirty, unhealthy ones; and they can't account for it.

God help us all—there is no love without fear—terrible fear. I suppose that is what makes love so precious.

Dolly

AUGUST 19, 1916

Dear Doc,

Just a line, while I'm in the midst of work, to tell you that I'm sorry I wrote that letter last night. I was so panicky and worried myself, that I never thought that it might worry you. Everyone laughs at me and my fear, but I can't get away from it for a minute. It's becoming an obsession almost. However, I don't imagine that we could be in a safer place than Lackawaxen and the children are fine, and I've given up all my plans and shall stick close to them. So don't you worry. Everything that can be done is being done.

No news from you for ever so long. I suppose that you only wrote to me as long as the people you wanted with you were here.

Will the children and I ever have you all to ourselves? I mean for good and all. I love you, but I hate all the others that keep you from me. Is there any hope for me to live on? I've been reading and studying and thinking quite a good deal, but my philosophy seems to evade me. I can't even get back to my

cynical one of this winter and spring, "To expect nothing from anyone, and to
be consequently pleased with the crumbs that are thrown."

Always

Dolly

As the weather warmed and became more humid in Lackawaxen, more
cases of polio were reported. When Zane wrote of his fishing and complained of the lack of things to do at Catalina, Dolly's patience broke.
Tucked into a long letter that she tried to make chatty and interesting was
her reaction.

AUGUST 21, 1916

Dear Doc,

   I haven't quite made up my mind whether or not you meant that letter
seriously. Somehow I think you couldn't so insult my intelligence. And yet it
sounds serious—it sounds like your childlike innocence. How can you be so
supremely egotistical and selfish as to drag your tender young friends and sensitive relatives to a "hole" like Catalina where there is "No nice place to eat,
no nice accommodations, no amusements, not one damned thing to do." You
see, I am quoting you. Poor Doc, poor Claire, poor Mildred Smith, poor Lillian,
poor Elma, poor Mildred Fergerson, poor Reba, poor, poorer, poorest Rome.
Oh my God! How I pity and sympathize with them! Why did they ever leave
their happy homes, or your happy home? Such a fate! I wonder if you remember your letter. It was a masterpiece. It should be published from an altruistic
point of view. Think of all the wives left at home (I don't know any) who
would be infinitely comforted and uplifted by its contents.

   Goodbye poor, unhappy, suffering man—separated by cruel lady friends
and a quest for big fish from enjoying the pleasure and perquisites of his only
wife, children, and fireside. Well, I'm still here. But if you can pray, pray for
us that we may come untouched through this epidemic.

Love

Dolly

Zane failed to see the humor, but the picture she painted of him was not
flattering. He became defensive, self-pitying, and accusatory.

Dear Dolly,

Your letter at hand. There was a lot of writing—words all over—but I did not like your letter. It has plunged me into the blues again. Perhaps all that about the children and that horrible disease was the cause, more than your satire, ridicule, contempt, etc. But the letter is not conducive to my future prosperity or happiness or well being.

I have worried about the kids. The feeling is beyond description. I ought to have almost the same pain for any children, but I can't. My own are a part of me. I will pray for them, Dolly.

You said a lot of things in this letter that I could not answer, if I tried. Perhaps I did write some fool stuff to you. God knows I'm crazy enough to write anything. I may be able to write beautiful letters, but not to anyone who has contempt for me. You say why don't I write them to you? And I reply because I can't. Your brains are too much for me. You see through me and my poor little dreams. You make me see that I am only a dog, a cur, when I could go on dreaming if my frailties were not so pointed out. You have made me lose faith in myself. I think I might have made some kind of a real success in life if I had been allowed to go on in my own way. . . . Your intelligence I grant, and your gift of seeing through people. You see all the rotten side, and none of the good. You could not even see that Claire was starved for some kind of love. She had never had a mother, or a father, or anyone to love her. And her "mushiness" as you called it, was only a crazy kind of longing for she knew not what. It was Mildred S. who showed me this.

One thing especially has wrought some sinister effect on me, and that is your contempt for my friends. The injustice of that has done damage.

I have forgotten your plans for the new addition to the house. Have it as you like. You'll have it all to yourself anyway, soon, so it does not matter.

This letter is no bluff, no vain glorious effusion, no morbid bid for sympathy. I am bitter, and strange for me I am growing hard. In my own way I've tried to be good to all I've cared for and I get only hell. I'd like to understand and to remember that this trip is different because I have Rome with me. But for him I could not go on. There is absolutely no need of me writing you

any more of this sort of thing. None! And when you don't hear from me you'll
know why!

As Ever
Doc

Dolly suspected this dramatic outburst was not only reaction to her letter. Other causes, namely those around him, were to blame. But she could
not let his accusations go unanswered.

SEPTEMBER 3, 1916

Chumpy!!

Why are you so sore at me that you can't think? Better get down to the
ground floor and analyze it. Who is making you sore at me? I haven't done
anything. Considering that I'm here crazy with terror and loneliness and misery, I've done particularly well by you.

Suffering either makes one callous, or softens. I suppose I can never make
you understand what torture I've undergone in the last months, and I don't
want to. It would be useless. Now is beginning the result and I feel as if it were
to be a softening. I feel as if, very little, the terrible hard rock in my breast
were beginning to be dissolved, to be washed away. It would be far better for
me if I would harden and callous, for I'd have more protection for the future.
There is still plenty of hardness and galling bitterness, of tendency toward
irony and sarcasm, that I find difficulty in repressing, and I fear it will take
years to overcome. If things only don't pile on me again when I am beginning
to emerge! And also—I still hate with avidity.

A strange thought popped in my mind this morning. I don't know if
it's safe to tell it to you but I'll take a chance. It came out of my thinking about
everyone I know and their motives. You know I've always had an uncanny
insight into people's minds and motives—an unpleasant sort of a gift. Well,
the conclusion I reached was this—that you, in spite of all the awful things you
do and the way you make some people suffer, are really intrinsically better
than most people because what you do is the result of no preconceived
motive, thought, or deliberation, but of habit and emotion. You do far worse
things than others but more as a child would in obeying an impulse. That

doesn't say you do less harm. You do more. But all the same there is a better germ in you than in most. God send that it develops and casts out the evil. You could be the greatest man on earth if you could conquer yourself, but that is a task for a superman. But even the striving would help.

Goodbye, now, dear. I can't help loving you when I see the children. Betty is hopping around in the sunshine like some big bright butterfly.

Au revoir

Dolly

Zane's newest protege, Emmeline, was left in Dolly's care for the summer. Emmeline was quite young and had a tendency, when around Zane, to be quiet, morose, pale, listless and to eat very little, and of course she had literary aspirations. Dolly felt that what she needed most was a normal and wholesome environment, and that summer she provided one, with tennis, croquet, horseback riding, swimming, and church suppers. With Zane gone Emmeline acted like any normal teenager. Attached to one of Dolly's letters was a cryptic message.

What would you say if I told you that:

Emmeline was singing at the top of her lungs while Mary pumped the piano—

That she threw a kiss to my mother when the train pulled out this Morning—

That she plays (or tries to play) tennis with us every day, also croquet—

That she is hugely enjoying her meals, and eats four times as much as she did—

That she has gained five pounds since you left—

That she is happy and appears so—

That she is making herself a dress—

Chew upon this![8]

Emmeline was to stay until the first of September and work on a manuscript, and Dolly was to help her with it as she helped Zane. Then Zane wrote and asked her to keep Emmeline with her until he got home. He was concerned, among other things, about some letters he had written her, and he wrote Dolly from the Grand Canyon to see if she could get them. She replied,

Dear Doc,

Just received your letter asking me to keep Emmeline until you come home. I'm afraid I can't and won't do that. It has gotten to the point where it is essential for our happiness, for the future, and for my life, that I live alone with you for a little while, and your goings away and comings home you must keep sacred to me and my children or else there'll be no me. When any one else is around you are entirely different to me, I am entirely different to you, and the third person, whoever it may be, gets impossible. Not that I don't care for E., but I care for the E. that is herself away from you, not the wild erotic creature you inspire. I'm just sorry for her then, and I hope she'll get over it. The other I am not sorry for, for they're worldly wise and know.

As far as the letters are concerned, I'll see what I can do. It's hardly fair to ask her to destroy your letters when you keep hers, is it? I'll see, tho. What have you written in a note to her? Have you written it yet? If you have I hope you haven't mentioned her staying here till you return, for it will put me in an unpleasant position. I had intended keeping her for some time yet, but not till you return. I can't. I must be alone with you for awhile, and I'll kill anyone who bothers us. All the rest have you all the time, share all your pleasures. If I can't have something, I'll have nothing. Can't you understand and see that? We can never get close together again and good companions as we were if there's always someone butting in. It poisons me and I can't be fair.

As for E.'s book—we are both working on that and it will be some time before that's in shape for typewriting, let alone publication. She has to work and work on it. The girl is too young, too inexperienced to dash off something and have it published on the spot. You'll do her a great deal of harm if you try to hurry the process. Her ideas of life are far from whole; in fact, some of them are decidedly unwholesome and biased. I think the quiet normal wholesome weeks she's had since you and your crowd left have done her more good than anything else.

I'm glad you're enjoying yourself, dear. You're the one that ought to enjoy it. But scatter a few of your crumbs of happiness my way, instead of throwing rocks and bombs at me all the time. I've had enough misery this summer. I feel like a drowning person who, just as he is beginning to rise to the surface to breathe the wonderful air, and is beginning to strike out and swim, has some giant hand shove him under again. Your last four or five letters have been like that. And all the time you're enjoying yourself. I'm not asking for happiness, just a little peace and cessation of active misery, and it's so easy for you to give!

Would you, could you, enjoy giving me a good time? You'd get more out of it than your wildest dreams could tell you.

For Always
Dolly

P.S. Emmeline just showed me the letter you wrote her. You're all wrong to take that attitude. She's doing her best and instead of making it harder for her you should be generous. The relation between you is impossible. It was founded on a lie and when that lie was discovered nothing remained. I don't say it was deliberate or conscious. And you say to Emmeline, "My two best friends, you and Dolly, have gone back on me." I am not one of your friends. I am your wife, and I'm the only one who has never gone back on you and who never will. Find anyone, friends, relatives, acquaintances, anyone in the whole wide world who has done for you what I have done. If you find anyone, and prove it, I'll gracefully yield my place. And you did mention to Emmeline to stay. Why didn't you ask me first? Why do you make things so hard for me? Won't you write her now, and tell her that you've changed your mind about her staying until you come, and not mention my having anything to do with it? And won't you try to be a real friend to the girl and to help her instead of making it all the harder for her.

Don't be afraid that I'd ever be disloyal to you compared to anyone else. For you to class me and make a sweeping assertion like that is awful. Please don't ever again. It makes any relation between me and your friends quite impossible. I could never even see any of them again, if you persisted in such a course. I am your wife. It is for you to say if you don't want me for that any-more. But as the long years roll on, you will find the truth of what I say. The past has proved it. I am the one that sticks, that has stuck, that will stick. One by one the others have dropped away, will drop away. The present ones are as transient as the past ones have been. Is it worth while then, to wreck what is real on what is transient, our years of work, of love, of companionship, our children? I say no. It's up to you.

Zane had already changed his mind about Emmeline, but for other reasons. The truth that Dolly wrote had stung, and he wrote an angry and cruel response.

SEPTEMBER 21, 1916

Greer, Arizona

Dolly,

Your communications received, and they were my finish. I have become obsessed the last year with the idea that the trouble between us is in part due to the German in you. It is too much for me. I concede the greatness of the Germans, their culture, their science, their metaphysics, their psychology. But God save me from another intellectual woman! Give me a girl like Claire, if I can't live longer without one.

I understand you now, and better than ever, what you never had and what you want in a husband. Well, I did my best which was little enough, I suppose. And now I pass. You can have the freedom you want and you can get the husband you want. I hope to God you find them. As for me, I'd rather go to hell than stand your scorn and bitterness and discontent any longer. If I must continue to be made to feel as you have made me feel lately, I do not want your love, or you as a wife, or as anything.

I know you have had hell, suffering, trouble, and all on my account. I should have never burdened you with myself and my fatalities. Still, I seem to feel that I can reproach you for two things, your persistent nagging and knocking, and scorn, and your blindness to the fact that if I had been helped in my way I might have made a great name. That is personal egotism, I suppose, but just consider the difference it would have made. It was too much to expect of a woman, that is all. No woman will stand for anything that excludes her from all. She would rather a man be a failure, so long as he was bound to her.

You have stood for more than any other woman ever did stand, but at the expense of my nerve, my dreams, and now my future. It is horrible for me to receive the homage and courtesy that I get everywhere when all the time in my heart I know that you consider me a whoremonger.

My friends are not what you think them. They all have weaknesses, as indeed the whole race has, but they are worth to me all and more than I have given them. If, as you say, they must fail me, one by one, then I say that when that day comes I am done for good and all. Nothing could have been any crueler, any more mortal a blow to me than for you to say that. These girls have kept something alive in me.

I have heard again from Emmeline. In these last letters, she is back again on her lofty pedestal, and I am not fit to touch her again. She says I led her too far and made her care too much. Well, she got exactly what she wanted. I was good to her. I saved her. I never built my place in her affections on a lie. Never. By God, I never did; and it is she who is to blame. She refused always to let me tell her anything. She swore she would share me with my other friends. When she came to L. and found she was not the all she had supposed, then she failed me.

Send her home at once. And get my letters. I shall write her and tell her to leave them with you. It is not safe for her to keep all those letters, written while I was trying to make her forget her unhappy state. They might hurt the children someday. So send the white-faced, two-faced girl home.

You need not answer this. I don't want to hear from you again. All your loyalty to me, and your standing by me (as you call it) and the rise from my earlier darker days, and the wonder of the children, all have been for naught, so far as saving me is concerned. It was a sacrifice on your part, for nothing. Unless you call the children something.

I will be home in October. Then we can settle the matter. I shall not stay long, but go to New York in November, and south for the winter. You must not think that because there is no mention of love for you and the children that this letter is no less than a death knell for me. I can never build anew, and my great Babylon is tottering.

Z.G.

Dolly wrote on September 25 that the letters to Emmeline were safely in her hands. Other than one more brief note, she did not write again until October 1, Romer's birthday, reminding Zane of the day his son was born.

OCT. 1, 1916

Dear Doc,

Seven years ago today our son—our oldest son—was born. Do you remember that night in the hospital? Will you ever forget it? I should ask. Every detail is as clear in my mind as if it happened yesterday. And the clearest part of it is of the time when we sat together in that third floor room holding tight to each other while the doctor calmly snored and the nurses sneaked away for a nap. And between the awful pains and the terrible weariness I would gasp "Never again" and you would echo, "never again." It was the first time, or I wouldn't have said it. I never did say it again, either, when Betty or Loren were born.

And our boy is seven years old today, fine, sturdy, and with a brilliant mind and a fine body. I can pat neither you nor myself on the back for this result. We're just lucky. But let's be more than lucky from now on.

We are putting these fine children into the world and they are worthy of the best in us. They are our future, our immortality, the rock on which our house is built. And it seems to be a pretty solid foundation, for in spite of the tempests and storms, the house has stood.

It was an earthquake that nearly brought it tumbling down this last time. That was the worst that ever—well, I won't speak about it. I haven't written to you since I had that letter because I didn't want to do so until I could conquer my bitterness and despair, and feel honestly that things were straight between us again. You were unjust and wrote without thinking, without half reading my letters. Well, never mind. It's past. Let the dead past bury its dead.

Goodnight

Dolly

CHAPTER 7

A Hyena Lying in Ambush

Z ANE'S ANGER had cooled by the time he reached Lackawaxen. Dolly was not the cause, but frustration with Emmeline and worry about indiscrete letters falling into the wrong hands. He reached Cottage Point in mid-October, stayed with Dolly until January, and this time, when he went to Long Key, he took Dolly with him.

She stayed only until his girlfriends arrived, a short week, then went home. Left with three beautiful women competing for his attention, Zane was oddly irritated. He wrote Dolly his concerns and she responded, taking the opportunity to point out the shortcomings of his friends.

JANUARY 24, 1917

Dear Doc,

Your letter just came. Every time I begin to struggle to the surface, something comes along and pushes me down, down, down into the depths again.

You are exceedingly unfair to shove the blame of your friends defection off on me, or to say that E. poisoned them is ridiculous. Don't worry that they've gone back on you—if there was anything in that they wouldn't be with you. And if they're making trouble for you, they're an exceedingly ungrateful bunch after all you do for them. And if, to quote you, "they might be so many rag dolls" for all the good they do you, you'd better send them home. Rag dolls at the Florida prices are somewhat expensive luxuries.

I say this—the girls know perfectly well what they are doing and what they are getting from you. If they didn't want to be with you, they wouldn't. For them to make trouble for you is ungrateful, to say the least. You didn't say what the trouble was—you say I knew they would fail you. That sounds specific and I certainly know nothing specific. Generally speaking, you know that I always have thought and always will think that I'm the only one who has always and will always stick to you. And I can't conceive how they can be in Florida and yet have failed you. Well, there's always a fly in the ointment—I think there must be bedbugs in mine.

Au Revoir

Dolly

And he wrote back,

JANUARY 29, 1917

Dearest Dolly,

That was an awful letter of yours, but I don't intend to let it quite finish me. I can't explain about the girls, but I will when I see you. And now that I'm over the shock, I guess I'm glad for their sakes. I felt pretty sick at the unhappiness of your letter. But I know that'll pass. We gotta stick together, Penelope, if I am away from home.

Love to all my family,

Doc

There was not much to keep Dolly in Middletown, and since she always enjoyed the city, she moved the children and herself to New York as she had the previous winter. A furnished apartment at 111th Street and Broadway in a large fireproof building that had comfortable, sunny rooms was leased.[1] The manager was accommodating, Romer liked his new school, and Dolly could renew old friendships and enjoy the sights and sounds of the city, especially the theater and the shops.

Talk of war was everywhere in the city. All of Europe had been at war wince 1914, but Germany's resumption of submarine warfare directed toward all ships in the war zone threatened to pull the United States into the fray, especially when it torpedoed an American ship on the third of February. Diplomatic ties with Germany were severed, and war seemed inevitable. Even in Long Key there were serious discussions of German actions and appropriate responses. Zane considered coming home, but Dolly felt it unnecessary and shared with Zane her shrewd analysis of the situation.

FEBRUARY 9, 1917

Dear Doc,

You ask me to write you what I think of the situation. It is this. Neither we nor Germany want to fight but as the situation now stands with diplomatic relations war will declare itself almost automatically as soon as Germany commits an "overt act of war" against us. Judging from the way Germany is now waging her submarine warfare she is trying very hard to avoid an "overt" act of war against us; but she also feels that this submarine warfare is her last effective weapon and she'll go the limit. If, in this crisis, the overt act should be committed, the bomb would be exploded, but both nations are anxious to avoid it. I notice that while Germany has been sinking ship upon ship, she has also been careful to save crews, etc. and that is what makes me think she is doing everything possible to avoid war with us, while at the same time pursuing what she considers her only course. On our side, I think the president, tho' taking a firm stand, and the only stand now possible, for us, will consider very carefully what he would call an act of war against us.

If war is inevitable, I can't see that it will be an active war at all. Like Japan, we are too far away to do anything but prepare and fortify ourselves as strongly as possible. Germany is certainly tied up and has her hands full, and I hope that our nation would not be so foolhardy as to try to send a fighting force over there. That is practically out of the question. Our line is preparedness and proper defense of our seabord [sic]. There is little or no excitement in New York, but there is a lot of quiet patriotism shown, and I think everyone worth his salt has come out strong in support of the president, whether he considers him right or wrong. I haven't heard of or seen anyone of even the most ardent pro-Germans who hasn't come out strong for the U.S. in this crisis.

Take it all in all, I don't think we need worry. Worry won't help anything.

The inevitable will come, be it peace or war, but while they're all so busy over there, they can't bother us much here.

So it's cold at Long Key? Well, it's somewhat colder here. Around our eyrie the wind whistles like a demon, but we have more heat than we can use. Goodnight.

Dolly

Much of their correspondence concerned business. Royalty checks from Harper's were sent to him at Long Key, and he forwarded them to Dolly. He negotiated with motion-picture companies to film his books, especially *Riders of the Purple Sage,* and worked on a manuscript about the construction of the transcontinental railroad called *East and West.*[2] *Wildfire* was released in January, and sales were exceptionally good.

Zane planned to go home at the end of March and wrote Dolly he had told all his friends his arrival date. This, and several other remarks, provoked a heated response.

MARCH 14, 1917

Dear Doc,

Your amazing, amusing, infuriating letter came this morning on the wings of a large and untimely snowstorm. . . . Do you realize that you have offered me a mortal insult? You say, "Lets be good comrades this year without a lot of K-F-S-ling." You imply that I'm—well, something unspeakable—a mink or something like that. Know then, my dear man, that you'll have to crawl around on your knees before I ever allow you to approach me again from that direction. Besides, my spiritual and intellectual nature is beginning to dominate to the exclusion of the physical. Some great and wonderful passion—but we won't discuss that now. Should I consider it my duty to further contribute to the race and my country by bringing more children into the world, I will investigate other methods.

Immediately after your above sentence ending with the word "K-F-S-ling," you say "Rome is going to have it out with you." Do you need your brother to protect you from your wife? Or is he perhaps to regulate our sexual relations. Perhaps he'll keep an engagement pad and a calendar, and every so often announce "Tonight's the night!" And will he have a stop watch to see that you don't overdo yourself? Oh Doc, how could you, how could you! The next sentence is "Now, dear, don't turn him down. For my sake, don't." Does he aspire to your position, or wish to act as substitute, perhaps?

About your homecoming. Since you have asked your friends to meet you, I couldn't think of intruding on such a touching scene. I magnanimously yield to them, since that is your wish. You know where I live. And remember—I repeat it—your comings home and your goings away are sacred to me and your children. When they fail to be we fail to be your wife and children.

Well, I'll be glad to have you back, and so will the children. I hope things will go well—and somewhat happily. If you'll just remember that I, too, am a woman, I think they will. And I can still subscribe myself,

Your wife,

(In name only)

"K-F-S-ling" was evidently a polite way of referring to their intimate life, or at least Dolly so interpreted it, and it appears that Zane was attempting to place their relationship on a platonic basis. Her angry response and obvious pain forced him to back down and claim he had been misunderstood.

MARCH 17, 1917

Dolly,

Yours of March 14 at hand, and I would rejoice if I knew I were to go to H- before I ever receive another such letter from you. Last night and today have finished me. I had a bitter quarrel with Rome, and worse with Reba, and still worse with Elma and Mildred. I fired them both.

Your letter was the last straw.

Evidently you took mine seriously. I did not mean anything about that K-F-S-ling, as you call it. And that about Rome was the business deal we (especially he) wanted you in. (But that's off now.)

I have been upset for days, and now I am sick. There is danger of a strike on the railroad, and we may be held here. We can't get away now, that's sure. But I hope to leave on the 22nd. If I am no better when I reach N.Y. I will go to a hotel. It did not occur to me that you would be insulted because I asked the girls (L. & M.) to meet me.

I realize from your letter that my case is hopeless, I am resigned to anything. I have lost my friends, and next will be my family. I seem to have a mortal deathly sickness within me. Poisoned! Ever since you came down here you have been satiric, bitter, and rancorous, except in one letter. And under the circumstances I think you had better not meet the train next Saturday.

Doc

In any event she could not have met the train. His mother was ill, and Dolly urged him to go directly to Middletown to see her. His visit there disturbed him.

April 3, 1917

Upon my return from Florida, I spent several days at my mother's home in Middletown. The visit was significant of the fact that a little time is remarkable in its effect or that I have learned to see more than formerly. Mother scolded and complained and ranted in a way as amusing as pathetic; my sister bustled about, important with her late responsibility as housekeeper, and she was lively, cheerful, and vain of her work; my brother was lame and half-ill, and the same pessimist as of old.

One remark he made shocked me, and it was that sister was fifty years old. I could not believe it. Yet I knew it was true. And I was appalled with the flight of time. In my dreams the years come and go.

When I went off to bed I lay awake for a long time. The house was dark and quiet. The old clock that ticked the hours away when I was a baby ticked at the closed gates of my memory, and the past of boyhood rose up.

Next day I remembered my wakefulness and the strain of thought persisted. My mother and brother and sister moved about the house; and suddenly all seemed so old to me. Old people, old faces, old footsteps, old pictures, and fixtures—all so sad, so revealing, so poignant.[3]

The following day Congress went into emergency session and for two days the nation held its breath while they debated entering the European conflict. War was declared April 6.

Perhaps the international situation affected him, or maybe his private life took its toll, but whatever the cause, Zane could not write. His thoughts were blocked and effort seemed futile, although his fame was greater than ever. *Lone Star Ranger* was on the bestseller list, and sales of *Wildfire* would soon put it there too. *The U.P. Trail* was scheduled for publication after its appearance as a serial. He had almost twenty books to his credit, but he regarded them all as preliminary, with the great effort of his life, a psychological novel, still eluding him. For thirteen years he had worked on *Shores of Lethe*, what he had earlier called *Mel Iden*, but much as he wrote and rewrote, he was not satisfied with it. And as he worked, he felt life slipping away.

April 14, 1917

Last night while I was awake, though lying with closed eyes, I thought of myself in this way: a vast, dreary, naked shingle of the world, dark and cold, under lowering clouds, with pale shadowy wastes of water on hand, and I upon this desert, naked, fleeing with wild eyes and hair upraised and clenched hands from pursuit! That is the living truth of my soul today.[4]

April 23, 1917

This then is what I face, defeat and loss. I can bear defeat, but not loss of all, not at one fell swoop! Loss of family, friends, loss of my power to write! Loss of virility, strength, eyesight! What horror! This war has upset my mental equilibrium. It is a bad time for thinking men, and fatal for an idealist.[5]

April 30, 1917

A hyena lying in ambush, that is my black spell. I conquer one mood only to fall prey to the next. And there have been days of hell.

Hopeless, black, morbid, sickening, exaggerated mental disorder.[6]

Dolly told him he needed exercise, that such morbid fancy was caused by lack of circulation. He was unconvinced.

His dark mood lasted until the middle of May, and only after it lifted did he write. He started another Arizona western, *Man of the Forest*, while in Long Key, made no progress on it after he returned, then worked feverishly through June and finished it. Too old for military service at forty-five but not wanting to let this opportunity pass, he planned a story about the home front during the war that would celebrate the values of patriotism, loyalty, and red-blooded Americanism. This would take advantage of the market for such books and sell well. It would depict Germans as scheming sabo-teurs who resented American success and values. He wanted to set it in the wheat country of the northern tier, and to gather material he arranged to tour the area on the way to California. Then he was to go to Colorado to hunt bears.

This time he took Dolly with him, as well as Dorothy Ackerman and Mil-dred Smith. It was the first time that Dolly accompanied Zane and his girl-friends on an extended trip. It would be an even greater test of her forbear-ance due to the fact that they would be closely confined on a train across the country. Their marriage, and her role within it, were clearly changing. This trip also heralded the waning of Elma's star and the rise of Mildred's.

July 7, 1917

It seems more than passing strange to be flying away from my "nearest and dearest." Again I have that feeling of a thread between my heart and theirs— a thread as thin as a spider's, which stretches as the distance increases and always pulls a little more and hurts a little more. Why must we always choose? Why must I leave my children or be left by my husband? It is far harder to be left than to leave.

Ida and Elma went to the train with us. I think, I know, Elma felt pretty badly, but she's spunky and proud. When we passed the house they were all on the back steps waving to us. I can't describe the feeling I had.[7]

More unlikely traveling companions would be hard to find: the author, his wife, and two admiring young women. For any ordinary couple the trip would have been doomed, any enjoyment of travel or scenery ruined by jealousy, arguments, and tears. But Dolly was resigned to sharing her hus-band, and her choice was clear: either accept them and their relationship to her husband or be left at home alone.

The railroad took them from Lackawaxen to Chicago, then across Min-nesota and North Dakota to Montana, reaching Glacier National Park five days later. Dolly kept a diary throughout the trip in which she recorded her impressions of the scenery, other people on the train and in the towns whom they met, and a few comments about her traveling companions.

Doc got fussy and angry yesterday because we stayed in the observation car for several hours. It was pleasant and cool and comfortable there, and at 4:30 they served afternoon tea. When we got back, Doc had an exceedingly injured expression on his face. He asked if the girls had talked to anyone. He's always worrying about them and that sort of thing. I finally asked him whether he didn't trust Mildred, but he'd trust Dot anywhere. Before I knew it, I burst out "As a matter of fact, Mildred is to be trusted every bit as much as Dot, and Dot always has a much more peculiar expression on her face than Mil has, when a man appears." The minute I said it I was sorry, but it's as true as gospel. Both of them are ready for fun of that kind; Mildred is more open about it and Dot is slyer. They've always done it, and the only reason they refrain from it now is because of Doc. Their expression when an eligible man appears is exceedingly interesting and amusing to me. And I don't blame them in a way. If they do nothing wrong or harmful, why should I quarrel with their way of having a good time. Of course they wouldn't pick up anyone when I'm around, but I claim it's the look and expression in their eyes and faces that invites men just as plainly as words would. And Dot has more come hither eyes than Mildred. Poor Doc, he takes things too hard. He'll have a great awakening someday. But I'm going to try as hard as I can to make everything pleasant for him this trip and I spoke to Mildred about it. She was perfectly frank and said she and Dot liked to get acquainted with new fellows, but of course they wouldn't do anything like that because of Doc. And Doc always blames the men for it. You'd think they were ravening wolves. I say it's up to the girls!

There was a beautiful young girl on the train yesterday. She had something of Allie Benke, Jo Munson, and Emmeline, but was prettier than any of them. When Doc saw her he remarked "It's a good thing Uncle Romer isn't on the train alone." As a matter of fact I would have trusted Romer sooner than Doc. Half an hour with that girl would have finished Doc, regardless of Dot.

Dottie and Doc are both off color this morning. Poor Dot has had four upheavals and Doc's been having awful dreams in which Elma tells him he's an old has been. That is abysmal tragedy for Doc, even in dreams. I lay the whole thing to the table d'hote dinner which Doc and Dot got away with. The diner was too crowded to allow our being together and Mildred and I ordered a light, conservative meal, but the other two were steered into the table d'hote dinner by which the road advertizes itself. They did it up from soup to nuts, and when Mildred and I left the diner, they were entirely surrounded by strawberry shortcake, whipped cream, and ice cream. No wonder![8]

After several days exploring Glacier Park, they left for Spokane, Portland, and finally San Francisco. News that Zane's mother had died reached them there. Zane was stunned. After his father's death he had assumed financial responsibility for her and his sister and had become very close to them. There was no way to reach Middletown in time for the funeral, and anyway Romer, Ellsworth, and Ida had made the arrangements, so there was nothing really to do but proceed with the rest of his trip. This included fishing at Catalina, with several magazine articles to be based on this, and a trip to Colorado for material on bear hunting. Zane and Mildred went to Southern California and waited for Lillian and Claire, who were coming out by train. Dolly and Dot returned to Lackawaxen.

Zane acknowledged Dolly's forbearance on this trip, which he realized must have been trying for her. While she was still en route home, he wrote,

JULY 25, 1917

Dearest Dolly,

Well, its over, and I'm back here alone. I feel sad. I want to thank you for being such a brick on this trip. I never really knew how fine you could be, and I love you more than I ever did. It was splendid of you, to be a good fellow, to enjoy it all. I'll not forget it, Dolly.

With best love,

Doc

But Lillian, Claire, and Mildred together made for squalls.

AUGUST 3, 1917

Dearest Dolly,

It is a bad mess here with the girls and I wish I were out of it. Lil's friends the Prestons have left Yuba. And Lil does not know what to do. Mildred has offended me for keeps, and last night Claire told me that my "other" friends were no good—that they did not care for me, and were only working me. This from Claire has about foiled her chances of ever getting any of my regard. Yesterday I told them that she would have to go with Lil or go home, and that caused a row.

Lil doesn't want her nor does Mildred and Claire has no place to go to in N.Y. I am pretty much disgusted.

Well, it won't be long, whatever I do. And while I can fish hard and go to bed early I won't be bothered much.

Love to my children.

Love,

Doc

At least the fishing was going well. Zane now chased big-game fish and landed his first broadbill swordfish on August 4, fighting it for almost six hours. This made up for a huge disappointment the day before, when he missed catching the world's record swordfish at 462 pounds. For days they chased it, and it took six baits from him, but Zane spoke of it to another fisherman who promptly quit his usual ground, invaded Zane's, and hooked and killed his fish.

Just before he was to leave for Colorado for the bear hunt, he wrote Dolly about Emmeline. Dolly had grown fond of her and had invited her to stay with her for awhile.

AUGUST 16, 1917

Dear Dolly,

I have not answered your letter, or written you the daily because I got sore. I was afraid your sweetness would not last. It just simply makes me sore, the way you nag and knock in letters. And I certainly will give you the dickens when I get home. You were absolutely a peach all on that trip, and then as soon as you got home—well, that's enough.

Dolly, the thing that gets me, and which has got to come to an end is this! You have permitted Emmeline to see that you held my friends in contempt. It was a great mistake.

I will not permit you to have Emmeline at my place anymore, either in N.Y. or L. If she is already at L. upon receiving this, cut her visit short. Don't make any excuses more. It is not often that I oppose you, or say such things. But when I do, I mean it. Her case must be handled differently, and at a distance. She makes fun of me and my friends to you, and to others. And she is dangerous to you and to me. That's all. Don't make any blunders, now!

I am not going to send you my love, but I love you anyhow. And if you ever write me another rotten line your home will be Denver.

Ever,

Doc

The bear hunt fizzled, even though much time was spent looking for bear and the scenery was beyond compare. He was anxious to go home, but even there little cheered him. Three things plunged him into the darkest spell of depression he had experienced in a long time.

The first was his mother's death, which had not seemed real to him until he got back home. He recorded his feelings in his journal.

October 17, 1917

Today I went to Middletown to visit my mother's grave. It was a melancholy autumn afternoon, subdued and hazy in light, and still and warm. We went through the cemetery to the far side where a wooded hillside had something of the aspect of a mood. The place was deserted. We walked down a grassy path to where a big evergreen tree towered, and here under this tree on the green slope was the last resting place of my mother.

I sat down beside the grave with slow bitter comprehending sadness. She was gone forever. When I saw her last she was alive and well, wishing me Godspeed on my journey, and from that moment to the time I sat beside her grave we had been parted. All I felt was that she was dead and gone and buried, that my boy and girl who are with me were the personification of youth and joy, that my brother who spoke with a terrible realization of the nearness of death, that my sister looked old to me.

The second was the end of the affair with Elma. Elma had been in his life for five years. Her dark hair, blue eyes, and small, strong figure had more than once been the inspiration for his heroines, and she added excitement, intrigue, and vitality to his life. But now his feelings for her had changed and Mildred took her place.

October 22, 1917

Yesterday I had a sad talk with an old and dear friend, E.J.S. We had not been on good terms for a year. It is settled now, and we will never be the same again. Where has it gone, the glory and the dream? Five years ago this month I met her, and never had I seen a more beautiful girl. Will October ever come without my remembering her and the sweetness of her charm, the allurement of her beauty, and the dreadful certainty of the death of love? Not death, perhaps, but change. I am losing more and more with every swift flying year. But I have gained the pain, the memory, the lesson: and I will be the better for all experience.

And finally, after moving to New York in December failed to lift his spirits, he ran into an old girlfriend one day, an occasion that would bring pleasant reminiscence for most, but for him it brought only sadness.

December 15, 1917

The other night I met an old sweetheart of mine, and had the opportunity to see her and talk to her. The experience was perturbing and sad. It showed the brevity and remorselessness of time. Ten years ago she was fifteen, pretty, sweet, shy, graceful, and altogether charming. Especially was she soft, fresh, radiant with youth. Many tricks of speech and mannerisms of act brought back that earlier freshness and beauty. Alas! The contrast with the present! She had grown stout, her face had broadened, there were lines in it, little wrinkles at the eyes, and creases in her neck. She was just as vain as if she were the sweet girl of ten years ago. Thus we have the tragedy of the years.

His mood was at its worst on Christmas Day.

December 25, 1917

This has been the blackest Christmas Day I have endured for nearly twenty years. The one I compare to it was when I was in Philadelphia, in college, and on that Christmas I had no money, no hope, no way to turn. I went out to Fairmount Park, climbed up on George's Hill, and then on a lonely bench, in the cold, I wept like a bitter and forsaken child.

Today I have not wept. But I have lain in my darkened room, ill in health, yielding to a long spell of depression, and let my mind go to sad and terrible thoughts. I could hear the sweet gay wild prattle of the children with their toys. Christmas, so little to me, was glory to them. I heard their pattering footsteps in the hall. And Romer ran to me with a present he had bought for me. I could hear it all with the door shut tight. And those happy sounds augmented my misery.

My wife's brother was there, his booming laugh and ponderous step unmistakable. He came back to me twice, not to forget me, to sympathize with me in what he thought my illness. He was full of the Christmas spirit and looked it. I envied him. The contrast in the reactions of his mind, his absorption in good will and love toward all, and my own terrible, driving passion. For I saw it all, saw the sweetness, wonder and joy of my children, the fleeting evanescent nature of their present, the pride and happiness of their mother, and the members of her family. I saw also myself.

Where are they, the glory and dream of my life? If I am not morbid and ill these days then I am lost. I cannot write. My novel lies unfinished and incomplete. I have not worked it out. I cannot work in the cold and noise and distraction of this city. Then, my Babylon is falling. All of 1916 it rose in dazzling radiant splendor. All of 1917 it has been falling, pillar by pillar. And now the beautiful keystone of the arch, that labor of love and time and years, is about to fall.[9]

1918

CHAPTER 8

Your Only, Wife

T HE WINTER OF 1918 was the coldest on record. New Year's Day the temperature fell to fourteen below in New York City, rising in the day only four degrees. The only place anyone could stay warm was in bed. Coal shortages caused by wartime demands aggravated conditions and there was terrible suffering all over the city. Zane's dark mood deepened. He wanted the warm sun on his face. On January seventh he left for Florida with R.C. and Reba, Ida, Claire, Mildred Smith, Mildred Fergerson, and Dorothy Ackerman and his mood immediately lifted.[1] Dolly stayed behind with the children.

JANUARY 11, 1918

Dearest Dolly,

My trunks came today. I had a good sleep last night, and have busied myself all day at this and that, so I'm beginning to feel pretty good. The wind has blown hard all day from the south, warm and nice, and my face feels soft. There are several kids here, and what fun they do have. It is such a healthy place. I wish mine could be here too. I suppose I will begin to worry about you and them now.

There is no news, but I am beginning to think of work. Write to me when you feel like it. I have bought $200 worth of nice letters from you. Of course, I did not make a deal for any number, and you may flim-flam me. But, why

can't we write like we used to? Simply because you married me? Poor
Dolly!

I will feel better when I know you have cheered up.

Ever with love,

Doc

By now Dolly was used to his absence and even enjoyed it.

Dear Doc,

I think I am recovering my equilibrium. I am busy—and I'm going to be
busier. That's the kind of happiness I get while you're away, and while it's limited, it answers the purpose of keeping me from active unhappiness.

I was thinking about myself and the difference between me when you are
home and when you are away. It's almost a dual personality. In the former
case I'm objective—my activities, mental and physical, revolve around you.
When you're gone, I get entirely subjective, independent, individual. I must
admit I feel much more powerful and purposeful, more able to accomplish
things, to express myself. I wonder which is better. The first is the more primitive, natural state of the woman with home, family, husband; the second of
the woman who accomplishes something in the world outside the home. They
can't combine in me; each state is separate, but I think that is your fault. You
absorb the personalities of all who come in close contact with you. It's not fair,
but I suppose you can't help it—and certainly the absorbed ones can't. Yet
they answer their purpose. It's a pet theory of mine that a genius needs to be
fed by many personalities, which he mashes and grinds up as a mill does, in
order to get the finished product. However, I refuse to be entirely ground up.

I'm glad you're enjoying your nice warm southern sunshine again—and
incidentally the beneficent sunshine of the presences gathered about you. It's a
cold, keen winter up here—no let up at all. Coal shortage continues here.

With love,

Dolly

Dolly loved the city. Her days were filled with activities. A few entries
from her diary show how she spent her days.[2]

Tuesday, Jan. 8

Peace—with a vacuum! Don't remember what I did. Oh yes, we had the four generations picture taken at Grandma's, a proceeding to try the patience of a saint. Mary and Marjorie came home with me, and in the evening we went to the And. Principally to see the "Rainbow Division."[3]

Wednesday, Jan. 9

Mary stayed.

Thursday, Jan. 10

Had Nelson and Elma to dinner and he took us to see "Flo-Flo" a rather uncensored production—but amusing and pretty. Poor Nelson, henpecked before he's even married.

Saturday, Jan. 12

I tried an experiment today. Took Romer to Damrosch's Philharmonic for children. He couldn't be quiet and he knew it all! Stopped at Uncle Theo's office, and as usual Romer asked questions all the time. Uncle T. was amused.

Sunday, Jan. 13

Cooky took children to Hoboken. Towards evening I met Miss Olsen at the Vanderbilt—Woman's City Club, where we had tea and an interesting talk. Then we went to the Strand and saw some kind of melodrama by Irvin Cobb, and a hash up of the Mikado.

Thursday, Jan. 17

Met Mama at 10 a.m. for a premiere of Arnold Daly in "My Own United States," a well-made production, patriotic and moving. Mama came home for lunch and in the afternoon I wheeled the baby up and down Broadway for several hours. Really a fine day. Elma came up for an hour or two.

Friday, Jan. 18

Jo Munson and Elma to dinner. Philharmonic with Grandma, Brahms and Beethoven's 5th concerts.

Saturday, Jan. 19

Went to Dr. Wolf's advanced Eng. Class. Very interesting. Reference to—only the unhappily married women succeed. P.M. "Lord and Lady Algn." Enjoyed it tremendously.

Despite the coal shortage and the measures taken to conserve coal, which included a five-day shutdown of all industries, amusements, and anything not absolutely essential to feeding the populace, Dolly enjoyed herself. Without Zane's demanding presence she could direct her own life, indulge her pleasures, and she could ignore his infidelities. But when she voiced her contentment to have him at a distance, Zane became concerned.

JANUARY

Dear Doc,

We're getting a touch of weather and war now; coal gave out and we haven't had heat yesterday or today, and may not tomorrow because Mondays are holidays now. We've managed by lighting all the gas jets and the gas stove, to keep from suffering, especially if we stick to the kitchen. But I shipped Romer and Betty to Larchmont with Julie and Mary this morning, and I'm going up myself early tomorrow and bring them home towards evening. We can keep Loren warm without much trouble.

Gee, I'm getting ossified with the cold. Wish I was under the palm trees with you. No, I guess I don't, after all. At least I know I'm alive up here. Life is pretty full and big for me just now, even tho I miss you. But I know you're there, and that you belong to my life, and that inevitably you'll come back to me and the children to stay, because you'll want to more than anything else, not because you must. And so, all must be well. Goodnight dear.

Dolly

He wrote back,

FEBRUARY 13, 1918

Dear Dolly,

I accept your Emerson proposal, and I accept it with full appreciation of its nobility and difficulty. You could do that if you wanted to. No doubt that would solve my problem. Anyway I would not accept it unless I felt that I could do, at least, a part of my share. I will be glad to do all that I can. The beautiful sentiments and confidences of your letter I cannot speak of now. I sort of shirk the responsibility. They are so big. I think I feel a good deal of what you want me to feel. I hope you will get something of what you need. But there is more than my work for me to consider, and that is you and the children. I am going to give you both more of myself, such as I am.

We must leave the question of the girls to future consideration. I am sure of your generosity there, as in other particulars. And just now I am prone to disregard the real value of the girls to me. Please think this over, so that we can talk about it when I come home.

You see, my ordeal was in part the giving up of my long cherished ambition to write the psychological novel. And now that I mean to follow my natural tendency, to express love of the beauty and wonder of nature, I will want to take you with me often. Rome suggested that I take him, you, and one of the girls on a trip into some wild place. Would you like that?

And I think I'd like to have you come next summer, providing I go, about Sept. 1, and go to Clemente with me. The Pacific would not make you seasick, and you would love Clemente. We could find a good place for the kids and Mrs. Koch, and then take the wild trip. The point is that I want you.

Ever

Doc

How ironic that the words that almost severed their relationship in 1912, "but I don't want you," were reversed in this simple statement. But the six intervening years had made a different person of Dolly. She knew how his moods changed, and she was cautious.

FEBRUARY 17, 1918

Dear Doc,

It's very nice of you to want to take me on trips, and of course you know I'd be more than glad to go provided all things are feasible. I know I can help you, and I also know that you have no one associated with you with keener appreciation than your wife. You see, I live almost entirely in the present, almost in the moment, therefore I perceive keenly and absorb readily the things that go on about me. You, on the other hand, are always a dream in the future. Therefore, I, with my present mind am the complement to you. We ought to do good team work.

Now, about those trips. There are only two things I want to ask you. I dislike asking those, but in your planning we may as well get things straight at the beginning. First, please don't include me in any trip with Mildred Smith. This is no reflection on or discredit to Mildred, simply I don't think I'd enjoy the trip, and it therefore wouldn't justify my leaving the children. Secondly, in that foursome, Rome, you, myself, and another, have the other no other than Dorothy. I can't see any harmony otherwise unless it happened to be Claire.

I suppose all this is in the nature of looking the gift horse in the mouth, that if I'm asked, I ought to be overjoyed under any circumstances. But I can't just see it that way. After all, home with the children, and plenty to do, isn't an unhappy place by any means. And it's paradise compared to association with incompatible people.

With Love,

Wife

Mildred Smith was now the favored one. Elma was not included on the trips or brought in as companion, but as she was a distant relation Dolly occasionally took her to plays and to dinner, and Elma worked with Dolly on some of Zane's manuscripts. Elma took the change hard, according to Dolly, but being busy did her good.[4]

Mildred was with Zane in Florida. Like many of his girlfriends, she too wanted to be a writer. She collaborated on a few chapters of the war novel, *Desert of Wheat*, much to Dolly's scorn, and in Dolly's opinion her influence was not an improvement. Chapters were sent to Dolly for editing as they were completed.

JANUARY 20, 1918

Dear Doc,

I'm worn out struggling with that awful chapter of yours where Lenore hands herself over to Kurt on a platter—so now you've got to at least share the agony with me. My God, what hit you when you wrote that chapter? It sounds just as if you'd had a "liebestadt" session with Mildred Smith. Lenore fades into insignificance. "Cool, soft pressures, white soft hands, arms, shoulders, dim starry eyes, heavy eyelids, white graceful images, reeling senses, brutal hugs, exquisite gowns, palpitating bosoms, sudden-flashing incredible portents, tremulousness, tumultuous, "Lenore Anderson!—You could not trifle with any man!" cried Dorn hoarsely! Hopeless love—physical rapture of senses, twisting black balls, chaotic black gulfs that turned into mixed metaphors, pulsating bodies, alive, intense, clinging—Some more black things, shapes this time. Angel's hands, distraught whispers. Black and shapeless parlor." And so it keeps on over and over, scrambled together in an awful mess. It's the limit when she faints from being hugged. The girl is flippant, indecently sensual, just where she should have been biggest and finest, and the fellow degenerates into mush. No wonder, after what she does to him.

I groaned and cussed and got violent and furious and disgusted. And I'd been looking forward to this particular passage because you'd spoken so much about it. I don't know what to do. Do you want to rewrite it? Or shall I try? It has some very good flashes, here and there, but most of it is the limit. And it's so important. You've made a beautiful character of Lenore all the way through—and just here, where she should reach her pinnacle, you've made a nasty little mink out of her. What possessed you when you wrote that chapter? It's erotic.

I'm simply scared to death to send you this, but it's absolutely necessary. You'll probably hate my insides, but I'm doing my duty. If this chapter ever got into print, it would dash all your really literary hopes, which are now beginning to materialize. Please don't write me a mean letter now and give me the dickens. I had to be honest with you—and one chapter is nothing in the sum of a really good book, but it's sufficient to spoil it if it's not right.

With much love,
Dolly

Dolly's advice was critical to Zane's success. Before he left New York, Harper's had assured him that he was their leading author and all the resources of the company were at his disposal. His royalties were enormous:

No other author's sales compared with his. But his idea had always been to win a public following with romantic novels that celebrated nature, then to write a powerful psychological novel of love, passion, and tragedy that would win him literary fame. Dolly shared this goal, but his publisher did not, and even advised that should he try, those different novels must be published only under a pseudonym. For thirteen years he worked on his psychological novel with no success, and he finally gave it up, indirectly acknowledging that his effort to write in that fashion was an excuse to be surrounded by beautiful young women.

FEBRUARY 16, 1918

Dear Wife,

I have gotten that great hold on myself. Dolly, rejoice with me. As far as my work is concerned, my ordeal is over. And that means, if I am to follow as intellect and passion direct, I must work so that you will be happier, and my children. There must be less and less of that part of my life that has hurt you. Less and less, until there will be none.

Now, Dolly, I am in deadly and terrible earnest, as I am when I am driven to my last stand. Let me forget my breakdown. I am ashamed that I hurt you by it. But maybe it opened your eyes. I will come home a new man.

Let me hear from you soon. With love to you and my magnificent youngsters.

Faithfully,

Doc

She wrote back,

MARCH 5, 1918

Dear Doc,

I can't answer your letters now, but I think you've misunderstood me again. No one has more faith in your possibilities, no one knows you and your potentialities, better than I do. And if you please, I did not mention your lady friends at all in discussing your possibilities. That's a thing which you have to settle to your own satisfaction. You know what you think they mean to you.

You must have what you think you need. After all, you are the member of the family with the message for the world, and the conditions must be the best possible for the transmission of that message. Whether I think that under some circumstances the message could be greater, bigger and more lasting, is hardly important if you are dissatisfied. And I'm not standing on my infallibility. I'm just your wife, the mother of your children, and as far as may be, your helper. I can and will adjust myself to circumstances. If in a way my individuality and perhaps some of my happiness is squelched, I can still feel that in helping you, being your wife, and bringing my children into the world, my life is not useless. These vague longings for more, the feeling of undeveloped power and possibilities are perhaps better squelched. But oh, how sweet they are!

Much love,

Dolly

He concentrated now on western romances and fishing stories and worked with motion-picture companies. His books were in demand by the movies, and he had no difficulty finding companies to film them. Fox filmed *Riders of the Purple Sage* and *The Rainbow Trail* on location in Arizona with William Farnum in the lead, and Samuel Goldwyn's company filmed *The Border Legion*.[5] But Zane thought there was more money to be made if he owned the production company rather than merely selling film rights, and he began discussions with Benjamin Hampton about forming a company, to be called Zane Grey Pictures. Hampton would do most of the actual work and direct the movies, but Zane would be an active consultant.

After two months of intense work in Lackawaxen's glorious spring, *Desert of Wheat,* the war story, was finished and another western, *The Mysterious Rider,* was begun. In June he went to California primarily for fishing, but since the movie industry was now located there, he also went to take care of some business affairs.[6]

JULY 5, 1918

Dear Spoofer,

Your long and passionate epistle at hand. It's awfully sad about you. When I had just about decided forever that you had changed into the dandiest woman in the world, what did you spoil it for? I sadly fear that German guy was right about women.[7]

I am pretty tired today. Have not gotten broken in yet. Then last night Mr. Hampton was over to see me, and he excited me. I will write you the details of the moving picture deal soon.

Ever,

Doc

JULY 8, 1918

Dear Dolly,

Mr. Hampton was over to see me. He said if I continued to live as I have lived, in the open, loving nature, loneliness, etc., that I could die the great writer of America.

I am beginning to feel better, and very hopeful. But I'll have to work as I never worked before. This big motion picture deal is going to make me stick to work. I will write you more fully as soon as I know the facts. The contracts are being made in New York by Mr. Stern, the Authors' League lawyer. When I get them and the details of the business to follow I will let you know at once.

This is a big opportunity for me, and I hope you will help me. You certainly were off your balance for a couple of weeks before I left. I hope you are well now and sane once more.

Weather delightful. Fishing good, but I have caught only two tuna.

Love to you and kids

Doc

JULY 15, 1918

My one and only love,

Mr. Hampton will be in New York soon, and he and Mr. Warner will probably arrange to meet you. I have suggested it. I'd rather you went to New York to meet them. Anyway, they will write you, and you will see what a big deal we are up against. I am very enthusiastic.

Have been thinking some of sending for Ellsworth, Ida, Elma, and Romer sooner or later. As I don't expect to have Mildred come at all and don't want Elma to travel alone with Romer, it really does not seem advisable to have them all come soon.

The fishing has not been very good lately, and I'm not killing myself. I am planning some books, and believe me, they will be corkers.

Adieu, fond wife. Write me when you feel happy. Love to all.

Ever

Doc

No mention was made of Dolly's coming along, but after such a cold and miserable winter in New York while he was in Florida sporting with his friends, Dolly decided that she and the children should go to California for the coming winter.[8] He thought it a splendid idea and that they should all go, his family and the "harem," as Dolly referred to the assortment of young women.[9] She worked on selling the Middletown house, while Zane looked for a suitable one in California.

JULY 16, 1918

Dear Dolly,

You are worried about the house I rented. Well, Dolly, I did my best. Houses are hard to get in Los Angeles. I took one when I had the chance. I'm scared to death for fear you will be furious and displeased. But it's in a nice neighborhood on the outskirts of Los Angeles, had a big sunny room and bath for Mrs. Koch and kids, and a nice room for you with a bath, and next to a sitting room I can use. There are a couple of other small rooms. The downstairs is all right, very cosy and cheerful. There is a tennis court near we can use. A good school near and some stores and flowers. We've got to take it, for I've paid a month's rent, $150, and I've got to work this winter. Savvy? You will love the climate and the fruit in California.

I will write again soon. Don't forget that I love you, in spite of all your faults!

Ever

Doc

Even though she expected to join him there, the last few weeks before he left were particularly hard on her, surrounded by the girls, and when he left with his brother and sister-in-law and several of the young women, she felt abandoned again. She wrote of her feelings, but Zane was incapable of understanding or of writing what she wanted to read and met her misery with only more demands.

Dear Dolly,

Well, I love you heaps this morning. The sun is hot and bright, the mountains gold, the mockingbirds are singing at my window, the gulls are screaming below, the sea shines vast and calm with the gentleness of Heaven upon it.

Your letter haunted me. Can't it be made right? Can't you be less feminine and still Dolly? Can't you be the wife, comrade, helper, mother? What is the use of that subtle side? I will never write overdeveloped, oversophisticated, oversouled books. They do no good. The good of my books is the elemental passions and the action of nature. They make men and women strive. Why cannot you learn from them? There, my wife, is a stunner for you.

I'm all in this morning. I've fished hard, and am tired. But every day I learn more, and feel bigger. If only I could hang on to you. Not just yourself, either, but your esteem, respect, faith. These I have forfeited, alas! All the same you've got to come back to respect for me, and faith, too.

I'd like to see you all. I'm asking you to cheer up, and be Dolly now. This is the first time since I left home that I felt right toward you. It was your letter. See how I respond!

Ever your

Doc

Dear Dolly,

Just back from Los Angeles. Have much news, but simply can't write you. There was a big, fat letter here, addressed in your writing. Not a damned word in it from you. I was simply amazed and sick with disappointment.

You are treating me shabbily. You are not doing the right nor the square thing. You are being dominated by a side of your character, which, if not changed, will ruin us.

I told Rome, and he said he fancied you'd never write him again. You see you are way off, all wrong in your ideas about him and me, especially him. If you imagine I would lie to you, you are to be pitied. Rome has never spent a moment with either of the girls, and very little with me.

I ask you once more, Dolly, to rouse yourself, and be the fine, wonderful, wholesome woman you really are.

Love to the kids

Doc

Receiving no response from her, real alarm entered his letters.

AUGUST 3, 1918

Dear Dolly,

Something is wrong. You are punishing me for my letters to you. Maybe you are hating me for something I said. Dolly, it's forgotten. It was never meant. It was only me. Always I am in mental strife, except when I work or am active. If I do not hear from you soon, I'll go mad. This will never do. Last June you were simply great. Now, what in the hell could have happened to change you permanently?

I absolutely and inevitably refuse to let you become like other women. All your hopes of life, all mine are centered in faith in each other, love for each other, comradeship and idealism. What you think you need and what I think I need are only agonies of the heart and soul.

I simply can't believe any hardness of yours can last.

That's all, and despite my hurt feelings I take consolation in that.

Ever

Doc

Dolly's silence was not because she was angry. She had been in New York taking care of her mother after an emergency appendectomy and had not even received his letters. When she returned briefly to Lackawaxen, she wrote explaining why he had not heard from her. More importantly, she wrote frankly and revealingly of her feelings and of their relationship as it had now become.

Dear Doc,

Since my mother was getting along pretty well, I felt I could take a few days off to run home and see my kiddies. I was very homesick for them, and it is a joy to be with them again and home here; even though it's just as mercilessly hot!

It's been a pretty worrisome time for me, and the great relief of feeling that my mother is practically out of danger, plus two or three nice letters I got from you, plus being home and seeing the youngsters makes me feel light hearted and happy this morning—a feeling that for a long time has been a stranger to me.

No, my dear, you don't understand me. In fact, you have never tried, or even imagined there was anything to understand. To you I am Dolly—your wife, the mother of your children, the bearer of your burdens. There are certain things you want me to be, certain things you want me to do, to love you and help you and understand you. But that I'm an individual that has a struggling, often suffering soul, you have never seen or understood. You ascribe all my reactions to physical things—that I should have no feelings except those prescribed by your conception of what I ought to be and do. But my most passionate ideals and desires—the ideal of a home, my children and my husband as my heart and soul see them, has never been at the border of your consciousness—at times my almost hopeless hope of that fulfillment seemed near death—but it was too vital to die, and now I see a faint glimmering, and my hope is renewed. You have that in you that will eventually fulfill my ideal; you have that certain rarity of soul that sooner or later will burn through the dross and egotism of habit that the years have laid on you. It has taken me a long while living with the physical you, and suffering through you as I have, to find the vision. It has come not only through development of you but also of me. There was a certain warmth and beauty in our relations part of the time this spring that has been one of the most precious things life has brought me—and in that lies the hope of all our future. And I cannot see failure. We have come so far together, through worse than hell and we must stick together to find the light.

There is another side of me that you fail to understand and allow for—and

that is the side of me that relates to love. Byron says "It's woman's whole existence." Yes, almost, even mine. What I do not get, I perforce supply to myself
mentally, but my physical possibilities are too powerful to be satisfied by my
mental dreams of love. It frightens me sometimes. I never can, and never will,
tell you some things. And yet I am sure that the physical relation has ceased to
exist between you and me and that all of that kind of desire is dead. I cannot
conceive of it any longer. But that is your fault. And yet certain things, instead
of perishing because of deprivation, grow stronger. Well, I suppose I'll have
to fight it out my own way, as I've fought out so many things.

Sometimes I say to myself—"What have I to do with such feelings and
such dreams of love and romance. I am getting on toward middle age" and
everything in me, mind, body, soul, laughs the idea to scorn. Why I haven't
had any of the things that are coming to me yet. Yet when are they coming,
and how? Somehow, tho, I'm going to fulfil myself—if not here, then
hereafter.

What on earth has Claire done now to incur your displeasure? Elma's and
my letters reek with reference to her fall from grace, but the reason is not
forthcoming, and I am consumed with curiosity. Was it a man? Of course, if a
lady falls from grace, cherchez l'homme.

Dear hubby, let me give you a bit of advice that applies not so much here
as in a thousand other situations, and that is one of the rock foundations
on which a successful marital mansion is built—the Grey mansion—always tell
your wife things first, before they get to her through some other channel.
They inevitably get—and you avoid, oh, so much. There's a very profound
psychological reason. Besides if you tell me things, it automatically foists upon
me an obligation and a sense of honor that would not figure otherwise.

Well, this ought to do for today. Day after tomorrow, I'll have to take that
hellish dirty hot trip to N.Y. again.

Goodbye, my dear.

Forever your
Wife

Their marriage no longer included a physical relationship. Whether he
did not want further intimate relations with her or Dolly did not want such

a relationship with him while he also had his affairs, we do not know for certain, but it appears to be what he wanted. He had broached the subject the previous year but backed down at her reaction.[10] Dolly was only thirty-five, far too young to be putting aside all thoughts of intimacy, and this must have been terribly painful for her. She indicates that she still wanted such things, that her desire had not died, and that the responsibility rested on his shoulders. But this was perhaps the only way she could retain some dignity. Dolly was now to be his sometime companion, mother of his children, business partner, keeper of his home, his voice of reality, nothing more. Love there was, but in a platonic and spiritual sense, not romantic, erotic, or sensual.

Zane was relieved to finally receive letters, but his salutation shows clearly what the relationship had become.

AUGUST 8, 1918

Dear Mama,

Two letters from you today. I don't know how to act. Was taken aback at the way you handed it to me. But on the whole I rejoiced at two, 2!, letters from my wife. As a consequence I feel fine.

We are stuck out here, Dolly, and you've got to come out. I apologize for whatever it was that hurt you. I didn't mean it. I do love you more than anyone.

Love, love, love

Doc

He urged her to come to California in subsequent letters. The salutation here is equally revealing, as is the reference to their being "chums."

AUGUST 13, 1918

Dear Old Fatty,

Gee, it's nice and cool here now. I wish you were here . . . I don't see how we can get away from the west. And I don't want to stay away from you and the kiddies for six months. I love you all too much. What have I a handsome, intellectual wife for, if I can't have her part of the time? And my beautiful youngsters . . .

Say, you and Elma championing Claire is too much for me, I fear. I will almost end up by weakening. Only I am thoroughly disgusted with

Claire and Mildred S. Fergy is all right, and I may have her come out to take the Arizona trip. In fact, I probably will, unless I change my mind again. But you are to understand that whatever I do in her case is because of what I feel an obligation.

As for you, well, you and I are going to be better chums than ever before. That means that you will help me, and I will do more, and care more for you.

Love

Doc[11]

He was most likely kidding, but that salutation brought a rise from Dolly, and the way she characterized herself in her closing showed that if they were no longer lovers in a physical sense, she was still his only wife.

AUGUST 19, 1918

You horrid thing, mean, nasty,

To call me "Fatty!" Anything but that! Its so undignified, vulgar, utterly loathsome. Fatty Arbuckle, etc. I've some names I could call you but I wouldn't be so undignified.

You are full of plans aren't you, dear one? But don't forget this one: that I and your children have you alone to ourselves for part of each year. It's very little, if you care for us. Otherwise nothing is possible for me. It is the one thing that is absolutely necessary so that I may "Carry on" as the English put it. It is what keeps living the part of me that appertains to you, my children, my home. If I can't have it, there's no home in this life for me. And don't think this is one of my morbid ideas. It is the life or death of what means most to me. Please don't forget it.

Your only,

Wife

So it was planned that Dolly and the children would come west in the fall. Romer, now nine years old, was not content to wait until fall but begged to go with his father to Arizona that summer to learn to hunt and live in the wild as his father did. With misgivings on everyone's part, it was arranged. The problem was how to get Romer to Arizona in time to take part in the hunt. Then suddenly, and to everyone's surprise, Zane's older brother, Ellsworth, seemingly a confirmed bachelor, wrote that he had married a wealthy Middletown woman, Ethel Stern, daughter of a department store magnate, and they wanted to come west as well. They could bring Romer.

AUGUST 22, 1918

Dear Dolly,

I am leaving in the morning for Clemente Island where I hope to stay for ten days or so. I wish I had some news about Ellsworth. His letter, saying he was to marry Ethel that day, sure was a stunner. He wants to come west, and as my other letter stated, I now expect him to leave on the 15th with Elma.

Be sure to send directions about Romer's food. Better send a package of zwieback and anything else you think I could not get at Flagstaff. Gee! I will be wild to see him!

With much love to all

Doc

Finally, five travelers—Romer, Ellsworth and Ethel, Ida, and Elma—left in September to meet Zane, R.C. and Reba, Mildred Smith, and Dorothy Ackerman at the Grand Canyon. From there, Zane, Romer, R.C., Elma, Mildred, and Dot, with Al Doyle as guide, departed for Arizona's Mogollon Rim and the Tonto forest to camp, hunt, and fish.

The Tonto had beckoned to Zane since his first trip there in 1915. It was a heavily forested region, rich in game and majestic scenery, with a bloody history as well. One of the most violent western feuds, the Graham-Tewksbury feud or the Pleasant Valley War, erupted there in 1887 and continued for five years. Its origins were unclear, and Zane tried to trace them but could not do so. Later, as he came to know the residents, many volunteered accounts that, unfortunately, differed, but on this trip in 1918 no one would talk about the conflict to a stranger.

SEPTEMBER 22, 1918

Dear Doll,

Well, here I am with a lame back, and large responsibility. We left Cedar, Ethel, and Ida at the Canyon for a day longer. We got here yesterday. Everybody fine except me.

Had a stack of mail here. One little note from you, and you swear you adore me. My dear, I know girls who would write me five times a day if I let them. Ahem! But, Doll, that joke about you loving me so darn hard is funny. Be that as it may I sure would like to see you before I leave on this wild trip.

Romer is some problem, but I love him. He is hard to manage. He does not like Elma. Yesterday Mr. Doyle took him home, and Romer was in the house talking to Mrs. Doyle. Doyle asked him who he came out with, and Romer told them, mentioning Elma last. He said, "Elma's not good!" Now that is fine talk for my boy. Romer wants me to buy everything he sees. I intend to make that kid behave before I get back to Los Angeles.

We leave here Tuesday. It is a great trip. I will get some grand material.

I don't know what else I can say that is news, so I'll close somewhat in a strain more to your peculiar liking. I will wire you upon my safe return from the wilds. Write me here up to Oct. 20. I look forward to meeting you with thrills and love and all kinds of feelings, such as you'd never believe. You are my one and only wife, anyway. You can't deny that. Love to you, Loren, and Betts.

Ever,

Doc

Dear Mother,

I will be good. Love from

Romer

The big trip was finally over, and Zane was in Los Angeles when Dolly arrived on Halloween eve with the younger children.[12] He met her at the train depot alone, and from there they drove down the tree-lined West Adams Boulevard to a bungalow on Western Avenue that Zane had rented for Romer and Reba. They had dinner there, with the whole family and the girls hovering around with a great air of expectancy, as if waiting for a great surprise to be sprung. A few doors away, another cottage housed Ellsworth, Ethel, and Ida. After dinner they all escorted Dolly to her new home, the magnificent Fitzgerald mansion, which Zane had leased for five hundred dollars a month. There they were installed with Dorothy Ackerman, Elma Schwartz, and later Lillian and Claire Wilhelm.

1919–1925

PART THREE ■ CALIFORNIA

CHAPTER 9

Penelope Has Taken
a Wandering Streak

CALIFORNIA'S GOLDEN SUNSHINE was paradise for Dolly. Romer, Betty, and little Loren romped all over the new house and lush yard, but their noise disturbed no one, because work was simply impossible at first. There was so much to discover, so much to do. The warmth called them all to play and seemed to diminish the pain caused by Dorothy and Elma and Claire. But such idleness could not last, and after the New Year and a week at Palm Springs, Zane settled down to write.

Work was never far from his mind. While fishing, he planned his next effort. He had three bestsellers, and *The U.P. Trail* was the number one selling book in the nation in 1918. Now that he had his audience, he could write his greatest novel. It would be a story of the desert and two brothers.

January 19, 1919

Today after years of plan, and months of thought, and weeks of travel, reading, I began the novel that I have determined to be great. It was with singular fire, sweetness, life, and joy that I began to write. None of that poignant worry, pain, fuss, or vacillation so characteristic of me at the onset of work.[1]

But work was often interrupted. A deadly influenza epidemic raged across the nation, hitting some areas in the West especially hard. First Ethel, Ellsworth's wife who was now pregnant, then R.C., then Dolly had flu-like symptoms. Then Zane developed a fever, but it was only a cold. All the family avoided the flu by maintaining a virtual quarantine about their house.

Even so, entire days of writing were lost to conferences about the motion-picture business. Ben Hampton was filming *Desert Gold* near Palm Springs and wanted Zane's advice almost weekly. Zane was to write the subtitles for the movie, and that took more time.[2] Then a streak of wildness in his oldest boy, noticed first when they hunted in the Tonto, flared again, and it was decided to send Romer to a boarding school.[3]

After that the house was quiet, with only Zane's thoughts to disturb him. Silence filled him with fear of failure, and he recorded his thoughts.[4]

> February 4, 1919
>
> When everybody was gone I tried to settle down to write. I did not sink into the blues, but I came the nearest to it yet. So near that I ought to record it as a bad spell.

> February 5, 1919
>
> Bad Day!!!

> February 6, 1919
>
> I have done no writing yet today, and hardly expect to. Conditions have been against me, and I was not yet strong enough to overcome them at once. This was D. birthday, and I hate birthdays.

> February 7, 1919
>
> I brooded and pondered and vacillated an hour this morning before I could accept the stab of starting to write. But at last I began, and wrote for nearly six hours. When I stopped, the dark mood, as if by magic, had folded its cloak and gone away.

Seven chapters were finished by the first of March, and the heart of the story approached. This was to take place in Death Valley, and to continue he wanted firsthand experience. He took Elma, Claire, and Dot to Palm Springs to watch Hampton film. Then the three women returned to New York.

March 12, 1919

I had a fine rest at Palm Springs. Camped out under the mountain—sat around the fire—walked in the moonlight—watched the desert—and profited exceedingly.[5]

March 19, 1919

This is the last night for Dorothy, Elma, and Claire in Los Angeles. They leave tomorrow for New York. I feel a sense of loss at the prospect of the separation. I have come to regard them almost as my own. They are young and full of life, and somehow inspire me. It will be a bad day for me when they are to come no more.[6]

The next day he left for Death Valley taking only one companion, Sievert Nielson, a Norwegian seaman turned prospector who had accompanied him on fishing trips and hunting expeditions.[7] They rode the Tonopah and Tidewater, a tiny railroad line, to Death Valley Junction, a collection of shacks clustered around a borax mill, and made camp there. In the morning they rode on horseback with the Funeral Mountains on one side and the Black Mountains on the other. As sunset approached they rounded a sharp curve and saw a vast, stark valley. Camp was made on the canyon floor, and the next morning they reached Furnace Creek. On the third night they slept on the west slope of the valley and met those who lived there: a farmer, a prospector, and some Indians. On the morning of the fourth day, they crossed Death Valley on foot. The distance across the valley at the mouth of Furnace Creek was only seven miles, but it seemed more than that and it took hours to cross. The return trip facing the sun was worse, but never had camp seemed so welcome.

Back in Los Angeles, Zane poured the mood of the desert into his story.

March 29, 1919

I have returned from Death Valley. It was a hard, but wonderful trip. I walked across that ghastly place and back again. . . . There has been much delay and obstruction in the course of my writing Wanderer of the Wasteland, some of it necessary, much of it needless. It was sweet to get back to wife and babies.

All of April he wrote, then when he and Dolly left for Avalon in May, he took his work with him. Finally it was finished.

> May 29, 1919
>
> It is midnight. I have just ended my novel, Wanderer of the Wasteland. 12 hours today—28 pages—and I sweat blood. Yet at this moment I feel strong, keen, passionate, still unspent. The spell is in me yet. I do not know what it is that I have written. But I have never worked so hard on any book, never suffered so much or so long. 838 pages. 170,000 words. I have been long getting the material, and five months in the writing. The only agony I feel now is the agony of dread. Have I written what I yearned to write?[8]

It was not his usual practice, but he dedicated the book to Dolly for her love, faith, spirit, and help in writing what he thought was his best work.
Once it was over he fell into another dark mood.

> June 5, 1919
>
> I have been unwell, and slowly recovering from my long emotional strain. Day after day I would fight to ward off depression and misery, and almost every day I was defeated. Yesterday and today I have become rational again. The tendency to drop back into hell is often present, but I overcome it, and presently I will be myself again.

> June 11, 1919
>
> The three weeks black spell is at an end! To my infinite shame and self-reproach I record here my defeat. My utter defeat! Yet I was unwell, worried, nagged, overworked, irritated, and distressed over things I could not control. Still I ought to have conquered.
>
> It is a terrible game, this ordeal of myself. Every defeat makes me rise more shamed, yet more determined.

When the mood lifted, the rest of the summer was enjoyed fishing in the waters around Catalina, with an excursion to Oregon for freshwater fishing on the first of July. Romer and Betty learned to swim, and Loren grew chubby and brown from the sun. In early September Zane took Romer, Reba, Elma, and Dorothy to Arizona for a two-month hunting trip in the Tonto.

Prospects for the trip looked good, but conditions at home worried him. War had ended the previous fall, and the armed forces rapidly demobilized, creating a surplus of employable men. Afraid that easy labor would lower wages, labor unions increased pressure, and their activity was resented by the returning soldiers. It seemed those who stayed home drew good pay safely, while the doughboys risked everything for a dollar a day. Subversives were blamed when a wave of strikes erupted in the summer of 1919, and many thought the nation on the verge of armed conflict. Zane sent directions for Dolly, should civic unrest occur.

Flagstaff Arizona

SEPTEMBER 14, 1919

Dearest Dolly,

I'd like to give you a hug. I'm feeling good, and free, and full of life, and my prospects for a story, and a hunt are big. Oh, Dol, I needed to get away! I am crazy to go off alone into the west. I promise you when I am alone every single day I will have fine and beautiful and grateful and loving remembrances of you.

About money, now. Put all the money you can draw between now and November, or till you see me, in cash in the safety deposit. And if there is any disturbance or riot or untoward circumstances, much as might happen, and is predicted, get the cash and both boxes and hang on to it. Conditions bad all over the country, with worse predicted. Be careful in that D—car.

I will be careful of myself and everybody. Don't let my wonderful kiddies forget.

Daddy

And don't you forget.

P.S. Don't tell Hampton that you can reach me at Payson.

If peace was fragile at home, it was absent in the hunting party. Elma could not get along with anyone.

One of the purposes of the trip was to search for information on the Graham-Tewksbury feud for use in a romance. Two earlier visits had netted little, but this time Zane found his story.

Beaver Dam, Payson

Tonto Basin

OCTOBER 6, 1919

Dearest Dolly,

We had a hard trip from Flagstaff to Winslow and out over the bare desert. It was hot and dusty. I caught cold and was sick for over a week. I am well now, and having a pretty good time. We got a bear cub yesterday, but the dogs killed it. I was crazy to have it alive to take home to Romer. We have gotten two deer and several turkey, so far. I saw 10 elk in one bunch. The woods are pretty wet yet.

Best of all I ran across an old Tonto Basin man, pioneer, named Elan Boles. He went through the Pleasant Valley War, and told us the story. It is a wonderful thing. The war really and truly was not between sheep men and cattle men, but between rustlers and honest ranchers. A good many men want to tell us the story, so we hear, for obvious reasons. But I'm glad Boles got to me first. I have a big novel to write, so that part is done.

Writing to you made me think of things—of you and the kids—and the flight of time. I had not been happy in mind, nor at peace. Your last letter put a crimp in me. But it was a fine letter, so I cannot scold you. I am wondering how you are, and if all is well. What of that D—automobile you got me to give you? I'm afraid of that. Well, I suppose if you write me you will tell me all the news. I hope you are well and working and having a nice time. On Oct. 1 I thought of Romer boy a hundred times. How I do love that boy! Isn't it strange how we love bad boys and men—and women? I hope Betty Zane is getting on fine, and that Loren is well. I sure have a noble and wonderful and lovable—and terrible family! Time flies, Dolly. Cheer up and make the best of it.

Ever with love,

Doc

The hunt netted five bears, a lot of venison, and many wild turkeys. It was hard physical work for the men and tedious for the women. When it was over Zane sent the others ahead while he went to the Grand Canyon.

El Tovar

Grand Canyon

NOVEMBER 13, 1919

Dearest Dolly,

Well, arriving here reminded me of our honeymoon, and I had a momentary pain in the gizzard. Not on your account, exactly, for you are almost as young, certainly more handsome, and a great deal fatter than you were then.

I am holding a sort of levee here. Everybody falls all over me. I hoped to come here and sit around alone and look on. But, alas, I find myself a sort of lion. There's a peach here—but that wouldn't interest you.

A little old lady with very sharp eyes nailed me to a bench, and engaged me in conversation. Part of this interview would interest you. She said, of course I was married. And I said: "Oh yes, quite, in fact, altogether!" And she said my wife must be a very brilliant woman. I said: "Brilliant, why she fairly scintillates, at times." And I asked her why she was so assured. And she said, "Because you're a great writer and no man could be that without such a wife." She asked how you looked and I showed the tiny picture of you with Romer and Betty as babies. And she said, "So young. Very pretty. You are much older, I see." At that I retreated, and went up with cold feet.

Still, it is very nice to be a celebrity. I daresay, because I'm just out of the woods. Soon I'll get tired of it. There are 10 books of mine on the book stand here, and 2 of Wrights, and 1 of other authors. Pretty nice, huh!

Please seal and drop this included note to Dot. I prefer, for a spell, that she does not know of my sojourn here.

Love to you and the kids. I surely hope to hear from you tomorrow.

Ever

Doc[9]

His celebrity was well deserved. Four of his books were on the bestseller list; *Desert of Wheat* ranked third in 1919. Income from book sales and magazine serialization exceeded one hundred thousand dollars annually, and profits from the movies promised to top even that.[10] The trouble that clouded his life with Dolly seemed to have evaporated in the California sun. His family was living in a mansion in Los Angeles, and even the circle of women caused little anxiety, although their novelty had worn off. Most of them had been with him for years.

Still life was not without its pangs. Troubling reports came from Romer's school. He was unmanageable, resentful of authority, and wild. At his new school he lied, cheated at games, and stole, the principal reported.[11] Zane felt he should stay home for awhile.

December 24, 1919

Time has flown by on wings. I have been well, but have done little or no writing. Still I have not fallen into one of the old spells. I have sort of fooled away the time, yet always with the thought in mind that I was going to work presently.

The children are wild tonight. Betty could not be chased upstairs. Loren came down without a stitch on and said he wanted to show me his "tummy." It certainly was a fine tummy. He is robust, strong, and a livewire if there ever was one. Romer is now decorating the Christmas tree. He grows keener all the time. I think the school is benefitting him. I do not feel so distressed over him as I did a few months ago. The children make bedlam; they make dreams or thoughts impossible. But they fill life, somehow, with joy, with sadness, with pride, with hope and fear.

After the holidays were over, Zane felt free to leave. He wanted to meet with his publishers, and they were in New York. Dolly went with him, and they enjoyed the city together.[12] Then Dolly went back to California and Zane to Florida, arriving at Long Key January 29 with Mildred.[13] There he wrote several stories about the Arizona hunting trip and a novelette, *The Wolftracker*. He also wanted to spend some time at Lackawaxen before returning to California.

When Dolly got back to Los Angeles she contracted flu, which turned into pneumonia, and was gravely ill for sometime.[14] All three children also contracted the illness, but their symptoms were less severe than Dolly's. Illness terrified Zane.

Long Key, Florida

MARCH 8, 1920

Dear Dolly,

No letters. Only a picture of Iris Hartwell. I'd like to see my young fresh wife! And Romer and Baby Lorry, and my beautiful Helen of Troy Betty. There's no news. Time flies along. I hope and pray you are O.K. now. Do you know, Dolly, that meeting you next time will be a terrible tremendous wonderful experience. Something warned me when you were so ill. I always know. Only I thought it mere dread. Well, keep writing me often, and you might, eventually, cut everybody out.

Love

Doc

Left in charge of business, new homes, and children, Dolly could not be timid or shy but had to be independent, capable, knowledgeable, and self-sufficient. These qualities steadily grew in her over the years, and a yearning for travel and adventure, denied for so long, became stronger. Part of her new-found liberty was the purchase of an automobile, which gave her freedom of movement in Los Angeles, although at this point she hired drivers for it.[15] Then she took short trips on her own to visit relatives. When in Middletown or Lackawaxen, she often went to New York, where her mother and grandmother and various other relatives lived. In California she took the children to Palm Springs to recuperate from their illness.

Efficient as a businesswoman and practical as a mother, in other areas she could not escape anger and sorrow. When she was unable to avoid thinking of Zane's infidelity, she grew bitter and wrote harsh letters then feared his reaction. If he was in a poor mood when it arrived, she got an equally harsh reply. But occasionally, when he was happy, he wrote loving, affectionate letters.

APRIL 6, 1920

Doc, honey,

You're a darling and I'm just flooded with love for you this morning. I got the answer to that bad, bitter letter I wrote you just after we got back from

Palm Springs, and it's the first time you haven't gotten sore, and returned blow for blow, and made me feel miserable. You understood! I had to write to get it out of my system, and ever since, I've worried about it, and about your answer, and I've had horrid dreams about wonderful, perfect men insisting on my marrying them because they said I was wasted on you, etc., etc. I never wanted to, but it seemed I'd have to, if they could prove it—and they always managed to!

And oh, joy, joy, joy that you're coming back to me alone. That worried me hellishly, because I wanted to be nice even if you did bring someone and I didn't see how I could stand it. I'm crying this minute. I don't know why.

Guess I'm still pretty nervous. One minute I'm down and out, the next I sing and carry on like a silly sixteen year old, without any pause, and the funny part is that I feel that way too. I've felt terribly young and innocent and inexperienced. Isn't that too foolish? And I blush like a fool, too. Am I going dotty?

I love to gather flowers in wild canyons, and I love to get down on a lonely beach. Oh, my! And I'm crazy to dance. Will you dance with me lots this summer? I'm going to golf, swim, walk, and dance to keep in good physical condition.

I'm thinking lots of Lackawaxen these days, probably because you are there, and especially of our first years there. How precious they are now, with their hard work and primitive conditions. Whenever I think of what we are enjoying now, I am thankful for those first years. Each condition is sweet and richer by contrast with the other, isn't it? And there's a sense of satisfaction in the fact that I did go through all that, that in a way, I earned the easier things.

Well, mine, exclusively in one or two things, I'll close with, oh, very much love.

Dolly

Zane wrote back from Lackawaxen.

APRIL 10, 1920

Dear Old Dolly!

This morning I was awakened by song sparrows and robins. Made three fires. Packed wood. Pumped the pump. The air was keen and cold, exhilarating and sweet; the valley of the mountains was purple; the black summits tinged with rose. All the past came flooding back, and what I wanted most and longed for with a pang in my breast was the woman who fought and strove with me here in this hard, barren, lonely place. You! This is home. This will always be home for you and me.

So cheer up, honey, and try to deserve your loving hubby. I will write you often.

Yours

Doc[16]

He was barely back in California when he and Dolly moved to Catalina. The island was one of their favorite places, and while he was in Long Key he had looked into buying a lot there and constructing a bungalow to be used during the fishing season. Most of the summer he fished in the ocean nearby, with one short trip to Oregon to fish the Rogue River. Battling swordfish was now a passion, and that summer he landed one weighing over four hundred pounds. When the season was over, he went to Arizona to hunt, but before he left the family moved into their own new home on the mainland of California in Altadena.

It was a mansion, surrounded by five acres of beautiful garden and trees: oranges, and flowers, and green lawn.[17] The house, Spanish in style with several stories and many rooms, was in the foothills outside Los Angeles just below Mount Lowe and Mount Wilson, and from it the hillside sloped down for miles toward the sea to encounter a lower mountain range, then another. On clear days the Pacific could be seen, and Catalina Island. It was a wonderful place for writing; Los Angeles was too far away to distract. Zane's study was a quiet, lovely place among the fragrant orange trees and the roses.

This time when he went to Arizona, Dolly set out on her own, venturing as far as San Francisco.

Hotel Ramona

San Francisco

OCTOBER 5, 1920

Dear Ulysses,

Penelope has taken a wandering streak. . . . I'm enjoying this trip, oh, muchly. It's the change I needed and I do so love this city. I cannot imagine a more beautiful one, not intrinsically, but in its setting. It fascinates me, and has a peculiar effect on me. I feel creative here.

Tonight, all alone, I crossed and recrossed that beautiful bay, and I cried with joy in the beauty of it. Do you remember how it always affected me? And this afternoon, when, the fog having lifted, we got a sweeping view of miles and miles of it, I couldn't tell you how I felt. For beauty, more than bitterness, makes the heart ache.

I've not wasted time, either. Strangely enough, most of the beautiful furniture I've seen seems suited to you, and I think I'll buy some. But here, as elsewhere, prices are sky high.

I'm looking forward to the home trip which begins Thursday. We'll take it through the big-tree region to Santa Cruz, then down this wondrous California coast. Oh, there is so much beauty in the world, my love. Only, I always feel we should be seeing and feeling it together, for we're complementary.

Goodnight, my restless one. Some day.

Your

Dolly[18]

Zane in Arizona was not as happy as Dolly was in San Francisco. R.C. and Reba were with him, as were Mildred and Dorothy, who did not get along. A friend from college days, Dr. Wiborn, and his wife were there, and Romer came along as well. When things did not go as planned, Zane turned to Dolly for comfort.

OCTOBER 26, 1920

Dearest Mine,

Mail came today, dated from camp Oct. 19–20th. We had been looking forward to it, and were all excited and pleased. To hear from you is for me like satisfying a parching thirst that perhaps you don't know you were afflicted with until you got a drink of wonderful cold mountain water.

I could not help being happy that you were homesick for me, but the unhappiness your letter expressed made me long passionately to put my arms around you and comfort you, to teach you what was real in life, and what would bring you peace. Often I feel as if you were like a child that needed me most, that I had to protect and shelter from the world. I do believe you need me more than even the youngsters do, and that is one of the sources of my perennial love for you. After all, the filling of a definite need is a very important thing in a woman's sense of happiness.

I am happy that Romer is improving and I hope you're feeling better about him. He is a wonder, but also a trial. I know. He used to drive me to hysterics when he'd come home from school. Bless his heart, I love him, passionately, but Daddy will always have first place. Loren and Betty are fine.

Ever your
Dolly

Over twenty inches of snow fell on Zane's camp in early November, and the women were sent home early with Romer, but Zane, R.C., and Wiborn stayed a few weeks longer.[19] Another heavy snowstorm forced them out through Phoenix some twenty days before they planned to leave. Still, the hunting portion of the trip was successful. The catch was one big bear, two mountain lions, three bobcats, and material for Zane's next novel.[20]

The Tonto forests were so full of game and the region was so replete with dramatic settings, unusual people, and intriguing stories that Zane decided to come each fall. He bought three acres on the Mogollon Rim overlooking the Tonto Basin and commissioned a hunting lodge to be built while he was gone.

By the middle of November he was writing in his magnificent new home in Altadena. It was the tale of the Tonto Basin feud, culled from the stories told by survivors. He wove a romance around the historical account and called it *To the Last Man*. He was now America's most popular writer. *Man of the Forest,* written three years before, was the number one best-seller. Wealth and fame were his; his name alone guaranteed a sale of at least a half million copies, and film rights sold for no less than twenty-five thousand dollars, sometimes twice that.[21] He had a luxurious home in sunny Southern California, a bungalow on Catalina Island, a hunting lodge at Lackawaxen, and enough money to fish to his heart's content. His wife seemed happy; his children grew strong. One morning he went into a bookstore in Pasadena and was disappointed to find none of his books. He complained to the shopkeeper, explaining he had been spoiled and such indifference was wholesome for him. She said it was not that they did not order his books, but that they could not keep them on the shelves, they sold so fast.[22]

He should have been happy, but he was not. He did not have respect from the literary critics.

November 23, 1920

Sometimes when I read a splendid review of some book I am at once uplifted and then cast down. I have never gotten the kind of criticism that I yearn for. My books do not receive serious reviews. Not one of those higher class of critics takes me seriously, if he ever reads me at all. I confess to a suspicion that my books are not read by the critical elect. Always this indifference to my efforts, to what I have tried to do, if not the result, has hurt me. . . . Someday I shall drive past this barren cold coterie of arbiters.[23]

Literary respect eluded him in spite of, or perhaps because of, his success. He thought of all his past effort as preliminary for his greatest work, which always lay in the future. At forty-eight could it be that his best work was already behind him and he was never to gain the honor, the reputation he desired? Perhaps he had attained all that was within his power, maybe growth and learning were spent, youth, energy, and vitality gone. Had he gained all only to find it dust?

Even New York, after Christmas, seemed lusterless.

December 31, 1920

I have just come up from the parlors and lobbies and streets, somewhat disillusioned, and surprised, and disgusted. New York has lost something on New Year's Eve. I did not feel the glamour as of old. Perhaps the lack of the white dazzling snowy streets like this night a year ago, accounts somewhat for my disenchantment. But I saw the crowd differently, or else it was a different crowd. Anyway, it was a motley, coarse, common crowd and all a kind of Bolshevik mob. The taxis sped and crawled and turned everywhere. Most of the people seemed to be riding. There was not a large crowd on the streets, especially, but such a jostling noisy confetti-throwing crowd as of yore. I can begin to hear the tin horns.

Looking out of this 21st story window I can see the lines of lights of cars creeping along, and the flash of the great signs, the gleam of the searchlight on the Times Tower, and all the reds and greens of the advertizing flares. But somehow it does not thrill me. The great city is there, perhaps, at heart the same, but it seems different.[24]

1921-1923

CHAPTER 10

The Froth of Enthusiasm

W HEN HE AWOKE the city was quiet, the crowds dispersed. He called on Dolly's grandmother and her uncle, then on Elma's family. He saw Claire, newly engaged. Social obligations accomplished, he turned to the business that called him east, hoping to resolve it quickly and return to California sunshine. Then something extraordinary happened.

It seems that I ought not put off longer the great task of trying to record what a marvelous thing happened to me in New York City, during the days Jan. 5 to 8. Even now I shall never be able to catch a thousandth part of the strength and strangeness and passion and splendor of my emotions. But I must try now before the memory crystalizes into a few unforgettable simplifications of fact. I should have written it all out at the time. That, however, was impossible.

I fell in love with another girl, almost a child.[1]

This is not a remarkable statement, considering the past. But it is something that has not happened for five years; and it is not possible now to estimate the magnitude or permanence of the emotion.

This girl seemed a creature born of my own imagination. A composite of Mescal, Lucy, Fay Larkin, and Allie Lee and Columbine Bellounds, yet unforgettably stranger and sweeter, and closer to me than all of them. It seemed not to be a sentiment. It seemed something long unconsciously waited for. Anyway, it came, and life was transformed, revivified, intensified, beautiful beyond all words for me to tell. It was not a sudden change. It took days. But there was a sure steady approach all the time to this tremendous realization.

Description of her does not come readily. That too will take time. Perhaps I do not remember her really well. But the vision I see in my mind is one of loveliness—a slender, infinitely graceful girl, whose every line was beautiful—whose eyes were dark and eloquent, smouldering with latent fire—whose mouth was strangely sweet and sad, small, full-lipped, imperfect of contour—whose face was pale olive-dark, oval in shape, haunting with a beauty of youth, fire, discontent and melancholy—whose bonnie head was small and sleek, and covered with wavy black tresses.

These are mere words. No more could I tell by them what she looked like than could I give one of the tones of her low contralto voice.[2]

Her name was Louise Anderson. She was from his childhood home, Zanesville, and in New York with her parents and at the same hotel as he. She wanted to be a writer, and when she heard that the famous Zane Grey was staying in that very hotel, she persuaded her parents to approach him. When she left four days later, he was no longer depressed.

When she left N.Y. on the night of Jan. 8 I went back up to the streets to find New York deserted. I was in a kind of trance. I saw, yet did not see, I heard, yet did not hear. What had been a roaring city of motion and gleam had become strangely silent, and obscured in gray shadow. No people, no cabs, no cars, no lights, no sounds. I wandered alone out 34th street, to 5th ave., up that street to 42nd, and saw nothing, heard nothing, but the dream in my soul, the bells in my ears. And that strange walk, so utterly without reality, so vague and illusive, so apart from physical action, rolled back the years. I ended it a younger man. Something had come back to me. And it did not leave me.[3]

Zane went to Lackawaxen then took the train back to Altadena. He became ill with a cold and expected his demons, depression and doubt, to appear to torture him. But when he thought of Louise and all the wonderful, thrilling things she had said and done, the demons faded. It did not matter that she was so young; she gave him a new beginning.

I am uplifted. It has come—the entrance to my last and most prolific and worthy stage of creative work. Whatever it was that happened was only a star on my horizon when I was lost in vague gloom. Whatever the folly of it, the pity of it, the strangeness and terror of it—it is true. By these things I know myself, and surely a little of my real nature dare appear in this record. Somehow love and inspiration are synonymous in my faculty of creative calm. I began that way. So I must end. Now I have the boy's romance linked with the matured passion and wisdom of the man. What I needed I have found. It does not matter what the fortunes of this last and crowning love of youth, beauty, life, nature, mystery as represented by this girl. I may never see her again. Or I may never have her affections. Or I may lose them and her. No matter what, the white living flame has come to my heart.[4]

Infatuation was channeled into creativity. In February he visited the Imperial Valley, the Salton Sea, Yuma, and Picacho for material for a novel to be called "Drifting Mirage."[5] When he got home, he finished *To the Last Man,* the story about the Pleasant Valley War, then started a sequel to *Wanderer of the Wasteland* but could not concentrate.

February 28, 1921

Today I learned that barring unforseen circumstances I shall have Louise A. with me this summer.[6]

That should settle my disturbance of mind.

For over a month I have been upset, wavering, wild, distraught, down in the depths, up in the clouds, and absolutely not myself. Of late I have been conscious of this derangement and that has worried me. I have done no work. I have taken no exercise. I have not gotten well of my cold, etc., as readily as I might have. And as for my brooding—I would be ashamed to record here the truth of my weakness and madness. All in all a wasted month as far as work is concerned.[7]

When Elma received a telegram that her father was dangerously ill, Zane took her back to New York, leaving March 12. While in New York he looked up old friends.

During this period I had a rather pleasant surprise in a meeting with Eugenie K.—the girl I used to wander with along the Delaware River at Rocky Rift, and who inspired in me the girl Genie of the Wanderer of the Wasteland. She was ten years older, a handsome, stylish, giving woman, married and happy. And I think I had something to do with her success in life. I met another girl, a newer friend, E.K.—and I found her ill and very low-spirited. Her confession to me was a shock from which I have not yet recovered.[8]

On March 23 he took the Pennsylvania train west to Zanesville, stopping there for the first time in twenty-five years. Places he remembered from his childhood brought back both pleasant and unpleasant memories, but most thrilling was the way the town cheered him as a successful and famous native son.

I was sought, praised, flattered, entertained as never before in my life. I belonged to Zanesville. I was a Zane. And these people, my old friends, and many new ones, were proud of me. The reception filled me with awe, wonder, sadness, and gratitude.[9]

He drank it all in. His last book was the number one best-seller, and the Curtis Publishing Company announced an unprecedented campaign for promoting his next one, something they said had never before been done for an American author. A "Zane Grey Week" was proclaimed for June, and his motion pictures would be shown in theaters across the country. Book displays in windows and newspaper publicity in every town of any size was planned.

But hard on all this flattering attention and good news came a poisonous review of his last novel in the *San Francisco Chronicle*. From the heights he plunged to the depths, and his last few days in Zanesville were not happy. Yet the trip was not a failure.

My anticipation of the train ride back to Z—was amply realized. I went there to meet Louise Anderson and never was there a sweeter or more fateful meeting.[10]

At first it seemed her parents would not agree, but in the end he persuaded them to allow their daughter to spend the summer at the home of a famous author under his tutelage.

It seemed that I must fail in my undertaking, and therefore fail in all things. But I fought, and fought, and threw all my force into the balance and I did not fail. I brought Louise A. west!!!![11]

It was perhaps no coincidence that Dolly took her first extensive overland trip by herself in April. To watch her husband, now forty-nine, infatuated with a very young girl was something she simply could not stand.[12] Taking Loren, Betty, her friend Hildred, and two drivers, Ed Bowen and Ken Robertson, she left a week after he returned, driving to Lackawaxen. They arrived in the middle of May.[13]

Driving across the country in the early twenties was not a simple matter. There was no interstate highway system, and those roads that did exist often were not paved. Bad weather could mean delays or being stranded. She kept Zane posted of her progress, and her letters gave no hint of her dismay.

MAY 13, 1921

Dearest Honey—

Home again! There never will be another house like this for us. I have wandered afar and seen many places, but none more beautiful than this.

All my love. Will sleep in your bed tonight. Don't know if I'll get much sleep. The smells—pungent, fresh, springlike, the birds and what they sing about, the thousands of memories, have filled me so full of emotions that I'm simply half wild and I long for you with all my soul.

Ever and ever

Dolly

At Avalon Zane was more and more enamored with Louise.

April 21, 1921

Tonight I sat here by the window in the moonlight with L. The sea glimmered out there, vast and shadowy; the surf dashed low against the shore; now and then a nocturnal seagull cried out his lonely call, the crickets mourned. And I talked and talked and talked.[14]

May 5, 1921

As I write here Louise sits beside me with her arm around me. This may be the secret of today's "Resurgam." It remains to be seen how deep and permanent the transformation is. But I feel something I never felt before. I have entered into the best of my life's work. I have found myself.[15]

By mid May he reached the high point of the novel, *Call of the Canyon,* and put it aside for fishing season, sailing out each day, sometimes taking Louise with him.

The previous year he had landed the largest swordfish of the entire season.[16] He was typically a quiet man in public, but on the subject of fishing he waxed eloquently for hours, much to the exasperation of other Tuna Club members. When a tiny woman, Mrs. Keith Spalding, beat his record with a 426-pound broadbill, each of the members of the club stood in line at the phone to inform him personally and to plant a few well-aimed barbs.[17] Zane's sense of humor deserted him, maybe because Louise was there, and he claimed Mrs. Spalding must have had help in landing the fish, a serious charge to these fishermen. The president of the Tuna Club informed him that he had sullied Mrs. Spalding's honor and must apologize or resign. He apologized, but the incident, along with a long-standing disagreement over line used for big fishes, left a sour taste. He eventually resigned from the club but not from fishing. For two weeks he camped on Clemente Island to fish the waters there, and at the end of the month went to Oregon for salmon and steelhead.[18]

In the fall he took Louise to the Tonto. R.C. and Reba, the Wiborns, Dorothy Ackerman, and his Japanese cook, Takahashi, went with him.[19] He wrote a brief note to Dolly.

SEPTEMBER 10, 1921

Got here after 5 days of hard riding and terrific heat. Last night we had cool mountain air. It was great. I am tired out but well again, and expect to reach camp tonight or tomorrow.

Love to all

Doc

They bagged only one bear and no deer, but to Grey that was of no real consequence.[20]

Days of hot golden sunshine, dry fragrant pine, still forests of spruce! I rode and rode, and climbed and climbed. We had poor hunting, but then I did not go for that.

The amber-colored Tonto Creek, and the jumble of huge gray boulders, and the dry brown ferns, and the giant silver spruce—Promontory Point with its deep canyons and black thickets—the long slope back of the Ranch, and the ride down Derrick, and the clusters of silver spruces above Leonard Canyon, and beautiful Louise.[21]

He finally wrote to Dolly, now in California after spending much of the summer in Lackawaxen. She had left the East in July, taking a month to drive home, stopping at Yellowstone and Crater Lake, then on to Seattle, Oregon, and San Francisco, finally arriving in Altadena at the end of August. His letters hinted of remorse.

SEPTEMBER 29, 1921

Dearest Dolly,

Well, we got back from Beaver Dam camp today. I am crippled. (Not bad.) My horse smelled a bear track in the trail and threw me. We had a fine stay at B.D.C. I got one grand big gobbler, 30 pounds! It was beautiful. Also got 3 others. Rome got 2.

I am sending out the mail tomorrow to Payson and sure hope to hear from you and Romer. I don't care whether or not I hear from any one else.

My plans are about the same. A trip to the Indian Reservation and one to Dude Creek after bear. I suppose these will consume October. I ought to be home early in Nov. I am still hanging fire on the trip to N.Y. but suppose in the end I'll go. Then when I get back it will be two or three weeks at home before the Mexican stunt. That also is undecided.

I think in this letter I have asked you to have some money added to my bank account by Nov. 1. I have $139 left. I sure will have a grand squaring up with you upon my return. I think you'll get most of the Nov. check.

But business and work do not seem to stick in my mind. I think a good deal of you and Romer. Not so much of the younger kids. Well, I do love you all. And my conscience hurts me more in the woods than anywhere else.

I know you are O.K. Somehow I seem to rely upon your good sense and wonderful capacity. Where would Z.G. be but for Penelope?

Do you remember when I used to meet you and walk through Central Park? Do you remember—oh, well, I won't make you unhappy with recurrence of the days that are no more. But—If I had only done more for you I'd be somewhere near feeling I had lived a good life.

Doc

And she replied,

OCTOBER 22, 1921

Dearest Doc,

The absolute certainty that mail was on the way finally today brought me your letters of October 8 and 15, stamped on the 17th at Payson. It's been a long time since I heard from you. "Long ago and far away." Sometimes you seem almost a dream to me and yet the time has flown. I have been so busy and occupied that the days escaped too, too fast.

My dear, I wouldn't know how to advise you on the Mexican trip. I should think it would depend entirely on your inclination and what you think you can get out of it, whether the huge expenditure will pay or not. But this, I beg of you. If you take the trip to Mexico please do very soon after you get here. It's too hard for me. It's a situation to which I have never yet been able to callous myself, that of not seeing you for a long time and then when you come back to have a mob around. It's requiring something almost superhuman of me. I can get away with the situation, but I suffer too much.

My soul is always lonely. I can't sit around with anyone and talk. I work and study evenings, and of course I'm always busy daytimes. I'm happy in my occupations, that is mostly. Life is rich, although the greatest treasure has escaped me. I wouldn't be human if I didn't long for it consumedly at times. But even so, I think I am happier than anyone I know, and I believe it's intelligence that makes me so, the realization and understanding of the values of life, and how to seize the best in everything. And there are a lot of people who care for me and by whom I am needed. The kiddies and I are still here for you to come back to. Maybe someday you'll come home to stay, and we'll have a real home of just our own. But don't wait too long, dear. I'm afraid even inborn instincts become atrophied from disuse.

Goodnight, man of my destiny. Yours so far, and always, I think,

Dolly

After a trip to New York then back by way of Zanesville, taking Louise home, he was again in Altadena ready to begin another novel.

November 29, 1921

Today I begin rewriting Shores Of Lethe. This makes the fifth time I have undertaken that novel. I wonder, has it always been a mistake? However that may be, the start was one of unusual strain, and tonight I find myself at low ebbs of spirit.

The intention to embody in that novel all the license of the modern day— all the freedom of the young people—the jazz and dance and indecent dress and rotten sensual stuff, has caused me to read the magazines on present day morals. And the effect has been to depress and sadden and hurt me terribly. I see so much more than I used to see. It may not be too late to write the novel, but I have been too late in one regard—the salvation of Louise.[22]

In the book was a modern girl of fifteen or sixteen, not the main character but an important secondary one who was tempted by the evils of the world. Louise was the prototype. Zane wanted Louise to remain as innocent as he imagined her to be, untouched by what he saw as the evil of the modern world, yet he, an older, experienced, and married man, was infatuated with her. As he introduced her to his world of wealth and unconventional liaisons, it was inevitable that she would be attracted to its lures. The irony was lost on him, but Dolly said the work was good.

He stayed with her and the children at Christmas, but Louise still haunted him.

December 4, 1921

Strange how after days of depression I emerge with something gained. Today I confessed to myself that I had been selfish, intolerant, and dishonest towards

Louise and Dorothy. It will have some effect upon my future actions, perhaps change me altogether.

My hours of leisure, moments, I should say, are almost wholly consumed by thoughts of L.A. and longings and doubts and fears. It is a shameful and tragic fact. I realize my childishness, my obsession, my draining habit of enchantment, my longings for the unattainable.[23]

December 24, 1921

I cannot remember a Christmas Eve that I was so utterly broken and miserable. The cause is my hopeless love for Louise Anderson.

The children and our guests assembled in the parlor to look at the tree and find their presents. For them it was a joyous occasion. Their shrieks of glee filled the air. Everybody entered into the spirit except myself. I could not. I was outside the pale. Betty sang and recited. Loren sang and played. They seemed the very embodiment of the happiness of children at Christmas time. It was an awful ordeal for me. I do not want any more Christmas Eves like this one.

And tonight I am in the depths. My heart hurts, my breast aches. I am tired, sick. I have not one anticipation. My absurd hope tries to raise its head, only to slink back into the gloom. This is a terrible thing—this horror of mine, and there can be only one outcome, unless I can conquer it.

Insanity, or breakdown—or death.

I have to confess that I am only getting what I deserve . . that I have never been fair. That I have at last gone too far. I have been taught a lesson that will endure all my life.[24]

Immediately after Christmas he came down with a cold, then tonsillitis, then intestinal flu. As soon as he could, he left for New York then went to Florida to write and fish. A short novel, "Tappan's Burro," was completed, and a new western, a novel of American Indian life on the reservation, was started. He planned to have Louise for the summer and wanted Dolly to assist him. Dolly issued a mild protest.

FEBRUARY 3, 1922

Dearest Mine Own,

Dear, you'll have to love me quite violently for the rest of your life to make up for what I've put up with for your dear sake. And that brings me to another point. Can't quite get my responsibility in the matter of making up to Elma and Dot what you impose on them in the case of Louise. Darling, how do you get that way? In all seriousness, you put it to me. Of course, I know what's happened. You've told them, and from now on they'll plague you. But this is up to me. And I'll have to think very hard and lots of other things, before I make a decision like that. Moreover, I thought you wanted them out here by August first. What has changed your plans? Will Louise remain later? Please be sure to keep me posted as to your arrangements. Perfect frankness is the only thing that will ever work with me, that is, provided you want me to do things for you.

Glad you have decided to have Ida upstairs. It will look infinitely better. And any old time you can't find all the opportunities you want will be a cold day in summer. I cannot give you any answer at all now about Dot and Elma, in fact, not until after I get East and see conditions of the trip. But I want to know your definite summer plans. Will you stay in Catalina all summer? Will you go back east with Louise? Any Oregon plans?

Ever yours,

Dolly

I'll be 39 Monday but I feel about 22 and I don't care how I look!

Few wives could so calmly discuss their husband's love affairs, but emotional reactions never made any impression on Zane anyway and distance made it easier. She was never meek, accepting, or resigned. She reacted as any wife would with anger, bitterness, hurt, and jealousy, but over the years she developed a way of distancing herself. She realized he would not change, but she must, if she were to hold on to any remnants of their marriage.

FEBRUARY 21, 1922

Dearest Dolly,

Yours of a week ago at hand. Dear girl, I despair of answering this wonderful letter. I can't even try. At best I can tell you that I shall trace every word you wrote in lead pencil over with ink so that I can treasure your letter always.

Honey, don't change. Be always as you are. My heaven, if you get any nobler, any more wonderful, how can I stand it? Please be bad. Please be selfish. Do something terribly human so that I can hold up my head. I welcome all you said about your life henceforth and bless you for it, and love you more than you know. And I will do more.

> Ever
>
> Doc[25]

She replied,

Ducky Darling,

Nowadays when I get a wonderful and enthusiastic note from you about some new trip you've planned, I want to laugh and kiss you. A year or two ago, I'd have wanted to hit you over the head with a club. Well, I'm glad you have so much enthusiasm. Whether its good sense is a different matter. It's nice of you to want to include me, but I don't think I could do it. In the first place, after being away from the kiddies so long, I'd be wild to get back to them. I'd moreover be full-up on travel. And I never could see traveling in mobs. I'll take my innings with you alone, even if it's only a few days.

It is the froth of your enthusiasms that is always planning these new trips. That is all right. But get down to the solid matter beneath. Your one aim and object in life should now be your work. You are now at the height of your power. You can't stay there forever, you know. So "Carpe Diem." All your life you have pandered to your own desire. Pander now, for a little, to your work. It will repay you so infinitely more.

I think I want you to take the kiddies over to Avalon in May when you go. I'll feel better so. I find now this thing is decided that my chief compunction is leaving them. But I know, with all of you, they'll be all right. You know, I'm always torn some way or other, always some little fly in the ointment to spoil the complete flavor of unmitigated enjoyment. Maybe that's what makes the brief moments so precious. I have so much choosing to do, now, you're putting this trip up to me means again that I must choose between you and the kids. Doc, I love you best on earth, but I have love and something more for them, responsibility and duty. I brought them into this world, and I must stick by them.

You have always evaded all your responsibility to them, to me, to anyone for that matter. Ida, the other day, grew quite awestruck when she spoke about your always doing just as you planned and pleased, when no one else she ever knew could. Well, in the first place, that's the power of your personality and then your complete refusal of responsibility and going ahead to your own desires. It's a wonderful thing to watch, impersonally, as I can see it occasionally. But I have yet to see that you extract much happiness from the process. Well, there must be some plan we're following.

As the years go on, I begin to appreciate how precious the love that we feel for others is. It is better to give than to receive. And my love for you, dear, enriches my life beyond measure. And it grows greater and stronger. The wildness is gone, the sex perhaps, the qualities in it that caused me bitterness and agony (not altogether though), and now it is almost the motive power of my life. I miss you, I long for you, at times I am unutterably homesick for you, and those are the times when I am restless and must go, but I feel a deep well of feeling in me that makes life worthwhile. Yes, I'm your old Dolly, and your new Dolly, and yours all the time,

Dolly

Zane was to have Louise in Avalon again, so Dolly would go back to Lackawaxen. The children would stay with him. He wanted her to bring two of the other girls back with her and meet him in Oregon.

He jumped from trip to trip as if chased by some phantom. He left Long Key for New York, then went to Zanesville to get Louise, then to Flagstaff.[26] The Wiborns and Lillian Wilhelm met him there.[27] Cars took them to Kayenta, then horses carried them across the Painted Desert to Rainbow Bridge. Weeks were spent on the desert before they returned to Flagstaff and boarded the train for California. He stopped in Altadena with a mob, as Dolly had feared, collected the children and their belongings, and by the first of May was settled in Avalon. Dolly was now free to leave.

MAY 3, 1922

Most Wonderful Dolly,

We arrived O.K. and I sure found both island and house attractive. The living room is simply a joy. I've worked like a slave, and tomorrow will have the job of settling down completely, and be ready for work.

Well, you are about to depart on your first ZG trip into my country. I sure thrill at the thought. You will have a great trip. I want to hear from you, just as soon as you get out. Honey, it's your turn now to go and see, and mine to stay home and work, and look after the children. If you do as well as I, and I do as well as you, it will be great. I'll do my best.

Let me thank you again for being quite the most wonderful and splendid and adorable woman, these last trying days. So long, Dolly dear, be careful.

Ever

Doc

First they went to the Grand Canyon, then to Williams and Flagstaff. They explored the Navajo Reservation, stopping briefly at Red Lake Trading Post. They arrived in Kayenta chilled to the bone and tired. That night everything froze, and it was still miserably cold the next day, so a visit to Betatakin was canceled. Dolly enjoyed the Wetherills' hospitality for several days, watching the Navajos and meeting missionaries, traders, and teachers. They left Kayenta May 12 for El Capitan, then they went on to Kansas City and across the country to Philadelphia, reaching Lackawaxen by the end of May.

From Lackawaxen Dolly resumed her long correspondence with Zane, by turns affectionate, disappointed, and exasperated. Avalon was a small village, and his entourage of young women was noticed and sparked local gossip. Zane caught wind of it and feared that members of his household were talking about matters he wanted hidden.

JUNE 9, 1922

Dearest Docalexis,

Got back to Lack last night after four days of rain in N.Y. And we left there in the rain, bringing Mother and the Smith family and a lot of truck besides. Up here it was comparatively dry, but the old Delaware was rip-roaring.

Lackawaxen is heavenly—and oh, I do have heart puttering moments when I think of you and the kids and all that happiness here. All the old places have their recollections and remembrances. And I do love you, my dearest, better all the time.

Lots of love to you and my babies.

Dolly

Dearest Doc,

You are eternally—in every letter—begging me to write you. My dear, I have written you—and when I do write, it usually takes me several hours because that seems the only way I can write what I consider letters. Of course, I could dash off notes like you send me in a minute or two, and do it as often as you do; would you like that better?

I brought your big picture and it dominates my room and every time I look at it (which is often) I say "Oh, I love you, love you!" And a flood of warmth and sweetness just goes pouring through my heart at the thought. Yesterday I thought that perhaps I loved you just as wildly as I did twenty years ago—but it's different. Now all the sting and the agony and suffering and restlessness has gone out of it. It is still ecstatic, but it's no longer dependent. You still do the things that used to make me suffer so terribly, but our love for each other seems to have gone above all those things—to be on a different plane.

Oh, I have my slip-backs too, and my gusts of fury at things. For instance, when I saw Dot's collection of beautiful clothes, and realized what they cost, a mad surge went through me for a second. I never had anything in a class with hers and Louise's things. And all the way across the continent we stopped at the cheaper hotels because you have to pay twice as much at the others, and you surely don't get your money's worth and it's extravagant. Now you know you wouldn't do that. Maybe you would, but your bunch of high-class traveling companions would probably pass away if they didn't have suites and private baths, etc. And I'm just as aristocratic and everything else as any of them—lots more, in fact. You are the most extravagant mortal that ever breathed the breath of life, and when you're away from me, there's no one to tell you or help you. But you're entitled to get what you want. You earn the money.

About Cooky: Of course she talks. So does everyone else connected with you. And the one who has always done the worst talking and done the most mischief and implied the worst is your own brother Ellsworth. Not maliciously, of course. And Cooky may gossip and gabble, but not in any unkindly way. She likes you too well for that. What do you think the island people have said about you all these years before you had your family? If I told you a few of the things I'd heard you'd jump out of your skin. Anyone in your position, if he were the most blameless mortal in creation, would be gossiped about, and your position has always been unconventional, to say the least. All you can do is ignore such things and laugh. If you can answer to your own soul, it's enough. If you can keep, as far as possible, from hurting those who love you or injuring the future of your children, why in God's Heaven should you pay any attention to foolish gossip. Nothing worse than has already been said about you can be said, and you're still living and enjoying your existence, and giving pleasure to millions by your writing. Cheer up, love, wifey is still with you and will be, to the crack of doom.

I am working on your MS. I can't yet give you any criticism, but I can say this: Honey, you're a wonder, and you're getting better all the time. You can paint better with your pen than many well-known painters can with a brush. And the soul and the feeling is there. Having seen your Navajo country, I just marvel at the wonder of your interpretation.

My advice is to let the Oregon trip go this year, if you see any chance for fishing. However, that's up to you and I don't care what you do. We'll have our usual tabloid form of meeting, I suppose, intense concentration of mental loving for a few minutes—and then goodbye. Oh, God, how I'd like to have you alone for a day or two. But such seems not to be my earthly fate.

Always
Dolly

Dolly also advised on business matters.

JUNE 27, 1922

Dear Honey,

I wasn't aware of writing you a nasty letter and your comeback this morning hurt me. I remember lecturing you about your attitude toward Betty's defections, but I feel that necessary. I don't think I ever say things to you unless I feel that it is for your good and for everyone's good. Even then I hate to, for the maintenance of that beautiful understanding between us means so infinitely much to me.

Don't worry about M.S.'s attitude. She's roasted everything almost that you ever wrote. You cannot expect "The Day Of The Beast" to be liked. I told you that myself. I told you I didn't like it. But it's powerful, and you felt driven to write it and I think it will have a big sale. It will hurt you with some of your readers, and you will get a lot of protestations. But they'll all swing back to you again. I'll wager everything I have. "Zane Grey" is unique, and they want Zane Grey. But this book shows versatility, at least. The ones that want your regular stuff will swing back the more eagerly to the next one. I can understand the publisher's point of view, too, but I think I see farther and more clearly. So don't worry, or get fussed or hurt if you get a lot of roasting on this book. In fact, if it's maligned, people will be the more eager to read it.

Don't get sore about Hampton. Don't ever allow yourself any personal getback at him, either by letter or in person. That's where you'll get in bad. He had so much legal justification in your own letters, etc. Steer clear! I ask you most earnestly and advisedly to do this. Of course, you may be justified in recourse to the law, but don't hurry into that either. Weigh the pros and cons. And above all, why worry and get excited and furious about it all. Why waste the mental energy and your own vital force over non-essentials? After all, you got yourself into it with your unbounded enthusiasm.[28]

Write me nice letters, honey. The one before this was so wonderful that I wept, I loved you so. Did you really mean all those marvelous things you said about me? Or were you jollying me for some fell purpose. Oh, I know you meant them. I have tried to be like that for you. But tell me just the same that you meant them.

Always your,

Dolly

Being left behind with the children was a new experience for him. For the first time all the domestic burdens of a complicated household fell on his shoulders.

JULY 24, 1922

Dearest Dolly,

Yesterday morning Sadayo came to my room at 5 o'clock, and said, "Mr. Grey, George is in jail!" I asked what for. Then she plunked down on her knees. I saw that she was terribly agitated. And she began to talk. It was hard to understand her, but the substance of the story is this.

She had been intimate with the Jap boy who works down the street. She had to tell George. The night before the three of them had gone to the golf links. George and the other boy got in a quarrel, and George shot him. Yesterday they sent the boy over to L.A. to be operated on. He was shot through the abdomen and has a chance to recover. Meanwhile George languished in jail and poor Sadayo is wretched. If the injured boy does not die I think Wiborn and I can get George out.

Say, my dearest, I am damn tired of the burden of the world without my old Squidge. That's all. Expect to go to Clemente for a few days, and upon returning will take Louise over to L.A. and get her started home. Time flies and soon you will be on your way west. I wish I was going to have more time with you in Seattle. But I'm grateful for a couple of days. I will get back to Altadena about September 25, or earlier, and be home a few days before going to the Tonto. Then I'll be home early in November for a spell. You'll have to be very devoted to make up for all this absence of yours.

> Ever your
>
> Doc

Even with domestic crises, poor fishing, and the comings and goings of his entourage, the summer was productive. He finished *The Vanishing American,* his novel about "the Indian." Over 150,000 words found their way to paper, and four months of steady work passed without one spell of depression.[29] It was a triumph, even more so as the critics had a field day with *Day of the Beast,* his psychological novel.

At the end of the summer Dolly left Lackawaxen with Elma and Lil in tow.

JULY 5, 1922

Doc Darling,

I'll attend to all the baggage business, etc. The girls are allowed only one suitcase each in the car—all of us in fact, and we'll be crowded at that. And I'll promise you no wicked men shall approach your innocents! Bunk! I'm younger and innocenter than anyone you know, old dear. Do you remember the morning (in bed) when you said to me "Dolly, you're the youngest thing I know." It's true, absolutely. I know it, too. But don't fall in love with me again. I couldn't stand the shock!

My God, Doc, you must think I'm a super-creature with the task you laid out for me for Elma—to make a sport of her? I'm afraid that's not in this world. She's getting more set and fussy and old maidish all the time. She's as bad as Lil when it comes to stalling around and wasting time. Well, there's one thing. She'll have to hustle on this trip. I'll wake her up before daylight, so she'll be ready. About that other business—I cannot broach that subject, but it will probably come up sooner or later, and then I'll see what I can do. You surely give me some hellish jobs, darling, with your lady friends.

Well, another note gone to seed. Gee, that makes me see red. I can't any more help writing you letters than I can help loving you.

Your young and innocent

Wife

She traveled by car to Seattle to meet Zane, where they were together only a few days before he went to British Columbia and she drove down the coast to Altadena. From Canada Zane went directly to Arizona to hunt again in the Tonto. The hunting was better this year, and he took home three bearskins.[30] The atmosphere among the Zane Grey outfit, however, was tense, with continual disagreement among Mildred, Elma, and Dorothy.[31]

Dolly, however, acquired a trophy of her own.

OCTOBER 31, 1922

Dearest Doc,

Much to my disgust and chagrin I've had to spend several days in bed. Yesterday I was sick as a dog. Chills, fever, out of my head. And in my lightheadedness my main concern was not to die, which I was sure I would do, but that some female would get to swish around in my new fur coat. And I kept saying "It's only charged, so it can be returned."

But honestly, the coat is a wonder, and I think my enjoyment of it is enhanced by a sort of forbidden sweets zest, for it's really not at all my instinct to spend so much money in one gob on myself. But then, you said it is a present from you, and you've never spent anything on me compared to others—that is personal—and if I'd had all the fun I should have had all these years, it would have amounted to much more, well, you see I'm making a lot of excuses.

But you must promise me one thing, or all the pleasure will be gone—that you will never, never buy any other female any kind of a fur coat. You see, whenever I think of anything nice for me, you go and buy the same thing for the rest of the tribe, and truly I'd rather wear rags. Anyway, as your wife I'm entitled to a few things better than the rest. I've never had any really fine, or expensive clothing. I could get four pair of shoes for what one of Louise's cost, and now that I have one thing very different, don't spoil it for me. I don't mean to be unpleasant, honey, but that's what's happened so much in my life.

Heavens, are you surprised at me? I am at myself. But a day's delirium focused on a fur coat must have had a peculiar effect on my mind.

Your weak and wobbly

Dolly

Back home in Altadena in the late fall, Zane finally got out of the movie business entirely, transferring his concerns to Jesse Lasky, who had brought the film industry to California. With this distraction gone, he worked on another novel, *Code of the West,* until Christmas. This was one of his happier Christmases.[32] Immediately after Christmas on December 26, he left for New York, where he stayed until January 14, meeting with his various publishers and with the Andersons, who had traveled there with Louise. Louise had entered Stanford, and Zane was paying for it at a cost of $656.00.[33] He then stayed in Long Key until the end of March, where he finished *Code of the West* along with several outdoor stories.

Dolly was pleased with his work but not at all happy with the way it was done. Mildred was doing some of the writing and editing. Mildred had been with him for years. She was willing to be eclipsed by others, such as Louise, but slowly acquired a greater hold on Zane than the others. Dolly felt most threatened by her. Mildred's smug self-righteousness irritated those around her, and they were eager to report anything that might discredit her to Dolly, hoping for an ally.

Dear Doc,

I'm sorry you're still fussing about that Mildred matter, as evidenced by the letter I just received. I'd put it out of my mind. If I let things like that fester and corrode, I'd be a sorry object. Suffice it to say that Dorothy, in telling me that, in no way changed my opinion of Mildred or influenced my attitude toward her, so don't hold it against Dorothy. However, where there's smoke, there's fire.

My dear, if I believed everything everybody said about everybody else in your little circle, life wouldn't be worth living for me, for they all hate each other's insides. Mildred to herself is a noble creature with nothing but the noblest motives, and at present she has you persuaded that way. That I see her otherwise does not affect the situation. I simply try to eliminate her from my mind. It's a little difficult because I'm so closely bound up in you, but after all, my relation is intrinsically and directly to you and with you. It's like brushing away a lot of cobwebs to see a clear image. It's taken me many a year to clear away and clean away all the mud and smears and dirt and cobwebs, but now I have my unobstructed vision—you to me, and me to you. It was undisturbed while you were with me here, but of course now that you are away the different influences are again swaying you. But don't let it matter, dear. There is to my mind only one situation where I could use all the claws and weapons of the "female of the species" and that is if anyone threatened our mental or spiritual unity or dependence. And then I could be just as unscrupulous as any other women you know, and that's not putting it mildly.

So just help me to forget Mildred by not mentioning her to me. I don't want even to think of her. That's one thing that the years have taught me in my relation to you—to think of you (my you) entirely dissociated from the people who surround you or spend their time with you. That was never a bearable thought. And my you no one can ever take away from me or even see, for it is the deep intrinsic self and soul of you that is a development of our relation to each other, our years with each other. No one can filch or steal it from me, even if it were Helen of Troy or Cleopatra. "Girls may come and girls may go, but I go on forever." If I never saw you again, I should not fear that any one or anything could erase my image from your soul. Even as you are to

me, so I am to you. This is no overweening egotism, but the indelible truth
that has emerged from the suffering and joy of years. Because of, in spite of,
and always.

Your

Dolly

He responded,

JANUARY 29, 1923

Dearest Dolly,

You certainly can write an inspiring and beautiful letter when you care
to. That is what you represent to me—the ideal Penelope. You are not without
a touch of Aphrodite, either! But such things make me glad I am alive, glad
that I have fought heritage, blood, early environment, materialism, and all the
rest. There are wonderful women. I've known one, at any rate. So don't worry,
my dear, about your place with me. It's as fixed as the north star.

Love,

Doc

Reassuring words, but Dolly was still anxious.

MARCH 27, 1923

My dearest wife—

Back again to Long Key. I have 4 letters from my Penelope, all but one of
them fine. That sad letter just makes me shrink. It hurts. Every time I think
of how you feel (sometimes) I am cast down. It has a bad effect on me. The
old sinking—the old self condemnation. That was my weakness years ago.
It will not do now. Yet, I should not complain. You have been so wonderful.
What's the use for me to try to tell you? You are Z.G. If I lost you I would lose
all. I wouldn't even try. And I cannot seem to understand why and how you
imagine that I could do anything but revere and adore you. I think that that is
not satisfying to you. A woman has a primitive side, and forever it draws
her back. My primitive side gives me the sensations that inspire my books, and
these sensations are what call to my reader.

If your heart is set on that trip abroad you can go. I'm not so stuck on your
taking it, and I will make a suggestion or two.

So darling, stop worrying until I get back. I am well, and O.K. I will read
your letters over again here, and also on the train north. And I'll now make a
stab at writing the letter you asked for.

Love

Doc

For the most part, however, Dolly was too busy to worry about Mildred.
She took brief trips to San Diego, Lake Arrowhead, and Carmel with the
children. What consumed her time most, outside of working on his manuscripts, business deals, and her own business transactions, was work on the
Altadena house. Before he left, Zane gave Dolly specifications for an addition that would include an extravagant study for him, and she supervised
the work while he was gone. Workmen wandered in and out of the house at
all hours for over a month, but when he returned he had his new study.

He immediately started a new novel that used the story of the buffalo as
a backdrop. He called it *The Thundering Herd.*

April 29, 1923

California seemed gloriously golden, fresh, fragrant and beautiful after the
cold, sordid east. The flowers and foliage were exquisitely striking to my eye
and the warm sun, the smell of the California desert hills, and the touch of
fog rolling up from the Pacific,—these gave me a feeling I have long missed—
the feeling of home. Perhaps California is home now. We have come to love it.

My place has wonderfully improved. The new tile roof, and the addition
built for my study, the new trees and plants, pleased me a great deal. Yet this
costly and beautiful estate seems strange. What a contrast from Lackawaxen![34]

April 30, 1923

I have begun to write again. Another romance! The epic of the buffalo. The
Thundering Herd. Where do I find these romances? That query has been
promulgated by critics and reviewers who have never been west. I see these
romances and I believe them. Somewhere, sometime, they happened. My
reward, and my faith in myself, come from the many letters I get from simple
readers—old women, and young girls, and boys, too, all with hearts full of
romance, all true to the child dream in them.[35]

With her responsibilities temporarily abated, Dolly left for the summer. Again she drove east, but this time sailed for Europe leaving the children with Zane. Once more it was a curious sensation for him to be left behind while Dolly was off on her own adventure.

May 13, 1923

The steamer Avalon has just passed out of sight on the way to the mainland. I watched it go with poignant emotion. My wife was on it—leaving for home and then to motor across the continent, and then sail the Atlantic, and motor over England and France.

It is a long and hazardous undertaking and I felt the meaning of it. We were rather late getting down, and the parting, owing to boat regulations, was hurried. I did not get another good look at her.

Then upon my return to the house here in the hills I watched with my glass until the boat left, and did not see her again. I imagine she was out of sight somewhere. She did not stand the parting very well.

Well, life goes on, and the farther it goes, the keener become hurts and worries. I can only hope and pray she will be returned safely and well.[36]

Mildred arrived after Dolly left, but letters followed Dolly all across Europe telling of the course of his summer.

MAY 14, 1923

Dear Mater Dolorosa,

I am back from my first climb. Am in pretty good shape physically, but my wind was gone.

Last night was punk. I nearly gave in to the blues. Refused to write—except a note to you—and read a little—then went to the movies.

Upon my return here I found out what home is without mother!

But I'll grab hold today, and if I don't show you something upon your return here then I am N.G. instead of Z.G.

Be careful—not ridiculously careful, but thoughtfully careful, and don't forget

Your

Doc

JUNE 11, 1923

Dearest Wife—

You are now on the big ship leaving your native land, and all of my heart that's not broken goes with you. It was hard to let you go. Be as careful as possible and have the best time that you can. This is your opportunity.

All fine here. The kids are happy and improving. I am well and in good spirits. Life seems particularly good to us. Be assured that often while I am in the Pacific, I will think of my wife on the Atlantic, and pray for your welfare.

Love,

Doc

JUNE 12, 1923

Dearest Wanderer of the Soul Land,

Your nice letter of yesterday sort of made up for a lot of neglect. I wrote you a letter before this to the steamer, but addressed it only care of S.S. Mauretania. I hope it arrived. Was glad to hear that your arrangements were going satisfactorily. It must be some undertaking.

We went to the movies last night and took the kids. Luckily the show was decent. We saw Richard Dix (the man who's playing Jean Isbel in my forest story) and I must say I like him very much. Also I liked Helen Chadwick. But the story was punk. No story at all.

Well, no news particularly. I wrote a piece about forestry for the American Forestry magazine, and a piece about background with photos for the Mentor, and now I'm working on a historical sketch of the cowboy for the Historical Society. Alas! What all this stuff will look like without your help, I can't guess. You should not run off from your poor husband. I hope you don't get seasick. It's so unromantic. Write soon.

Love,

Doc

Business followed her, for there were publishing houses and publishers in England to visit.

Dearest—

Will try to catch you with one more note, though I haven't anything to say except I love you like h—now you're leaving me. Isn't that just like me?

My MS is finished and I guess it's pretty good. I'm sure Mildred and I worked on it enough for Currie, at any rate. I will send it soon.

I have an offer of 50 pounds for serial rights of Tappan's Burro from Curtis Brown. Isn't that cheap? I suppose anything in England is better than nothing.

Put this address in your book

Curtis Brown

6 Henrietta St.

Convent [*sic*] Garden

London

and call on him. Meanwhile I'll answer his letter and refuse the offer. Find out what is paid the English authors, etc., etc.

Now be sure to see that man Jeffries, and if he is any good you had better make a deal with him to handle my stuff, all kinds, serially, of course.

See Sir Earnest Hodder Williams (Hodder and Stoughton Publishers)

St. Paul's House

Warwick Square

Get all the angles you can.

And write me about them. After that your work will be done.

Love, kisses, good wishes, prayers,

Doc

Mildred left for Arizona on a vacation of her own when Louise swept in. Zane took her on a tour of California.

Dearest—

I blew in here last night, in knickers, tanned, needing a shave—and they didn't want to let me in, I guess—especially the dining room. But I wrote my autograph in a book, and Magic!

Say, Dolly, I know now why you love to motor all over.

Miss A—is having a grand time. L—is kidding me. She says "Ain't nature grand?" at the big trees. At Carmel when I said something, she replied "Yes, it's wonderful. Let's go." Some blase kid! I'll say—Here she fell for the place immediately.

Will get to L.A. tonight. Tomorrow see Lasky in important council—and next day Avalon. And there I'll sit down, believe me! I'm about through dear, and—

Hope you are having a glorious time. I thought of you yesterday afternoon. I am getting very loyal to my wonderful and adorable wife.

Love,

Doc

Zane's problems were only beginning.

· JUNE 28, 1923

Darling,

I am back here. Everything fine. The kids great. I was sorry to have only one letter in 10 days, and that one saddened me. So you're going abroad to make yourself a better wife. My love, you're quite wonderful enough. I don't want you any different. That sort of hurt me.

The Andersons are here, and the kids are overjoyed to have Louise to play with. She loves them, and that part of it is fine.

I have only a note from Dot about seeing you off on June 17.

By the way I want you to fetch Dot back with you when you come west. Don't holler now. I seldom impose anything on you. But that I insist upon. Please write me your acceptance.

I have arranged with Lasky to take him to Kayenta and Nonnezosche, about September 10 or 15. We are going to make Vanishing American into a $500,000 10 reel picture, the greatest Indian picture ever to be made. I will see about $50,000 in advance.

Love, kisses, hugs, etc., especially etc.

Your,

Doc

Dear Dolly—

Bad news. I'm sorry to have to tell you that I am sunk. Things have been bad for days. And the climax came yesterday, with some added knocks.

Currie roasted h—out of Thundering Herd, and incidentally informed me that my recent stories had been inferior to those before, and returns for his magazines were steadily diminishing.

He asked me to rewrite last of novel. This I am afraid I can't do. You see it is the tragedy of the buffalo. He wanted me to devote more to characters. It's the old story of the magazine editor thinking of popular appeal. I should never have let the story go without your seeing it. This is my last bitter lesson.

In the same mail there came a half page from the literary section of the Evening Post containing a stinking ridicule of the Wanderer of the Wasteland. It is long, and the most villainous thing I ever read. It made me ill.

Add to that the fact that I cannot get money due from Lasky. And also that the situation here regarding Louise is intolerable. She is all right. But I should not have had her again. She is a worry instead of a help. Mildred really helped me. Now some Zanesville boy is coming to Avalon to see L—, and as I understand it for a week's vacation. She says he only cares to dance!

I shall send her home just as quickly as I can get somebody to take her; and lacking that I'll take her myself.

I'm sorry that I must distress you with my troubles. But if you were only here! I never needed you so badly. I hope your trip is worth it.

Forever,

Doc

My dearest Penelope,

My troubles multiply. I wish I didn't have to tell you this one.

I gave Elma $500 in January and $500 in April. The understanding was that I would pay her way through college, and in the event that I gave up the A's she would be the same as usual, and in any event go on working for me and stay home.

I am just in receipt of a letter announcing her intention of marrying in Sept.

Three times she mentions the surprise it must be to me. The lucky (?) Gentleman is one Nagle I met at her house last year, and I asked her a rather pointed question. She laughed it off. In April I asked her if there wasn't someone she was interested in, and she said No!

If she had trusted me, and had told me I would have taken it well enough. But a deliberate double-cross like this is a humiliation I have never suffered before. She writes as if she expected me to be pleased as Punch, and do favors for her.

You, with your great heart and understanding of the frailties of humanity, and the inevitableness of life, will be sympathetic and get her point of view. But if you could have a look at me now, after 24 hours of shame, you would not be so sympathetic, I imagine.

But my dear, like Tappan's Burrow I shall weather another vicissitude of life. And, I am certainly sure to appreciate my one or two remaining friends.

Sometimes I feel an amazing sensation, as if I suddenly saw myself. It's strange. And I don't like it. Imagine a vast lonely flat drab place with all things of huge proportions, and myself as a tiny little mite wandering here and there. Then I have another sometimes. You loom as large as Betelgeuse!

Love,

Doc

JULY 24, 1923

Dearest,

Just a line. The tide of my unhappy state has turned. The thunder bolts have ceased raining down, and a few good things came.

Lasky paid up and made a deal to go to Kayenta with me to see about Vanishing American. Will make Call of The Canyon and Heritage of The Desert this summer and fall.

I love you dearly, and need you a hell of a lot. But I guess I've weathered this storm. All well here. You have a good time or I'll never let you go again.

Love,

Doc

Dearest—

I had another fight with Mildred. It was about Elma. She made me see that
I must write to Elma—a congratulatory letter. She said you would make me
do it. And I daresay you would have. So I have written a nice sweet lying letter
to the d— white-faced [illegible—] and do not feel particularly virtuous therefore. So that is ended.

I am glad to tell you that I have heard from Dot, and she will be glad to do
what I want her to—which particularly is to come west with you in the car. I
was worried. I was afraid she too would turn me down.

Dolly, don't linger in the east. Come along soon so you can get home by
Sept. 20 or 25. The d— machine won't run much longer without you. Still, the
kids are wonderful and Hildred very good and capable. It is poor old Docco
who has gone to wrack without you. Everybody else seems to be fat and contented. I love you dearly and hope and pray for your safe return.

Ever

Doc

Dolly wrote mostly short notes, not out of anger or pique, but because
she was busy recording her observations and impressions of all that she saw.
Occasionally she wrote a longer letter. Visiting Paris, full of expatriate Americans, she spilled out her enthusiasm to Zane, along with some wise advice
regarding Elma's desertion and apparent fraud.

Dearest O'mine,

Paris at last! Got in yesterday P.M. and found that the hotel to which I
had written a couple of weeks ago for reservations had been booked up for
months. Rather alarmed, I got them to give me some other hotels, and
by sheer luck managed to get the last two rooms here. The place—Paris—
is chockful of Americans, and one hears more English spoken on the streets
even, than French.

It took me two hours to read the stack of mail I found—much to my joy.
Letter from Elma announcing her forthcoming leap. I do think she worked

you rather unfairly in a sordid mercenary sort of way but perhaps she figured it was coming to her. At any rate, personally, I can bear her no resentment, but considerable from your point of view. And I hope she does get a little happiness, as I think she has been very miserable ever since she was deposed by Dorothy and successors.

Doc, you want me to cold shoulder her. If I were able to do that, I would have been able to do the same thing to all your friends in the past for far more vital reasons than that they were marrying some other man and deserting my husband. I appreciate to the fullest, and know exactly how you feel; and my heart always aches for your unhappiness. Nevertheless, I think that marriage is the only solution for Elma, whereby there is the least possibility of her getting a little happiness out of life. She would never have had it hanging uncertainly on to you. No woman can, especially if there are any others on the scene. Therefore, my darling, forget yourself, and be glad that she has her chance, even if she did pull your leg. You needn't be enthusiastic, of course, or give her twin beds, but don't begrudge.

And God knows, if she doesn't make a go of it, you'll probably have her back on your hands like the others. The size of the man she's marrying gets me. He's nice enough, but when he borrowed Ed's bathing suit, it hung on him.

Sorry about the change of plans concerning Dorothy. I hope to God that you change it again so she won't have to come with me. It means a lot of bother all around. It means a lot to me, of course, if there's no way out, I'll have to, but it spoils my trip more or less.

Wandered around alone all morning just looking into shop windows. Wonderful city. Love unto eternity.

Wife

Her absence made it clear to Zane how much he relied on Dolly. She handled the income tax, the bank, the publishers. She edited his work, and manuscripts that had passed her scrutiny were never returned. She advised him on his affairs of the heart and mothered him when they went awry.

The passionate affair with Louise burned itself out, its end sealed in Louise's own hand.

SEPTEMBER 4, 1923

Doc—

I have very little to say to you as you forbade me to speak of the dishonor of opening my mail. I am very sorry that you should pass such low judgment on my attitude towards Dick. I really expected you to say such vile things though because you have always interpreted other people that way and there is no reason why I should expect you to be more lenient in my case.

All I can say is that I am sorry for any suffering that I have caused you. That is what worries me, not the very childish threat you made in Mother's letter. Please remember, Doc, that I am no longer a child and should you care to make trouble for me I can repay you ten fold. It seems that we can no longer remain even friends so I say good-bye.

Louie

At least he landed four broadbill swordfish, to the chagrin of the Tuna Club.[37] He could hardly wait for Dolly to return, but when she did in early September, he left almost immediately. He was obligated to go to Arizona to help Jesse Lasky find locations for the filming of his books.

Zane met him in Flagstaff in early September, bringing Mildred with him, and they toured the areas he had described in the romances: Keams Canyon, Kayenta, the Rainbow Bridge, Monument Valley, Navajo Mountain, the Gap. Later he spent some time on location where *Call of the Canyon* and *Heritage of the Desert* were being filmed.[38] When Lasky left, Zane and Mildred went to his cabin in the Tonto, where he hunted and took notes for more western stories. They left Arizona in November, Mildred returning to New York and Zane to Altadena.

But he could never stay in one place longer than a few months. He was in New York again for New Year's Eve and wrote to Dolly,

DECEMBER 31, 1923
11:58

My dearest treasure,

I am alone, and thinking of you, and that I shall try next year to show you somehow something more of love and reverence than in 1923.

The din is tremendous—sad—wonderful. Your home city, my love, where you were born!

I am here, but I am with you, at home.

This old year was hard for me. I am glad it is over. I have suffered. I have renewed hope and strength from you. And so—I write—at the last second.

My Dolly, I hope and pray you have a Happy New Year.

Zane

*Lina Elise Grey, called Dolly by family and
friends, 1890s. Courtesy Loren Grey*

*Pearl Zane Grey at the University of
Pennsylvania, where he studied dentistry
on a baseball scholarship in the late 1890s.
Courtesy Loren Grey*

Dolly and daisies, circa 1906.
Courtesy Loren Grey

Right: *A dapper Zane Grey during his*
college years in the late 1890s.
Courtesy Loren Grey

Facing page:
Dolly with parasol at Lackawaxen
before their marriage. Courtesy Loren Grey
Bottom: *Zane Grey at Lackawaxen, circa*
1910. Courtesy Loren Grey

Dolly with a bass caught in the Delaware River close to Lackawaxen before their marriage. Fishing was not one of her favorite activities. Courtesy Loren Grey

Dolly artfully posing at Lackawaxen, circa 1906. Courtesy Loren Grey

*Dolly and Zane at Lackawaxen, 1906.
Courtesy Loren Grey*

*Dolly and Zane at Lackawaxen,
1906. Courtesy Loren Grey*

Dolly at Lackawaxen, circa 1906.
Courtesy Loren Grey

Lillian Wilhelm, Dolly's cousin,
circa 1908. Courtesy Loren Grey

Lillian Wilhelm, Lillian's sister, Claire (also Dolly's cousin), and Zane Grey, circa 1915. Courtesy Loren Grey

Below: *Lillian Wilhelm, Zane Grey, and Claire Wilhelm at the Grand Canyon, circa 1915. Courtesy Loren Grey*

Elma Swartz and Lillian Wilhelm,
Lackawaxen, circa 1912.
Courtesy Loren Grey

Elma Swartz, Claire Wilhelm, and Lillian Wilhelm at the cottage in Lackawaxen where the
girls stayed, circa 1912. Courtesy Loren Grey

Lillian Wilhelm, Claire Wilhelm,
and Elma Swartz in a canoe on the
Delaware River at Lackawaxen, circa
1912. Courtesy Loren Grey

Elma Swartz in a field of daisies at Lackawaxen, 1912. Courtesy Loren Grey

Top: *Lillian Wilhelm, Claire Wilhelm, Elma Swartz, and Emmeline Jones at Lackawaxen, 1916. Courtesy Loren Grey*

Bottom: *Emmeline Jones, Elma Swartz, Lillian Wilhelm, and Dorothy Ackerman at Lackawaxen, 1916. Courtesy Loren Grey*

*Dorothy Ackerman, Long Key, Florida,
1916. Courtesy Loren Grey*

*Mildred K. Smith, Lillian Wilhelm, and Dorothy Ackerman at Catalina Island, circa 1919.
Courtesy Loren Grey*

Above: *Loren Grey (age four), Dorothy Ackerman, Betty Grey (age seven), Zane Grey, and Louise Anderson at Altadena, California, 1921. Courtesy Loren Grey*

Right: *Louise Anderson and Zane Grey at Catalina Island, 1921. Courtesy Loren Grey*

Facing page:
Top: *Louise Anderson with a black sea bass, San Clemente Island, 1922. Courtesy Loren Grey*
Bottom: *Louise Anderson and Zane Grey enjoying watermelon by his touring car, 1923. Courtesy Loren Grey*

Mildred Smith and Zane Grey
at the Grand Canyon, circa
1914. Courtesy Loren Grey

Mildred Smith, Catalina Island, 1920s. Courtesy Loren Grey

TOKAANU HOTEL

TOKAANU

(Lake Taupo,) N.Z.

April 20   192 7

Dearest Wife —

Cable from you today "Sending Money."
That's all. Well, did you include
your loss? and what bank did you
send it to? My dear love, I fear
you are sore. Well, I'm sorry. I
sure did not have it figures right —
the expense I mean. I shall have
to work the harder. Never you fear,
I shall not let you suffer for my
extravagances. I'm afraid I'm
a little hurt at that cablegram.

Love

Dad.

THE WORLD-FAMED SALMON TROUT FISHING GROUNDS

Letter from Zane Grey to Dolly, April 20, 1927. Courtesy Loren Grey

Top: *Wanda Williams in Tahiti, 1933. Courtesy Loren Grey*
Bottom: *Dorothy Grey (Romer's first wife) and Brownella Baker* (on the right) *in Tahiti, 1934. Courtesy Loren Grey*

1924-1925

CHAPTER 11

The Female of the Species

AT THE STROKE OF MIDNIGHT, Dolly wrote to Zane.

Altadena

(HERE DEC. 31ST, 1923)

(IN N.Y., JAN. 1, 1924)

Dearest,

Funny, isn't it, to be living in two years. My physical self is here, but of course my mental or spiritual self has been spending the last hour or so with you; and your telegram assured me you'd be alone at midnight to wish me a happy new year. Were you awake or were you having one of those dreams about me? At exactly nine here which was twelve in N.Y. I had my eyes shut, and the tears (not of unhappiness but emotions engendered by the depth of my love for you) were oozing through my eyelids a bit; and then what do you think I heard? The tremendous diapason of sound which means the birth of a new year in the greatest city in the world. The most wonderful sound on earth, I think, for it carries and conveys all the pinnacles and depths of human experience and emotion, and all that re-echoes in me when I hear it. I wondered whether I seemed to be hearing it because it was smiting your ear.

We had a warm pleasant evening around our fireplace while the rain poured down outside—a sound that always enhances the comfort of indoors. I don't feel so forsaken and lonely tonight as I usually do on New Year's Eve when you're away. I think it is because you're not with someone else, and perhaps because I have reached the conviction that your love for me is really a thing apart—that no other relations you had could ever touch or degrade—as mine is for you. I mean sort of infallible to outside influence—but the strongest, most permanent and dominating influence in both our lives. Is it that to you?

Well, beloved, in spite of the warmth of my emotion, my nose and toes are icy—and I don't just relish crawling into that cold damp bed without you. But sleep is wonderful. Last night I dreamed a thrilling romance of which I was the heroine.

You're my one and only and I'm your only

Wife

Despite his infidelities, distance, and misunderstanding, Dolly remained loyal to him. She endured his constant wandering in the world and in matters of the heart and rose above it, distancing herself from the torment as best she could. She was no longer young, and the years of strain and three babies had changed her appearance. She was now a business partner, mentor, advisor, and comforter rather than a wife in a traditional sense, even advising him how to handle his troubles with women. But she still had deep emotions and fought fiercely to maintain her place with her husband, first and separate from all others. Zane, in turn, placed her on an ever higher pedestal, even while he continued his dalliances with her rivals.

Since the summer of 1917 Dorothy had been closer to Zane than the others only to be deposed by Louise. Dorothy had not born that rejection well. Now Zane told her that even with Louise gone they were not to resume the old relationship. Mildred had taken her place.

JANUARY 7, 1924

My Dearest,

Yesterday I met Dot at 9:30 and was with her until 4 o'clock. I expected it to be another ordeal. But it was not. Dot looked fine. She was well, cheerful, and had a good hold on herself. She had changed, somehow, and reminded me of how she used to be years ago. She has been having a good time, mostly with Fergy, Laverne, and Mick. Mick's engagement was broken last summer,

and he seems a different man. I sort of gathered from Dot that the old friendship had been renewed.

Dot told me that something you said or did the last day at Altadena gave
her the spirit to get through with it. She said she could never be grateful
enough to you. Well, to me it is only another instance of your beauty of character. I think my love and reverence for you grows as the years pass by. I may
lose D. presently and it will hurt. But somehow I was relieved, glad that she
was as she was. I have a genuine affection for Dot, and I want to repay her for
her loyalty to me.

We called on Elma. Ye Gods! I don't know how to express myself. Elma is
working for her husband in a back office of a building on East 43rd street. It
was a strange thing for me to see her there, with her husband, and to talk with
them. Life is so queer, funny, terrible. Thank God I don't want to know life or
write realism.

Still it must be life when I have a feeling that without you I couldn't go on.
Somehow I have an unmistakable faith in your loyalty to me, in your sympathy
and love. Perhaps I'll soon get back my feeling for what it is that makes me
thrill and write. I haven't done a lick of work in the week I've been here. But I
promise you I'll begin. When I write and read, or fish, or ride, or when I am
home with you, the painted windows shine again. With unutterable love,

Doc

Mildred Katharine Smith had been with Zane since 1915. Originally
from New York City, she had dark hair and flashing dark eyes and was
twenty-five years younger than Zane. Dorothy was to stay on as a secretary
and to come with him to Long Key, much to Mildred's chagrin. Mildred was
jealous of Zane's attention and fearful of rivals. With innuendo and hints
she tried to erode Zane's opinion of Dorothy.

Dolly advised,

Altadena

JANUARY 18, 1924

Dearest,

I was just on the point of beginning this letter to you when Hildred came in
with yours of the night before you left N.Y. You don't know the longing that

goes out from me to get my arms around you and comfort you and smooth things for you when you are sick, or distressed, or worried.

But I won't go into the matter of the girls again. It is useless. Only don't take it so seriously, for some way or other it will work out. Only this I say to you; no woman is ethical, can possibly be, in the relationship in which these girls are placed to you. So you will have to ignore that part of them and get what is worthwhile to you out of your personal contact with them. In a certain sense you have idealized every woman you have ever come in contact with—made her something to fit your momentary need—rather than grasped at all their real characters or relation to the world. It was when the latter considerations impinged on your "dreams of fair women" that trouble always began.

Your friends have always been nice, more or less normal girls in the ordinary walks of life, but in their relations to you, they have become just the biological "female of the species" and in that manner have reacted to each other and used their claws. It's perfectly natural, has always been, only because to you they are different, you haven't grasped the fact that it's history repeating itself. Not only in the race, but in these particular individuals. Aren't they all perfectly sweet and nice and lovely when they have you all to themselves? But let some other female get a little of your attention and Zowie!! I can't blame Dorothy. I just feel sorry for her, for she's reacted in the way natural to her. Naturally she is a sweet and wholesome and normal girl, but she's had more than she can stand. The Anderson affair knocked her flat, and then, just as she was trying to get up comes this almost greater blow.

And Mildred Smith has reacted in exactly the same way as all the rest with the modifications of her particular makeup. What is so unforgivable in Mildred to other women is the assurance of righteousness and superiority. It sticks out all over her, and enrages her adversaries. I find that the fighting spirit in the human species requires a blow for a blow, a hurt for a hurt. The Christlike spirit of turning the other cheek never manifests in a battle of woman against woman for a man. That's where nature gets in her deadly work.

Well, I think I'll desert the topic. It lends to no open sunlight at present, and my sole aim has been to help you to clarity. I think the best way is to let things take their own course. Inevitably they will. But in this, as in everything, remember that my love is with you.

Well, the work is stacked up for me all over the house, so I'll leave you for
the present. But since it's your home, and your wife, and your work, you see
it's only the letter I'm leaving.

Ever and ever

Dolly

There were two things Zane could not countenance: disloyalty and drinking. As a boy he had promised his mother he would never drink after his
older brother Ellsworth had fallen victim to this vice. His aversion to alcohol increased over the years, and he would not allow any of those who surrounded him to so indulge. Loyalty he required as well, which included,
among other things, strict adherence to his wishes. Mildred contrived that
Zane should discover Dorothy had committed both sins. Dolly continued to
write loving and helpful letters full of advice, and these in turn invited Zane
to write frankly of the frustrations created by Mildred.

JANUARY 19, 1924

Dear Dolly,

Yesterday I got a letter from you that hurt very deeply, yet it is a beautiful
letter. I'm afraid it is beyond me. I can't reach up to it. I feel that my anchor is
slipping, or that I'm skating on thin ice. What in the world is to become of me
if I can no longer go to you with my troubles? Of course, you are bored to
extinction.

As I see it, the relation between you and me is closer and more beautiful than
ever. Nothing threatens it, not from my side. That I have been going through
some kind of awful distress only makes me more dependent on you. Lately the
only thing that has mattered to me was to get at the truth of things which have
mystified me. Naturally I have written what was uppermost in my mind. But
your letter makes me shrink and cringe, and long to hide my face.

It is my honest desire to be fair that has caused this last upheaval. You
claim I am swayed by one more jealous woman. It may be a painful matter
to annoy you, but sooner or later I shall prove you are wrong. As far as
Dorothy is concerned, I have been laboring under a delusion in some regards.
You always said I invested my friends with something they did not have.

The last exposure came through a conscience stricken Claire. I told you, didn't I, that I was the one who gave Phil the money to save her? Well, Claire jeopardized her own happiness by confessing that she drank whiskey cocktails at my cottage in Lackawaxen, with Dot, Fergy, LaVerne, and Mick. Dot said, "I hate the stuff, but I wanted to be a good sport." That was proof that she had drank before. That night Claire heard someone slip downstairs softly. For some reason Dot had put Claire in the little front bedroom, while she occupied a cot in the dining room. Claire went to sleep and was awakened, scared by a loud noise. She yelled. Dot answered, "It's only Mick come down for a drink." The next morning Dot was rather flustered and explained that Mick had come down to get a drink, fell over a chair, woke her up and then sat on her bed and talked a little. I see no reason why Claire should risk her own happiness by lying about her own drinking. This happened last summer.

It dovetails with queer intimations that I have had. I see now how Dot was scared badly, yet felt she had it on Claire. But somehow the truth always works out. This explains Dot's queer reaction to what I said about Elma's dirty trick on me. For years I have held up Dot to my friends, and they, knowing she was getting away with murder, were disgusted. At that it was two weeks before I could choke this last thing out of the girls, after Claire had confessed it.

If you knew how I long for your respect and admiration you would understand the humiliation I suffer, when you write as in your last. I have always told you about all it was possible to tell. I am no different being away from you, except that I have to write instead of talk. And I repeat that if I cannot make myself well, happy, industrious, very shortly, I shall come home.

This situation would have been nothing to handle, if I had not wanted to be tolerant, kind, sympathetic, and helpful. Think of how I suffered because I was hurting Dot, and all the time she had this on her record. If I had known that I wouldn't have suffered. Now I recall what you said about Dot having a pretty good time at home. But I prefer to think that her letdown came very recently—last summer at least. For years I have tried to train Dot against drinking. I believed I had.

I will not bother you again with revelations and circumstances such as these. I'll go it alone. If you think I am an utter fool you will find it necessary to change your mind. I think I can get out of this, and keep out of future

trouble. I have faith in myself and despite the successive shocks of the last
months, I still have something of an ideal left. But one after another, Louise,
Elma, and Dot have betrayed me. It hurts to stand poorly in your estimation.
You are my wife. And if you can't do more, just love me always.

Ever

Doc

Dolly did not care for Lillian or Claire and found Mildred intolerable,
but Dorothy she liked, and she rose to her defense.

JANUARY 28, 1924

My Dearest,

The letter I had from you Saturday distressed me, first on your account,
then on Dot's. Now, listen, old dear, I am not censuring you, whatever I say. I
never look down on you or despise you, or think less of you. Because I know
you, the inner and essential you, stripped of all relation to everything and
everyone else, that can never change. I may disapprove of things you do, may
tell you about it, but that can make no difference. Always remember that.
Being human, we are all prone to mistakes, misjudgements, wrongs. I should
think less of myself if I let pass things that would wreak injustice. But that does
not mean I'm judging you. I know your reactions and the motives behind
them, and in spite of everything, perhaps because of everything, I love you. To
know all is to forgive all. But even that is too severe, for it is not even a matter
of forgiving. I have nothing to forgive. So when I say things about your
friends, it must not affect in any way the relations between us two.

With that preliminary, I approach the matter of Dorothy and the others.
First, a "conscience stricken Claire" is a thing that doesn't exist. Second, if
Dorothy did drink whiskey cocktails to be a good fellow, or for any other reason (and I don't yet admit that she did), what of it? That's a mild reaction
to what the poor girl had to suffer for so long. And I know that Dot would
have no shady relation with Mick. Claire has ever had facile adaptations to the
easiest way of the strongest influence. She lies easily. Certain pressure was
brought to bear on her, your and my disapproval, or worse. As far as I want, I
didn't disapprove in the least. I know her and even with her insincerity, I like
her. She has no power to hurt me. Lil, well, I won't say what my opinion is of

her. Those two, with Mildred Smith, have damned Dorothy to you, when, as a matter of fact, Dorothy has always been more faithful and loyal to you than all the rest put together. And I think their telling you the cocktail business and the other, even if it were absolutely true, shows how despicable women can be to gain their ends with a man. It's just proof of everything I've told you.

Listen, honey, I'll tell you something that may make things easier for you. You have always set impossible standards for the girls with whom you've been associated. You've wanted them to be impossible angels and saints for you and they've really tried to be. And therefore they've feared mortally to let their human reactions and mistakes get to your ears. Now, being merely fallible human beings, as we all are, they've done things innocent enough to most people, which would be utterly damnable to you! Do you remember the fine girl in "Flaming Youth" who joined the naked swimming party because she wanted to be a "good sport" even though she hated it? She was good and fine, although her motive was mistaken. Well, I could tell you things about every girl you ever knew which in no way affected their intrinsic loyalty to you, and yet which if you heard about it, would make you lose all faith in them, because you have set an impossible standard. Think what a weapon I've had and not used, because my sense of justice and proportion forbade my getting rid of anyone in that fashion.

And so I say to you, because you want me to view Mildred Smith through the same rose-colored spectacles through which you are now seeing her, that you are doing Dot a bitter injustice. You don't have to go on with her, but at least be fair to her, and consider the position in which she was placed. Neither do I want you to give up Mildred Smith, if she fills a present need for you. But don't, unless you want me to lose what little respect I may have for her, let her and Lil and Claire form a combination to injure Dorothy in your eyes. I know just this—that if you knew everything about all the girls that have come into your life, judged them all by their mental, physical, spiritual makeup as it reacted to life, you'd find that Dorothy stood very high. I should say that Elma, by actual deed, would have been the most bodily virtuous, but that's nothing to her credit. She had not the disposition, nor the temptation, ever. Essentially, there was less loyalty to you than in a more impulsive temperament that broke the letter of your law.

Don't let these things worry you or dig into your peace of mind. Cease to worry about what I think of Mildred. Again I tell you that the letter in no wise changed my opinion of her. Do you remember the letters she left in the cottage that Mrs. Swartz found? If I hadn't smoothed that out, there would have been merry H—! And that letter, beloved husband, would have sent any other wife to the divorce court. I remember I laughed, though I was furious at the carelessness, for it involved so many people.

You're all right with me, darling, if that will make you feel any better. Just forget about the rest of it where I'm concerned. Go through with what you have planned as cheerfully as you can. I don't want you home disillusioned and unhappy. Home is always here for you when you are ready to come, but I want you to feel that it's the best place on earth to come back to, not a tie that binds. So don't worry about us, or it, or me. I eke some happiness out of life.

Always yours
Dolly

Almost everyone associated with an author thinks that they, too, can write, but Mildred did have some ability and collaborated with him on several pieces—for example, *Desert of Wheat*, which was written in 1918.[1] This was the chief reason Dolly felt threatened by Mildred, for up to now no one could displace Dolly in the role of first critic and literary helpmate.

FEBRUARY 23, 1924

Dearest Doc,

It was a good thing that I received a couple of letters from you at once for in opening the later one first, I mitigated the unpleasantness of the earlier. Let's stop fussing about the Mildred-Dot affair. We each have our own convictions and we can agree to disagree, or better still, eliminate it as far as possible in our relation to each other. Just one thing you said I cannot let pass. You said Mildred would not, and will not, take anything away from me. You just bet she won't! Not because of her magnificent magnanimity, but because she can't, no, nor anyone else. I'm beyond the point where anyone can take anything concerning you away from me, nor can anyone give you anything that I can in any way, shape, or form, or anything that I have given. So that doesn't worry me. Only I don't care about anyone laboring under misapprehension.

Let me know when you intend going into the Everglades and if there is any possibility of your getting home before May 1st. My plans depend on yours, you know. Now, as always, lovingly,

Your

Dolly

Dorothy became engaged in the summer to the same young man who had visited at Lackawaxen.

Fishing was good in Long Key, and quiet days by the endless ocean and limitless sky were all inspiration for Zane. Harper's wanted another outdoor book, which he titled *Tales of Southern Rivers*.[2] He began a tale called *The Fisherman*.[3] He planned to spend five years on *The Fisherman*, and there were many places he thought he should visit to gather material: Nova Scotia, possibly even the South Pacific. Royalties poured in: $1,550.43 from McClurg; $192.58 from Grosset and Dunlap for British royalties on *Betty Zane*, a check from Lasky for $10,000.00; another from Grosset and Dunlap for *Betty Zane* and a baseball story written earlier, "The Red-Headed Outfield," for $1,335.31; another from Curtis for $30,000.00.[4]

More literary negotiations continued, this time centered on his novel *The Vanishing American*. The agreement was that it would run as a regular January feature and its publication was to coincide with the release of the film made from the book, but Harper's was reluctant to publish it because of its negative view of missionaries and because the ending, a marriage between a Caucasian woman and a Native American man, might offend the sensibilities of some readers.[5] It had been run as a serial in 1922 in *The Ladies Home Journal* and had created a public outcry. Harper's was also concerned about the release of the motion picture simultaneously with publication, fearing it would detract from the readership. Zane reworked the manuscript, changing the ending by having the main character die in abrupt and mysterious circumstances and eliminating much of the negative material regarding missionaries.

He was in California by the end of April and after only a few days at

Altadena went to Avalon for the summer with Mildred. At the end of summer he traveled to Nova Scotia, and Dolly adjourned to Avalon.

Once before he had fished the North Atlantic, in 1913 when Robert Davis had taken him there, and the sport of Atlantic salmon and giant bluefin tuna was tempting.[6] He had designed special tackle for the broadbill swordfish off Catalina, and it had worked magnificently. Captain Laurie Mitchell, a Nova Scotian fisherman who held the world record for giant tuna, urged him to try the tackle on them.[7] Zane had his Florida fishing launch, a twenty-five-foot boat equipped with two engines, revolving chairs, and rod sockets, shipped to him.[8] Romer, R.C., and Mildred went too.

The trip was successful beyond his wildest imagination.[9] On August 13 he landed a 608-pound tuna, the second largest ever caught, and he wired Dolly the news. One week later, he set his first world record with a bluefin tuna weighing 758 pounds. On the last week of the trip, he fished one of the inland rivers and caught two Atlantic salmon on flies.

Big-game fishing was an important part of his life, and his world record proved his ability. To go further with it, he needed a ship. He wanted his own ship, "a beautiful white ship with sails like wings," one that would take him to distant seas, and in Nova Scotia he found it.[10] The *Marshal Foch* was a three-masted schooner, used as a cargo vessel but never as a rum runner (that was important to him), that could be refitted as a fishing yacht and was available for seventeen thousand dollars. One hundred and ninety feet long, with a beam of thirty-five feet, it drew eleven feet six inches of water. Dolly was skeptical.

Avalon, Catalina

AUGUST 29, 1924

Dearest Doc,

Well, firstly I wired you my disapproval of your Oregon trip, and my disapproval grows as the details of your plans dribble to me. I should say to take eleven people on a camping trip into a rain-soaked country would be a good way to kill off a number of them with pneumonia, providing they didn't go hurling off the precipitous slippery roads first. Doc, those roads were dangerous even in good weather, and there are places you couldn't climb in wet, even if they were safe. You know I seldom interfere with any of your plans for trips, but I don't consider this a safe one and should worry all the time about you.

Now about the ship. Never knew you were even looking at more than one, so your telegram was somewhat puzzling. However the part about depositing the $16,000 for you by Sept. 1st was clear enough. I'll do it though it will pretty well clean me out. Not a cent came in since you left and the only money you have given me in months is that $9,000 just before you left. I'm hoping there will be a windfall before the income tax is due on September fifteenth. According to the New York Times you are having your boat refitted in N.Y. Why? When labor was so infinitely cheaper in Nova Scotia. Did anyone ever tell you that it would cost you a fortune to bring that boat through the canal? It costs the Manchuria $11,000 for a single trip. Well, Pa's rich and Ma don't care! That is, if the children don't starve.

Well, goodnight. I love you muchly.

Dolly

Words of caution fell on deaf ears—in fact, they did not even arrive until after the deal was closed. Zane renamed the ship the *Fisherman*, had it refurbished in Halifax, and hired a captain and crew to sail it through the canal when repairs were complete.

He came home by way of Oregon against Dolly's advice, but none of them caught their death of pneumonia, nor was anyone hurt. Dolly was not happy all the same.

OCTOBER 3, 1924

Dear Doc,

This is the third time that Reba and Sadayo have heard from their respective spouses, and I haven't had a word from you. It makes a pretty humiliating situation for me. I'm really beginning to believe what I get from all directions, that M.S. won't let you do things. Perhaps she's put an embargo on correspondence with your wife. If nobody were getting mail, I wouldn't mind, but if Rome and George can get it out, there must be some reason for your not doing it—and I know it's the people you're with.

No word or sign from Dorothy. Lasky sent the last Code of the West check and first Thundering Herd. The Grauman Theatres have been running a very fine screen ad about you, in connection mostly with "The Border Legion," which appears next week.

Well, there's no particular news that would interest you. Hope you are getting some fishing. Hear Rome caught some steelhead. Are Lil and Jess back with you, and what was wrong with them?

Love,

Dolly

Dolly hoped he would stay in Altadena for awhile, but her wishes were ignored. As soon as he returned from Oregon he went to Arizona, not for his usual fall hunting trip, but for an unusual event taking place there. For years Arizona had placed a bounty on mountain lions; consequently, their numbers were severely depleted. Ranchers on the North Rim of the canyon thought this a great boon, as their cattle were safe from attack, but without the natural predator the deer native to the area increased far beyond the ability of the land to feed them. By 1924 the browse of the North Rim was exhausted, and the deer were starving.

Forest officials and other interested parties devised a plan to drive the deer, as if they were cattle, from the North Rim down into the canyon then to the forests to the south.[11] Since he had already filmed two of Grey's stories in the region, Jesse Lasky wanted to capture the drama for use later. Zane was aware of the plans, wanted to participate, and convinced Lasky he should finance the whole thing in order to have the film rights.[12] A small army of almost forty cowboys and over a hundred Native Americans were hired to drive the animals, and they all converged on Flagstaff in early December. Zane and his entourage were mounted on horses and ready.

That it was a failure did not detract from the dramatic potential of the drive, but it did add the element of tragedy. Zane blamed inadequate preparations, lack of drivers, and the unexpected refusal of the deer to behave like cattle, and he bewailed the fate of the deer now to be shot to reduce their numbers.[13] But he had great material for a story.

He was home for only a few weeks to spend Christmas with Dolly and the children, then off again, this time to meet his ship at the Pacific port,

Balboa. The ship had been refitted to his specifications.[14] The aft cabin extended over the forward hatch and now contained eight staterooms and saloon. Galley and crew quarters were new. Below deck were a combined saloon and dining room, four bathrooms, a darkroom for photography, a tackle room, storerooms, a large refrigerator plant, and half a dozen staterooms. Behind these was the engine room, which contained two Fairbanks-Morse driving engines, an engine to generate electricity for lights and fans, another for the compressed air that forced water over the ship, and an emergency engine. The ship carried three launches and was stocked with every kind of tackle that money could buy and ingenuity devise. It had left Nova Scotia early in December 1924 and reached Santiago, Cuba, in twelve days. From there it sailed to Jamaica then Colon, Panama, where it ran aground. It was put in dry dock at Colon and was found to have stripped the keel. Grey fired the captain and put Captain Sid in his place. The *Fisherman* reached Balboa January 17, and Grey sailed two days later from Los Angeles on the SS *Manchuria*.[15] With him were R.C. and Romer; George Takahashi; Chester Wortley (Lasky's favorite camera operator); Lillian Wilhelm and her husband, Jess Smith; Claire and her husband, Phil Carlin; Mildred; Romer's friend Johnny Shields; and Captain Laurie Mitchell.[16] Zane wrote Dolly from Balboa.

Balboa

JANUARY 29, 1925

Dearest Dolly,

Had a wonderful trip down, 9 days of fine weather with only one bad day. I wrote over 100 pages, under terribly uncomfortable conditions, and when I finished I was so crippled—back—legs—bones, that I could not stand erect. Excuse me! I have sent off the rest of the MS and hope you get the $25,000 pronto.

Romer was fine on the trip, except for one or two little things. He got to chasing a flapper. So did Johnny. And this little flapper fell awful hard for Chester.

There was a rotten crowd on board. They all tried to hobnob with me, and fell down hard.

Panama and Balboa are very beautiful—and muggy. You would perspire and expire here.

My boat is wonderful, but the expense drives me crazy. I just have to work hard to get it back.

Well, darling, I am rushed, so adios. I will go out and cable you now. We're going off on a hard, rough trip, but I hope it will be safe. I'll be careful. Love to you and my children.

Doc

He was gone four months, first fishing the waters of Cocos Island, where seabirds stole bait from the mouths of fish and sharks mangled hooked fish before a catch could be landed. Galapagos, five hundred miles west of Ecuador, proved no better for fishing but provided dramatic photography and exotic animals. The Perlas Islands were also poor for fishing. Further north at the small Mexican fishing village of Zihuantenejo, close to Acapulco, sailfish and marlin provided good sport. At Cabo San Lucas on the southern tip of Baja California, he set another world record with a tuna weighing 318 pounds.[17]

Life on board ship was good for more than fishing. The long, monotonous voyages with no distractions were excellent for writing, and Zane finished several stories. A romance set in the Tonto Basin, *Under The Tonto Rim,* flowed almost effortlessly, but having nothing but ocean around him and the rhythmic motion of a sailing ship as it rose and fell and rolled, he had to write of fishing. The story of the voyage he called *Tales of Fishing Virgin Seas.* He also began a northern California novel for Currie.[18]

Home was not as conducive to writing. After a few weeks in Altadena, he went to Catalina for the opening of the season and began another western, *Forlorn River,* but there were too many distractions. Tourists bothered him at the house he had rented in Avalon, and he caught a cold that lingered.

JUNE 26, 1925

Dearest,

I woke up this morning with a severe pain in my right temple and my right nostril closed, and aching all over. I have caught cold again, and I declare this is the limit. I've been well only a few days since my return to California.

You'd laugh if you were here. This place is overrun by curiosity seekers. They annoy me frightfully. Some of them are decent people, but most are rude and will peep right in the windows. We never calculated on such a thing. No writer builds himself a house in a public place, where the crowd can get to him. And that is what it is here. I am very much surprised and dismayed. I have been extremely annoyed many times. Many people take the place for the Indian Museum advertised before. I made Glidden put up another sign but it doesn't appear to do any good. We have not found a remedy yet, and I see none except to let them come and not answer the door. I'll have to cover my window.

I wired twice to Trinidad, wrote three letters to La Junta, two to Kansas City, and the rest to New York. Don't say I didn't either. This mail after stuff is bunk. You never get anywhere you say you will, until before or after. Well, I'm not cross, but I'm sick, so goodbye.

Love,

Doc

Dolly had gone east again to spend the summer in Lackawaxen and New York, most likely because Mildred was with Zane. All three children were in summer camp, so she traveled alone. She was more concerned about Mildred than ever and blamed her for the breakup with Dorothy, but Zane rose to Mildred's defense and accused Dolly of being jealous and manipulative.

JULY 2, 1925

Dearest Wife,

It's lucky for you that I'm too sick to raise hell with you. Your letter of June 29 sure added to my misery. Three days ago I awoke with my right nostril closed and a fearful pain over my right eye.

I think your letter fine and wonderful in a way, and nasty in another. If what you think is true, there's only one thing for me to do and that is go back to the old way. But I think you exaggerate. No woman runs me, unless it's you. And even you can't when I don't want it. Perhaps I am unjust to Dot. I'll remedy that, and rely on your say so wholly.

Mildred is not the cat you imagine. I hope you will come to see this in time.

If not I'll have to prove it to you. We've not had an unpleasant word until your letter came, and when I was fool enough to tell about the towels, and that it really was a new fellow. We didn't fight then, but it was unpleasant, because she read my mind, and I was thinking what you wrote. Mildred did not undermine any other friend. I did that myself, for the reason you know, and for what you wanted. Much that you wrote is true, and your writing it proved it even in your case. I'm sorry I blabbed to you. Now you wait till I do it again.

Please forget this. I shall be guided by you as always, except in some particulars where my very soul is in jeopardy. Then I hedge. I think I know you to be the sweetest and finest woman who ever lived. And you've got a streak that makes you human. Please forget what I wrote and write, and I'll do the same.

Love

Doc

It seemed that Mildred might even have the ability to turn Zane against Dolly, something no one else had ever been able to do. But he was ill and he missed her, and something about the way she had left bothered him.

JULY 16, 1925

Dearest Dolly,

It has bothered me not to know where you are, to have telegrams returned. You went off on this trip like a woman sort of driven out of her home, and bewildered. I don't see any good reason for that. You certainly never got all the telegrams and letters I sent you.

Everybody has been as good and kind to me as possible, but I don't think I ever wanted you as badly as this last month. Ida and Reba, Rome, George, Captain M. and Mildred have all been perfectly wonderful. But I have been contrary and irritable and dissatisfied. Perhaps when I return I'll be O.K. There were so many annoying things besides work and illness.

Love,

Doc

P.S. I will leave here about Aug. 30 and Altadena about Sept. 1. You must plan to be home my love.

Lackawaxen

Dearest Doc,

Returned here from New York Friday evening. It's always restful and fine to get back.

I don't believe I've written you since you wired about the operation. You did not specify, but of course I took it for granted the trouble was your tonsils, otherwise I would have been scared silly. But I wrote you that your bad tonsils must have been the cause of your repeated colds, and so it turned out.

I'm not going to comment much on the contents of your very surprising epistle where you told me M. had kept and opened one of Dot's letters to you, and a year later showed it to you to prove Dot's duplicity. Where's the logic of that? If Dot was sending you a letter she was telling you what was in it, wasn't she?

Better be careful. Anyone who'll purloin a letter will do other things. Anyway, I'm numbering mine on the inside so please see that the consecutive numbers reach you intact.

Saw Elma in New York. She is very thin, but looks well, and really beautiful. I offered Mrs. Schwarz and Bergman this house for the few weeks after I leave. Poor Mrs. S. loves it up here, and I don't think she gets much change. Elma may get up for weekends.

Dot's young man and his mother were up for the weekend—very nice people they are. The more one sees of the boy the better one likes him. Dot seems happy and perfectly sincere, and her future mother-in-law evidently likes her very much.

Please, dear, if you think you want me back, let me know. I'd hate to think you needed me and I'd not know it. But a tonsil operation isn't serious and I just can't be pessimistic about it.

Went to theatre almost every night in New York, but there's still plenty to see. Eugene O'Neill's "Desire Under The Elms" was a primitive, striking, terrible play. Brutally frank, of course. "What Price Glory," very different in conception seemed to strike the same note. They interested me intensely.

I will be in N.Y. again July 27 to August 1. However, if you want to address your mail here, I have it forwarded.

Goodnight, honey. Keep cheerful and well, for life would be a desert for me without you.

Ever

Dolly

Zane had his tonsils out in mid-July and recovered swiftly. He was soon fishing and making plans.

AUGUST 15, 1925

Dearest Dolly,

Yesterday I licked a broadbill swordfish, 309 pounds, so I must be well again. R.C. had one the day before, 343 pounds. You should see the crowds on the pier. Simply a circus.

I've got over my terrible morbid spells, and am cheerful again. For God's sake, help me to hold on to my old self. You have no idea of the terror I feel in the moods I had.

I got a dandy letter from Dot which I answered, and I sent her a check. I did not mention the past trouble, nor did she. I think we can be friends again, and I want to help her all I can. And at the same time I want to be decent to all my old friends.

Mildred is well again, but in unhappy mind because of the gossip most probably emanating from Dorothy. She heard from N.Y. friends who heard directly from Hildred that you had no use for her. I have lied about this. But I fear she knows I lie. It's a question of honor with her, and if there is any foundation for this talk she'll sever her connections here. She'll do it, too, and I think that would hurt me. Won't you be gracious to her when we get to Altadena? Imagine me asking you that. My God!

Love,

Doc

Mildred's fine hand was behind this. Now Zane thought Dolly had wronged her and Mildred was an innocent victim. Zane was so smitten that he asked his wife to be gracious to his latest lady love! Insulted, Dolly responded from Chicago, now en route to California.

Dear Doc,

I think you will want to apologize for that last letter I had from you. I don't think if you had thought, you would have said that I ever insulted any of your friends. I have always treated Mildred Smith with utmost courtesy, and if she says anything else, she lies. I would feel myself besmirched if I insulted any one of your friends.

I am going to the root of some of the things you say Hildred told Mildred when I get back. I have always been extremely careful not to say or indicate anything derogatory of Mildred in front of, or to Hildred, for I know Hildred liked her, and I wanted to do nothing to spoil that liking, or even embarrass it. I have a silly sensitiveness that has always prevented me from doing such things.

Mildred has a peculiar mind. It seizes upon some act or fact and builds a structure upon it that may be entirely false. But she has always been convinced of her own infallibility and she's managed to convince you.

No one more passionately desires peace and good feeling between us than do I, and no one will do more to preserve it. But I can't and won't swallow injustice, and you do me a terrible injustice when you write as you did in that last letter. Therefore, I think you did it thoughtlessly.

I didn't make one scrap more fuss over Lillian or Claire than I did over Mildred. Why would any indicated liking for Dorothy rather than for Mildred or Claire or anyone else make any difference? No one on this earth likes everyone the same. If Mildred had nothing whatever to do with you, she would appeal to me no whit more than she does now. You know it has always been that way. I can't force myself into an enthusiasm I don't feel for her. I'm not a hypocrite. But I repeat, and most emphatically, she has always been treated courteously by me. I consider myself a lady, at least, even if you and she do not.

We're a little south of our intended route, for yesterday the radiator began leaking so badly that we had to stop in each town to fill up with water. It's been mended several times, but I guess it's beyond help now, so we have to have a new core, and deemed it advisable to come here to get it, rather than miss out at a smaller place. From here we'll drive west to Springfield, Illinois,

which is on our route. If the weather holds, and we don't get mud, we ought
to get across pretty fast.

Love

Dolly

More and more, Zane's world encompassed only Mildred and Dolly was
excluded. Business decisions were made without notifying her. Editors
asked her about stories she had never heard of, and she discovered they
were works on which Mildred and Zane had collaborated.[19] She felt superfluous in her own home.

SEPTEMBER 2, 1925

Dear Doc,

Am enclosing a couple of letters of importance. Was extremely surprised at
this McCall letter. You never mentioned this to me. Is this "Desert Bound" the
N. California story? You said something about writing for the American, but
not a peep about McCall. Are you sure you're clear with Curry? You said you
wouldn't go into these things without consulting me, you know. I presume this
is all right, but you do get into a lot of trouble, you know. Moreover, I think if
you were switching to McCall, you might have gotten more. However,
$50,000 for future isn't bad. But my advice is not to tie up to any definite con-
tract until we talk it over, for prices are going up all the time. They're crazy to
get you as you're the most popular writer living and they ought to pay for the
privilege. You said "American" only offered $40,000. I hope you didn't prom-
ise them anything, for then you're in bad with McCall again, and if you quit
American, they'll be sore. For heaven's sake, be careful. It worries me. If you'd
just not do things until you consult me, you'd be better off. It doesn't hurt to
make people wait. The longer they wait, the more anxious they are to get you.

I wish you'd told me that you told Reba she could put her chauffeur in my
apartment over Labor Day. I had told Mary to rent it, for I built those places
for income, and at this rate they'll be nothing but expense. Not that I mind
Harry's having a few days vacation, but I would like to be consulted about my
own business affairs. After this, make those things subject to my approval,
will you? I have the feeling that Reba thinks I have nothing to say about any-

thing, and that she's of more importance to you than I am! She told me she had a lot of things to attend to for you at Avalon! I got the impression that Reba wasn't keen to have me go up to my own house, for she asked me if I was going to, and when I said yes, she said, "Well, you know, Rome invited Dr. Greengo over Labor Day." "Oh," I answered airily, "I don't mind that. I like Dr. Greengo," but maybe she thought Rome wouldn't like having me!

Ever,

Dolly

Rogue River

SEPTEMBER 6, 1925

My darling wife,

Your last letter is something I thank the Lord for. I hated to go on this dangerous trip without such assurance from you. It softened me, and lessened the hurt, and made me sorry for my temper and nagging. That is all I need to know—what you wrote. You have nothing to fear, if you care that way. I cannot always do as you want, and this last trouble has been trouble only because you would not see it with your usual clear fine tolerance and wisdom.

I forget and neglected to tell you a hundred things. We never got beyond our quarrel. Alas! What foolishness! I forget all about the Avalon matters. You must not mind Reba. She was fine and useful to me this summer. Don't you care. I'm sorry about the house for Labor Day. You are there today, or up at our new house. I hope a thousand frumps come up to look at my wife. Then you will see what I had to stand.

The enclosed letter from McCall's amazes me and tickles me too. I planned that story on the Fisherman, and went on with it at intervals until I fell ill. McCall's pressed me again. So, with careful instruction and construction I had Mildred finish it. Of course her name will never be connected with it, and no one but you will ever know. I forgot to say that the story is about Lillian, with Jess, and others figuring in it. Modern, of course. Burton's reaction to it amazes me. But it proves what M. can do, and it is very encouraging for M. Please do not mind, Dolly dear. I must and I will help her to some kind of success in life. She needs some encouragement, God knows.

I have played fair with Currie. My deal with him ended with the Forlorn

River novel, northern California setting. He went abroad without a word about renewal. Of course he felt sure of me. But I cannot see myself sacrificing lots of money just because he advertizes me big. Other publishers will do the same. As for Schuler and Country Gentleman, I'm pretty sore at him. He was rather nasty because I used some photos and notes about the Galapagos trip in newspapers. They are hard businessmen, and want it all. I promised Schuler a short story, but that's all he'll get.

Crowell, editor of American magazine, offered me $80,000 for two novels. I promised them, and will be glad to deliver them, one or both, in 1926. Upon my return home we can talk over the McCall offer. But it looks good to me. I think we ought to grab that next year.

Please write Mr. H.P. Burton, editor, for me, and find out when he means to start Desert Bound. Deposit the $35,000 to my account.

Now, my girl, take some time to think, and write me at Gold Beach. I send you all the love any woman is safe with.

Doc

SEPTEMBER 9, 1925

Dearest Doc,

Returned from Catalina last night, but spent the night at Mary's and did not get here until almost noon today.

Sorry about Mildred, but exasperated too—and at the tone of your letter. She's wrong again. Hildred didn't have time to be cold to her, for I hustled her right off because Stewart, who had just brought Mildred, was leaving, and Hildred had no way to get home except with him. Then, when Hildred phoned, she asked me to tell Mildred she was sorry she hadn't been able to get up again to see her and say goodbye, but their car was in the shop, and with all she had to do, she couldn't manage it.

Mildred had gone to bed, or I thought she had, so I kept the message for the following morning. Then, in the rush of your departure, it escaped my mind entirely. She's a liar if she said what you wrote me that I said over the phone. Nothing I said applied in the least to her, but her usual egotism applied it to herself. I begged Hildred to come up to see me, as I would be all alone, but I never said anything that she could misinterpret in that way. She was just sore and that's the way she took it out. She surely is a troublemaker. Everybody is right about that. And let me tell you, Hildred is far more loyal to Mildred than M. is to H. Mildred is always saying things to queer Hildred with you, and Hildred has never, to anyone, said anything unkind or derogatory about Mildred. Now I know if it had been real friendship, it wouldn't have made any difference. I don't think she's lost as much as she thinks she has. As usual, her imagination has distorted matters. Why can't she be a sport and live up to her choice, instead of making you and herself and everyone who comes in contact with her miserable and uncomfortable. She'd be much better thought of. I want to be kind and nice to Mildred but she makes it all but impossible. She's the most ingrown, egotistically selfish human I've ever had any experience with and she seems to get worse. She can't be pleasant or decent unless she has her own way. She gets it with you, but that doesn't satisfy her.

I'm not roasting Mildred. And I'm not sore when I say these things. Nor am I sore at her. She'd probably be horrified if she thought anyone had such a conception of her. But every word I've written is true and I know it and say it in an unprejudiced way. Some day you'll know I'm right. I think in your own soul you know it now. But it's no reason why you should like her the less, or be less kind to her. But it is a tremendous reason why you shouldn't let her bias you and jaundice you toward the rest of the world, why you should take her valuation of all things, why you should be so utterly small as to threaten the things you occasionally do—like insulting Hildred and ruining the lives and happiness of some other people. Nobody is fighting you about Mildred. She's getting no more talked about than any of the others who ever traveled with you, but she makes more fuss about it. But there are times when the show pinches.

And don't make any mistake about me. I don't want you to give up Mildred. Indeed, rather than have you feel injured on that score, I'd prefer to have you give me up.

Now, wake up, my dear. I don't want to interfere with your friendship with Mildred, but it's not going to absorb me and my life. If you keep looking always at her point of view, you'll turn lunatic. She's made you believe that the whole world has turned against her on your account and that it's up to you to make up to her for it. Well, that's all wrong. In this world, we get what we give. She took what she wanted. If she sacrificed what she thought was the friendship of people she liked she did it deliberately. If she cared for you in any degree as she says she does, she'd forget about herself and her wrongs and troubles occasionally, and think of your comfort and peace of mind. She'd be a sport. But she hasn't it in her. If you do anything she doesn't like, she's not slow to call you insulting names! And even if you deserved them, it's the one thing I'm not broad-minded enough to ever swallow. She does not know you or understand you or she never could have done that. A jealous woman cannot see the truth.

Well, if I die and am crucified for it, the great man shall triumph. You must live up to your work, to the great good you do through it. If that weren't in you, you couldn't create as you do. How terrible it would be to disappoint and disillusion all the millions who believe in you so wonderfully. You can't, and you won't. I won't let you. And if there is any sacrifice, it will be that. Believe in that side of yourself, and don't let anyone warp you from that belief. You have made mistakes, the bad part of you has often triumphed over the good, but you have never been what she has called you. Moreover, the relations you have had with other women have been no more wicked than you have had or are having with her. Don't let her convince you of that. Don't let her make sordid reality of what was a dream to you. All those people loved you. There may be little excuse according to ethical standards, but that is the great excuse. So don't belittle them.

As long as you want me

Your Dolly

Zane's plans would take him farther away than ever. Not long after the maiden voyage of the *Fisherman,* he received a letter from C. Alma Baker of Bay of Islands, New Zealand.[20] Zane's fishing feats were famous; his well-known name and his world records were a combination that attracted worldwide attention. New Zealand boasted wonderful sport for fishermen, but few knew of it. All kinds of game fish were in abundance: striped marlin, giant black marlin, mako and thresher sharks, and smaller varieties as well. If the famous Zane Grey would fish there and help them publicize their attractions, the government of New Zealand would help with the expenses.

What a marvelous opportunity! New Zealand's fishing season was from December to March, their summer but the coldest months in the Northern Hemisphere. He could fish Catalina's waters in summer, have Oregon or Arizona in the fall, and spend the winter and spring in the South Pacific.

The *Fisherman* could not make that long a voyage without being re-outfitted, and there was no time for that, so Zane left on December 25 for San Francisco then caught a commercial ship to New Zealand. The preparations were hard on Dolly, who depended on his being home for Christmas at least, and the parting on Christmas Day was sad. New Zealand was very far away, and Mildred would be with him. She might never see him again—or worse, she might never be a part of his life as before.

DECEMBER 29, 1925

Dearest,

I think you were a thoroughbred that last day at home. Somehow you always finish well. Of late you have distressed me very much. But you have made up for it. I wish I could tell you how much I appreciate you, and love you. It is quite beyond me. And that is saying something.

This great Babylon, no, I should not call it that, but this beautiful, rich, all-satisfying edifice I have erected, and which I now enjoy, is something you have as much to do with as I.

Work hard, Dolly, and get things done. Don't start too hard. Work up gradually, and then stick. You have so much to accomplish. I am losing that awful feeling of desolateness and callousness which haunted me. I believe I can make this a great success. If I work hard and you work hard the time will fly. So long, dearest Penelope.

Ever

Doc

In San Francisco Captain Mitchell, Mildred, and Zane boarded the SS *Makura* for the South Pacific.

Dearest Dolly,

I have not been very well today. Just escaped cold or grippe in San Francisco. I ache all over, and feel pretty badly. I could not find the salicylate pills I asked you to pack. They were always good for anything. I smashed my right thumb in the door. It hurts dreadfully, and makes it almost impossible to write. Then I tried to make myself agreeable to a man on board who claimed to know the Wetherills, and I had my feelings hurt for my pains. I got to spouting about big fish, and the damned fool said he wondered how so old a man as I dared to be so strenuous. He said I surely must be 60. Ye Gods!

I did not go to dinner. It was quite an occasion, they told me. Everybody dressed up. After dinner I told Mildred about the man speaking of my age, and she said she did not wonder, considering I did not shave. I guess I'm a misfit among people. I wish to God I was back home.

The sound of the sea outside is terrific and appalling. It makes me think. I have read considerable. The English custom of baths, meals six times a day, dinner at bedtime, inspections, and a lot of other bunk give me a pain. I know so little of how other people live.

Happy New Year, my dearest wife, my anchor. I have absolute faith in your power to make it happy. 1925 is gone for us, unto the beyond. Here is my promise to make 1926 greater. Try to work hard, Dolly, dear.

Love to you, to my children.

Doc

1926–1939

PART FOUR ■ SOUTH SEAS

1926-1927

CHAPTER 12

To Know All Is to Forgive All

T HE VOYAGE TO NEW ZEALAND took nineteen days including
a stop at Papeete, the capital of Tahiti. Notes Zane made on this trip
formed the basis of *Tales of the Angler's Eldorado: New Zealand.* Arriving at
Wellington on January 18, they were received with full honors by the New
Zealand government. The Wellington papers reported that Mrs. Zane Grey
was with him, however, and would receive special attention.[1] It took some
explaining regarding Mildred's presence instead of Dolly's. Nevertheless,
Zane was treated as a celebrity.

JANUARY 19, 1926

6:30 a.m.

Dearest Dolly,

Arrived O.K. yesterday. Sent you a cable. My cold is bad again, but I think
when I get where it's warm I'll get well.

Gee! These funny people! Not a soul up. The streets are deserted. I got
rather a favorable impression of Wellington. Big bay with hills around. City has
a foreign look.

I must say that they are running me to death. The government wants to
extend me everything free. Yesterday I had the Prime Minister's car! You
should have seen people look. I talked till I lost my voice. Had to do it, because
it seems New Zealand and Australia read more of my books than of any other

writers. The worse is everybody wants to run my trip or go with me. The three fishing places are fighting about it.

This morning at 7:30 we leave for Auckland. I tried to get reservations on board one of the ships sailing in March or April to Vancouver. All gone! It beats the dickens. I will sure be stuck if I want to come home earlier than planned. And I'm afraid I want to come home now. It's so terribly far away. I feel so lost. That 19 day sea voyage did it. Lord, why did I leave home.

I'll write you often and tell you what I'm doing anyway. It amuses me to find out who Z.G. really is.

Love to all,

Romer, Betty, Loren, you,

Doc

After a short stay at Auckland they traveled to Russell, in the Bay of Islands, and from there to Orupukupuku Island. He described the city to Dolly.

Russell

JANUARY 24, 1926

Dearest Dolly,

Have been here two days. It stormed this morning. This place is very quaint and beautiful, quite small, and much the same as Avalon. The one boarding house—a queer rambling place of many rooms—is full of people and kids— just plain people.

There is absolutely nothing I can eat, and I'm starved to death. There is no Aunt Jane's that is decent. You would die of constipation in one week. The people drink tea, and eat all the time, 7:30–8:30, 10:30, 1 p.m., 4 p.m., 6 p.m., 10 p.m., and yet they seem not to need toilets. It's a mystery to me. And bath—my God, they don't have baths in this country!

Here all the women, young and old have shingle bobs. The kids and young women do not wear stockings. Morning and afternoon dresses without stock- ings! I don't know whether or not they are moral, but they look easy to me.

I must say that they have been most interested in me. Women come up to me on the street and ask to take my picture. I have autographed a thousand albums. I hurried away from Auckland to get away from attention.

You can bet this trip will do one thing, anyway, and that is make me appreciate my own country, my home, and family. So it will be money well spent. I have to fight homesickness all the time. 7,000 miles from home. It's awful.

Love

Docco

This was the farthest he had ever been from home, and distance made it easier for him to write of his feelings for her.

FEBRUARY 15, 1926

Dearest Wife,

Your letter, mailed the same time as your other mail, did not reach me until Feb. 13. That was a bad day. I had a rotten day in the sea, and came home to be overjoyed at sight of your letter, then crushed by its contents. I told you what you might be up against, though I hoped for luck. My dear, all I can say is this. I will repay you for all your trouble and expense.

The thing I wanted to write you fully about had been in my mind lately, but I'm afraid your letter side-tracked it. It was this. The many wonderful beautiful thoughts and emotions I have about you and the children. I ought to put them in some permanent form for you. I might die away from home. Then you would never know. It is a distressing thought. On the boat for hours out on the sea you are in my mind, grateful, beautiful loving remembrances. At night in the silence or when the wind and sea roar I lie awake in my tent with thoughts no stenographer could even transcribe. I am so much away from you all and life is so short. I have done so ill with my talent! What might have been! What a name I might have made! What a home I might have fathered! It was in me, but I had no start. And now when my youth returns nearer and I am fixed on the North Star in my ways it is too late. When I am home I have fine feelings, of course, love, pride, and all, but nothing like what I am trying to tell you.

Love and kisses,

Zane

The fishing portion of the adventure was successful beyond even his imagination. Captain Mitchell got a world-record black marlin at 685 pounds, and Zane caught the first broadbill swordfish ever landed in New

Zealand waters at 400 pounds. By February 22 he had caught eighteen swordfish, and Mitchell nine. In all his party caught over a hundred striped marlin with weights up to 350 pounds, and Grey set two world records with a 450-pound striped marlin and an 111-pound Pacific yellowtail.[2]

Grey's success, his methods, and his scorn for New Zealand methods stirred controversy.[3] New Zealanders used a variation of freshwater fly-fishing rods and reels that had been developed in England, with the reel underneath the rod, tackle that seemed primitive to Grey, and he unfortunately said so. In addition while Grey trolled—that is, while he kept the boat moving at a rapid pace so the bait was close to the surface—the New Zealanders drift fished with live bait and caught only a few fish. Grey's critical remarks were published in the New Zealand papers and created an uproar.

Grey and party left Russell at the end of March for Roturua, where they attended a Maori concert and Zane was honored with the name "Maui," which they told him signified a great fisherman. After several days of sightseeing, they motored to Wairakei, a beautiful resort nestled amidst huge pine trees that had grown from seedlings imported from the United States. This was followed by more sightseeing, particularly of fishing holes, then on to Taupo, a small town on the shore of Lake Taupo, source of the Waikato River. Fishing spots were hard to find, as the lake was crowded with vacationers, so Zane and party decided to go to the mouth of the Waihora River in Western Bay. The river and lake were known for salmon and brown trout, originally rainbow stock from Oregon. After several days of fishing, the party moved to the Tongariro River. While most of the New Zealanders fished near the mouth of the river, Zane made camp several miles upriver near the Dreadnaught Pool. After a week at Tongariro River, he returned to Wellington and sailed for California at four o'clock in the afternoon of April 27 on the SS *Tahiti,* arriving at San Francisco in mid-May.

Dolly's winter was not as pleasant. Romer ran away from his school in late January with his chum Ed Mix. Taking the car, they reached Phoenix, had tire trouble, left the car, and started walking to Texas. They got as far as Tucson but ran out of money, could not find jobs, and slept in the desert. Dolly wired them money for tires and they returned home, eating humble pie. Then Dolly fell ill, Loren went away to school, Loren's tonsils had to be removed, and the income tax absorbed her time and energy as well as the usual business with publishers, editors, and movie producers. To top it off Zane asked her to have an addition built onto the Avalon house and to supervise the re-outfitting of the *Fisherman* for long sea voyages as well. Not only did the responsibility worry her, so did the expense.

JANUARY 12, 1926

Precious Lamb,

I've been faithfully forwarding your stuff, but have been so busy that I couldn't write. You certainly left me with enough work to do!

That dog-gone ship worries me like the dickens. There is so much more involved in what you ordered than was at first apparent. For instance, the canvas of the deck house (or whatever it is) has rotted and the thing leaks and will have to have a complete new roof. It was a rotten job in the first place. And then there are lots of other things. The cost will run into the thousands, and it's not worth it, and makes me wild whenever I think about it. Ed has started the job, and tennis court, and your room all together, and the money flows out like water. Courney's bill, almost $1000, studio $1700, and so it goes on. I don't know whether Crowell is going to send on that money or not. Didn't you tell him you were going away? He telegraphed and wrote about the novel, wanting you to cut and make some changes, and when I wired back that you'd left, he sounded pretty sore. Anyway, I told him he could do the cutting and changing, or if that didn't suit him, I would. He asked me to give him the authority, which I did by wire, also letter and told him he didn't have to wait for your approval. What I hope is that he doesn't hold up on the check. I presume I'll hear from him soon.

As soon as I get a chance, I'm going over to Avalon to get things ready there. Lasky sent the $15,000 check for Deer Drive, but asked for immediate payment of the bill.

Well, that's all the bad news I can think of. After that I suppose you won't care whether I still love you or not—but I do.

Dolly

She also planned another trip to Europe, booking passage on the *Berengaria*, which sailed from New York June 2. She left California May 22, only one week after Zane returned from the South Seas, with Ed Bowen and Ken Robertson going with her as drivers. Stopping at Zanesville, she looked up the Andersons.

Hotel Zane

MAY 26, 1926

My Dearest,

It's late and I'm fiendishly tired, but I suppose you'll be wanting to hear from me. I wired you a minute ago, but this will supplement the telegram.

We rained in here (Zanesville always weeps when I come) about 9:15 p.m. Someone told us this new hotel was completed, and I was glad enough to get away from staying at the antedeluvian and dingy Clarendon. Anyway, could I resist any place named like my best-beloved? It's a very nice place and they gave me what must be the bridal suite, with two bedrooms and a sitting room. I wonder if I'm supposed to sleep in all three beds!

Well, I immediately phoned the Andersons and Louise came down with some of her young friends and they fished Mr. and Mrs. Anderson and Eleanor out of the movies (Desert Gold, it was), so I had use for the reception room!

Louise has grown taller and older, looking much more sophisticated. She's very charming and handsome, but has lost the "wild, sweet youth" which was, to my mind, the most fascinating thing she possessed. She said she was beginning to feel old having celebrated her twentieth birthday. Then Mrs. Anderson and family came and Louise and friends departed. By the way, Louise wore a perfectly marvelous opal necklace which no one but you could have given her! And it must have cost a fortune! (You devil!!!) I'll make you buy me something that costs ten times as much—No I won't darling. I'm your wife and the mother of your kids—and what are all the gems in the world compared with that?

Well, Mrs. Anderson gabbled some, also Mr. A. Poor futile people. They seemed wanting to grasp something that eluded them. Mrs. A. spoke about Louise having been "out" so long, already twenty years old and Louise talked abut the lack of society facilities, etc., in Zanesville. I got the impression that the end and aim of their existence was for Louise to make a good match— something desperately to be striven for, and difficult or impossible to accomplish. Louise said she hadn't settled on her career yet—that she had given some dancing lessons. Eleanor seemed youthful and sweet, and Jeanne had a lovely baby, they say.

But I'm afraid you've done them more harm than good, for you've given them a taste of luxuries they crave and which they may not have dreamed of if you hadn't happened along. It's all the froth of life, society, clothes, wealth, connections, etc. that the woman instills in them. I think Louise looked really well, altho Mrs. A. suggested that she was delicate.

There wasn't much of a personal nature, for there wasn't the opportunity—and anyway it would have embarrassed me dreadfully. All this was for anyone to read who can—and so I interpreted it.

Well, old precious, I must stop and get a few hours of rest. We start very early and can't go fast on account of breaking in the new car. I hope to be in N.Y. in two more days—that is, the 28th.

Someday I want you to bring me and the kids here, and take me to all your old haunts. This country always arouses tremendous emotion in me. I can see you as a boy, with mighty dreams, running around in the beautiful country, fishing the brooks and the rivers and developing the genius which made you what you are today.

Good night.

Always

Dolly

In New York she visited Dorothy Ackerman, Claire and her new baby, and Elma. She hurriedly took care of what business she could, but the Memorial Day holiday hindered. When she sailed, Dorothy and Elma were at the dock to see her off. Her European itinerary, enclosed in a May 30 letter to Zane, was ambitious.

Figure about three weeks between Catalina and Europe in mail. Air mail L.A. to N.Y. 2 and ½ days.

All mail may be sent to c/o American Express Co. 11 Rue Scribe, Paris, France, but below are approximate dates of arrival in other towns, where I shall have mail forwarded and may be reached in case of emergency.

June 8—15 Hyde Park Hotel (Cable—Highcastle, London)

June 18—Amsterdam, Holland—c/o American Express Kalverstraat 101

June 23—Lucerne, Switzerland, 4 Haldenstrasse

June 27—Genoa, Italy—c/o American Express, 17 Piazza Nunziata

July 1—Rome, c/o American Express, Piazza de Spagna

July 6, 7, 8,—Venice—c/o Cook's Agency

July 15—Munich, Germany—c/o Cook's Agency

July 20, 21, 22—Berlin, c/o American Express, 55 Charlottenstrasse

July 24—Cologne, Germany—c/o Cook's Agency

August 1—Paris, 11 Rue Scribe, c/o American Express

Sailing S.S. Aquitania, Cunard Line, Southhampton, G.B. August 14th.

Her new car was shipped with her, so Ed and Ken could drive her across Europe.

Zane settled in at Avalon, fishing and writing.

MAY 1926

Dearest Hunky Beans,

It was terrific going to the Pasadena station with you. Luckily you had sense enough to send me away. You were so nice and sweet that it almost killed me to let you go.

All okay here, with most of the unpacking and fixing up done. It is certainly the finest place now I've ever lived in. It is 100 percent better in looks, utility, comfort. My room is just what I wanted and needed. I wish though you hadn't made that wall in a kind of stairway leading up to the roof. George caught some kids climbing right up to the roof, walking up in fact.

I have an offer from Roy Long for the New Zealand story, providing I postpone book publication. Will wire Hoyne I want to accept. Probably by the time you receive this the matter will be all settled.

The work on the Fisherman made the most wonderful improvement. I am simply delighted. Please tell Ed. All the Avalon boatmen want to go to New Zealand with me. I saw a big broadbill swordfish the day we came over. Yelled at him!

In a few days I shall be hard at work, and will stick till July. I have read over your instruction book. It was almost as funny as mine. We sure can get a kick out of that.

Phone just now. The tax assessor is after me. I don't know what to tell him. I'll bawl it up sure. I suppose he wants valuations on this property. I have forgotten what you rated it before. I am apt to make such people sore, and never ought to have anything to do with it. Will let you know the results of my interview.

With much love,

Doc

He protested mildly at her journey.

MAY 26, 1926

Dearest,

I have been doing a number of things this morning. Feel full of zest. Don't know whether it's because of work or fish!

Don't know what to write you either. I will be in L.A. on June 2, the day you sail. Will send you a message.

You have reversed the usual order of things. It is not Ulysses who is leaving "There gloom the broad dark seas." But this time for Penelope!

I used to lean on the rail at sunset, and watch the sea. I used to think so often of you at night, when I was on deck, peering out unto that roaring unknown. I shall pray that you have a safe voyage and return. Do not worry or get blue. This is your vacation. You need it.

With endless love,

From your

Husband

Dolly had barely returned from Europe when Zane was off to Oregon, taking R.C., Romer, and Loren. He first visited the Rogue River in 1916 and found the fishing excellent but did not catch any steelhead.[4] In 1925 he explored a more primitive area of the Rogue River and discovered Winkle Bar. While Dolly was in Europe he bought land there for eight hundred dollars.

After Mildred and Zane returned from New Zealand, Mildred left to visit her family back east during the summer, returning to California in the fall. Appendicitis required surgery, so she did not go with him to Oregon but stayed with Dolly at Altadena while she recuperated. She complained constantly, even blaming her suffering on Zane!

SEPTEMBER 14, 1926

Dearest,

Was glad to get your wire from Marial, saying that you were feeling better. Everything is going well here. Mildred is up and down stairs and walks around the garden. The nurse is still here and I'm wondering how long she's going to stay. I know Mildred blames her illness on you (As Mrs. Koch always used to blame hers on us), but I don't see that by any process of reasoning she can blame you for her crooked insides. It wouldn't be quite decent, would it?

Went to see Don Juan last night. I don't think I liked it very much for various reasons. Barrymore is magnificent, if a little stagy, but he radiates coldness. I'm not prissy, but the amours of men are rather disgusting to me—the deliberate amours. I suppose, being what they are, they have to have 'em, but why disclose them so deliberately on the screen? Every man would like to be Don Juan, I concede. I often think the poem influenced your life powerfully. Of course, there's this difference—that you really cared more and stuck to 'em longer. I believe you have always had to live in a romance of which yourself were the hero—I can see the things you read—beside Byron, Michelet, forming a path for you. Your own powerful personality, your predilections worked in with these. You're a great man, honey, and you're coming out of it to be a fine man also, but it's rather appalling to look back. There is still a threatening and sinister influence in your life—a weakening one to your genius—but I have faith in the strength of that genius. It must not be diluted or belittled by other influences.

Ever

Dolly

Zane left Winkle Bar September 27 arriving home the 29th. Almost immediately he left for Arizona, taking Betty, Romer, and Mildred with him.

They stayed only three weeks and were home by Thanksgiving. Meanwhile Dolly worked on his latest manuscript, *Stairs of Sand*.

But the South Seas beckoned. This time he wanted to stay over eight months, the longest time yet, from late December to early August, taking the *Fisherman,* newly outfitted for long sea voyages.

He sailed in late December, taking R.C., Romer and his friend Johnny Shields, Mildred, and Captain Mitchell and his wife. By the end of January they were in New Zealand enjoying the fishing, this time off Mercury Bay, and Zane worked on a new novel. In a letter to Dolly he described his schedule.

Mercury Bay

FEBRUARY 17, 1927

Dearest Dolly,

I have yours of Jan. 20. Fine and dandy! It's a satisfying letter, despite your complaints. My God, darling. Consider! I get up at daylight—6 o'clock now—write till 7:30. Then I fish till 5 or 6, and write in my notebook after supper. By 7 pm am exhausted. When an off day comes, such as today, I write more on my book. 13 pages today! And my hand is tired now.

We are having great luck. 70 fish in all, beating in 6 weeks our previous work here in 10. Romer has done most remarkably. 22 fish in all, and some of them big. I have 28. Had a slump lately. But I'll make it up.

I'll write again for this boat. Love and kisses and things. Bless your dear old heart! I'm well, and carrying on. Love to my kids—My Helen of Troy and my young author.

Doc

He was warmly received again and accorded the celebrity status of the previous year, but there were flies in the ointment. He had written his criticisms of New Zealand fishing methods in his book *Tales of the Angler's El Dorado: New Zealand,* which had been published during the time he was gone. With his arrival the controversy flared again.

Bay of Islands, N.Z.

FEBRUARY 21, 1927

Dearest,

Your letter this time was long, sweet, fine and made me happy. I positively die when you send me bad news and disapproval. Just think! I have been happy ever since it came.

There's lots to write if I only had time. I get up at 5, write from 5:30 to 7, eat breakfast, fish till 5 or 6, come in, clean up (at times) eat, and rest a little, or write some more. So I haven't the time to write letters, such as you want and deserve. But as I told Betty, I think of you many times, with the utmost love and prayer.

Last night Col. Stapleton Cotton called on us. Tonight Sir Thomas Bridges, another big English war officer is calling. No wonder Governor Morris (who was here) gave me a few little digs. Sir Thomas is Governor General of Australia and he said I have made New Zealand known to the world as had no one else.

Baker is very jealous, and I fear giving over to the cheap few who are hostile to my presence here. They have split the Cabinet and N.Z. politics wide open because plans were made for me to take the Duke and Duchess of York out fishing. I fear it will become too strong for those who want to give the Duke such an honor. Ahem!

You can do what you think best with the play. I wirelessed you to that effect. Am sending revised MS. If that does not go through we will write one which will. We may as well clean up some of this easy money. Needless to say I was overjoyed to hear you were willing to try to put it on. For God's sake, darling, don't forget that you said so. M. was very surprised and touched. Grateful, too. Dolly dear, she is not quite so bad as she has been represented. I hope you won't realize that too late.

I will write notes oftener after this, to prove how deeply pleased your letter made me. So far, honey, I am up to my job. It's a H. of a big one, but I'm sticking. With love and kisses, and many thoughts.

Yours ever,

Doc

Mundane matters marred his enjoyment. The radio was not working properly, the syrup soured, three engines went bad, the weather was foul, and expenses were far higher than he had planned.

Auckland

APRIL 2, 1927

Darling,

Well, they almost cleaned me out here. When I got here I had $11,000, and now I have about $3,500 left. We bought supplies for five months, and need only meat and fresh vegetables occasionally. The ship's chandler bill was amazing to me, and something not calculated. It was all the ship supplies for work, repairs, etc—a big item I had overlooked.

I am pretty sick tonight. Such waste and lack of economy! But honey, I can't manage it. I should have a good sharp man as steward and manager.

Try to see your way to hold yourself in readiness to cable me bank credit at Wellington about May 20 or so. I may not need it. But I am afraid I will.

If I can sell the pictures we will not be so badly off. I think I can. We will have some wonderful stuff. Even if I only got $10,000 for the two reels. And we think they will be worth $20,000. The whole trip will stand to cost about $75,000, of which $50,000 has been spent, practically. I will stall the salaries off until the ship docks in September at San Pedro.

You have no idea how terrible this is for me just now. I'll recover. But I am determined not to lose money on this boat.

Stick to me beloved! I could not carry on without you. We sail at 7 o'clock tomorrow morning, if weather permits. I've lots to tell you, but not this time. Love to all.

Doc

Dolly saved the day.

Tokaanu Hotel

Lake Taupo, N.Z.

APRIL 20, 1927

Dearest Wife,

Cable from you today. "Sending money." That's all. Well, did you include your love? And what bank did you send it to? My dear love, I fear you are sore. Well, I'm sorry. I sure did not have it figured right. The expense, I mean. I shall have to work the harder. Never you fear, I shall not let you suffer for my extravagances. I'm afraid I'm a little hurt at that cablegram.

Love,

Doc

After six weeks fishing the Tangariro River, Zane left New Zealand May 20 for Tahiti, arriving at Papeete May 31, and planned to sail home September 5.[5] Trouble followed him, this time from Mildred.

Tangariro Camp

MAY 16, 1927

Dearest,

I don't know how long it is since I wrote you last, but it seems long. There have been some upsets in camp for me, a couple of small ones, and one hell of a big one. No use to revisit it here, but I'll tell you upon my arrival home.

I came very near breaking camp and making tracks for home. But after considering I find I have to get some good stuff in the South Seas or else give up any hope of future trips. That I cannot make up my mind to do yet. If I do come home on the Tahiti it means selling the Fisherman, and firing the whole outfit.

We have had wonderful fishing, especially Capt. M., Romer and myself. R.C. monkeys around, and does not fish right or long enough. Naturally my condition of late hasn't made him any happier.

Your long letter of April 18 was surely a life saver. It was a very inspiring and splendid letter, and it came just at the right time. I have absolutely kept my word to you about the writing, and I will never publish a word again that you do not go over. Part of the trouble with M. was that I refused flat to accept any change in my MS, or anything written in by herself. It is all right for her to correct any errors, and to cut when necessary. But I absolutely refused to listen to her ideas of what was wrong here and there. So we quarreled. She has sworn a dozen times that she will quit her job upon arriving home. I certainly do not want her any longer unless she changes. We'll see. But in case she stands to her guns, I will have to have somebody else, and that puts me in a quandary. Where in the world can I get anyone who will suit me. I would be afraid to let you select a secretary for me, because she would either be lame or married and certainly ugly. Anyway, sufficient unto the day, my dear. I swear by the Gods that work and wonderful work is my determination. Pray for me, and stick to me.

We break camp Thursday. This is Monday, winter in N.Z. It blew like hell last night. So long sweetie, until my next—

Ever

Doc

R.C. went home early, and Zane booked passage for the rest of the party on the SS *Tahiti* for both July 25 and August 22. If things did not go well, they could take the earlier steamer arriving in San Francisco about August 6. Although the fishing was good at Tahiti, he was eager to get home, so they took the earlier ship.

Dolly passed the long, lonely months from January to August in her usual way, editing and polishing Zane's manuscripts, handling business affairs with publishers, editors, and motion-picture companies, and maintaining the structure of their lives. No matter how many times he left, every time was an adjustment.

JANUARY 9, 1927

My Dearest,

Reba tells me that a letter must be gotten off today to make the New Zealand mail from Seattle or Canada. I do not want any possible chance of keeping in touch with you to go lost, so even if it's only a few lines, I'll write. Somehow, in the beginning, it's very hard for me to write. Your going is too recent, and the wound still too raw—and when I write it brings it all back and I cry all the time I'm writing. It's silly, of course, but I wouldn't have it otherwise—for if I didn't feel that way, I wouldn't love you so much. I've been working all the time—sent off the "Forlorn River" about a week ago, and last night I finished going over "The Call Of The County." It's a wonderful story. I'll have to have it typed, and then I'll send it to Burton. I've heard nothing from him yet about the book, and it worries me, as I need the money. There are still a number of big bills, insurance, and the other day came a turn down of the 1922 income tax and demand for over $10,000. I don't know what it amounts to. Turned it over to Masters. So I've been occupied at least. But back of it is that hellish loneliness which it always takes a while to overcome. Even the children, home for the weekend, scarcely drive it away. It's you, of course. But what a wonderful thing that after all these years and happenings, it could still exist, stronger than ever!

This doesn't seem a very cheerful letter, but you mustn't worry about me or let it depress you. I shall be quite all right. I may be homesick and lonely for you, but in my soul I know that we belong to each other in a way that nothing can ever touch—nothing. And that is the greatest miracle of my life. I've had so many—wonderful things that always are miracles to me that I should welcome a little misery just in way of contrast.

Dolly

Disturbing rumors about an imminent divorce worried Zane, who heard them even in New Zealand, but they did not ruffle Dolly. Even in the liberal atmosphere of the twenties, in the midst of glamorous Hollywood where the movie stars took advantage of looser divorce laws, Dolly did not consider divorce a remedy for her unconventional marriage or a solution to her husband's habits of romancing beautiful women. In a series of letters designed to lay Zane's fears to rest, she wrote of her view of their marriage. In them, for the first time, she directly referred to his infidelities, but she assured him she never doubted his love and downplayed the significance of his affairs.

Altadena, California
JANUARY 23, 1927

My Darling,

Yesterday the mail came from Papeete, with Romer's postcard, your manuscript, and a couple of rather depressing letters from you. Also the cables from Wellington and Auckland came during the week. I am glad you reached everywhere safely and found the Fisherman "fine but expensive." Ye Gods, you didn't have to cable me that. I've found that out in my perennial broke condition ever since you took her on. Or was that a gentle preparation? Well, I'm not worrying, so you needn't. Only be sensible, darling. And get the most out of the boat—if you can't physically, then mentally, spiritually, any old way. If, all things considered, you can say, "Well, she's worthwhile," why then, what's the money?

And don't worry about that silly divorce business. It's not a scandal, as you dub it. You know that divorce has never entered my mind. I can't conceive of such a thing when we love each other as we do, and always shall. And divorce would never solve any problems for you and me. We're past that age and stage. No, darling, we were made for each other and we'll stick together always, here and hereafter. Why, even if we weren't bound by indissolvable ties, by the children, by your work,—do you think I'd give any female the chance to get you? I'd shoot her first with buckshot.

As for my European trip causing the trouble, I don't think it, for I went to Europe before under the same circumstances, and I've gone East every summer for five or six years. If anything, I'd lay it to Mildred's prattle about being your literary assistant and being so indispensable to you. She sure must have spread that thick all over the country. It comes back to me from the mountains and cities, the desert and sea.

Well, enough of unpleasantries. Except that you leave me far, far more than I leave you, and people talk, of course, always have. It might not be a bad thing for us to spend more time together—especially at Avalon some summer.

Burton finally sent the check for "Stairs of Sand," after I got worried and wired him. Also the enthusiastic telegram which I enclosed. You had scared me about the length of the story before you left and I imagined all sorts of things, so his wire was a great relief. I'm anxious to get at "The Avalanche," and would have done so today, but Loren and Betty were home, and I didn't have a minute to myself. And these letters cannot be delayed, or they won't catch the boat leaving soon. But don't imagine my lingering over it, for I need the money too badly!

Mr. Herzburn phoned Saturday to make an appointment with me to see Lasky tomorrow. Wonder what he wants? Metro G. are making a pre-revolutionary picture dealing with the opening of the wilderness. As usual Paramount has let them get ahead—but I'll tell Mr. Lasky so, and suggest

Betty Zane to him again. I'm afraid the interview will be too late to get to you in this mail, but maybe not.

I don't see how you can stay away nine months, though! Aren't you afraid I'll forget you? Life seems terribly flat and stale and unprofitable at present. I've got to fight out of it, because I just can't stand this frame of mind. And I've always determined not to be dependent for my happiness. I wonder if one becomes so as one grows older.

There's a letter here from Bessie Barker. Can't I forward even that? I wouldn't let anyone tyrannize over me that way. I suppose old B.B. has false teeth and looks like her mother did twenty years ago. By the same token, the romance probably still blooms in her heart. Oh, those bad, sad, mad days! You'd always whistle coming home from the D.H.[6] at night, and I could tell from your whistle what you'd been up to! You don't have to whistle anymore, sweetheart, to give yourself away! "To know all is to forgive all." And I love you, knowing all. You still lie to me occasionally, and I know when you do, and it hurts a little now and then. But you needn't. For my love is too fundamental for that. You could kill me, but not it. Nothing could root it out, even if I were wild about someone else and untrue to you. And I know yours for me is the same—for you've been wild about other women and untrue to me physically.[7] But never spiritually or mentally. And you never can be. I know it in my soul and that's why I should laugh at the world—at "literary assistants." And mostly I do, but sometimes I get mad, because of the dishonesty.

> Always and always
>
> Your wife

She continued this theme in her next letter.

MARCH 22, 1927

Darling,

After I mailed my letters to you yesterday, yours came from the Makura. She sails again tomorrow, and according to newspaper postal listing, there is still time for me to write you an additional few lines. Your letters were loving and cheerful. We ought really never to write each other anything but nice letters, for I guess we have the same effect on each other. When I get a bad letter from you, I go down into the depths. Well, I hereby promise you something—that, if I can possibly avoid it, I will never write you with anger or disapproval in my heart. I may have to tell you things that I consider you ought to know, but it will be when my love can control my output, as it were!

I saw "Dancing Mothers" as a movie, and it was well done, and made a lasting impression on me, so that I've never forgotten it. That is a rare thing for a motion picture to do to me. However, in the movie, she turns down the man, tho she loves him; but she goes away by herself, unable to stand the selfishness of her husband and family. I got the impression that perhaps she was giving them the chance to see the error of their ways, and might return. But the case isn't similar to mine—as I can see—and though I could feel the woman's suffering poignantly, having partaken of it in some respects, I could not react as she did—at least I don't think I could. That story of May Sinclair's that we read before you left, struck me more closely. However, my reaction is again different. I think if one has enough love—and enough intelligence, one can encompass any situation. However, there is one great factor in our case— I have never doubted your love for me, and your need of me. I know you need me more than you do any living soul—or dead one—I know you realize that, and even if you didn't realize, it would nevertheless be fact. And that need is not only material, but mental and spiritual. No one understands you as I do; and I know, as I know that I am sitting here and writing to you, that no one can ever take my place with you. I'm afraid I'll have to confess that that fact means more to me than even the preciousness of my own giving of love, per se, but in a way that it is an emanation. Other things pass—other people, as they have with the years; but some day you will understand that our love of each other, and need for each other has been, and is, the rock upon which our lives are founded. For me that rock is beautiful and blossoming always— you have still to discover its preciousness. You are still a wandering Ulysses, questing for the unknown, seeking the magic isles, dallying with romance and physical love.[8] But like Ulysses, the Kingdom of your home and your Penelope, and your three Telemachus's are the most precious things on earth, and you'll discover that sooner or later. Ask yourself, for you know it even now, what significance your adventures (not only material) would have, if there weren't the background of home? When I look at things whole, I do not worry. You must fulfill your destiny, must satisfy your longings. Possibly, if you were the perfect stay at home husband, you would not be a great man. We have to take the bitter with the sweet, darling; "thy fate and mine are sealed," so, though there may be petty stings of gnats, even what the world would call unfaithfulness, what most women would leap at as grounds for divorce, these do not count in the whole scheme.[9] I do not deny that, being mere woman, I have not burned in the fire of Hades, tasted the bitterness of death, wanted to torture and slay. But even for those things I am not sorry. We must live all of life to understand all, or no, that isn't it. Rather there is a wisdom and an understanding that is gained from misery and sorrow that we could not otherwise achieve. The thing is not to let it make us callous, and hard, and embittered.

I believe you are a great man, a genius; and by that token, I believe the greatest of your adventures, the spiritual ones, are still before you. You have not even tasted the "sweetness of reward" that those will bring you. In a sense, you are still a child, still groping and seeking your way. I can see, but I cannot live your life for you. We grow by our own experiences, but we can grow faster if we can comprehend, and garner the result of those experiences. Perhaps the surest sign of your genius is its power to remain true, and sweet, and untouched by the intrigue and plottings and bickerings with which you are continually surrounded, the demands of personalities smaller than your own, the selfseekings. I have often warned you about M.S., but, after all, while she may affect the physical man, she cannot touch your soul and its child, your genius. Of course, the physical man, and his reactions to the world, is not to be slighted or minimized. He is the house of our minds and souls. But my faith tells me that your genius will come through triumphant. I know no one can kill that. And therefore I predict that the best of life is still before you, the sweetness, the real significance.

Well, time fugits, and this must go. If I could only put into words all that I feel—all that I know. But I have not been given the power. There is so little we can say in words, and they are our only means of communication, of physical communication, that is. But there is an understanding, a telepathy, a sympathy on which I rely. It will get to you through my love.

Always
Dolly

Zane's business grew more demanding and complex. Dolly handled all of it, even more so when he was inaccessible. A flurry of letters shows how complicated the business was and how crucial was Dolly's role. They also reveal the ever present irritant of Mildred.

MARCH 21, 1927

Darling,

The Makura sails Wednesday, so it behooves me to hustle. I just got off a bunch of radios. Saturday I had two from you. The radio does make me feel easier.

Finished up the income tax in good time, altho it almost did finish me once or twice. All those terrible figures. I think the headaches came from my eyes. It was a couple thousand more than last year.

I was figuring the other day, darling. Recently, your earning went over $2,000,000. Quite a lot to get out of that old head of yours, isn't it? I suppose most people would consider just that material fact of money a wonderful achievement. But I'm considering what's behind it—what it means. It means that you are a tremendous factor for happiness and pleasure and uplift in the lives of thousands of people. If that isn't greatness and success, what is?

Well, out of the total, Ma has managed to invest about a quarter of that—i.e., counting our properties, etc., what I should say assets. And that is figuring cost, not what we could sell them for. Really, considering what a spendthrift you are, that isn't so bad, is it? Aren't you glad you have me? For if you didn't, you wouldn't have the assets! However, I hope you consider me your greatest, regardless of money. Do you?

Love always

Dolly

MARCH 29, 1927

Doc Darling,

I was summoned to Lasky's again the other day and I've been chuckling ever since. They are wild to get "Open Range" for a picture. Can you beat it? Naturally, I had to tell them that it had already been made as "Born To The West" but I also added that you had had to change it somewhat, and that it had sufficient material for a new and different picture. Which shows several things! I also told them to look it over, with a different story in mind. Of course, they can't have it until Schuler is through. And it's only a possibility, at that. They're crazy about "Nevada"—as is—I wrote you about that and the fact that Lasky said changes would be unnecessary.

Yesterday McGlynn sent a check for $60.00 on the first week's tryout of "Hell-Bent." He said he never got less than five curtain calls—and hopes to make the Orpheus Circuit, which will be a big thing. Well, even $60 a week isn't to be sneezed at! It's lots more than lots of people have to live on, though of course, it wouldn't probably supply your bait. But, every little added on to what you've got looks good to me, for I'm studying the business of money—making and investing, rather closely this winter. I think I'll be making some nice profits presently.

Au revoir, love, hugs, kisses,

Dolly

APRIL 2, 1927

Beloved Husband,

My dear, I've been absolutely faithful to your commands. The manuscripts were finished and went off long ago. Your employees' wages got paid on the dot, even though I starve myself. I work till my head whirls, all to the glory and comfort of my husband! And that reminds me—do not forget your solemn promise to write nothing that I do not see before publication. I find so many things that would cause people and critics (are critics people?) To react unfavorably, things that never occur to you, and seem unimportant, that really do not change your message or meaning, and yet that may be inter-preted to your harm. For instance, if you had let me go over your New Zea-land book, you would not have incurred the enmity that you have. That's my job, darling—to be a buffer between you and the world you don't understand. And it's only in the little insignificant things that you fail. The soul of your work, the good you do, the greatness of it, stands intact. It is like some won-derful gem that may be a little blurred or indistinct and needs polishing and rubbing and understanding to make it shine forth in full glory. Don't forget that

I am official polisher of my beautiful gem! Mildred is clever, but there are innumerable things she does not know, either of life or literature. And in certain directions she has done you active harm. I dislike to mention these things, but your work is more important to me than I can say. I want you to realize your own ambition—to make the carpers recognize your greatness. I know it is there—I need no convincing but I also know the things that make or break with them. And it takes such a little slip to make one slide over precipices. And then there is all the climbing to do over again. We'll ram your power, your significance down their throats! Perhaps that is a small reaction; for after all you have the people that really count—your great widespread audience to whom you mean everything, and the others are less than nothing. But even for them you must grow constantly bigger and better to justify their faith in you, and their love of you. Many of them cannot discriminate; would not be able to tell a surface difference. But your power has always lived in your emotion, and your ability to get it into your books and thus transmit it to your reader. Now, as you grow bigger, finer, express yourself better, the quality will be transmitted into your writing. A book lives by its universality, its significance for life—that is, its power to uplift, to inculcate standards and ideals for many. There seems to be no doubt that you have this gift; but you must never stop striving. Paradoxically, if we stand still, we go backwards. That you must never do: You must be "one who never turned his tack . . ."

Herzbrun telephoned me for "Nevada" this morning, so I took it over. They've been crazy to get it, and it can be made at this time better than the others. Things are pretty satisfactory over there of course. I have to keep after them about money all the time. I finally got second payment for "Drums Of The Desert," and he promised me the "Nevada" first this week.

Don't know that I'm greatly taken with "Beckyshibita" as a name for a book. It's striking, but I'm afraid nobody'd understand it, and the selling might be retarded. Personally, I'd be drawn to a name like that, but I doubt that the average reader would.

Briggs wrote yesterday that the swordfish-tuna book was twice too long.[10] Guess I'll enclose the letter. I'm trying to get in touch with you now by cable and radio about it, but if I can't I'll just try to do the best I can in the way of making a decision. I suppose the best solution would be to separate into tuna book and swordfish book and publish the swordfish book first.

Well, fini to this letter for now.

Always for you

Dolly

MAY 1, 1927

Dearest,

There is a chance that this may reach you before you sail from Wellington, therefore I am making a duplicate copy to send to Tahiti in case it does not. If you have a chance to think this over you can write and give the message to Rome to bring to me.

First, Paul Reynolds, a literary agent, has been telegraphing and writing me, asking whether you would sell a story to a big woman's magazine for $60,000 less 5% commission, $2500, making a net to you of $57,500.00. This seems to me a pretty good offer. Would you be free to accept it? I have asked you before when you had to give Crowell another story. "Nevada" has just ended. Last month "Open Range" commenced in the "Country Gentleman," and he's not due for anything else until 1928. McCall's has not even begun "Stairs of Sand," so you seem to be pretty free, unless the American must have "Becky-shibita." I analyze the situation this way: I think you have become a tremendous circulation booster and all these magazines are crazy to get you at almost any price to put them over big as you did the American with "Nevada." I didn't ask Overton what Collier's would pay, but I think I shall write him now and tell him that you were offered $60,000 for a serial, and see what Collier's would give. It's too darn bad that you always tie yourself up to so long a period. You're the biggest thing on the map right now, and can dictate terms. However, if you made promises, you must stick to them, and if American is to have another serial at $40,000, why that settles it. When was that to be delivered? This is important.

Schwartz was out here recently and I had a talk with him. They have finally put through the deal for "Wildfire" and "Golden Dreams," and will pay the $8,000 odd dollars on the former. They are beginning "Nevada," but want to substitute the payments already made on "The Deer Drive" for "The Tonto Rim." I said I had to have your permission for that. So let me know about that. They're talking about "Open Range" with great enthusiasm. I told them again that it was the changed story of "Born To The West," so that they can't accuse us of putting anything over on them. But if they insist on having it, they can do so on the same terms as the others! More and more I come to the conclusion that it's your name and titles and stories they want, and the plot doesn't make a very material difference. Witness "Nevada" which Lasky refused to have me change.

You need not have cabled Harper's about the revision of the fishing book. They are sending it back to me for that purpose. This long absence of yours has at least done one thing—forced me to become more thoroughly conversant with your business matters, and given me a clear vision of things that seem to have been a bit vague before. But lots of things crystallize as we get older. It is a compensation of the years. One learns more all the time, and wisdom and judgment increase.

Please excuse the messy letter. Stenography was never an accomplishment of mine, especially when I tried to write as fast as I have today. But there is a chance of your getting this at Wellington, in which case you could think these problems over longer. That's all.

Much love

Dolly

P.S. Just looked up the McCall contract and you're not due to deliver another novel to them till 1929.

MAY 13, 1927

Darling,

Since I wrote, I had the enclosed letter from Crowell, and answered as you will note. If we can put him off until you can write another book (say by the end of the year), I may be able to swing a $60,000 deal on "Beckyshibita." What do you say? But you must live up to your promise to Crowell, and perhaps he'll make an awful howl now. I'm afraid "Beckyshibita" might not be popular as a name. Names count so much for your things. I think the reason

Laskys are so crazy to get "Open Range" is just on account of the name. I was over again the other day to talk over the "Nevada" scenario, and they've already announced "Open Range" in their advertising for Nov. 1927. I told them repeatedly that by no chance could they release that picture before it was finished in the "Country Gentleman" and they promised to stick to that. That was the most profitable mistake I ever made, darling, for they will have to pay you all over again for it. The more I discourage them, the more they seem to want it. I get an awful kick out of that bunch over there. I don't think they know what they're doing half the time, except as regards grinding out pictures. They're trying to do everything to please us, though.

If I were you, I'd tell Schuler that I wouldn't give him anything hereafter except first American serial rights. The Authors' League says anything more than that is old-fashioned. And we could be making money on syndications, etc., as I have frequent inquiries for those. Of course, you can wait for that until you get home, but I'd certainly put it through then.

Another thing, you must be sure to answer in this letter either by writing or verbally to Rome: Is there any reason why I shouldn't take a run to N.Y. with Betty, starting June 20th and returning about four weeks later? Any chance of your getting home before that? I'd go by train, of course, and take your manuscript with me. And I'd see that everything was left in good shape.

I'm having a big luncheon tomorrow for my alumnae. We've all been working hard to get everything in order, and the place looks fine. The roses and other blossoms have been gorgeous beyond words, but a very hot spell struck us yesterday, and I'm afraid it has done some damage.

I feel as if there were a lot I'd forgotten to tell you. There probably is—but I may think of some more before I mail this. Just when will you be home?

Love—and always
Dolly

Dolly did take a quick trip to New York in June, visiting her mother and grandmother. In August Zane returned and went almost directly to Avalon with Dolly, most likely to put a stop to the divorce rumors. Mildred traveled east to visit her mother.[11] In September Zane took Dolly, Betty, Loren, and Romer to Winkle Bar for a couple of weeks. At the end of September he went to Arizona for his annual bear hunt. With him were Mildred and her mother, R.C., Captain Mitchell and his wife, Tommy Deforrest and his wife, Ken Robertson, Ed Bowen, and George Takahashi.[12] Three weeks of hunting were planned. A month later he was in Phoenix, on his way to California to stay at home for awhile.[13]

1928-1929

CHAPTER 13

Dear Old Comrade of the Years

FOR THE FIRST TIME in some years Zane visited Long Key, arriving at the end of January. It was a quiet time for fishing, long walks on the beach, and introspection in the balmy, almost enervating warmth, and he completed a manuscript there.[1] R.C. and Mildred were with him.[2]

He stayed six weeks then traveled to New York City, stopping for a day at Lackawaxen. Ten years had passed since last he was there, and the empty, familiar rooms affected him.

FRIDAY, MARCH 18, 1928

Dear Old Comrade Of The Years,

Lackawaxen today is hauntingly memorial of you. I went into the attic. And there you might have been yesterday. I saw a rubber off your corsets. And a lot of paint brushes, cans, etc. that you placed so and so. And all around the house your presence follows me. It is like things I have read of familiar places that lacked the living spirit.

I am here only for a day. Have packed a Morris chair (my old one) and a box to send to Avalon.

It is spring. Bright, sunny, but cool. A high wind roars through the pines, the rivers are white, the forests are burning, the smells are sweet, tangy, fresh, of wood smoke and trailing arbutus, and earth.

Not for many years have I had the sudden consciousness of what you mean to me. Old Comrade! I am not greatly conscious of any deserving thing from you, but I do know that absolutely in spite of all contradictory evidences, you are the main spring, the strength of my being. You have made me some wonderful force to spend my energy in the ways that I seem driven to do. But as the years go by, and you grow, and the children grow, and I have my trials and agonies, and my wild dreams (such as I am bent on now) and as I live more and feel more, and go from place to place, from one home to another, from absence to return, all the times my mind so full, I know clearer and clearer what I feel for you. It is not explainable in words. It is not the fussy little mush husbandy love women need. It is great. And I do not care a damn that I do. This is true.

And I repeat that your attitude of late (with a couple of days exception) has helped me make my strange driven life easier, my passionate hopes more stable.

The miserable face you showed me when I said goodbye has finally faded away, and now I remember you as you look at your best. Sometimes you look so young, sweet, handsome, bright and keen as a shining light. I can't understand why you get those cross spells that make you ugly and worn.

I am gradually recovering something. I will be my best self soon. And I hope to return to the coast ready for work, study, travel, play, everything.

We are not going to see a great deal of each other this year, I'm sorry to say. And this letter is to ask you to help me make the best of what we have. A little time in April—in August—in November.

I'm going back to N.Y. tomorrow. Will write you. But this is the letter I want you to take to your bosom. Really I have a great and wonderful love for you.

Doc

When he reached New York, he wrote again.

MARCH 1928

Dear Old Lackawaxen Sweetheart,

I have just gotten back from Lacky, sunk, all-in, uplifted and cast down. I wired you from there.

We had hell getting there. New time tables—new regulations. No. 1, no stop. I had to use the old Z.G. stuff to get us the train at all. Then we got off at Pt. Jervis and motored up. But they stopped No. 2 to let us on.

The place has grown up most wonderfully. It is a forest. It is a jungle. The trees are splendid. Oh, that is the way I wanted it then. I was overcome with the beauty, the sadness, the loneliness, the desertness of it all. Oh, Dolly, the rooms are haunted. There are our spirits there. I thrilled and I wept. I recalled everything. I felt the cold of the old cottage, I saw you in bed, I heard Romer's tiny wail, I heard the wind, the river. For the first time I went into the room where my mother died. Something strange came over me there.

The dust, the dirt, the decay, the river reproached me. Why have we not taken care of those places? They are a first and great part of our lives. Love, struggle, work, children, all came to us there.

I am sort of strangled. I could scarcely walk into this hotel. It was a poignant, uplifting and singular experience for me, which I shall remember all my life. We must go back for a summer. I shall remember every detail to tell you upon my return.

I picked out some pictures, books, fish, etc., that I want Charley to pack and ship to me by freight. I can use a lot of that stuff in my new quarters.

Everyone was fine to us. I was delighted. I had no idea I was a hero there. But I am. And I am proud of it.

Perhaps the strangest impression, of which I was not conscious at first, is that going back after all these years—going back alone, I mean, and changed as I am, drew me in a circle back to the days of struggle, of agony, of growth. It would be great for me to return there, and stay a while, to roam, and walk, and dream, and ponder. It would be a spiritual consumation, a realization, a most splendid experience for my creative power.

I must close now. I'm exhausted.

Love,

Doc

Leaving New York, he returned to California and stayed in Altadena for the month of April. In May he was fishing in Avalon. But Dolly became ill, and her illness did not go away. It was decided that she needed an operation, but this could not occur until she regained strength.[3]

Dearest Doc,

You haven't been gone very long, but I wanted to send you Betty's letter, and to suggest, that if it seemed to be easier for you she could be at the hospital with you while I'm being operated.

Dr. was up again, and now he says that it wouldn't be as safe to have the operation until I've recuperated from this siege. I've lost so much in the last few days. I'm pretty anemic again. And I have to get over that condition as he wants, if possible, to avoid blood transfusions. So there may be some delay, but you can go ahead with your plans just as if this thing weren't looming, and when the time comes, you can come over for a day or two. After I'm out of danger, there's no earthly reason for you to stay in town. You can fish your head off!

I have loads to do, and I've cheered up, so everything is O.K. I'm looking forward to my Greek tragedy and my Aristotelian catharsis tonight! The play is Hippolyte.

Au Revoir. Much Love

Dolly

Zane was terrified of any hint of serious illness and surgery but not terrified enough to rush to her side. Of course Dolly encouraged him to continue with his own plans.

May 25, 1928

Dearest—

I slaved like a dog today, but the minute I got through the black cloud settled on me again.

I was awake a good deal of the night, and Oh, my God—my conscience, my misery! There is no use to lie to you, or to deceive you, even if I could. I am down in the depths and scared to death. But I swear I will pull out and use all the strength of my mind, and my love for you, to help you in this trial. I don't believe God could take you from me at this time of my struggle.

Anyway, I have faith in you—that you can fight your way through very

much worse things than this. So for my sake lift yourself to meet it tri-
umphantly. I am a goner if you don't. I never really knew how much I did love
you. You see you have belonged to me—the Keystone to my Bridge, and I
never dreamed you'd get loose!

Love and kisses,

Doc

Surgery was to take place June 19 at Good Samaritan Hospital in Los
Angeles, and Zane took her to the hospital the day before. The next day he
went back with R.C. and Romer to see her off for surgery.

At nine o'clock I saw Dolly at the last moment. She was bright, cheerful, cool,
game as a thoroughbred. Pride overcame my fears for a little. Then I saw her
moved down the hall and into the elevator to go to the ward upstairs to take
ether. She said, "I'm all right."

Somehow I got over the first hour, or through it. When the second began,
the minutes dragged. I paced the gloomy hall. My mind whirled, yet outwardly
I appeared calm. But I could not sit or stand still. Romer stood it well for a
long while, but at last he weakened. He talked incessantly about everything
except Mother.

When Dr. G. came down, it was about time to save me from collapse. He
reported that the operation had been imperatively necessary and that it had
been successful. Something caved in in me, but I could thank God. My consciousness was such that I cannot now recall the thoughts I had, the prayers,
the agonies.[4]

By July 4 Dolly was declared out of danger, and Zane felt free to leave for
a nine-month sojourn in the South Seas, missing Christmas with Dolly and
the children. Dolly insisted her illness not stand in the way. Still in the hospital when he left, as her recovery took longer than expected, she was disappointed about not being able to see him off. But even in the hospital her
expanding business affairs occupied her.

Monday

Doc Darling,

I forgot to speak to you about something yesterday, and that is your account. Will you let me transfer it to my bank "The Altadena National?" You see, I'm a director now, and chief stockholder, and expect to make at least a 25% profit a year. But we want good accounts and big ones, and the more we get the more we'll flourish. So you should give me yours. I'll guarantee you perfect safety and as much interest as you'll get anywhere, and all the conveniences of business. I think we'll be able to give Frances Mitchell a job a little later. Bob Vesey is going to be manager and he's a live one and very popular and he'll take a lot of the big money with him from the other bank. And you know Altadena is a very wealthy community. Well, anyway, if you want more details, ask Ken. But write me and tell me that you'll do it. I hate to see your nice fat account working for a big soul-less corporation when it might be working for your little wifie!

I've decided to cheer up. It was rather a fight, but I've decided I'm a good fighter after the way I managed myself for that operation. I was even cheerful about the possibility of having to carry on the fight in the world hereafter!

I'm not getting any encouragement yet about getting up, but Miss Sutton says Dr. Cochran wants to be doubly careful now that you are gone. This morning they painted my wound with Mercurochrome making it more handsome than ever. But Dr. Cochran said he didn't suppose I wanted to go in for muscle dancing! By the way the name of my operation is a "Hysterectomy," so if anyone asks tell them that. It sounds quite elegant. "Hyster" comes from the Greek word meaning "womb" and I immediately made the deduction that "hysterics" must have the same derivation. I was right, for the ancient Greeks believed hysteria had its origin in the womb. Pretty wise deduction, n'est-ce pas?

This is a long letter for an invalid, even a recuperating one. Just had a postal from Romer. He'll be in S.F. tonight.

Oodles of love from

Your
Wife

Zane responded,

Hotel Ramona

San Francisco

JULY 10, 1928

Dearest—

I don't know about transferring my bank account. I'll think it over. It doesn't
look wise to me to put all our eggs in one basket. In any event I wouldn't do
it unless my account was guaranteed. I'm sure surprised to find you own a bank.
Good God! What next! I'll bet you build the Boulder Dam.

Your letter was most cheerful and bucked me up. Ed ran over a dip yesterday and I nearly shot out of the car. Busted my head. I had a bad day, but
rested easy last night.

Romer seems particularly fine, and it thrilled me through. God, I'm fond of
him! He is coming to meet us in Sept., leaving Sept. 5. I will have to pay
his passage $495 to N.Z. and return. You can give him a shock and charge it
to me.

Well, as always, you've helped me along. Suppose I hadn't had the courage
to ring your bell that first time!

Love and Kisses

Docco

This time Tahiti was his destination. He had stopped briefly at Papeete
on his first venture to the South Seas in 1926 and did not like the city,
although the island enchanted him. He found the heat oppressive, the
crowd around the wharf seemed made up of the world's undesirables, and
the constant imbibing of alcoholic beverages appalled him.[5] The women of
Papeete, however, he found delightful.

The Tahitian women presented an agreeable surprise to me. From all the
exotic photographs I had seen I had not been favorably impressed. But photographs do not do justice to Tahitian women. I saw hundreds of them, and
except in a few cases, noticeably the dancers, who in fact were faked to impress
the tourists, they were modestly dressed and graceful in appearance. They
were strong, well built though not voluptuous, rather light skinned and not at

all suggesting negroid blood. They presented a new race to me. They had large melting melancholy eyes. They wore their hair in braids down their backs, like American schoolgirls of long ago when something of America still survived in our girls. These Tahitians had light-brown, sometimes nut-brown and chestnut hair, rich and thick and beautiful. What a delight to see! What pleasure to walk behind one of these barefooted and free-stepping maidens just for the innocent happiness of gazing at her wonderful braid![6]

In 1927 he had fished off Tahiti for a few weeks, just enough to whet his appetite for more. Broadbill swordfish, marlin, and sailfish were abundant in these waters, as well as tuna, but few had fished there. Those who had had used indifferent methods in his opinion.[7] He had left the *Fisherman* in the harbor there the previous year, so this year he sailed to Tahiti on a commercial line. R.C. and Reba, Romer and his friend Bob Carney, the Mitchells and their daughter Frances, and, of course, Mildred were with him. Zane left Dolly with instructions to build an addition onto the Altadena house that would be a study for him, and more directives came with his letters, along with questions about business, reports on fishing, and complaints over expenses and inconveniences.[8]

Papeete, Tahiti

SEPTEMBER 11, 1928

Dearest,

Two months today since I left home! Time flies, and I'll soon be back with you again. Gee, but I'd love to see you.

Your wireless message of Sept. 1 and 4 caught me at Paiatea, and I was sure delighted. When we arrived here yesterday there was a fine letter from Cedar that came on a freighter. It had a lot of good news, and Rome and I are consequently happy. First, over your recovery, so wonderful, then over Ellsworth's good spirits, and finally over Loren's 14½ pound yellow. Chip off the old block, Dolly! I should say—blocks.

We had a fine time in the Leewards. Got some fish, and pictures. Photographed the Fire Walkers, natives who walk over red hot stones. It is a stunt, and a religious rite. Also the Fish Drive, which beat anything I ever saw. 300

natives in paraus chasing and catching fish in a natural trap where the reef runs around to an island.

I have decided to abandon the trip to the Paumotus, on account of the risk. We shall confine ourselves to Tahiti from now on.

Romer is doing very well indeed, a great improvement over last year. Only twice has he been uppish. I seem to get along so much better with him, thanks to your advice. He and Bob are crazy about photography, and I mean to say they have reason. They miss their meals to take pictures. Bob is a fine chap. Junior is doing well, also. Romer has not had one spell of dumps, that I noticed. He is contented, and indefatigable. R.C. is all right, better than I had hoped for. The rest of this outfit pretty fair.

About your messages. I sent wireless answer that I would take $75,000 from Burton for 6 short stories, 12,000 words each, and deliver first in Dec., the rest next year.

I am ahead in my novel, The Drift Fence, and up to date in my fishing notes. I shall do even better from now on, as I expect to get rid of the ship and a lot of this crowd.

Don't forget to start the addition as soon as you are settled at home. And make that a swell study for me, hon. Then I'll stay home a little.

Don't let the studio people put over any more jobs on me. Both Avalanche and Sunset Pass have to be made in Arizona, with Lee Doyle handling locations.

If you can give me any news about my books, etc., I'd appreciate it. Not that I am discouraged at all! But I just wonder when I shall have to stop writing fast and furiously, and settle down to real serious work. Remember, Dolly, that I trust you to tell me when I should do this. I'm not afraid of my stories, but I am of the publishers, editors, and reviewers.

So long, old girl, and stick to your job. Lots of love to Betty and Loren.

I will write you again before steamer time.

Doc

Camp was at Flower Point on Tahiti Iti, the smaller island connected to Tahiti by a land bridge.

Tahiti

SEPTEMBER 13, 1928

Dearest Doll—

We are back at Taroia, and today worked a gradual exodus from the Fisher-man to our camp at Flower Point. By the way, darling, from my porch, high up over the sounding sea, is to be seen what I regard as the most beautiful and magnificent panorama I have ever seen. Some day I shall attempt description.

Romer and Bob have gone looney over their cottage, which is high up, across the glen from mine. All day they have toiled at fixing up, and packing things.

I shall be glad to leave this ship, though it has been a vast improvement over the former two trips. Nevertheless it is congested, noisy, dirty, buggy, smelly, etc. I expect to turn it over to Father Rangier on Oct. 15, for $30,000. Hope to get cash. If it is a cable transfer I may instruct the bank to get in touch with you.

I have not missed a day since July 31 working some on my novel, The Drift Fence. It has mostly been done between 5 am and 7 am. Get that, Sweetie! I find my mind remarkably clear early after I get up. It's hard to get up in the dark every morning.

Love and kisses

Doc

Flower Point

Z.G. Camp

SEPTEMBER 27, 1928

Dearest—

I finished The Drift Fence. 466 pages, 57 days. Never missed a day! 5 am to 7 am, most of the work, though I had a few stormy days. It was some stunt. If the work is good, I sure have discovered something.

We left the ship four or five days ago. It is glorious up here. Cool, breezy, above sea and canyon, with the mountains close, and the reef booming its grand melody. And I've had something I could eat. On the ship I ate nothing, and got thin. Our stores are sadly depleted. First by theft of those on board, and then by bugs, etc. We lost all our flour, cracker, and stuff that was not sealed. I ordered it for the tropics. Lost about all the jams, cookies, etc.—things we can't buy here. I do get sore at those bolsheviks I have to hire in the U.S. The natives I have are simply fine.

The deal for the Fisherman is about settled, except that I must wait till end of Oct. to get the money, which will be paid to you. I don't intend to sign the bill of sale until you cable that you have the cash. It will be a relief, if I get the blooming thing off my hands.

I have rec'd your several radios and they were worth what I have to pay for the operator. I was just thrilled that you called Amber's Mirage beautiful and powerful. I think next I will begin one of the short stories for Burton, if you radio that he accepts my terms. As the offer came from him I suppose he will do so.

So far the fishing has been poor. Romer has 4 fish. Mitchell 5, and I 2. Possibilities look great. Time flies too fast. Here I have been gone over two months.

That was good to hear about the new part of the house going up. I hope it will be big enough. If you cut down on that 75 feet length I will kill somebody.

I shall describe the scene from my porch some day. Perhaps I will send you my notebook description, when I write it, and you can keep it. The moon is full tonight. I can't tell you how it looks, but if you were here, I'd bug you till I broke all your stitches.

I hope you are fully well now, honey, and happy. My God, that was a few days for me! I'll never get over them.

Love and kisses

Doc

SEPTEMBER 17, 1928

Dearest Dolly,

I'm pretty tired, and I'm afraid a little depressed tonight. Last night, after reading your letters I was in seventh heaven. But I'll be O.K. in the morning.

There's nothing specifically in your letters to answer. I'll radio tomorrow night. Tell Ed I don't need a stairway. My goodness! In case of fire couldn't I get out of a window? But build the blooming place of brick and cement, if that's not too expensive. Keep to my specifications in regard to dimensions. Have a bridge from my room next to our sleeping porch. Put a big light closet in the first room, and it should be twice as big as the one upstairs. Also, cabinets, etc., in that same room. The study should be a peach, and have everything. But as far as taste goes you can use your judgment, if it comes to a pinch. Ed knows what I think I would like about size, windows, safe, fireplace, window seats, book cases, cabinets, lights, etc.

I'm delighted with the prospect. It'll keep me home more. I was also delighted with your sweet, dutiful, loyal letters. But you always give me an intellectual puzzle. I'm afraid most of that is above my head. I'm just a poor sap who can feel but not think. That is why so much of the literature, and what is written about literature, perplexes and aggravates me. By the way, send news about my literary affairs, business and otherwise. Anything encouraging, if that's possible.

You did not tell me if Paramount is filming Avalanche and Sunset Pass in Arizona, under Lee Doyle's guidance for locations. If they are not they'll sure have a lawsuit on their hands when I come back. That was the pitch, and I had it put in the contract.

Looks like I may have to have Father Rangier's bank in San Francisco pay you that $30,000, and upon receipt of your cable I'll turn the ship over to him. Expenses run high. I'll be glad to get rid of this old ship and the ones it takes to run it. Repairs are always being made. My camp is about done. Romer, Bob, and R.C. are up there. I go tomorrow.

Today I saw the most wonderful fish I ever saw in my whole life. I think it was one of the new species broadbill, with the bill underneath. It made four jumps, with incredible rapidity, and covered over 100 yards! I might catch one, so the ship, the expenses, and the misery are justified.

I think that picture of Jeannette that you sent Romer, is disgusting. And that isn't old fogyism or hard and fast judgement. I am less influenced, however, by those around me than I used to be, and I am surely learning from Romer. But an indecent bathing suit is not a theory or an idea. It's something that reveals all the nude body. It's ridiculous not to know that nudity invites sexuality.

I do think of you lots and lots. Out at sea, at sunset. Mostly in the dark before I go to bed when I look out over this wonderful ocean and listen to the grand roar of the reef. It about kills me to think, but I can't help it.

I hate to say goodnight. I'd give a lot to be with you a little. It sure takes guts to stick to this job. With more love than ever.

Doc

As the trip progressed, troubles increased. The sticking point appeared to be Dolly's resentment of Mildred's constant presence, her increasing importance in Zane's life, and her influence on Zane's work. When Zane built Mildred a house in Altadena patterned after the pueblo-style Catalina house, it was too much to bear.[9] She wrote him of this, and he replied with a long and bitter letter.

Camp

OCTOBER 14, 1928

Dear Dolly,

Your long awaited letter (?) on hand. It turned out to be but one, the beauty and profit of which are for the present spoiled by your vituperation. I had hoped, and believed, that when you had your——————cut out it would remove some of your bitterness. But alas, it didn't.

Things have come to a sad pass of late. And a resume of them would sound like a catalogue of disaster.

First, I have had 2½ months of very hard and wholly profitless fishing.

Secondly, there has been a continual and daily list of miserable little dealings, etc. I have had 18 men—natives—at this camp, and 20 people on board the Fisherman. There were several cliques, and I got the short end of every clash. I would not annoy you with a record of the squabbles and stealings. The one bright spot on the schooner was when I got her sold.

I have been deceived by this camp location, as Capt. M. was. The other day our water went dry. There have been a number of irritating circumstances, chiefly concerning the apparent and actual cost of things and labor. On the face of it at first the camp looked very reasonable, in fact cheap. But it has actually amounted to considerable.

We were deceived about the time to come here. Oct., Nov., and Dec., was drummed into us last year. As a matter of fact, Dec., Jan., and Feb., are the months. That upset me much. And the last few days the continual dropping of drops of water have begun to wear on the stone.

Then yesterday, the 13th, I had three jolts, in quick succession, and I went down for the count.

The first was news of the remarkable and unprecedented run of swordfish in Avalon in late September, 29 caught. And oh! how those bastards are laughing in their sleeves at me. They have cause. Jump claims 4 fish on light tackle. Of course he is a rotten liar. Everybody knows that. But the Tuna Club will uphold him, and all my efforts to show the vile sportsmanship of that out-fit will go for naught. Romer's employee, Emil, who never fished in his life before, caught one of those broadbills very easily. Caught it as all of them are caught. In a way we call crooked.

The second jolt was your letter and the third was poor tragic broken-hearted Romer, who came to me for sympathy, if no more. That little gold-digging slut has thrown him down! . . . Well, more of that anon.

The letter that M. read I let her read, and so I told you. But she saw me slip it out of sight as she came into my room, and asked to read it. As I had not read it I took the risk, and it was a crazy love letter from that D—South African fool. You would believe to read her letter that I had been deeply intrigued. Well, I hadn't. Only my old weakness momentarily stirred.

To conclude about M. who really had been fine this trip. We have had only one ruction of late, and that was when she was down about her work. I talked the suavest I could. Then she grew wild and said "I can't ever succeed. Even Hildred knows it. She told me I never could succeed because of Dolly's hate!" I swore this was a damn lie, that you were too splendid and noble to poison your soul with hate. She laughed at me in scorn, and said I knew nothing about you or any woman. Well, maybe I don't. Thank God, I am not intellec-tual, or analytical, or bright, or anything but simple minded.

Again and for the last time I think you have exaggerated M.'s claim about my work. She acknowledged that she had claimed to be of assistance to me. But even if her friends or folks have augmented that claim, even to the extent of starting gossip, I doubt that it can ruin me. If such things could ruin me I would have been ruined a long time ago. Work talks for itself. These editors are not going to buy poor books, and I shall never make another blunder.

If there were pencil marks on the margin of Amber's Mirage I never saw them. When I got your radio about this last installment I was upset. You gave

no specific suggestions. And I did take M.'s advice about a little of the rewriting. To be honest it helped me to get her point of view. In the last paragraph
she advised that I change the wording to read plural instead of single; to wit
"the souls of men must climb."

About the house in Altadena, she is in despair about the expense. And I
really believe I will have to take it off her hands, by giving her what she has
paid out on it. Several thousand on building, and somewhat more on furnish-
ings. And that's that.

You say you don't know how long you can continue to stand the things
you have to swallow with me. My dear, you are finding that out rather late in
the day. And it is a total reverse of what you told me before I left.

Yes, Reba is a hard pill for you to swallow. She used to be for me until I saw
the uselessness of being sore. Now I never think of her shortcomings. She
knew I intended to get Rome a car and I would not put it beyond her to dig
you a little. Women are so kind! But please acquit Rome of any of the things
you intimated. Only the other day he asked me anxiously, "Are you sure it's
O.K. with Dolly, about my Christmas present? Because I wouldn't want it
otherwise." And I, like the poor sap I am, not only told him it was but I actually believed it. Reba sold bonds and pawned diamonds to get me money.
Rome gave me many a dollar of his hard earned salary, earned by the hardest
kind of work, and then poorly paid. Baseball! He saved $600 a year, and we
got it all. Thank God I have made that up.

Of all the things I ever did in my life, I mean of the few worthy things, the
standing by Ellsworth I put first. I have saved him from——————well, you
know. That deed of mine will be recorded somewhere.[10]

My poor family have always been a source of rankling irritation to you.
Small wonder! We had some good healthy backwoods blood, but no more.
If you put store on culture and the amenities of life you should never have
thrown yourself away on me. I always told you that. I have stuck to my
people. At that I never hated yours.

Somehow the sting of this letter of yours, the reiterated scorn of Rome and
Ida, has sunk deeper than ever before. I understand the bitterness of life, the
hardening as the years go by.

Before I forget, I was the one who chose a Stutz for Rome, and I asked

Ken's advice. How perfectly amazed was I at your littleness! You ought to be pleased that I can afford to buy him the safest car. I swear to God no one has begged me to go out and buy them something that you have. That is ridiculous.

That's all very well about you blowing off steam occasionally, or clearing the sultry atmosphere by a thunderbolt. But this time I have been about destroyed. Such things should be left for direct contact. I was longing for some kindly helpful newsy letter. Did I get it? Ha! Ha!

So instead of a thrilling fishing and photographing stunt this trip has become an ordeal. It is a fight. Work, of course is a saver. My own zest and joy have flown, and may never return.

There is little more that I can add to this. I am pretty sick. Such for me is not unusual, but it seems unusual this time. I wonder how much I can stand of trouble. Last night my heart hurt; it beat slowly as if tired; and the thought persisted that perhaps I would not be required much longer to fight the odds. That may seem morbid, in writing, but last night it seemed clear.

But to conclude—this trip was a crowning blunder. There's one chance in a thousand that it can be pulled out, and I'm taking that, more for Romer's sake than mine.

With love,

Doc

His bitterness was most likely prompted by poor health, as shortly after this he became ill. Once back to fishing, he regretted his outburst and sent a conciliatory letter full of grandiose plans, some of which included Dolly.

Taroria

NOVEMBER 25, 1928

Sunday

Dearest—

I am a little better each day, and have begun to pick up. My food doesn't taste like sawdust. Yesterday I walked some. Perhaps I will try fishing tomorrow. Only eight days left to fish.

Yesterday a wireless came from you, dated Nov. 21 requesting me to remember the date (that is, to think of you today). I wondered why you speci-fied that day particularly. I think of you everyday. Then I remembered that your birthday is on Jan.6, and Loren's in Sept., and Betty's in May, so it couldn't be that. Finally I deduced it down to some kind of an anniversary, and from that to our wedding day. Well, it's a long time back, and if you are happy to remember it, I am glad.

When I get home we will have to do some tall talking about future plans. First whether I shall go on with this big game fishing work for three more years. Or not. And in the event I don't what shall I do? And in the event that we decide to go on with it I submit this program for your consideration. As you know 1929 is pretty full already. I'll get home in April. Go to Norway in May. Return early August. Take Betty's crowd to Utah and Arizona in Septem-ber. Take my hunt in Tonto in Oct., Jan., Feb., March 1930 I will return here. Aug., Sept., Oct. (part) go to Winkle Bar, on which trip you will be cordially invited.

1931 May, June, July, Aug., Sept., Marquesas and Paumotos. This will necessitate a new ship, etc.

For 1932 plan a trip of 8 months fishing around Australia.

In this event we might do something wonderful. Say I take you, Romer, Betty, and Loren, and go abroad, seeing England, at least one Scotland river (salmon river), France. Then ship aboard one of the big liners for Sydney. We would see the Mediterranean, Suez, Port Said, Aden, Red Sea, Indian Ocean, Calcutta or Bombay, Singapore, some of the islands, and the Straights. At Sydney I will go aboard my yacht which would meet me there, with Romer and Loren, and you and Betty could hop the Aurangi for Suva and Honolulu. And at Honolulu hop the City of Los Angeles for home.

This is an ambitious trip, darling. But it has many attractions, educational and otherwise. The whole four years expenses would be considerable, counting the new ship. But it could be done, and it would not be hard or exacting, or keep me from the West or my work till 1932.

You can think it over. You have plenty of time. My main idea is to see Romer out of the woods and get Loren started. Maybe it wouldn't be practical to take Loren. Anyway, consider it for what it's worth. I, or we could save every dollar of the expenses before 1932. So that's that.

I might fetch you down here for a month in 1930, if you liked the idea. It would be a great experience for you, and the weather is delightful, provided you keep quiet. 1932 is as far as my fancy can roam. After that I would be content to fish for minnows and trout, and let Romer and Loren do the big stuff.

Well, darling, I'll write you again, of course. My address will be Auckland, N.Z. General Delivery.

Love to all

Docco

P.S. I wonder how my house is getting on.

In December he sailed for New Zealand for several months of fishing. Dolly, Loren, and Betty celebrated Christmas together, with Zane and Romer still in the South Seas.

Altadena

DECEMBER 23, 1928

Doc darling,

Rome got in yesterday afternoon, but I didn't get my mail until this morning. Naturally I was on pins and needles till I received it. Your radio from the ship reassured me as to your recovery from the flu, but radios never say much and I was anxious for something more ample. I got it! If in nothing more than your plans for the future. They are rather breath-taking, my dear. I will have to digest them at my leisure.

It will seem strange and lonely not to have you and my firstborn for Christmas, but I am having the Christmas just as if you were here. I had my mother come on for a couple of months from the east with Mr. Kuster. The change in her shocked and surprised me. She is a feeble old woman, Doc. Somehow I cannot realize it. I think she's just let go somehow, mentally. She can hardly walk, and yet I don't think there's much wrong with her physically. Just sort of a nervous breakdown. They only came yesterday morning, and are in the bungalow. I felt that I ought to ask her, although it's not going to be so easy for me. Mr. Kuster looks fine, and is cheerful. He is absolutely devoted to her and does everything in the world for her. It's terribly pathetic. She looks and acts almost old enough to be his mother.

You'll laugh when I tell you what we're doing this minute. Loren and I are both sitting in front of the fireplace in my room. I'm writing this and Loren is writing a story with a big writing board across his lap, a la Daddy. The radio is singing Christmas hymns. Betty and Pete are wrapping Christmas presents.

Say, old Galapagos, do you realize your daughter is very talented? She has a marvelously poetic imagination and writes beautiful poetry and other things. Very high brow. They say she has a brilliant mind. But she's very much alive, nevertheless! And she's so beautiful, that she can wheedle all sorts of clothes out of me against my principles when we go shopping. She says, "Oh, mother, just let me try it on." And she does and that settles it! Latest is a black tulle evening dress in which she is absolutely delectable. You sent her quite a lot of presents. Did you forget the opal ring you left for her? She's absolutely crazy to know what it is that you left in the deposit box.

I had almost decided to take Betty and Loren to Europe while you were in Norway, but I fear the time will be too short, especially if you leave on that riding trip September first. However, I'll see. May go to B.C. or somewhere else.

My dear, don't ever worry about your reading audience. No magazines are going to pay $65,000 for a story from you if you are waning. I was in Bullocks book department yesterday and on all sides I heard people clamoring for Zane Grey. I'll take my oath that by and large you're the biggest seller in the world right now, despite any Bookman lists. I don't know how they get them anyway. Well, you can't slump if you want to keep up your new addition. I get scared whenever I look at that enormous place and think of what heat and light it will consume—let alone the building. Why Doc, it's just about as big as this house! But you ordered it and let it be on your head! But it's perfectly beautiful. Poor Edd worries because it's costing so much, but I tell him it's absolutely being built according to your specification, which it is. A place like that can't be erected for nothing. The tiled roof and concrete are on now, and they're beginning on the interior. Yes, darling, you'll have secret chambers (Not potties) but you've forgotten that your wife is not nosy or inquisitive like the other people you are accustomed to. I have no desire to pry, no interest even. It's only for safety that I should be able to get into all your things. Anyway, the workmen know what they're building. Honestly, do you think you deserve such a perfect wife? I know I should raise some hell just to show you and make you appreciate me.

Crowell was delighted with "Drift Fence." The only objection he could find was that the girl was too young, but he can easily make her a year or two older. He sent me the first half on payment and I'm to get the rest after Jan. 1st which I wanted that way.

I can't write more now, I'm afraid. So, good night, beloved. In spirit we will be together as always this Christmas. I hope you and Romer will be together. That will be two-fifths there and three-fifths here of our whole. And a whole it is—an entity. If there were no other tie remaining between us, there would always be that one—those three flesh of our flesh, and spirit of our spirit, the well-born because they are children of our love and no accident. They are not perfect any more than you or I are perfect, but oh, they are precious.

Love always, my darling, from your wife,

Dolly

Now in New Zealand, Zane located his camp at Mercury Bay, on the east side of the north island. Conditions here were better, and he was optimistic, but on Christmas Day his thoughts turned toward home.

Camp Mercury Island

Mercury Bay

DECEMBER 25, 1928

Dearest Dolly,

We have been here three days. It was hell getting here, and our stuff ashore, and camp pitched. But it is the most beautiful of all the camps I ever had. I won't attempt to describe it. The ti trees are in blossom, pink and white, and very fragrant. The pohotakaisas are in bloom, and vivid scarlet, the color of the red eucalyptus we have in our yard. These trees are very large, like a huge chestnut, and the forest just behind and above camp is so dense you can't see through it. Below is the sea, and out the many islands, of all sizes and shapes. The bell birds and tin birds would alone make the place fascinating. Altogether it is wonderful.

We have caught 6 mako, the great jumping shark we came after. 250, 275,

300, 325, 400, 360, and 580 pounds. This is truly luck, my big mako of 580 pounds jumped magnificently, but I was too scared to think of photographing.

The people of Whitiangi have been exceedingly kind and courteous. One man sent us turkeys for dinner, another flowers, and all sorts of mail, paper, etc. We are most decidedly in favor in N.Z. at the present writing.

I have not yet gotten wholly well. But am gradually improving. That brand of flu in Tahiti was fierce. We heard there were 3,000,000 cases of flu in the U.S. I don't believe much I read out here.

I am working again, mostly from 5 a.m. to 7 a.m. I write my fish notes at night.

On December 28, I entertain Mr. and Mrs. Sir John Cecil. She was Cornelia Vanderbilt. I'm going to take her out (in a boat I mean, of course!) and let Cappy take Sir John. We will sure give them a couple of exciting days.

I forgot to mention that the new book is a sequel to "The Drift Fence." Title—"The Hash Knife Outfit," which you may not like.

Well, this has been a queer Christmas for me. Rather sad, I think I have found myself picturing you and Betty and Lorry last night, this morning, today. I hope you are well, and happy. God bless you all.

Love

Doc

Mercury Island Camp

JANUARY 20, 1929

Dearest Dolly,

Your letter of Dec. 23 has put the joy of life in me. It was just lovely, and I soared. Why can't you write me that way oftener? I would adore you— presently, not that I don't anyway. All you said about Betty and Loren was recorded, so don't think I'll forget it. I will be terribly glad to see you all again.

Romer is well, fine, busy with cameras and fishing. Only now and then he breaks out about what he'll do to girls when he returns. I am well and strong again, but not busy. I'd like to stay this way. You'd admire my figure.

The ladies are in the South Island, and we have been alone for over two weeks. It's the first time I can remember camping without feminine jumbers, and it's bad, because it shows the difference, and that all troubles of mankind emanate from his rib.

Fishing not so good. I have 15 to date, some big mako. The last was 446 lbs.

That is funny about Crowell finding fault with the heroine's age in Drift Fence. He is a funny little old woman about stories.

I was sorry to hear about your mother—very surprised, too. Life is sad. I hope she gets better in Calif. Rome said you were just fine—better than for years. I'm sure glad of that.

You sort of scare me stiff about the new addition for myself—the new study, etc. I thought it would be too small. Honey, I didn't mean I wanted secret places to hide things from you. But from burglars and such. I am not afraid to leave the study to you, considering Ed has a rough outline of what I require. Fire place, seats, bookshelves, etc., etc. But that tackle room downstairs—the end toward the big trees must have all sorts of flush dubs. Tables, racks for rods, shelves, closets, flat bench about 2 feet high for the purpose of holding my tackle trunks off the floor. These, of course, need not be stationary. Just plain benches, or movable seats for trunks.

Move all my tackle from your sewing room to this new tackle room as soon as is convenient. The black cabinet also. This should be done while you have some husky men about.

I don't know what I'll do with the downstairs room toward the street. But the upstairs, one or two rooms (I don't know which) back of my study, should have one big light closet for my outdoor stuff. And at least one side of one of these rooms should have a million drawers, a la Lackawaxen. Also window seats, and in short, my darling, places to put things, not only what I have now, but what I expect to accumulate. So use your head, my dear. This new place ought to settle me for keeps.

Money holding out pretty good. I hope I can make what I have do. But expenses are high. Romer has cost a pretty penny this time, but he's worth it.

I am writing every morning 5 to 7. I get up with the larks. Lord, I wish you could see this place.

Much love, Dolly. I'll write again soon.

Doc

Nine months was the longest he had been away. The trip had its disappointments, especially Tahiti, and its pleasures, but he could not declare it a success.

Mercury Island Camp

MARCH 6, 1929

Dearest Spondulux,

Our time grows short. We have had bad weather lately, and fishing has been poor. 95 all told! But that's some total. We'll make it a hundred. I'm tired, I guess, and will be happy to be on the way home. I'll write all the way so the time will fly.

Probably will be stone broke when I do get there. It sure is fine to think of coming home to my frugal and speculating little wife. If you are also broke there will be some explanations in order. Any more of these investments just to keep money from me will create a vacuum somewhere.

I will be, as usual, full of plans and work. It will be sort of tough on you, because my return means only a lot of love making to you. Ahem! However, it will be glorious to see you. I don't seem to dread the long ride home. I wrote 200 pages the last time—I hope I can beat that this trip.

I will arrive home April 13, on Saturday, so you can have Betty home. I will be glad to see her. 9 months! My God, it's an age. And I have accomplished nothing! We will have to be together most of the time while I am there, so you can let me go away again.

I am well, and all right otherwise. You will see me not very long after you peruse this.

Love and kisses,

Doc

P.S. I've asked Doc and Betty Wiborn to go to Utah with us. You help it along. Ask them out for Sunday 14th.

He arrived home in mid-April and stayed only to the end of May. Then he left for the East Coast and another fishing adventure, this time in Nova Scotia. While in New York, he called on old acquaintances, dutifully visited Dolly's family, and met with publishers and editors.

JUNE, 1929

Dearest Helpmeet,

I saw Claire yesterday. She is fine. Wonderful baby. I will see Uncle
Theodore again, and if possible see your grandmother and mother.

Saw Swartz of Paramount this a.m. I had very little to say. He will make
an appointment with Mr. Lasky for me. Also saw Mr. Rose. We had a fine talk.
I agreed to write him three novels for $55,000—1930, $60,000—1931,
$60,000—1932. Delivery June 1 of each year. You may not approve of this,
but I feel that it is not so bad, considering that I do not want to lose the Curtis
Pub. Co. He was well pleased. I will only have to work a little harder, which is
nothing for me.

I am feeling pretty good. Oh, yes, I saw Anna Wood yesterday. Had a
shock. She is twice your size!! She drove me in her car—scared H. out of me.
Hit one car in the behind, and that was all I wanted. I met her mother, and
also her little girl—a sweet child.

No letter from you, since that first one. You're a fine wife. Write to Liver-
pool, Nova Scotia.

Love and Kisses,

Doc

She replied,

Monday,

JUNE 3, 1929

Doc, darling,

There has been plenty of communications from you, but in rather confus-
ing order, since wires, air mail, and regular mail were all mixed up. However, I
managed to follow! It's seemed most dreadfully lonely since you left. I've been
working very hard, though.

Last Wednesday and Thursday we spent at Avalon lending our distinguished presence (ahem) to the opening of the new Casino. It's a magnificent
building with a marvelous dance hall. Your little wifie danced every dance, and
enjoyed it! We were seventeen at the house, so it was quite a party to feed.
Romer's party consisted of eight.

I'm glad N.Y. is bucking you up—literarily, that is. There's no reason why it shouldn't. Your wire from Lacky made me homesick for it. I wish I were on the way there. I hope you've seen my mother and grandmother. I don't think I'd forgive you if you didn't. And I'd try to hurt you as much as you'd hurt me by not doing it. And that would be a lot. However, you won't fail me, I know, and I'm just silly. Uncle Theo says grandma is looking forward to seeing you.

Naturally Harper's, Chenery, Crowell, et. al., would be fine to you. But why send the poor souls chasing to California to see me? Did you get any money from anyone, or are they sending it. I need some P.D.Q. for the income tax.

Romer is doing well, tho chasing as hard as ever. He has a terrific driving force and energy, and manages to accomplish a lot. Lorry is getting more and more involved with his pigeons. He is secretary of the club and conducts a heavy correspondence. Your beautiful daughter payed us a couple of flying visits. She's written a highly-commended poem recently. Doc, what have we hatched? Do we deserve all this? These marvelous children, particularly? An old N.Y. friend was here yesterday. She was much struck with our beautiful places (Catalina, too), wonderful children. She patted me on the shoulder and said, "You deserve it, you've worked hard for it."

Goodnight, my very dear one.

Your,

Dolly

And now Zane,

Dearest,

Your letter, air mail, June 3 simply made me happy. That is the way you ought to write me occasionally. Of course I saw your mother and grand-mother. Cost me $7 for taxi and $10 for flowers. So there! I wrote you about seeing them. Hope you get it.

Perhaps I did wrong to sign up with Rose. But I figured it over very care-fully, and think I can deliver the stories. If I hadn't done that I'd have written the same three stories for $150,000. As it is I talked him into $175,000. It was the three that got the raise. I'm sorry though if I displeased you about Chenery and Crowell coming out there to see you—they wanted to, they like it.

Write me here till June 24, air mail, then write to Halifax, Nova Scotia until further notice. I was thrilled at what you said about our three children. They have got me going, too. I love them terrifically.

Don't forget to have a spring lock put on my hall door leading to my study. Don't forget anything I told you.

Today I caught my second Salmon, 11½ pounds. Gee, it was sport. I can't wait for Romer to get here.

No, it wasn't funny, Anna Wood driving me. Nor Elma either, though she can drive. But her dress was way up over her enormous legs, still beautiful, by the way, and I near croaked. Damn modern women anyway!

The frogs are trilbing. All same Lacky.

With Love,

Doc

In her letters Dolly sounds busy and content, but she was not happy. Always there were new sources of pain. Mildred's Altadena house, built for her by Zane and located where Dolly must see it every time she ventured out, was a constant thorn in her side, daily reminding her of her rival.

Altadena

JUNE 21, 1929

Doc Dearest,

Well, guess I put it over once more. A letter from Chenery said he and Crowell would pay $75,000 for stories. But he wants to come out anyway to talk over a more definite association. I'm perfectly willing to do that, but think we can manage a sliding scale arrangement. You see, they are crazy to have you, and that's because I've worked you up the right way to them. They're good magazines, have plenty of money, and it's a good association for you. I wrote them quite a Machiavellian letter, with the stress upon every word raised to the nth power. Sounds conceited, but really I'm not. There's a right way of doing things.

In fact, I'm rather depressed, and in a "what's the use" frame of mind. I've been harboring a horrid suspicion recently that so many letters and telegrams from you meant you were trying to cover the M.K.S. trail—that you were sending her a lot.[11] I keep thinking of what the telegraph and post office people think for they all know you. That building for her in Altadena was the most bonehead, and for me, the most humiliating thing you ever did. Moreover, I've been bombarded with bills for books and things you were sending her.

It's very hot—but one doesn't suffer like in the East. Romer graduates this afternoon. I got him a fine watch chain and knife for a present, and will send him off to you tomorrow night. He really is a wonder, and I've trained myself not to let his peculiar ways bother me. He's really been very sweet recently.

Loren is the prize. You ought to see the way he listed and packed his duffle. Romer's and Betty's are all over the house, and I'll have to do it for them in the end. But not Loren. It's ready to go Sunday and it's been ready since last night. I leave Monday. I do love you honey, and maybe I'll stick to you—if you persuade me that you can't live without me—but no lying!

Dolly

It was now Dolly's turn to enjoy an adventure of her own, a trip to Canada with a cruise up the coast of Alaska. Romer joined his father in Nova Scotia after graduation, and Loren and Betty had other plans, so Dolly was free to go. She left in late June. Her boat, the SS *Prince Rupert*, departed July 1 from Vancouver with stops at Prince Rupert, Juneau, and Skagway, to return nine days later.[12] No doubt her vacation was more enjoyable than her husband's.

Grandy's Brook
Newfoundland
JULY 6, 1929

Dearest Dolly,

We had hell getting up here, long cold ride on the sea, seasick and freezing, being towed in skiff for eight miles to the mouth of this river, then up for a mile more, to a night in a little cabin. Next day rain, and a walk up the river, wading, crossing bays and islands for miles farther, to a place where we are camped. We did all in the rain, and all last night it rained cats and dogs. The outlook was dismal indeed. During the night I was pretty discouraged. Next day sunshine, and a roaring river. We had to fix a camp that was habitable. It was a job. Flies and mosquitoes by the million, hungry as wolves. We built fires, which alone made the job possible. The mud was a foot deep, brush wet, trees thick. But we cleared a spot, and unsightly as it is it will be possible to stay here a few days. I have five guides, and we are all working like beavers. The pool in front of the camp is a wonderful one, where we expect to catch some salmon. By the way, the flies are bad now and I am wearing gloves and headnet, while Romer is taking a motion picture of me. It is all adventure, and hard as hell, and not much fun, except to remember. I have done pretty well with my notebook, and if we get some fine photos of the river and leaping fish I will have another book.

Today you are somewhere in Alaska. I hope and pray safe and having a good time. I really ought not let you gad about like that.

We plan to stay here a little while, then return to Burges where our schooner awaits, and then go on along the south shore. May we have success! I am storing up energy for the great task this winter. I must write four novels by June 1st. Pray for me. But I can do it, Dolly, and two of them will be long and historical, and all of them must be good.

I thrill at the prospect. I certainly thrill at the thought of home again, and my dear family, and my wonderful study. I will take much joy in fixing it up more and better, and sticking in it a lot. I must have a stenographer to work at the house, to mind the phone, and protect me while you are out six days a week. Which you are! This letter will be a long while in getting to you, but it bears my endless devotion honey, and my prayers for your well being.

Love,

Doc

The Nova Scotia trip was over by mid-July, but Zane was in California only briefly before leaving for a long trip through Utah and Arizona, taking Romer and Betty.[13] By August 30 he was in Green River, Utah, where Lee Doyle, Al Doyle's son, met the party and guided them through Monument Valley, Robber's Roost country, Bryce Canyon, Zion National Park, Grand Canyon, Havasupai Reservation, and finally Flagstaff.[14] From Flagstaff the Z.G. entourage toured the Rainbow Bridge, where Fox Studios was filming *Lone Star Ranger*. With him were Captain Mitchell; Miss M. Thomas, an artist from Scottsdale; Mildred; son Romer; Robert Carney; Ken Robertson;

daughter Betty; Virginia Nash; George Takahashi; and J. Nasurka. While he
was gone Dolly made a very quick trip to New York, daringly by train and
plane, which got her there in only forty-eight hours.[15]

In Flagstaff Zane met with Tom McCullough, a member of the State Fish
and Game Commission, and expressed his regret at the lateness of the opening of the hunting season in the Tonto and the fact that the black-bear season was not open. From there the entourage moved to the cabin in the
Tonto Basin. Taking two teenagers on such a long trip proved taxing, physically and emotionally. Expenses worried him, as did Romer and Betty, the
hunting was plagued with problems, and worse, the Arizona that had capti-
vated him had disappeared. It was now modern, up to date, and overrun
with tourists, many of whom ironically may have wanted to see Arizona
because of reading a Zane Grey novel. All this put him in a sour mood.

Monday

SEPTEMBER 30, 1929

Dearest Dolly,

I was foolish enough to be disappointed not to hear from you—except the
wire and note. I ought to know by this time that you will not do as I'd like. As
for myself, I couldn't write.

I had made up my mind to show my West to Romer and Betty, and under
most trying conditions I did it. Our last ride (horseback) from Segi to Kayenta,
Monument Valley, Noki, Argon Rock, Piute Canyon, the San Juan, Surprise
Valley, Nonnezosche, and Navajo Mountain was simply epic. But it damn near
killed me. It was too much without rest.

For that matter we were all knocked out, and Betty, Virginia, Bob and myself
were very sick for a day and a night. It might have been only nervous exhaustion, and it might have been ptomaine poisoning. I never vomited so. And my
bowels were awful. The intestinal antiseptic saved us all from serious disorder.

Betty turned out so much better on this part of the trip. Only a couple of
slips—one of which was taking a bath in a sulphur spring. The youngsters
slipped off from us in Surprise Valley. They returned vomiting their heads off.
Served them right. They went in bathing, nude of course, but I hope not
together.

You are no doubt right about Betty. I told you how sorry I felt for her and that I understood. I was furious because of the risks they took. I did not attribute any immoral act to Betty or Bob. Mr. Robertson said "You must let nature take its course!" He was a distinctly bad influence upon the youngsters, as was proved when he left us. He is some queer kind of pervert. I have never been so sore at anyone before. Bob is fine. But I'm afraid he is not so involved as Betty is. However, it is nothing but puppy love. Personally I hate this monkeying of the kids in plain sight of everybody. Maybe that proves it's all right. But I feel they don't care a D—for anybody.

I shall never come back to Arizona. The main reason for which is that the country has been ruined by motorists. The Navajo are doomed. The beauty and romance of their lives dead. Still I got material for several stories of bygone times.

I am going to rest in the Tonto and finish Red Rock Ranch, then hunt a little, and come home. I feel the need of you more than ever in my life, but this separation has made me less sure of you. Still I do not need the kind of help that you persist in flaunting in my face. Perhaps I ought not write more. I am worn out, yet I do not feel depressed or morbid.

Betty and Virginia will leave here on Oct. 10. Romer will wire you. I am sure a few days more will be all right, and Betty coaxed so hard. It's strange how I love those two, when I know they do not love me. I am convinced that never before have I kept my mouth shut, or inhibited my wishes and fears as I did on this trip. Well, enough of that until my return.

Your one bit of news about $5,000 advance on each story for Chenery meant little for me. I would have preferred an agreement for five years at the same price.

I have spent a lot of money on this five weeks, about $2,000 of which went for blankets, baskets, silver, etc. for presents and my study. My last mad fling at that sort of expense! Perhaps around Oct. 15 you had better put some money to my account. I am pretty near the end of my tether.

Hoping you are well, and rested now.

With love,

Doc

Two weeks prior to the great stock-market crash, he wrote almost pre-sciently of money troubles.

OCTOBER 14, 1929

Dearest Dolly,

Romer is going to Payson tomorrow, to mail letters, so I will take advantage of his extraordinary and wholly unnecessary act to write and mail you a letter. This, by the way, is the way Romer does things. The expenditures of money uselessly and absolutely without reason except because he wants to has become a very serious thing.

I am sorry you are broke. You always are broke unless at a time when I have just given you some money. Your big interests have absorbed all the cash and credit you can get, and threaten to absorb mine. But, nothing doing, anymore, my dear. It's more important (to me) that I buy the stuff I want and take the trips I plan, than for you to buy this and that for investment.

I shall turn in the green Lincoln and the truck, and get another car as soon as I can afford it. No more trips with cars. I shall probably get a driver, also. I have never had one, when I wanted it, and had to rent a car. It seems foolish, too, because I will only be going out once in a while, outside of meeting you down town every week, as usual. But so I feel about it now.

You pitched into me pretty hard about the expenditures on this trip. Well, this trip was mostly for Betty and Romer, and I planned it to cost about $2,500, outside of what I have to pay for the Haughts. I spent that much, almost, for blankets, I know. But that is my last splurge for such stuff, and as well my last trip to Arizona. The blankets are such beautiful, the finest and best bargains I ever had. Wait till you see them! About half will go for Christmas presents.

As I told you, I have overdrawn my bank account somewhat, and it will need to be replenished. Besides that I'll have salaries to pay, upon my return, and several husky bills. So it will take around $15,000 to make me square. I have one more chapter on the McCall novel, assuming that I am home inside of two weeks, we can figure on getting that $50,000 by a month later. That's the only money I see in sight, and it's rather dim, at that.

I hate to borrow, more than you do. But if you continue to go south with all the money that comes in, as fast as you get your mitts on it, well, there'll be something more to pay, and that will be hell!

This discourages me horribly. We will have to talk it over upon my return and do something. It is certainly rotten that you and I should quarrel over money. But we shall, I fear. I never get a d— cent of money you earn, even if you do pay endless bills of mine, and you do get part of mine. I don't care a d— for the California community property law. If we have to conform to legal ways, we are no different from a lot of other rotten married people. Personally I won't stand for that sort of thing. I'm not sore, or do I feel mean, or anything, except that I do not like the way you are doing things. That is my privilege. You've had that stand toward my peculiar way of doing things for 20 years. You've been most gracious and fine about it, too. But I don't like this financial game you are in. Especially does this bank matter annoy me. I earn most of the money, and I intend to have more to say about its use. So that's that. As to the future, of course if I do not go ahead with my plans, we'll have no need to bother our heads about money. We can just let it accumulate to ruin Betty and Loren, as money has almost ruined Romer.

The season opens day after tomorrow. We have seen some bear sign, and lots of turkey and deer. But I'm leary about hunting here. There's a new road, and the woods will be full of these—————! Tin-can, auto hunters with shot guns. I'll try to have everybody wear red hats and coats, and be careful. But I don't like the chance. And I'll never come back here again. I've camped at this spot since 1918. It is sort of haunted. The old order changes. We have no more real hunting parties, or hunters. Nor fishermen, either. That is, great game fishermen! I look to Loren to carry on my work.

This is not a very pleasing letter. But it's your own fault. Why didn't you write: "Well, dear, I'm broke too, but I'll dig up some money for you. Don't worry about that. Have a good time. Be careful, and come back to work like H—." Now that would have been the way for you to write. Instead you say, at the close to try to live up to my greatness. I'll take you at your word. But I don't feel happy. Lots of love,

Home soon,

Docco

P.S. Edd Haught came back from Phoenix yesterday with bad news.

There is a concerted deal on to run me out of this country. Next year they will make a game refuge under the Rim, taking in both my properties. It looks like petty politics and personal jealousy. I was refused a special permit and insulted publically by the State Game Warden. The Game Commissioner of Flagstaff, a two faced—who pretended to be friendly to me over there, got up in the meeting on Oct. 5 at Phoenix and roasted me vilely. There is a bunch of Winslow hunters who have killed loads of game, breaking every law, and they have laid this on the Z.G. outfit.

Ken Robertson made a crack in Flagstaff that has materially aided my enemies. He was heard to say; "I'm always glad to beat it out of Flagstaff. The sheriff might get on to the fact that Bowen and I got our licenses by claiming to live in Yuma." This is a fact, but I did not think Robertson would brag about it. God damn him anyway! That is another thing added to the many I have against him.

There are other details of this mess, but I'll tell you upon my return. I ought to break camp at once. I ought to have more sense than to stay here longer. But I'd disappoint everybody. However I don't think I'll hunt myself. I'm sorry that I must report utter failure, so far, of this part of the trip. I wish, oh, I wish I were home.

Much love

Doc

He did not get much news in Arizona except what was in Dolly's letters, so he was probably unaware of the stock-market crash on October 29, its rally the following day, then the rapid plummet over the next few weeks. He was in California in November, where surely he heard the news, but he could not have imagined how it would affect him. Dolly, with her acumen in investment, could hardly have missed this ominous portent. He worked at home to the middle of February, feverishly writing the novels he had promised by June 1, and spent Christmas of 1929 with his family.

CHAPTER 14

I Love You Till It Chokes Me

HUDDLED IN HIS STUDY, Zane was largely unaware of what was happening across the nation, but Dolly watched with sinking heart. For a time conditions seemed to get better. The stock market recovered a bit, and the employment situation brightened, but banking and business slowed. After a few months unemployment again soared, with a million more people out of work, bringing the total to four million. By late spring stock prices fell again, industrial production declined, construction slowed, banks and businesses failed, and farm income dropped.

Nevertheless Zane departed February 18 from San Francisco on the R.M.S. *Makura,* bound for Tahiti.[1] He wrote Romer from on board ship about a two-part trip he planned for the fall of 1931. The premise of the trip rested on acquiring a new yacht to replace the *Fisherman I* and included stops at Cape San Lucas, Zihauntenejo, the Marquesas, Tahiti, the Leeward Islands, Christmas Island, and Hawaii, a trip of about ten months, then home for seven. The yacht would be sent via the Panama Canal to the Mediterranean while he and Romer visited New York, London, Paris, and finally Marseilles, where they would meet it and sail to Cairo. It would then be sent to South Africa through the Suez Canal while they took train, boat, car through central Africa. They would join it at Beira and sail to Madagascar, Sumatra, Java, Australia, the Solomon Islands, New Hebrides, across the Pacific, and finally home to San Pedro, taking eighteen months in all. Hard reality eventually made this trip impossible, yet he continued to dream while the nation plummeted into the Great Depression.

When he arrived in Tahiti, it was all he remembered.

Flower Point

MARCH 8, 1930

Dearest Dolly,

I wrote 17 pages today, and now feeling virtuous shall write you a letter. It is 7:20. The moon is gorgeous, the sea mournful and beautiful in its ceaseless swish and surge and boom, the perfume of flowers fills my cottage.

I have had bad sunburn on cheeks and forearms. Cappy [Capt. Mitchell] has been laid up for four days, unable to get about. He has suffered acutely. He wore shorts fishing on a blistering hot day, and he sure got a burn from above his knees down. He can scarcely walk. We must be careful of old Sol. At night it is so cool, so sweet, so balmy that you would never believe the day had been hot. A wonderful shower came down about three and cooled the air.

The Guilds were here for several days.[2] They are really very nice. Mr. G. confessed to me that I had straightened out his bad habits and that he was happy about it.

I feel somewhat blue about our fishing prospects, otherwise I am fine, and I shall make the trip profitable. I feel a long way from you, yet very close. I can see you. And Loren and Romer and Betty. When I was home you all drove me crazy. But now that I am away I love you till it chokes me. These things here—I mean the physical things—rouse me to profound emotion. I think it is good, so long as I try to express myself. I forget the burglars, earthquake, automobiles, etc., until I come to write you.

Love ever,

Your Doc

Dolly's letters brought grim news. Not comprehending the dire financial straits of the nation, he suspected that the source of his money woes was closer to home.

Flower Point, Sunday
MARCH 30, 1930

Dearest Dolly,

It was just as I expected—your letters crushed me. Yet they appeared to be your usual loving kind of letter. I think I have worried a good deal about my situation. 1930 surely started bad, and it keeps up.

Robber's Roost must be a flop.[3] It never occurred to me that the motive was really rape. Most all of the present day novels are worse than rape. But I'm glad to get a chance to correct the blunder. You should never have let it get by you! I'll gladly correct and do what's important.

However, that did not hurt me as much as the other jolts. It looks like our great trip is cooked. And that makes me so sick I can't stand up straight. I'll never get over it, if I cannot go. You're very good to jolly me along but as a matter of fact I cannot see much hope. Paramount wants me to justify them, let them out of it. I saw that long ago.

So with my magazine profits eliminated, and the motion-picture income stopped where in the world will I get $300,000 for a ship and trip, and money to carry on my current expenses, etc.?

I managed to crawl out this morning, but I wanted to die. It seems most selfish of me to ask you to see me through this thing. If you don't help me I shall never be able to accomplish it. Romer's letter was the only note of encouragement I received. Dolly, I am very much afraid that there are certain influences at work against me in my own home. You may deny this, or even ridicule it, but all the same I feel it is there, and think I can prove it. This is the last thing on earth for anyone to attempt with me and certainly the last thing you should attempt to conceal.

This is a poor letter, and I shall try to write another before mailing day. If I don't you will know that I've gone under completely. I rather imagine, however, that that is unlikely to happen.

Much love,
Docco

He fished Tahitian waters for several months. Captain Mitchell and his wife and daughter were there, as was Mildred. Long days went by without any sign of fish, but on March 13 he landed a 618-pound silver marlin, a new species, which he named,[4] and on May 15 he caught a 1040-pound record striped marlin.[5] He also caught a 63-pound dolphin, beating his own world record set in 1926 in the Galapagos,[6] and a 450-pound shark.[7] All in all, when he returned in mid-July he declared the trip a success.

At home there were changes. Romer had eloped with his girlfriend, Dorothy Chasen, who was, according to Zane, a young, beautiful, fine, and sensible girl, studious and economical, with nothing of the flapper about her.[8] Romer was twenty and Dorothy nineteen. Betty, at age eighteen, was engaged to Bob Carney, Romer's friend.

Although much of the nation was out of work, and for many there was not enough food to eat, Zane purchased another yacht that summer. He had heard of one for sale, the *Kallisto,* a three-masted schooner manufactured by the Krupps of Germany, reportedly for Kaiser Wilhelm II.[9] He went east to look at it, agreed to purchase it not knowing exactly where the money would come from, renamed it *Fisherman II,* and hired a captain and crew to bring it to San Pedro to be reoutfitted. Once prepared for a lengthy cruise of up to a year, the yacht would be sailed to the South Seas, where Zane would board it. It was hoped it would be ready to sail December 30, but that was not to be. Instead, it did not even leave port until March 1. Not only was the purchase of the yacht a tremendous strain on finances, the retrofitting was exorbitantly expensive.[10]

Production of more books and stories was the key to his finances, at least so he thought, so he concentrated on writing. In late August Dolly and Betty motored east, leaving Zane in Altadena with Loren. Romer and his new wife were in Oregon, and Loren was often away visiting friends, so Zane had plenty of quiet time to think and to work.

After writing throughout the fall, he left before Christmas for the South Seas. Mildred was not included, as there had finally been a falling-out and acrimonious final breakup in October 1930.[11] Their relationship had always been volatile. Her literary ambitions and perhaps her ambition to displace Dolly, as well as disagreements on a myriad of topics, led to many arguments. Her verbal attacks became more shrill, and Zane ended the relationship, but not without occasional pangs of regret.

With him instead were two young women, Carrie and Berenice Campbell, and eventually a third, Dorothy Wideman. He wrote from on board,

DECEMBER 26, 1930

Dearest,

Presently I will wireless you that Richard is himself again, except for the shame of having made you unhappy. Bless you, dear, for your loyalty and help and love.

I slept 10 hours like a log on Wednesday night. Christmas day I reveled in presents. Say, honey, you blew yourself for me, didn't you. Gee, that watch and the clock! I love them both, especially the latter. Thanks ever so much.

I was deeply touched at Romer coming up to see me off. He was different somehow. When he stood below, looking up as the ship started his face was so young, boyish, eager and uplifted! I had a tremendous rush of feeling, and suddenly realized that in him was embodied all I was leaving. My eyes filled and I couldn't see. Miss C. said, "Why Z.G., you are crying!" and so I was. She has been perfectly fine. I am embarrassed a little, at dinner, because she is so stunning.

The guild wrote me good news. Carrie wrote me some womanly sense.

She said I belonged to my public, to get myself another secretary, and if I didn't like her then would drop her overboard, so I could get another.

I will write you again, or sure from Papeete for the next boat.

Love and gratitude

Doc

DECEMBER 27, 1930

Saturday

Dearest,

I just sent you a wireless. Final advice. "Richard himself again. Send Betty Bob Feb. if possible." Zane

After thinking it over a lot that is how I feel about that. There is only one thing I can find in the way—a little additional expense. But you can stand that, darling, for Betty. Bob will more than pay his way. He will get some grand pictures for me. Betty will fit in somehow. She will have to work. Miss C. just loves her.[12] I hope you decide favorably.

Four days out, and I feel o.k. again, except for that horrible twinge now and then.

Your presents were dandy. It's always an event to open a present from you. I love the watch. The razor I will save. I have one more box to open.

I have begun to think in terms of work again, and that without undue suffering. I don't want to get started soon, though. If you think The Trail Driver is good let me know pronto.[13] I do hope so, but I'm doubtful about it. I wrote that under terrific driving stress.

I will write you from Tahiti for this mail.

Love and kisses

Doc

JANUARY 2, 1931

Dearest Dolly,

I got Bob's wireless this morning. He said coming Feb. hurrah. And I say "Hooray." It seems very likely that I will send the Mitchell ladies home, and let Bob and Betty have their stateroom on the yacht. Mrs. Mitchell said quite snippishly that she did not know whether or not she was going on the yacht. I daresay this is because I flagged Francis [Frances] going. I am sure Betty and Mrs. Guild could help Miss C. with the typing. Anyway, that's the dope.

I am well and fine, and almost all that dark horror is gone. I have only one objection to Miss C. and that is the same I have to Betty and her friends. They simply have no modesty. In Miss C's case she is so strikingly beautiful in a bathing suit that the effect is startling. All of which she is surely unconscious of. By the way when I read Bob's wireless to her she clapped her hands, and said "Goody, Goody! More fun!" Which is a pretty true indication of her type.

Well, so long, darling. I'll write from Vauroo Sunday.

Love,

Doc

SUNDAY, LATER

Dearest,

Here's another point. Since the Mitchells are out I'll need a stenographer. Neither B. or Betty can be nailed to a typewriter all day. There will be a lot of such work. So I'm engaging a stenographer friend of Bernices [Berenice's], a

Miss Dorothy Wideman, whose address is 1419 E. Marquette Rd., Chicago. She will not be any expense to me getting to L.A. and she can come on the yacht.

Put her in R.C.'s stateroom, down with Loren and Capt. M. She is also a teacher, and can help Loren with his studies. I shall pay her $10 or $15 a week after she gets here. She will be instructed to write you and phone on her arrival in L.A.

I have wirelessed Ed [Bowen] to start the yacht on March 1. Not earlier. This will save some expenses and she will not arrive too soon.

Darling, I hope I don't have to write any more instructions. Please explain to Bob that Miss Wideman is to have R.C.s stateroom until she arrives here anyway.

Much love,

Doc

Once the arrangements were made, the trip began auspiciously.

JANUARY 14, 1931

Vairoo

Dearest,

Everything fine except the expense problem. Carrie and Berenice have discovered that Mrs. Moran fed my fine stuff to the men last year. We found it out because I let Carrie handle the housekeeping and the Chinese cook. Then the roar went up. They had been accustomed to taking what they wanted from the store room. Now we make Sverre check on everything. I suppose there'll be mutiny, but I don't give a d—. This also put a damper on the Mitchells ordering whatever they wanted for meals. Carrie sure knows her stuff. She's for me, and she and Wallace will save me thousands of dollars.

I caught the first marlin—a dandy of 360 pounds. Also had another on the first day out so have been fishing 4 days. It has rained almost continuously. It's roaring on the roof now. I love it. All same Lacky.

Carrie told me that Mrs. M. [Mrs. Mitchell] said that MKS [Mildred K. Smith] was tremendously interested in my new secretary and wanted to know who and what she was. Mrs. M. did not know of course. But she had to prom-

ise to write M. Carrie said M. thought she knew who it was. Well, she didn't.
Gosh, I hope that old stuff is over!

I have my plan made for "The Lost Wagon Train," and shall begin it soon.
It will be great to hear from you on Jan. 31.

Love and kisses,

Doc

At home Dolly tended to business, making arrangements to acquire
funds to finance Zane's adventures.

Mon. Eve

JAN. 18, 31

Dearest Doc,

I have just finished writing to Harpers on the subject of borrowing $50,000
from them at 6%, and giving them as security an extra book to be published
this year outside of the regular contract, the indebtedness to be paid off by the
receipts from the book, as they come in and from out end too. I think it's a
pretty good scheme, and I don't see how he can turn it down on the basis on
which I put it up to him. If he does that, it will tide us over until I can sell
another story. With what there is left and that, the boat should be paid for and
on its way to you, and I can get this weight off my mind. Its like an old man of
the sea.

I think I'm feeling better altho I am still very tired.

I didn't congratulate you for your birthday, so will do it now. I wish I could
have sent you something but I was too sick. I know that you will feel—and
really be—years and years younger than you have on previous natal days. May
the year bring you happiness in the fulfillment of your cherished plans. Whatever I can contribute to that end, I will.

Much love,

Dolly

(Over)

P.S. This evening's papers have headline of hunger strikes and unemployment parades and rioting in San Francisco. One wouldn't think such things
possible on this West Coast. I wonder when things will ease up? Again: if

Harpers or any one else want your confirmation as to any deals I am making to borrow money, please back me up. I won't do anything not strictly safe and legitimate!

In Tahiti Zane had his annoyances too.

JANUARY 23, 1931
Friday

Dearest Dolly,

It has rained continuously for 10 days—a deluge. My boat was nearly flooded, and I've given up fishing for the present. Here is a fine chance to work on my novel. But I can't yet. Not to see the sun is horribly depressing, and the everlasting roar and drip of rain like Lackawaxen on a November day!

This is the rainy season, they say, and it may last a few weeks. Well, if I last I suppose it'll be OK.

I'd have written you oftener, only I was afraid I'd give away how things are with me. And they are awful. Just think, I haven't the slightest desire to fish and I am appalled at myself. This can't last, of course. Either I shall pull out, and give in, and come home. I have a sort of yearning for you and your comfort, though I'd be ashamed to face you.

I will say for B—that she is not only the loveliest girl I ever knew, but the nicest, sweetest, and finest, in every way. Nevertheless I should never have deluded myself enough to fetch her. I'll tell you why some day. Three weeks tomorrow we have been here. It seems an age. Mrs. M has politely informed friends of Mrs. Guild that she will not go on the yacht without Frances. She knows of course that would come back to me. Frances is really nice, and I could not ask to have a more uneffacing person around. Cappie and Mrs. M., however, do not like the new state of affairs, especially the regularity and economy.

Well, darling, more the next time.

Zane

Zane's problems in Tahiti involved money; however, Berenice and Carrie took matters in hand, eliminating waste that had counted up to thousands of dollars on previous expeditions.

Flower Point

FEB. 4, 1931

Dearest,

Two days more and your birthday. Many happy returns, and I do hope you are your old self again.

There is a new regime here at Flower Point. Bernice has taken over the finances, and things are happening. She has stopped the leaks, the graft, the needless expense. And she is going to cut the whole D—bunch. It is a novelty, for someone beside you, to try to save me money. What did you write this girl? She is inspired. She says "I'll know where every D—red cent goes!" She's a wonder. Well, I'm sort of scared, because pretty soon I'll want some money for something. I'll bet she doesn't give it to me without a good reason.

Everybody has to accept a cut, or walk the plank! This was B's idea. My Gawd, imagine me thinking of such a thing! But it's sense. Maybe Captain Wallace can do the same with the yacht outfit. If so, we'll save a lot.

I am very anxious to get your next month report. Ken reported favorable conditions, bank okay, etc. R.C. said the worst was past. But these are only opinions. Suppose it's not true! I won't borrow trouble, but I'm plainly worried.

I don't think there's any doubt but that I will send The Lost Wagon Train on the April ship. It will be a great novel, and any editor would borrow money to buy it. Then I'll tackle another.

The Mitchell situation grows worse. Mrs. M is the limit. You'd never believe she could be as nasty and catty. I suppose when she finds out that I won't take her—presumably because of her ill health, that she will be furious. I have not had any work for her. And B—thinks she should not be paid for nothing. I gave Cappy $950 in Dec., paying him through Jan. He said he needed money for taxes, interest on loans, installments, etc. Well, he tacked me for $450 in Feb. for the very same expenses, he said. I wouldn't advance it. Then he went to Haw Guild and said I sent him, and asked for $450. Haw let him have $250. Capt. told me he only needed a hundred or so which with what he had would tide over March debts. It's pretty fish, to say the least. I am amazed. Yet this sort of thing isn't new. I can see now how M.K.S. put all these things over for the Mitchells. And now they won't work. I like Cappy as a fishing partner, and really need him for that. But I doubt if he is really worth so much money as

I've been paying him. I see it now. I've been a sucker, as usual. Well, there does not seem to be much change of my continuing one. For which we can thank Miss C—

I'll write again soon.

Love,

Doc

After their wedding February 16, Betty and Bob Carney sailed for Tahiti to join her father for the cruise on board *Fisherman II*. There was some difficulty in communicating exact departure and arrival dates, particularly with the lag in mail, so Zane was not certain they were coming until they actually arrived in Papeete February 28.

Camp 2:30

FEBRUARY 28, 1931

My Poor Darling,

I was so glad to see Betty and Bob that I could not speak. Really had given up! Some Tahitian who once worked for me (and stole from me) said "Your son is on board!" I forgave him for being a thief.

The ship was docked when I got there. Betty looks stunning, so well and happy. Bob looked like a million dollars. They were dippy. The Guilds, the Mitchells, came on board, and of course Berenice was with me. Maybe she wasn't glad to see Betty! We had a grand lunch at Guilds then motored out to camp. Bob and Betty enchanted with their cabin.

I am distressed about your illness. R.C. gave me a bad report about you. Said you did not recover as you once did! My God, Dolly, "are you flopping on me" as the grave robber said to his wife? It positively shrivels me up to think of all you've gone through. Dearest, for my sake, if for no one else's, brace up and be your old self!

All accounts of the wedding were received here with thrills. I'm glad it was so nice. Ida raved. And now our baby Betty is a wife. Dolly, where are we? Loren's letter was a scream. That kid will keep me pepped up.

According to Bob and R.C. the yacht is a peach. But great heaven, how can I be happy on a thing that has crucified you? All this talk about flu and

antrums is baloney. You had a breakdown! I can't think about the yacht now.
Maybe later I'll write what I think.

The first letter I opened was only an enclosed clipping of a picture of B—
published in the N.Y. Times, with an announcement of the proposed trip on
the yacht and her work at writing up the log, etc. The photo was fine, and the
write-up very nice. But this clipping had been sent to Mildred from N.Y. by
Claire. I recognized her handwriting and—wrote on the margin the rottenest,
vilest, most poisonest and hideous words I ever read applied to me. I was sick
in an instant. More about this later.

All will be well with me now, dear. I couldn't fall down now. I would never
let you sacrifice all that and suffer as you have suffered, and not make up for
it. That part of your distress due to financial difficulty I can remedy, thank God,
by work, and I'll do it. The rest you must trust me for. Bernice is a God-send. I
regret the letter and the need of the radio replies. But they relieved the situation. Darling, your faint satire was lost upon me. The readjustment to a new
condition has been a terrific strain. But it is done now, and you are still alive,
and according to Ida and R.C. on the mend. Why didn't you tell me?

I will be keen to have your next letters, about the yacht, your trip to Frisco,
and lastly the financial situation. Ed did not say much. But I see that he wants
to get the D—yacht off his hands. No wonder! You have both been sportsmen
in the finest sense of the word.

No more news. Tomorrow I'll write again. My faithful and wonderful wife.

Ever your

Doc

Perhaps because his daughter would soon join the entourage, Zane informed Dolly that his relationship with Berenice had entered a new phase.
Berenice evidently began her employment as Zane's assistant, but that relationship developed into something additional. In a letter dated February
16, Dolly wrote,

You pulled a boner by putting air-mail stamps on your important mail. They
didn't arrive til this morning (Monday) and all the letters with plain stamps
arrived Saturday noon. Consequently I couldn't send wire to you till today, and

didn't know what you were driving at and had terrible nightmares about it all and was afraid to open your letters this a.m. You can certainly think up queer and awful situations to put me into. I supposed I should say "God bless you, my children." However, since its nothing more than I expected, it wasn't a shock. But to ask my permission! And after it was "fait accompli." Tell Berenice I'm too sick to write her this time, but not to worry about my reaction.

On February 17 Zane wrote to Dolly, quoting her radio,

Your radio just came. "yes, okay, provided boat sails. Love, Dolly." I didn't get the "boat sails" but the rest was enough. Thanks, Dolly dear. You are a brick, a thoroughbred, a wonderful woman, a magnificent wife. And I love you till it hurts like hell.

The Berenice situation settled, Zane faced another distressing and potentially embarrassing situation with Captain Laurie Mitchell and his wife. The friendship between them stretched back over ten years to just after World War I. Mitchell, originally from Britain, had settled in Canada, marrying a French-Canadian woman.[14] Grey had met him while fishing off the coast of Nova Scotia. Like Zane, he was an avid fisherman, at one time holding a world record for tuna. He became a friend and an employee, in charge of Zane's boats and other property in Tahiti. Mitchell and his wife were also quite friendly with Mildred and remained so even after the relationship between Mildred and Zane had soured. This contributed to the problem. The friendship cooled on this trip, and as time went on matters became worse, ultimately coming to a head in an ugly confrontation.

When fishing off New Zealand, Zane had given orders that Mitchell was to stay nearby, at least within sight with the glasses.[15] But when Mitchell went out, he gave the order to his boatman to go on out to sea and leave the rest. The boatman said he was sorry, but Zane had given him orders to stay within sight. Mitchell was reported to have said, "I get enough of the damn Yankee blighter at night at camp without having him all day too." Evidently some other negative statements had been reported to Zane. Mitchell sensed the coolness in Zane, probably having some idea of what was happening

from the Guilds, and took an opportunity to speak to him, offering a reconciliation, but Zane refused to talk to him. Zane then wrote him a letter stating that he did not like the way Mitchell had been fishing and that he expected him to be in sight and photograph and get material for the book
with him. He also told him that he could not consider taking him on the
cruise unless he would accept a substantial cut and he could not pay Mrs.
Mitchell a hundred a month after this month, as he had no work for her.
He concluded with the statement, "If it's impossible for an Englishman to
have a friendship with an American, then for Christ's sake say so and let's
end this farce." He did not wish to discuss it but wanted Mitchell only to
indicate yes or no. The Mitchells did not appear for breakfast. They came
to lunch, but Zane did not. Later Mitchell and his daughter, Frances, went
to town. The next evening Zane received a letter from his attorney on Tahiti,
Brault, asking him to come in immediately. Mitchell had been in to see
Brault and another lawyer and intended to sue Zane for all or a portion of
a year and a half's wages. While there was no contract, there were letters
that indicated an expectation of employment. Mitchell could tie up Zane's
boats for months.

A meeting was arranged, and the attorney tried to negotiate a compro-
mise. Zane said he could afford no more than two hundred a month, but
Mitchell said he could not live on that. Past offenses and perceived insults
were aired. The ante was raised to three hundred a month, with Zane sending Mrs. Mitchell and Frances back to the States, paying half of Frances's
expenses. With some prodding from the attorney, Mitchell agreed to this,
but he later reneged.

MARCH 15, 1931

Dearest Dolly,

I have written pretty hot letters to Bowen, R.C., etc. and guess I'd better
cool off to write you.

The facts in the Mitchell case are these. After I called him for failing to do
his duty by me in the fishing, he quit, and left the camp with his women. I did
not discharge him. He went to the British consul and a Papeete lawyer. My
lawyer, Brault, effected a reconciliation in which Mitchell accepted $300 a

month, and would go alone. Subsequently he went back on that, as I wrote you, and then came the frame-up on Miss C. and scheme to get Mildred back in dominance of the situation. It failed.

Well, I could not risk a trial with Mitchell here, and had to settle paying him $2685, and also giving him my new launch Skyblue II which he took as equivalent for cash $5150. She cost $6500. Now they are trying to get me to sign papers making this money an indemnity for discharging him. Also trying to get me to sign over the tackle Mitchell kept. All because they are leary now of an action in California. Mitchell snorted at my hint of so doing. "You can't stand the publicity!" Meaning of course he will throw dirt, and give to the newspapers stuff that would disgrace Mildred and Miss C and ruin me. Oh, he is surely a fine type of English Gentleman. I am absolutely certain now that he is a liar and a thief. He was drunk twice that we know of, and evidently drank right along.[16] I am well rid of the Mitchells and the Guilds, and despite being gouged for so much I am still the gainer on the whole cruise by around $5000.

He is selling my fishing tackle here. You remember that he did that before, and that I bought back one of the reels. This is a bitter pill for me to swallow. I sure would like to know what a court would say to the tackle question, the expense fetching the Kallisto around, the disappearance of the supplies, and this extortion of $8000 and more on salary unearned or uncontracted for. But if he can get the papers to print that he quit because my morals were such that he could not allow his wife and daughter to stay in my camp or on my yacht, and such rot as that, I think he'd better be left alone. Of course, he may publish that sort of thing whether I sue him or not. He is rotten enough. Mildred, like a damned idiot, told him her relation to me, and so he can prove it.[17] He would not care about ruining her, or anybody. So it is a delicate matter for you to decide.

I'll bet Ed and Ken will hop. Frances called Ed a "low-down dirty skunk." And Mitchell accused them of getting rich off you. That's funny. Mitchell is a stupid, bull-headed, treacherous Englishman. That says it all. He is also weak. He is dominated by the women of his illustrious family. They are all anti-American. He had everything to gain and nothing to lose by standing by me. So had the Guilds. But they quit. Well, so far as fishing is concerned, they never will be heard of again. I'll be in $25,000 a year (counting Miss S—

expenses) and I can spend that on my own kids.[18] I don't think I'll suffer greatly at the loss.

I'll write more, of course, before the next northbound steamer leaves. I hope to heaven you are well and O.K. once more. I'm worried about you. This will be a long week, waiting for the yacht, Loren, and news.

All my love,
Doc

He wrote again on March 16 that the matter was closed, the papers signed, and the check and deed for the launch handed over. He added gleefully that Mitchell could not sell the boat as he had thought he could.

Berenice noted, in a letter to Dolly, that one of Zane's concerns in this whole mess was Mildred and her opinion. She wrote,

The night we had Brault's letter, Zane said, "Well, if he goes back on this next boat and talks I'll certain write some letter to Miss Smith." It seemed to have absolutely no bearing on the situation so I asked why. "If he goes back and tells her I'll certainly want to tell her my side of it." Even as he said it he had the strangest, far away look and I honestly don't think he was conscious of what he said or how it sounded to me. I changed the subject. For him I think it is pitiful that he should still care for one who has caused such havoc in his life.

At the end of the letter, she added,

Going back to the story again I think I'd better tell you, to justify Doc regarding what he said, that at all other times when he has talked to me of the lady he seems to hate her intensely. I don't believe there is immediate danger of his changing his mind about her.[19]

The yacht finally arrived, bringing Loren with it, and the Grey outfit set sail on what was supposed to be a grand cruise. But even in calm seas, the *Fisherman II* rolled badly.

Dearest,

I don't know what kind of a letter I can write on this rolling B—of a ship, but I'll try. The sea is not rough, just a little trade wind, but Oh, my God, how this boat rolls. B has been in bed all the way and so have some others. Betty is green in the face. Some of the men very sick. I am feeling rotten. I don't know what on earth (or sea) we'll ever do in a storm. We just had an unpleasant incident. They washed the deck above. Our portholes were screwed tight shut yet the dirty water poured in to spoil beds, etc. I think we will find that the L.A. Ship Co. gypped me plenty.

Please deposit this check to my account. That will leave me just about even, or maybe a little overdrawn. I will hardly be able to cash a check in Suva. But I still have a little currency which I can use.

If you have not mailed me some money you will have to cable me some. I'll send you a radio. By the way, those radios of mine have been mostly baloney. I'm afraid I'll have to quit sending them, or else tell the truth. The fact is that I am so disappointed and discouraged, I'd quit but for the kids. They are having a swell time.

I have not been able to write while at sea. That is a great blow to me, because so much time will be wasted. While we are at anchor I'll want to fish and prowl around the reefs. And I had hoped to keep up my writing while we were moving. Why, I can't sit in a chair! There is a good deal radically wrong with the yacht, Dolly. It must be the small boats. But she would not be of any use to me if I couldn't carry them.

This, of course, is just the beginning of the cruise for me. Perhaps I can work out things.

The Tongas were beautiful islands. I would have liked to stay there weeks. We reach Suva tomorrow, where we pick up fuel and water, and then go on to New Caledonia. My catching the world record sailfish, 1170 lbs., beating Mitchell's set me up again. If I can only get hold of myself! But I have so much to bear. I am down to 136 pounds, and going down. I have some kind of infection on my left arm. Itches like hell. Hope I haven't leprosy.

All your radios have been depressing. We get the press news. And there are

many claims that conditions are better in the U.S. and bound to improve. Anyone would think you wanted to keep me in the blues.

I hope you are well, and that Romer and Dot, and the kid are fine.[20] We
never hear a word about them. It's kind of tough.

The Mitchells are due in Frisco today. I think I'm worried about what that
yellow dog will put in the papers. Will write from Suva.

Love and kisses,

Doc

Money problems, Mildred, the Mitchell mess, and disappointment in
the *Fisherman II,* the center of so many of his dreams, to say nothing of what
had been spent on it, by some accounts over three hundred thousand dollars, made this trip one of the worst Zane had undertaken.[21]

July 10, 1931

550 miles off San Pedro

After six months of strife in the south seas I am nearing home, worn out in
body, but still unquenchable in spirit. This trip has been remarkable for
trouble. Despite its one great white light it has ended in failure. My financial
ruin appears certain and otherwise I am facing the crisis of my life. I am prepared for the worst, and know my clear stern resolve. I will not be crushed by
all this disaster, this continuous disaster from last October to the present, one
thing following another in augmenting fatality. Life, of course, is uncertain.
But while I have it, and the flame still burns, I laugh at mistakes, betrayals,
troubles, hates.[22]

He docked in California shortly afterward and stayed in Altadena through
most of August with some time at Catalina. In September he tried Idaho for
material for a book but also to hunt and fish. He took Betty and Bob, Romer
and Dorothy, and Berenice. He wrote Dolly from Myer's Cove, near Challis.

SEPTEMBER 14, 1931

Dearest Dolly,

All fine and dandy, except the expense. I can't keep it down. Today we
came back from the lake, and tomorrow will go into the forest. We had to get
a permit from the Governor.

The kids are wonderfully well and happy. I hate to think of quitting now, when we just got started. I never saw Betty so handsome. Dot is simply wild with pleasure and thrill. Berenice came and she makes the thing fine for me.

If I was not so worried about you, I would be happy myself. R.C. will read my letter to you. The Smith thing is rotten. Perhaps you have read the stuff—the latest. Bob's mother wrote him.

But to come back to the unpleasant financial thing. Today I made more bills. Gorden $59.60, gas and oil. Hunting license $174.00 and money to everybody. I will be overdrawn by Oct. 10, when I settle up, if you don't clap some money to my account. Where in God's name you will get it I don't know. But I have a blind faith in you. These bad days you seem my prop and inspiration.

One good thing at least, my dear. This awful mess I have drawn us into makes me realize my blunder and your loyalty and love. Don't ever think they are wasted. I never loved you so well or so gratefully. Write me to Myer's Cove, via Challis, Idaho. And tell Loren to write also.

With infinite love,

Doc

A dispute over federal income tax complicated their money woes. Dolly had worked on the taxes for the past ten years to try to iron out the situation. The dilemma centered on what could and could not be deducted as business expenses. Grey wanted to deduct the yacht, his fishing and hunting equipment, and trips that were connected with business in some way. The Internal Revenue Service did not see it his way, even though Grey was writing, publishing, and earning money from books based upon his travels. In 1922 Dolly paid eleven thousand dollars for past-due income tax.[23] In 1923 I.R.S. officials demanded the Greys' papers and account books.[24] The Greys hired a man to help them with the taxes, and Masters acted as a go-between, not letting Zane see the officers (which would have been disastrous) and going himself to San Francisco to try to iron it out. Finally, an inspector was sent to talk to Zane. Dolly was away, however, and Zane refused to talk to him, having his friend Wiborn talk to him instead, as Wiborn was good at "jollying such guys."[25] As he wrote in 1924, Zane detested the tax, the Internal Revenue Service, and more.

Dearest,

   Your mention of the income tax, and a glance over this Tribune statement, made me freeze my gizzard. If they stop our equal division, and my expenses, as seems probable, I will be ruined. I think it monstrous that I have to pay an enormous sum out of my earned income to a pack of political hounds. Have you read the latest disclosures from Washington? That oil scandal! It is enough to make a real American lose his head. The times are bad. The war left greed, selfishness, lawlessness, and crookedness paramount in the hearts of almost all men. I fear my patriotism has been dealt a blow from which it will never recover again. Life is a battle—a fight against your fellow men, just as much as life in the sea, or on the desert, or in the jungle, it is a struggle for existence. If I would dwell upon that I would lose my idealism. But I forget, and in that there is hope.

Love,

Doc

In 1922 the Greys paid forty-four thousand dollars in income taxes.[26] By 1924 the amount required was fifty-four thousand dollars. As Zane's income increased, so did his taxes and so did the struggle with the Internal Revenue Service. In November 1931 Dolly and Zane went to Washington to contest the government claim that they owed four hundred thousand dollars in unpaid income tax.[27] As soon as they arrived they received an invitation from President Hoover, for Hoover was a Zane Grey fan. They were invited to lunch with the president and the first lady and remained talking until four o'clock in the afternoon.[28]

This did not resolve the matter. The Internal Revenue Service continued to examine Zane's finances and demand back taxes. Nor did it help his financial situation. Magazines, with their cash flow restricted, would not pay as much for stories, and when they bought them they were more demanding than ever before. *McCall's* had him write and rewrite, mainly to stall payment.[29] Zane signed with RKO Pictures but would not receive any money from that until September 1932. Having nothing to spend, he stayed in California and worked on three novels, *Thunder Mountain, Knights of the Range,* and *Wyoming,* all written in the winter and spring of 1931–32.

In late May and early June he traveled to Roseburg, Oregon, to fish the Umpqua River and there was hit with a crisis. Berenice, who had accompanied him to Tahiti the year before and to Idaho, had left his employ to get married. Zane had been infatuated with her, and for a time she had replaced Mildred in his work and also in his affections. She now pressed him for payment of a contract he had foolishly signed and threatened to take the matter to court, which would result in devastating negative publicity. Zane's books were marketed as works that could be read by all ages, that were safe for children and adolescents, and above all, that promoted middle-class values: endurance, honesty, chastity, family. Should it be made public that Zane's own life was not based on these standards, he would be ruined. At this particular juncture, when the nation's businesses, including the great publishing houses and the magazines that bought Zane's work, were reeling from blow after financial blow, it was difficult enough to sell the works of even established authors like Zane. Such publicity could be his death knell. Dolly was horrified.

JUNE 9, 1932

Dearest Doc,

I received your letter today, and am glad for what pleases you and sorry for what does not. I am rather edgy as I've had a very hard week with work on income tax and a lot of business that was none too pleasant. Then just now Berenice telephoned me (from Frisco) at length about the contract you'd made with her and the fact that you had returned her letter (with signs that you had read it). That phone call must have cost her a small fortune because she kept on gabbling so long.

I have always told you to refuse to accept letters at the source or even to take them and not read them. Anyway, she told me a lot about that contract and that you had insisted on it (to protect her, you said) and that there was no stipulation in the contract that if she left you, you were not to pay it, and that now she needed the money very badly because she had told Harry he could go to school, etc. on it. And now she couldn't pay the bill, etc., etc.

I told her I know nothing about it except what you'd told me and that was that the contract was to be in force only if she remained with you. However, that isn't the way you wrote it, and she has you on it, and suggested putting the matter in her attorney's hands. I told her that would create a lot of unpleasant publicity for herself as well as for us, and she said yes, it would. However, she didn't say she wouldn't do it. She said you even wanted to give her 15% and 10% and she said 5% was enough. I told her that you had said that the jewelry and stuff you gave her was valuable and she said it didn't amount to more than a couple of hundred. I said, "How about the ring with the three diamonds?" (Anderson, which you told me you gave her) and she said she never had anything of the sort. I told her in my income tax return, I would apply the Ford and typewriter against that debt, but she said they were presents! However, I shall still do it. That Ford was in my name.

I told her we had no money, which is true enough, and I told her I couldn't do anything, that the matter was between you and her—which it is. This is some of your dirty linen I can't wash, I'm afraid, old dear. I told her I'd write to you and she said she'd write again and telegraph you and this time I advise you not to incense her by sending back her stuff. You'd better calm her down some way—not threateningly, for she's the kind that would cause trouble and untoward publicity. Tell her that though you didn't mention it in the contract, it was hypothecated on the fact that she was to remain with you, and that you felt all you had given her and which she had not offered to return would surely settle any obligation—which you didn't think there was. I don't know—you have to be very careful. It's a dirty Mess—but at least don't inflame her as you've been doing. Tell her that even if she did put it in the hands of her attorney, your present lack of funds would nullify any attempt on his part, and that usually attorneys mean suits, and any suit would be just as bad for her as for you—that is if she mentions attorneys to you.

And if you ever make a contract again, God help you. You've done it to your sorrow and confusion several times. Look beyond the end of your nose— or your infatuation. Don't put anything in writing. I think we'd better have a regular partnership agreement that no contract you sign regarding your literary output is valid unless I sign it. Not that it will do me any good, but it may protect you. Human relations are unstable, my dear. A few you have proven—life and the years have proven them, but for you to fatuously put yourself in the hands of people like Mildred and Berenice proves that you need a guardian.

Well, I don't know what more to say on the subject. Not knowing the contents of her letter, I don't know how to counter it. You might talk to Romer. He has a legal mind. I can think of many defenses if it actually came to court, but that is unthinkable because of the stink it would make. And after all, you made the contract. You insisted on a written contract when you could have given her money if you wanted to. Same way Smith. And it's bound you and never her and after all, very little of that story was hers. I pruned most of her stuff out of it. But by signing that contract you admitted that she had much more to do with it than she actually did—and that is bad enough.

Hereafter, my dear, let the literary end of things remain strictly in the family. Here's an angle that has just come to mind. Half of all profits are supposed to be mine under the partnership. Therefore if she enforced the contract she could perhaps only get 5% of your share of the profits and a lot of things could be charged against the profits. Just how was that contract worded? And perhaps in view of the partnership, your signing was not even legal. I don't know.

I am intensely weary. All day yesterday, from 7:15 a.m. when I had to leave here, I was downtown until 10 p.m. I was honor guest (with Mary Pickford) at the Women's Banking Convention (500 women from all over the U.S. at breakfast in the big ballroom of the Biltmore). I was the only woman bank president there. I don't know if there are any more of the species. Anyway, I was amused to find that it is quite distinguished. God knows, I never wanted the doubtful honor, but it was forced upon me. Well, "me and Mary Pickford" had to do considerable autographing. Seriously, though, it was an impressive and inspiring gathering and I was glad I went. But between you and me, the fact that I was Mrs. Zane Grey counted for ever so much more than being a woman bank president—even though the combination seemed overpowering! Tell the kids. It's funny, I think. Had quite a talk with Mr. Giannini, and that was important.[30]

Well, we've weathered a lot of storms, but presently we'll be riding serenely again. But sign no more papers!

Lots of love,
Dolly

Her lengthy letters speak eloquently of the work she did for Zane, not only handling his business affairs, but also cleaning up the remnants of his indiscretions.

JULY 22, 1931

Dearest Doc,

Even if I had been up to it, I would not have had the time to write you these last two weeks. The kids in college have what they call "Hell Week." Well, the last week or so has been my "Hell Week" and then some. In the first place I was in court for two long hot days being sued for a deficiency judgement on a trust deed on some property I had to let go and lost the case. But there was some crooked work and we may be able to appeal. Then everybody to whom we still owe money has been getting after us, particularly Hoyns on the Corn Exchange Note for $38,000. I told him it was absolutely impossible to pay off anything at this time, and why. There has been voluminous correspondence on that and apparently this thing is making it difficult for Harper's to borrow the money they need to carry their booksellers, etc., etc. I explained our situation very carefully to him, and that we were conserving every possible cent to get out of the woods and on our feet again, but it apparently didn't have much effect. Then I wondered if by chance you had written him or Briggs about your New Zealand plans, etc. It has an exceedingly bad effect on all creditors to even know that you are on a fishing trip. They don't understand these things. I try to explain that your expeditions are being financed with an end to motion pictures.

Then, as I said before, everyone else got after me. Everything that could possibly go wrong went that way, until I had that terrible madhouse feeling again. I thought "if I can only get over to Catalina for the week end, I can shake it off," and then who should walk in but Berenice and her husband! Well, my dear, that is a serious situation, and one which you certainly handled in the worst kind of a way from its inception. She brought me a photographic copy of that note you had made to her. Why, when you were at it, didn't you sign away your whole future, your family and tell her she had written all your stories, past, present, and future? Because you sent back her letter and wrote her harshly, she was about ready to take the thing to court, and believe me, if she does, you will get all the worst of it with that note, and with what she can prove. You couldn't get to first base with her opposing you with a jury. Your contention that you would pay her only if she stayed with you was not mentioned in the note, and if you tried to pull that argument, it would boil down to your infatuation for her, and all the dirt that would follow upon that. It would be unspeakable, a thing you could not afford. You could never hold onto Wanda under such circumstances.[31] Do you remember how you worded that note? Among other things you gave her practically all the credit for the book "for the plot, incident, dialogue, and inspiration" to quote. You know that none of the story was finally hers. Well, we talked and talked, and she was more or less adamant. I said it was none of my business and that you had repudiated the matter. Her husband was there all the time, and that more or less tied my tongue. We got nowhere that day and I had to leave for Catalina with the manuscript. I told her I would get in touch with you again to see what could be done, and we left it at that. Then I came over here, but I could not sleep all night and I finally worked out something. So I went back again Sunday, phoned her and said I wanted to speak to her alone, that there were certain things that the presence of her husband prohibited me from saying because I wanted to give her a break. She said it wasn't necessary as her husband knew everything, but she consented, nevertheless. So she came, and I put certain things up to her pretty flatly, things that I know she wouldn't want her husband to know, even if he did know everything, as she said. I made her a proposition to give her my note in place of yours, for that is a very incriminating document, and I stressed the surety of my note as opposed to your repudiation. I got it down to a discussion of a settlement for $1500 over a period of time, and she sort of wavered on that, as I explained that I considered the Ford and typewriter as part of that payment. Then her husband, who was again called in at this juncture, happened to mention the 10% you had promised on royalties, and she was all off again. Well, there was no use discussing it further at that time, as I was getting all on edge, so I said I'd write her my proposition—which I have done. If she does not accept, we'll have to settle with her in some other way. She doesn't balk at a lawsuit, except as a matter of inconvenience and expense. I think she'd love all that publicity as to her contribution to your writing and being your "literary assistant" and you surely gave her plenty to work on and to sustain her in that note. Also she has the letter in which you promised to divorce me and marry her. I laughed at that when she told me (although I felt more like weeping) and said you just said that to get her back at that time. But there, if she wanted to use it, she has the basis of a breach of promise suit against you, and despite her marriage, it could be worked up very nicely. But I am sure she is not unscrupulous, although if this thing ever comes to court action she'll use any weapons she can—and I'd bet she'd put it over with any jury, even of women. But that is what we will have to avoid—or what I will, for I've again had to take the burden upon myself. Her husband is pretty decent about the whole thing, and says it is her business, not his, unless it comes to a law-suit, in which case he would have to take a hand and back her up. He, too, resented your attitude, although he did not say so in so many words.

Now, my dear, for a little summing up. You promised me never again, after that Smith involvement, to give any papers or documents to anyone. But you went ahead and did it, and never even kept a copy so that I could have some-thing to work upon. If she had not given me that photograph of your note, I would have been absolutely at a loss to know how to proceed. Now I know the absolute necessity of getting back that paper in some way or other. Then you again leave me at a loss by telling me untruths or half truths about the whole situation. I am not nosy. I don't want to know things that don't concern me. Mostly they are exceedingly painful for me. But if, when this business came up, and we discussed it, you could have given me a little more informa-tion, I could perhaps have advised you so that things would not have come to this pass. Bernice denies ever getting any valuable jewelry from you. She said she sold one ring for $45, but when I mentioned the three diamonds of Mrs. Anderson's ring, she denied ever having seen them. Moreover, she said she spent $800 of her own savings to bring her brother out here. You told me you had paid all his expenses. It puts me at a disadvantage to make certain claims and then to be told you had lied about them. I know she had jewelry, money, and clothes from you, but she minimizes that. Now I want you to make a list of everything you ever gave her, what it cost, so far as you can remember, and everything she got outside of her salary. I want unvarnished, unembroi-dered facts. I may not be able to prove anything, but at least I can have the psychological advantage of knowing what I am talking about and being able to state facts. This fencing around and making assertions that you are not sure of gets one into deeper trouble. To give the devil his due, I don't think Berenice is at all unscrupulous, but she went ahead with certain arrangements for her brother that she has to pay for. Then her husband cannot, during this bad period, make any collections, and they have even had to move into a cheaper apartment, so that he can not help her.

If by any chance she writes you again, send the letter to me, and not back to her. There is nothing that so infuriates people and makes them your enemies. I'll do my best to get you out of this thing now, but so help me God, if you ever again sign any papers with anyone, I'll do something drastic. I am doing everything I possibly can, in every way, to pull us out of a dangerous situation, but I must have some cooperation from you.

I feel fairly cheerful again and determined not to let anything get me down. I am sorry that I have to write you all these things but I don't see how it can be avoided. You will have to do your share toward keeping us off the rocks, and face the situation courageously and cheerfully. If I could bear the burden alone, I would do so cheerfully, but I can't so you must help, if only to the extent of not undermining what I have been able to build up. And lastly, please forgive my rotten typing. I have had to go very fast and not stop for mistakes. My love to the Wiborns and Wanda, and much for my firstborn and yourself.

Still your

Wife

P.S. The next time you offer to get a divorce from me, let me know, will you?

The book in question was *Wyoming*. Berenice claimed she had contributed and thus was entitled to a share of the royalties according to the contract Zane had written. Dolly said she had edited out all of Berenice's contributions. In fact the story was based largely on Berenice's youthful adventures when she hitchhiked to the West. Dolly was able to settle with Berenice for $1,500, and the matter was never taken to court, nor was there any negative publicity about it. Zane's career and reputation were saved, thanks to Dolly.

Zane's gratitude was short lived, for his pride was injured. He really did not understand economic conditions, those of the nation or his own, so he did not appreciate all that Dolly was doing to keep the family solvent. He began to suspect that there was a conspiracy to keep him short of funds and that his business was mismanaged. Prompting this concern was Dolly's wish to incorporate, which would give Zane less control but might avoid bankruptcy. He wrote Dolly to that effect from Oregon. Her patience finally snapped, and she wrote a blistering letter.

AUGUST 20, 1932

Dear Doc,

Bob just brought down your letter from the P.O. Frankly, it has made me feel pretty bad, and I think I have just about enough misery without getting it from you. For three years now, we have been fighting a very terrible situation caused, not by our own blunderings, which were bad enough, but by an economic condition that has affected the whole world. The battlefield is strewn with the dead and dying but we are still fighting on, and victory is now in sight. We cannot let down unless we want to lose entirely, but if you think you and Romer or anyone else can carry it on better than the present "lineup," I shall be more than happy to be relieved of the responsibility. I am pretty tired. I have been on this job day and night for several years, watching and studying every angle. I have no brief for Bowen. He has made just as bad mistakes as the rest of us, but he has learned and profited by those mistakes in experience to the point of not making them or any similar ones again. He has handled our creditors as no one else I know could or would have handled them. Even now they have continuously to be placated and soothed. If you wish that job, you may have it. I won't do that. That business is so humiliating to me that it drives me wild to think of it. Romer might be able to do it, but he has shown no conspicuous success in his own affairs, and has had so much adverse publicity that people don't trust him, merely because of that. To the general public he is still Zane Grey's son, the son of a rich man who has gotten himself into all sorts of messes. Romer has learned an awful lot, but he still has to show it and to deliver the goods. I love my son, and it is my greatest hope that he will develop his potentialities—but I don't agree with him that they are along the lines of running this corporation. We are still a long way from being out of the woods, and this is not the time to throw a monkey wrench into the business, which you are well on the way to doing when you write such letters to me as this one. Do you, by the wildest stretch of imagination, think that I am doing all this for myself, or perchance for Bowen? What am I working for, if not for you and the children, to pull all this out of the fire. And what will Bowen get if he does not make a success of what he is trying to do? He gets a fair salary now, but believe me, he earns every cent of it. He is liked and respected by all people with whom he has business dealings, except perhaps a few whose personal deals he has crabbed because they were not good for the corporation. I did not take the final steps in the formation of this corporation until our attorneys—Lloyd Wright himself—assured me that he considered it the only way to save our bacon.

I have admitted to you that you were not the only factor in our downfall—that I got into some pretty bad messes, for which I myself was to blame, but I also claim, that if things had gone on as they had been, if the book market and the magazine market and the movie market had not failed, if the bottom had not dropped out of real estate and investments and securities, if cities and counties and even the United States had not almost gone bankrupt, we would never have known the difference. I know that 90% of my own investments were perfectly sound and that under ordinary circumstances, I would have made a lot of money on some of them. We still have some good real estate and that, as much as anything, caused the Corporation Commissioner to grant us our charter. I admit and so does everyone else, that your name and reputation and literary output far outshadows these other things in potential value, but they are what are called intangibles, and legal minded people are wary of intangibles. I heard Mary Pickford make a plea to bankers on that very subject.

You say you asked Romer three questions. If you asked him 300 you could not get at the root of this business. I suggest that you study this situation thoroughly, that you make all possible investigation, that you attend directors meetings in our attorney's offices, that you go into the details of what we have done and accomplished, and then if you are satisfied that the "lineup" is not right, that you get someone else to run the business that will satisfy you better. You may agree with Romer that he is the one. You may think that some stranger, at an enormously larger salary, would take the personal interest that Bowen and I have done, that would work day and night, regardless of time and weariness, that would lose precious hours of sleep figuring and wondering how in the world to solve all the problems that arose. Possibly now that the worst is over, someone else could take the responsibility and make a go of it. I am not even sure of that. I tried to get your brother to come in as director foreseeing this very situation, so that he could know everything that transpired and everything that was going on, so that I wouldn't be the goat and get thrown at me that I was unduly influenced. But Rome's own affairs were in such bad shape that he was unable to enter into it, or get permission to do so from the people with whom he was tied up. I have never shirked responsibility, but I thought that if he got in you would take his word for what we were accomplishing and doing, and not have to rely on mine, or on that of others who were adversely influenced. If you are not satisfied with Bowen's conduct of the business, you are at perfect liberty to make any change you wish, but at least, you must be fair to him, and just not say you don't want to talk to him or see him or have anything to do with him. If you are dissatisfied, or wish to make accusations, or to kick him out, come out with it and be straight and above board. It is your business and your corporation and you should be intelligent about it. We can no longer look back and wail about mistakes we have made in the past. It will take everything we have to meet the future. I say, let the dead past bury its dead. That's what I intend to do. I have had more grief and trouble than I could absorb, and I am going to make a change. I shall no longer be motivated by fear, as I have in the past. All of you have taught me a rather bitter lesson and that is that I can get along alone. As a matter of fact, it's what I have been doing most of the time. The business is my responsibility and as long as I am connected with it I shall do my very best, and shall see that everyone else does the right thing. If I am relieved of that, it may be relief to quit. I have been in that office on every business day since you left, I have watched everything minutely, and I know just what is going on. Personally, I think it would be extremely dangerous to make any changes at the present time, but rather than have you distrust the present setup, lack confidence in Bowen, I would tell him myself to get out.

You can do as you please, but ask yourself just what plans you have that are constructive, if you do not wish to go on in this way. I wish you could spend a week, or even a day in the office and see all the problems that have to be met, and most of them connected directly with you and your properties, income taxes, boats, books, pictures, etc. At last we are really beginning to get a little organization into things. Take foreign translations, for instance. Harper's handled that, and payed commissions to several different agents besides what they got. Now we are getting to making our own negotiations and contracts and ought to increase that revenue substantially when conditions improve. It was absolutely haphazard heretofore, and there was no way for me to do anything. That is only one small thing. I could tell you dozens of ways that we have saved money and put things on an efficient basis through the organization. As a matter of fact, we could use several more people to work in the office and could keep them busy. More and more we shall be able to make the best of our assets, and to develop new ones. This Zane Grey business is really an enormous one and has grown too unwieldy for me to handle by myself. The income tax alone drove me crazy. I have worked for months with Doyle on it, am still doing so, but now he has it well in hand and is relieving me of the terrible responsibility of it. In fact he has already saved us about $8000 that we would have had to pay on the 1929 tax.

I could go into endless details on the multitudinous things that affect us and how we are handling them. They are day to day and hour to hour problems that no one who does not live with them and has not lived with them constantly can understand and handle to the best advantage. For instance, would you be willing to turn over to some stranger the handling of all your literary work, contracts, the knowledge that I have gained of this end of it in 25 or more years? The situation is a ticklish one, even for you. If it is not handled with the utmost finesse, disaster may result. And just because of conditions. Yours is still the most popular of all names, but it has to be kept that way, continually built up and enhanced. That is one of the jobs of the corporation. I found out why Harper's would not publish a July book for you. It was because they brought out this other western, I am sure.

Well, it's up to you. Either you will have to trust me and my judgment, have faith in the organization and those who are working in it, or find someone to take my place. "A house divided against itself will fall." It's a new deal all around and those that are going to continue to wallow in the past and its errors, are going to fall by the wayside. And don't think that I wouldn't be willing to lay down this burden and see if I still can't find a life of my own to live. But I wouldn't be a quitter on what I consider my job. But if you thought I was not fit any longer, that I was capable of being "unduly influenced," why that would be the time for me to stop. It would let me out without hurt to my own conscience.

If this business comes through with young Vanderbilt, you and Romer will have your hands entirely full. You had better consider this in connection with making any changes in your business organization, for you would have to be on the job. Have you considered into whose hands you would put everything? Do you know of anyone who would carry on while you were going around the world? Those are the questions that you must ask yourself and to which you must find the answers. I don't think I would be capable of doing it all over again with a new set up. I don't think I could ever teach and instruct and work with and agonize over a new organization, aside entirely from incurring the danger of wrecking this one by abandoning all we have so painfully built up. You would have to take the responsibility for that yourself.

Sometimes I think I would have much more peace if I ditched it all, but it would be such a pity to wreck everything after all these years together, after all the building and fighting and struggle. We are neither of us finished, by any means, and there is still much future, but it would be a crippled one for either of us separated. But that's what it is bound to come to if you again express such distrust as you did in your letter—indeed, if you feel it. I have been totally loyal to you—to Zane Grey—all these many years. My mind has not weakened to the point where I can be influenced by anyone against my own judgment; that is outside of you and the children. No, rather has my will strengthened. I am too cautious now, too suspicious. I let nothing get by me. Another thing you must not forget and that is that as a corporation, we have a board of directors, and that no one or two people can put anything across.

I send my love. Despite these upheavals, it seems still to survive.

As ever,

Dolly

Zane confessed that he wrote the letter in a terrible state of illness and depression.[32] He conceded Dolly's expertise and admitted that the wisest course was to heed her advice, even on the matter of incorporation.

_1932-1935_

CHAPTER 15

Give Us This Day Our Daily Bread, O Paramount!

I F   T H E   E C O N O M I C   P R E D I C A M E N T   of the country was desperate before, it got worse. Unemployment rose from seven million in the fall of 1931 to over eleven million in the fall of 1932. The fortunate who still had jobs took drastic wage cuts. Between 1929 and 1932, five thousand banks failed and over eighty-five thousand businesses closed their doors.

Zane and Dolly were not immune to the disease that ravaged the country. The publishing houses, magazines, and motion-picture studios that had provided their prosperity in the twenties suffered as much as other businesses. Zane and Dolly's fortune diminished and all but disappeared, as did almost everyone else's.

Except for the first five years of their marriage, Zane and Dolly had enjoyed financial security and eventually enormous wealth. This allowed the luxury of houses, yachts, cars, travel, servants, and comfort. Insulated by such wealth, the normal stress and strain from their peculiar marital relationship was muted. Zane could live his adventures with the company of his feminine companions, and Dolly lived her own life at a distance from his. But with the wealth slipping away, not just their fortunes were threatened, but also their union. Perhaps this explains the numerous lengthy and contentious letters.

Zane departed mid-November 1932 for a fishing trip off the coast of New Zealand then later Tahiti. Travel and adventure were as necessary to him as breathing, at least so he felt. They inspired his writing, the basis of all he and Dolly had built, and fishing was a treat he believed he had earned, and it too generated income. Dolly agreed but also knew that his mood and thus his writing suffered if he could not get away. The specific purpose of this trip was to shoot motion pictures of big-game fishing, which, it was hoped, the movie studios would purchase.

So she helped with preparations, which included taking Wanda Williams, his latest flame, and Doc and Betty Wiborn with him, and she cheerfully waved good-bye November 18. Four thousand dollars cash was all he took for expenses, which they both knew would last only a short time, and neither of them knew where more would be found. Ten days later he crossed the International Date Line and wrote to Dolly.

NOVEMBER 28, 1932

Crossing The Line

Dearest Dolly,

Well, old pardner, we are getting along. Nearly to Samoa. Suva about Wednesday and Auckland Saturday. I have done pretty well with my work. Most of the passengers got off at Honolulu. That place is a tourist joint. Pretty in the country. But Tahiti makes it drab and tame. The people left on board are Australians and New Zealanders mostly, this type: "Bah the way, Mr. Greeye, do you happen to know my friends John Drinkwater, Stanley Weyman (who has been dead for years), Stephen Wicken, etc." Bologna!

Nothing more unpleasant than the men trying to ogle Wanda has happened. She doesn't even see them. I could just sputter, telling you of her poise, her calm sweet poise. And she sure is a lady of quality. Betty has some grand gowns and the two of them hold up the good old U.S. okay. Funny how as soon as I leave home I begin to appreciate it and my native land.

I am beginning to fear we will be stuck in Auckland on Sunday. More expense. That $90 I had in American cash is about gone, I don't know where, except advances to Emil and Andy, and a few things picked up in Honolulu. At that I didn't have any taxi bill to pay. Maybe some of it went at the dock in San Pedro.

I'll write again soon.

Love,

Doc

Upon arrival in New Zealand he wrote again, the first of many letters whose theme is money or the lack thereof.

Pobootakanbai Camp

Whitiangi, New Zealand

DECEMBER 11, 1932

Dearest Dolly,

We arrived at Auckland on Dec. 5, after a lovely voyage. I wrote almost all that I had planned.

My launch Frangiapani came out to meet the ship. I was simply flabber-gasted at sight of her—the finest fishing launch I ever saw. If the pound had stayed at $4.84, as it was when I ordered the launch, she could have cost $17,500. But I got her for about $14,000. Collings, the builder, stuck me for 314 pounds for extras, insurance, etc. But I think I got off pretty easy. I had intended to have larger mast and sail made for the trip to Tahiti. These were included in the extras.

I will send you receipts for utensils, chemicals for camera men, hardware, hotels, taxis, and truck and cars to Whitiangi, and the boats and men needed to get here and put up camp. It took 14 men in all, three days, and was some job. Altogether it made a hole in my little $4000. Upon receipt of this send me a draft for $1000 made out to Bank of New Zealand, Auckland. Mail it to me. This will not reach me until end of Jan. and the Jan. 15th sum of $2500 will not reach me until Feb. I think I can manage on what I have till then. But if what I expect turns out—that the gasoline people here refuse to charge my gas to the Standard Oil in L.A.—I will sure be broke pronto. By the way that letter Ed got me was surely a letter boosting my credit, which I did not need here. Read this over twice, darling, and don't fold up under it. I was afraid to land in N.Z. without $10,000.

This camp is the most rugged, wild, and grand of any I ever had. We are high up from the sea, on a hill covered with giant pobootakanban. The view anywhere is wonderful. The Wiborns and Wanda are crazy about it. We have had three days of storm, hence no fishing as yet.

Here is hoping you have a Merry Christmas and a Happier New Year, and a success of our latest venture. Somehow I know it will. I haven't had a doubt since I left. We will have a turkey dinner here and of course exchange presents before dinner.

Love to all

Zane

At home Dolly faced economic collapse. It was impossible to sell stories to magazines and publishing houses, as they had no money to buy them. Movie studios could not afford to pay what was owed on old ventures, much less start new ones. They all had creditors who pressed them for payment, just as Dolly demanded payment from them and was in turn pressed by her own creditors. To protect their assets she convinced Zane that they should incorporate, and the process began in the fall of 1932. Details were left to her, and she worked on it at the new corporate office located at 3580 Beverly Boulevard in Los Angeles.

Altadena

DECEMBER 6, 1932

Dearest Doc,

Ever since you left, I have been a business lady. You know I planned to spend about three mornings a week at the office, but instead I have spent every day and all day in my new quarters, and then come home and worked till after each midnight. And to tell you the truth, I think it saved my life or my reason. With one thing and another, I was about sunk.

At first it seemed a perfect chaos down there, but gradually things are shaping up. I think the Romer situation would never have been solved if I hadn't gotten on the job, and now I can understand why Ed was so keen to have me down there. Romer was going ahead in his usual royal fashion, making the money fly, trying, I suppose, to live up to the newspaper characterization of our offices as "palatial." Now I think we have made him see reason and he is working along enthusiastically, with fewer lapses than usual. I am beginning to hope that we can put the thing across. Money is as scarce as hen's teeth, and I don't know where in the world it's coming from, but somehow our lives are always saved at the last moment. Paramount paid for the third picture they're making so I stuck away your first month's salary. By the way, it was not due until the 15th of December, as the corporation did not start until the 15th of November, and we have to be careful from the legal side. So, instead of crediting your account on the 1st do it on the 15th, beginning Dec. 15th. That won't make an iota of difference to you.

I hate to tell you this, but you must know sometime. Dot has left Romer. She told me she could not go on as things were, and I don't blame her, though I think I feel it more deeply than anyone else. I miss her and the baby terribly, and, of course, Romer does not live at home any more. I see him every day at the office, though. They were both here for dinner on Sunday, and it seemed like old times again, but Dot is very firm in her decision. It had come almost to a split several times before, and Romer would come home oftener and turn over a new leaf temporarily but then would lapse again. It really wasn't any life for her and the baby, and it is better that she should make the break now than later. Maybe someday they'll get together again, but nowadays women don't stand for the things they used to. Why should they? Dot is living at home with her parents.

I need you more than I used to. Every time you go away I miss you more. Well, I'm weeping now, so I had better change the subject.

Betty and Michele are thriving and happy. So far, Bob shows no indication of ever being anything but a one woman man, and I don't imagine that particular problem will ever bother them.

I hope you are having a wonderful time. At least you are well away from all this mess. Forgive me if I ask you to be as careful as possible with money, as it may take awhile for any to come in.

Love,

Dolly

The corporation held all assets, received all monies, and paid all debts, including salaries. Zane, like Dolly, received a salary, so he was unable to spend as he had previously unless the board of directors approved. Unused to any restraint, he tried to hold on to his finances, making impossible demands on Dolly.

Whitiangi, N.Z.
JAN. 12, 1933

Dearest Dolly,

Your letter was a shock.[1] I have not recovered yet. But if I had not had such marvelous hold on myself I would have had such a set-back as I have not experienced in years.

I am on a new tack. I quite appreciate that better men than I am have gone down in the crash. But I am not going down. I have too much power, too much momentum. The best possible thing for me, at this crisis of my life, was to get away and have a chance to recover from all that nearly wrecked me. You are not helping me as of old when you do not take me seriously. The importance of my present work and development will have lasting influence upon my future. If I am just another "also ran" I must be thoroughly disillusioned.

No one at home, except R.C., wrote me a word of optimism. And little about affairs. You were all to write me and send me reports of progress. I will not consent to being a figurehead, a mere name. The lack of information coupled with your dreary humdrum mention of a few things was like a blow in the face. The few words about finance, about money, were ghastly. I wanted to double up, to cave in, to slink into one of those Maori caves and let my bones mingle with the dust of forgotten savages.

I am not scolding, criticizing, ranting, or anything except trying to tell you that the spectre of the money I have wasted, thrown away, given to rotten people, is haunting me. And it must be dispelled. I cut my budget to the bone, knowing I hardly could get through on it. And I let those few figures speak as impressively as possible. Already the one date is past, and Jan. 15th is close at hand. If that money is not here by Feb. 1, or soon after I will be horribly situated. It will be much worse than if I was home.

Darling, don't rob a bank, and don't worry yourself sick. But send that money here and to Tahiti as listed in the book I left you!

I told you that I would never come back until I had carried successfully through these over-advertized projects of mine. That may seem strange and foolish to you. But I was deeply mortified and shamed by all that failure—and particularly to the publicity given to it. I hate my own government. It would seem easy for me to be come an anarchist, which is incredible.

I told Wanda that I would not come home, and she said she would not come without me. The Wiborns, of course, would not stay indefinitely. I will not think of this again, so as not to give it any place in my mind.

I am writing and working splendidly, and our picture work is great. But, my dear, this letter had to be written.

Lastly, I want you to get over grief, trouble, worry. You can apply your wonderful energy and mind without that. This last two years almost wrecked you, too. I am haunted often by your tired, tragic face, and it hurts me terribly. Yet it is a dear face! You must be superhuman, Dolly, it is quite possible. Don't admit defeat, doubt, fear, any more. I love you quite marvelously more for all this trouble.

Ever

Doc

So insulated from the reality of the situation was he that a trivial disagreement with Wanda affected him as much as the news from home.

Whitiangi, N.Z.

JANUARY 16, 1933

Dear Dolly,

It has rained torrents for five days after a terrible gale. The boats had to run in for shelter and we are about out of food. Other things, more important have gone amiss, also. I overheard the Wiborns and Emil discussing news they read in N.Z. papers about the latest developments in the U.S. The plan to double income tax of men with incomes—the refusal of the Democrats to aid Hoover in any way to help overcome the depression—that the bottom had not been reached by any means—that big business would be stagnated, etc., etc. Then add to that the quite incredible fact that Wanda and I have had our first difference. It was my fault. I grew irritated at her flattering comments on

Theodore Dreiser's book The American Tragedy, and I criticized sharply and perhaps unjustly. She promptly told me where to get off. It had always rankled a little that she admires Dreiser, Cavil, Mencken—that group of agnostics, and I never could understand it. She has not read one of my books since she was fourteen. I apologized, of course, and I will not make the same mistake again.

All of which succeeded in accomplishing what your letter began. This is the first time since I have been studying Science that I have fallen.[2] And it is with a stronger look at it. I don't ever remember to have felt as I do now. But I can clearly see that I should never had undertaken this trip. I was surely mad to risk coming down here with $4000, which is practically all gone. But you know me. I could not—I simply could not see the ghastly facts for me. I see them now. The idea that I should get away for the sake of my work was all baloney. Probably it would be better for me not to write at all during this period. Not that I did not want to write and could write but that evidently no one wants my product. I was buoyed up for a while by the conviction that it was only the depression—magazines retrenching, etc., but I now see it differently. And I had as an anchor our new plan—the corporation. It seemed sound, reasonable, good. But if the conditions at home make it impossible to borrow on that asset I am infinitely worse off than before. Besides, I am in a strange hostile country where the possession of money is the only factor that can insure liberty, let alone comfort.

Bowen never wrote me at all.[3] As another mail boat has arrived since your letter without any other mail I assume that for the present I must take no news as good news. Well, I don't. I take it as an indication that I am a mere figure-head, and in spite of all sense, reason, loyalty, I am assailed by the old doubt.

In going over your letter I found something I had skipped or failed to grasp. That about your not paying my salary until Dec. 15, cheating me out of two weeks. Because it was Dec. 1 that I settled that deal. And I do not see why it should not be as binding as the papers you had me sign. Why did I not have you sign papers to that effect? This may be silly of me, or even worse, but I am in black despair. I am so sick of this horrible mess that I have got myself into that I am quite tired of carrying on the struggle. I am no god—nor any-thing different from other men. I invited disaster, and wasted a fortune on other people when I should have saved it for my wife and children, and to help my brother. That is the inexcusable insupportable truth. I give you my word it would not make so much difference—this shameful miserable lack of money—if it was not for that fact. I could give up my fishing, my writing, and come home to die. But that would never wipe out my blunder, my dishonor, my treachery, my ingratitude.

You need not answer this. I will know perhaps before you get it, how things are coming out for me.

With Love always

Doc

Dolly had in fact written him two additional letters, both containing details of the business and a dose of good sense. Ed Bowen, now general manager of the corporation, had nearly sold three stories to Fox Studios, but at the last minute orders came through from the East that nothing more was to be bought and that Fox would not make any more program pictures. Fox had lost millions the year before, as had every other studio.[4] *Collier's* rejected *Knights of the Range,* but Dolly was going to try *Cosmopolitan* next. Then, toward the end of January, RKO Pictures went into the hands of receivers, followed closely by Paramount.[5] Paramount owed the corporation ten thousand dollars, due in four payments beginning February 1, but with the studio bankrupt, those funds might not be forthcoming. Conditions were bad all over the country, with food riots in Chicago. (Dolly cheerfully suggested she plant potatoes in the backyard.) Betty and Bob gave up their house and moved in with Dolly.

Zane had not received those letters, as they arrived on a later boat, so he had no idea how grim the situation was nor how heroically Dolly was working to save the business. He was the key to the entire enterprise, however, and if he crumbled, so did all the rest. He could not give up, and Dolly wrote encouragingly to him.

At the office

FEB. 13, 1933

Dearest Doc,

Your letters of Jan. 12 and 16 just came in. It hurts me to think you were so miserable, but I could see that your mood was induced, for the most part by your falling out with Wanda, and I know that by this time that will all have ironed out. You said some very unkind things, e.g., something about being cheated out of your salary. I don't care what date you put on your check-books. You can continue to keep writing it down on any date you please. But if we can't get any money we can't give it to you, and if legally certain dates enter into the formation of the corporation, we can't help that either. I just can't give you any idea what we have been going through. I sometimes won-der just why I hang on at all. I certainly don't get much incentive from you, my dear. And the children, except perhaps Loren, are just as well off without me. However, we are so well off compared to most people that I sometimes think I ought to be ashamed. But this burden of debt, and nagging creditors is, at times, more than I can bear. And yet, they are far from unreasonable, or else they would have closed down on us long ago. They are being harried and pressed too.

Just when there is going to be any relief for this condition, no one knows. Bob told me this morning that some of the biggest people in the country said we weren't anywhere near the bottom yet! The only solution for us is to accept an entirely different conception and to shape ourselves to it. You can't fight a rip tide. You must allow it to carry you on, adapt yourself to it—or sink. You must continue to fix your mind on the spiritual rather than the material, as you have recently been doing. Essentially, that is in your nature. Perhaps this is meant for a great lesson to us. Perhaps we have all worshiped Mammon too much and the material and luxurious things he could bring us, whereas the things of the spirit and what is really worth having cannot be bought with money. You cannot buy love or friendship, and that has always been the hypothesis on which you worked. When you strip yourself of your false pride and your wounded vanity, and really trust your friends, you will find something you never dreamed of. And that applies to all of us here, too. We are working with everything in us to keep up the whole structure, and it's up to you to help. You are the foundation stone, and if you withdraw your support, everything will topple. Sometimes I wish it would and that I could find oblivion under the ruins. But I'm fighting on for you and for the great name you have built up, which is even greater than you are. No matter what the state of affairs, the name, Zane Grey, has lost nothing—again, spiritually. You, the man, must live up to the name you have created. You can't quit. You can't be anything but great. You dare not. In that sense, you don't even belong to yourself, but to the millions to whom you stand for an ideal. And that, after all, is also the answer to my problem. I can't desert that Zane Grey to whom I have dedicated my life and I'll continue for fight for him, and, I hope, for you.

This should reach you in Tahiti, where problems of the world should bother you very little. If the worst comes to the worst, you can live off of coconuts and fish, and be much better off than we are here! I'd better explain that that is meant to be funny.

Love, as always,

Dolly

The weather in New Zealand was not good, nor was their reception, all of which contributed to Zane's mood, so the party moved on to Tahiti sooner than scheduled.[6] Either the move or Dolly's encouragement or both worked, and he wrote a rare introspective letter to Dolly that reveals much of his torment. This did not deter him, however, from showing more concern for Wanda than for his wife.

Flower Point, Tahiti

MARCH 12, 1933

Dearest Dolly,

Your last letter, Feb. 13, ended with an appeal that staggered me, and caused me to put off replying until I had time to think. You will remember: to wit, that the great name I had built up had lost nothing—that spiritually I had not lost—that I must live up to what I had created—that I couldn't be anything but great—that I did not belong to myself but to my millions of readers to whom I am an ideal. That, lastly, I was an answer to your problem, as well as my own, that you had dedicated your life to me and would go on fighting for me.

These were the strongest words you ever said or wrote to me. I grasp that you were driven to it by fear I might crack. Probably the letter I wrote Edd when I was sick and wretched in N.Z. accounts for it. Or perhaps the one I wrote you.

Well, I confess I wrote terribly because that is how I felt. But I would never have gone the limit. I realize that now. And as you got me out of rotten N.Z. I am myself again, stronger for it all, somehow strangely awakened.

That you thought you had cause to appeal to me like you did is at once staggering, shameful, and yet it made me warm deep within. If you and all of you depend on me—on my nerve to stick, and my power to write—you need never fear for the result. I am glad you wrote that. It hurt, but it has done something to me.

So far I have gotten, Dolly, but I am not out of the woods by a long way. I need more than thinking. I need someone working on me. At night when I awaken is the worst time. But still this is infinitely better than ever before. I wonder why I am here—what the sense of it is—how can I ever pull out and get back my passion to fish—to hold on to my reputation? I feel then mostly poignantly homesick, and a longing for you and the kids and home. It would be all right if you would stay well, happy, and live until I get home. But fears beset me. In daylight, nothing phases me—but at night! Sometimes I think of the years. So many now! And that this idea of mine, about being young still, with work and achievement ahead of me, is merely a dream. Not reality! And I suffer.

I suffer remorse because I never was a good husband or father. That I lack something. That I am to blame for all that is blameful in my children, for what you have had to suffer—for the harm the years have made in you. And it is hell. But if I am given a chance I can atone for all that—in part. I passionately repudiate any hint that I have not loved you—and the children with all that is best in me. That, of course, is not enough.

I feel like a little lost child in the dark. I never grew up in the sense of reality. I am still dreaming. I catch myself dreaming. I do not know how to face the hurts, the stings, the shocks, the losses of life. If I lost any of you now, or R.C., it'd about kill me.

So you will see from this that my feelings have grown this trip, and that I am plumbing the deeps of life. I haven't intellect enough to understand myself.

Another source of pain is Wanda. She has had so much strain, such a hard time on the sea, such worry over me and my troubles, such earnestness to work out my problem in Science, that she has worn herself out. She is a shadow of her old self. And it scares me stiff. She has been the most wonderful girl. I never knew her like. The Wiborns rub her the wrong way. It is because she is honest and they are deceitful, fussy, mean, little and even jealous. They try to work me in their suggestive way, and she sees through it.

This letter, you see, concerns nothing but the inward me—my sorrow and fear and hope and struggle. It seems sort of pitiful to me that at this late day, when I am stranded here without much hope of seeing you soon, I should find out I needed you all. But so it is.

Dolly, as long as you believe in me and my work I shall go on. There is not the slightest doubt of that. But just how to go on these days of revolution and chaos I don't see.

With all my love

Zane

In another letter he spoke more specifically of his plans, of conditions in Tahiti, of the money situation, and of Wanda.

Z.G. Camp

Vairoo, Papeete, Tahiti

MARCH 6, 1933

Dearest Dolly,

Yes, I will play ball with you all. But as for pinch hitting, how can I save the game when none of you gets on base? I see that I am called upon to knock the ball over the fence. If somebody pitches me one I will do it.

Your Jan. 13 letter and your Feb. 13 letter arrived here on the same ship I came on, but did not get to me until five days later. If I had received yours and Romer's Jan. 25 letter in N.Z. they would have about cooked me. But Tahiti is different. N.Z. is cold, sticky, inhospitable, and the people hate our guts. Here all is sunshine, flowers, color, beauty. You would not dream of a sordid world going to hell. All the same Tahiti is broke and in precarious condition. My bank, the Chin Foo went up the flue. There is only one other, the Banque of Indochine (I think, but am not sure) and the manager confided to me that he was not taking checks of many Americans. But he was courteous and fine when he cashed $100 for me. Brault informs me that Papeete is full of beach-combers. People have flocked here to escape the depression. Well, they can't escape it, although they won't freeze or starve.

I can manage on $1000 per month, I think. This means cutting down every possible way—my natives to 15 francs a day, my cooks (Chinese) to $20 and $10 a month. I don't know what grub will cost, but we can't live on fish and coconuts, as you facetiously suggested. We must have meat once a week—chickens once—2 doz. eggs a week—milk, etc—and they cost here. Gasoline and kerosene are my greatest expenses. We have to cook and run the lighting plant. And I have to fish, or I could not stay here at all. Gasoline is high. Freighted out here 17½ cents a case! And a good engineer will be expensive. Ice used to cost $190 per month. We haven't had any yet. But we must have a little.

I am not going to consider any other way. For my main reason, I don't think the Wiborns would stick if we don't fish and have a reasonably good table. And as Wanda swears she will never leave me here alone, you can read-ily see the critical situation. I don't want to hurt Wanda's good name.

Wanda is splendid—a marvelous help. You are wrong about crediting my let down in N.Z. to a fight with Wanda. We have never had a fight. But once she protested against my bad mood. Lord knows what I would have done without her. But the strain, the worry, the need to work as one and for me eventually wore her down. And she was seasick all the way here. She is thin as a rail, and fragile. But she thinks Tahiti perfect—absolutely perfect. She had a queer scientific slant on her seasickness, and attributed it to her weakness in not being able to ward off Wiborn's insidious undercurrent of thought. He wants to be first with me—to influence me. I shouldn't wonder if Wanda is right. Anyway, she will gain here. I shall be particularly careful of her, and to keep her from worrying about me.

This ought to do for today. I shall write again about my work, and the more personal things.

With much love

Doc

P.S. You should see our Ford car. It costs me $33 per month! It runs. But oh, my God! How it rattles and jolts. It nearly kills me. How the mighty owner of Lincolns has fallen.

The Wiborns went to town in our Ford. Wanda and I dodged the ordeal, and waded on the reef looking for those small shiny shells. We found 200. Wonderful to relate the Wiborns and Emil and Martin got back safely. No stores or banks or individuals in Papeete would take checks, drafts, American Express checks, or money! When good old U.S. bills, greenbacks and gold certificates, are refused, then the U.S. is not so d— good after all. In fact it's pretty punk. The rumors in Tahiti are staggering. American banks all failed. Government taking over everything. America ruined. Credit gone, the dollar on the toboggan. Roosevelt ordered session of Senate in which they are to declare $2,000,000,000 dollars in paper to be made and floated at once. Etc., etc., etc. It sounds like a lot of baloney to me. Wiborn took it pretty seriously. Said it might be Morgan after the government, or vice versa.

Dolly, it must be a queer, chaotic time at home. I'm so d— sorry you have all this, all the time. But I'm thankful that you seem to be getting hold of yourself, and fighting without agony. That makes me happy, dear. Just you use your brain and wit, and get Romer and Edd to help without suffering or undue strain. Worry, anxiety, dread will only add to difficulties, not help them. If you don't find a way out of this hell, I will.

Zane

This last statement was false bravado but revealed how little Zane actually knew of the situation or the business. He simply could not understand why the money was no longer there and blamed Dolly. Dolly's long letters spoke dismally of conditions in the United States, the finances of Zane Grey, Inc., and their personal relationship.

MARCH 13, 1933

Dearest Doc,

Truly I don't know what is going to happen, but neither does anyone else. The whole nation is pinning its hopes on Roosevelt. One state after another was closing its banks to avoid runs and the people losing all they had, so Roosevelt's proclamation to declare a bank holiday for the whole country was a logical and constructive move.[7] But it means that most people had no money at all. I had a little cash—enough to keep us fed for a while, but then we're down to bedrock anyway, $50 a month or less is all I take for Loren's and my food and personal expenses, and once or twice a week we even go out. True, we get two movies for 15 cents nowadays!

Drastic measures are being promulgated against hoarding of any kind, so that the people will have to drag out their hidden stores and put money in the banks. It is said that all gold and gold certificates will be called in, and that after a certain date will lose value, and that there will be large fines and imprisonment for sticking money away in your sock. However, having none stuck away, or even in sight, such decrees fail to touch me.

The income tax department still goes on its merry way, making life miserable for me. After examining the 1930 tax, they decided to disallow at least $100,000 of our losses. Just how much tax this means, I haven't the nerve to inquire. That's where the corporation helps. Our bookkeeper is an expert and will fight it out for me. Eventually we may still lose but it is putting off the evil day. After ascertaining that this year's tax would be between $12,000 and $13,000 with just nothing with which to meet it, I got an extension for ninety days. What will happen at the end of that period is beyond me to prophesy— but "The Lord will provide"—or as the Scientists have it, "Supply is infinite." But how to find it? Then today comes a note from Hoyns saying he doubts the Corn Exchange Bank will renew our note, now reduced to $25,000, and if they couldn't, he would wire us for it! That to me was just hysterically funny. We can't even pay the interest. They'll have to take it out of our 25% which, by the way has now been deflected to pay off the income tax attorneys; also 20% of all other income, but as there hasn't been any other, they haven't kept from starving on that. Harper's has been keeping all of the 75% of what came in to pay off what we owed them, but as they endorse our note to the bank they are responsible, and there is just nothing they can do about it. Today, too, to disprove that 13 is my lucky number (it being the 13th) Pictorial returned Horse Heaven Hill. I never had any confidence in that story, although I did work on it after you left. Essentially it didn't have the stuff. Now we have still to hear from Burton on Knights Of The Range. I simply do not let myself hope any more. The trouble is, we cannot shoot these stories to editors too fast. They get together and discuss things and if too many Zane Grey stories are floating around New York without a place to light, it will create a bad impres-

sion. I know both Chenery and Pictorial will buy a Zane Grey if they can get
one to suit them, but I want to consider very carefully before I submit another
to them. You must see that you get plenty of plot and action at the right spots
for climaxes of weekly or monthly installments. You always had an instinct
for that. Also, get away as much as possible from your former stories and characters. Drift Fence was the January book. Didn't I send you one? It has had
exceptionally good reviews. It will be followed, naturally, by The Hashknife
Outfit. Harper's prefers your original name. I have prevailed upon them to
issue it as a Christmas book this year in order to get the Christmas trade. They
would not do another July book though I begged them to, in order to pay off
more of the debt. I think I'll rub that in on Hoyns.

Now to get to the movie situation. Paramount Publix went into receivership
and Paramount Pictures went on making pictures. We were cooking up a deal
for remaking some more of the old pictures (at a greatly reduced price) when
this banking holiday came joyously along, with all its ramifications. No one
knows whether any of the studios will remain open. They are all practically
bankrupt. They want the actors to act without pay, or on a small proportion of
their former salaries, or give up pay for a month, or what have you? One
hears a different story every day. They might just as well act without pay, for
one can't cash any checks anyway. Herzbrun is in N.Y., whether bounced
or still on, I know not. Mr. Karp, his successor or temporary substitute, told me
today that he thought the deal would go through, so we still live in hope.
We are also hoping for the Rogue River film, but it's so hard to find the money
to get it in shape, the release, etc., etc. Also the wherewithal to make the additional scenes for a consecutive story to carry it along and hold suspense. There
is some wonderful river material, but that alone won't carry the thing.

Don't worry about your boat. We probably couldn't give it away at the
present time as yachts seem to be considered more a liability than an asset
nowadays. Bob read the other day how a former millionaire sunk his palatial
yacht in the Sound because he couldn't even give it away and couldn't afford
to keep it. What bothers me is where the money is coming from to take the
trip. With things as they are now there is no chance of selling stock in the Corporation, and apparently little chance of selling anything else. There is one
thing I am sure of, and that is that I am almost at the end of my rope where

this debt business is concerned. The only reason that I have weathered it, is because we formed the corporation, and the only reason that we have held on so long is because of the corporation. All these people were about ready to close in. Believe me, I'd rather take a job as someone's cook than keep on with this kind of burden. You'd be surprised at how often I try to think out what kind of work I could find if it were necessary. I am afraid that my life job has been too highly specialized for me to be good at anything else. And jobs of any kind are so scarce. At that, I think I am more necessary to you than Peter, for instance. Maybe you would give me a job as cook. You always liked my cooking.

What gets me more than anything else is your attitude that we have oodles of money that we are withholding from you. My God, there is nothing we would like better than to keep you doing anything on God's earth that you wanted to. You say in your letter "that you could go against me never occurred to me until the Suva mandate and the messages to New Zealand. They were terrible." That is the most amazing thing I have ever heard—that you should hold the failure of money to carry on as a personal fault of mine, as a going against you. I suppose you would have considered it more loyal of me to say "Keep going, Doc, have your heart's desire" and leave you stranded somewhere at the ends of the earth. And yet you tell me you were thankful that I got you out of New Zealand.

I hold with Wanda absolutely that if what you want is right and the best thing for you, you will get it inevitably. I am doing everything in my power to help you get it. You can't, by the wildest stretch of imagination, think that there is anything in all this for me? What do I want of this huge place, this empty shell. I can't even pay the servants to keep it up. What do I want of the yacht, or of the office where I go day after day to worry and to scheme and to wonder where we're to get the money to keep you going, to pay our debts, to keep from losing all the things that are such a burden to keep. I am per-fectly willing to go on as I have been, serving you, helping you, fostering that which you have to give the world, but I can't do it if when I'm faced with a terrible decision to force you to an action you don't like, but on which your actual survival depends, I am accused of disloyalty and cheating and going against you. And in a lesser degree this applies also to other people who are working for you. For God's sake, show me that I am not doing all this in vain. Words won't do it—actions must. I don't mind getting along on less a month for Loren and me than your least hireling, and Loren is learning things he would never have to in better times. But I do mind fighting a losing battle . . . not in that which is material, but in those things that are wellsprings of our going on, our excuse for being. When those are gone or destroyed . . . well, then things will be ended for me. Moreover, if you know of anyone who can administer your affairs to better advantage than this corporation, or anyone who could run the corporation better or cheaper than the present incumbents, we would be more than happy to yield.

Readapt yourself to present conditions. It is only age that cannot change, and you are not old. You have the youth and flexibility still to conquer, but you have fallen into ways of self-indulgence, into vanities of position. Believe me, no one is too proud to retrench in these days. It is those who do not when they ought to that are looked down upon.

Love,

Dolly

Zane's response filled two letters and shows his mental state, conditions in the South Seas, and his own precarious financial position but again demonstrates clearly that he had only a vague idea of the money situation or, after all these years, Dolly's feelings.

MARCH 28, 1933

Dearest,

Your long, poignant, terrible letter came three days late. I don't know what to say. You write "not words, but deeds." I don't blame you. I lay awake all night. The thundering surge beneath my window seemed a dirge of my hopes. I never wanted to see the light.

When I read about the income tax demand again I felt the roots of my hair burst into fire. God, what a hideous thing!

But what wrought me most was your sorrow, your resignation to anything. I have brought you to this sad pass, and nothing I can write will do any good.

Nothing here will interest you unless Wanda's state. She is about failing. Her health and beauty are gone. All these months of strain have done it. She is mental. She feels so deeply. And she has tried so hard to help me. She is the kindest, sweetest, truest girl I ever had with me. She refuses to go home and leave me here.

The unsupportable thought for me is that I may never see you or the children again. That hurts more and more. I know you don't believe it, but I do love you all.

Ever

Doc

P.S. Ed's letter also was three days late. Like the others it was ambiguous, uncertain in regards to money. The only definite fact was that I could be sure of $300 per month for expenses. Only promises about salary! I was depending upon my salary to use for expenses here. To repeat. I had $600 in my L.A. bank and $96 in my Altadena bank, on Jan. 1. Both you and Ed wrote me of deposits of salary to my account. I have drawn checks for only $700 or 800 since Jan. 1. If deposits have been made, as you wrote me, I have some money of my own you can send. So I wrote to Ed to cable me what the bank would stand on April 10. Care, Banque de Indochine, Papeete. I also told Ed and Romer both that I am afraid these deposits have never really been made. That means four months without any salary. Of course you can't deposit money when none comes in. But if you have only deposited $1000 or $1500 since Jan. 1, that would save me. I shall wait till April 10 before giving up here. I don't know just what giving up means. I'm afraid that to send away the Chinese cook and the boatmen will mean the Wiborns would not stick. I may be wrong. But they are for themselves.

What you say about Horse Heaven Hill, the editors, Harper's, etc. was all disheartening. How to think without doubt, fear, worry, grief is beyond me. I can't be a Christian. I can't see God reflected in myself. But I am keeping on trying to think right.

Zane

Dearest Dolly,

The mail ship has been delayed, so that I can get you another letter. You will not be so happy to get it, darling.

Donald's bill has just arrived, for 5 weeks, and it's for food, hardware, lumber, gasoline, etc. etc., and it's over $500. Of course nearly $300 of that is for gas, which will last me a couple of months. This gas was ordered, and the other bills started upon my arrival here, when I thought I had some money of my own in the banks. Recent letters from you and Ed make me fear I haven't. But if what I had on deposit Jan. 1 is there, and the deposits you and Ed wrote about, I can still weather things without asking for expense money. If not——

——! We are doing our damndest. But we can't do a thing with the Chinamen. They want this and that ordered for the table and the lunches.

To be brief, I couldn't get along here at all on less than $1000 a month. I'll pay that out of my salary if you can stand it.

To give up fishing means so much that I simply bolt at the thought. It means to give it up for good! That means no big cruise, no more trips. I question whether that's wise. It would mean my finish. And if you need my work to help carry on you have got to keep me fishing.

Poor Wanda is struggling with the food and servant problem. It is a tough one. Betty [Wiborn] refuses to help. She is sore about the N.Z. business. But if I had not taken it out of their hands we would have lost our help, and that was not to be thought of. The Wiborns are a detriment instead of an asset.

I want my own family in on this job. Do you understand? If the deal goes through with the Vanderbilts, as I think it will, I'd find some way to come down, or send the W's home before we started.[8] But that won't be easy. Doc is making as much out of that trip as possible. Writing everywhere!

Well, enough of that! There must be a way out.

I'll pay these bills by check, after this boat sails, and if the merchants will accept the checks, which I doubt, they will reach you when the next steamer arrives. Or in 6 weeks, unless the Union S.S. Line quits, which is the report here. They are not hauling any passengers or freight. Copra is dead. And their mail order expires this month. We hear that the Union line is not booking any

passengers for April. That'd been tough for R.C. or Betty if they had planned
to come.

Meanwhile if Ed can cable me some money out of my bank account (you
see I harp on that. But G—D—it! I had at least $1000 there without any
deposits at all.) I will be able to keep on fishing.[9]

So long, Dolly dear. I'm not sick or blue or discouraged. I'm just plain mad.
I daresay you have been the same. But I still have faith and hope that I won't
crash here. If you could sell a story and send me $5000 I would be O.K. and
could go to the Paumotos and get a good picture in the bargain. If!

Much love and many kisses

Doc

No relief was in sight.[10] Small amounts of money trickled in from Paramount for remake rights, but Dolly feared that would dry up any day. The
income-tax attorneys insisted on 25 percent of what Harper's was still sending and 20 percent of everything else. She could not sell another manuscript, and even the magazines were so much in the red they were unable to
buy stories. She placed her hope in Roosevelt and approved of his measures, which included pushing Congress to cut expenses; restoring beer,
which brought in huge revenues and employed millions; and ending hoarding.[11] She remained optimistic, at least when she wrote Zane.

Zane fished, and despite his annoyance with the Wiborns, Wanda's inabil-
ity to tolerate the tropics, and financial woes, he maintained his position in
Tahiti. He met and became friendly with Governor Herse, who invited him
to Apatakie for fishing. He naively proposed to Dolly a month of fishing
there, allowing him to take motion pictures at Rangaroa as well, which could
be done, he said, for a mere five thousand dollars. Dolly, he wrote, would
have from May to August to raise the money. He visited with Charles Nord-
hoff, a British resident of Tahiti and author of *Mutiny on the Bounty* among
other novels. Zane was still writing and by the middle of April completed
two-thirds of a new novel.[12] He hid from reality and worked but upon occasion questioned his faith in himself.

Tahiti

MAY 4, 1933

Dearest Wife,

I must be starting another letter to you. Somehow I can't help it, although I am certain you don't read half I write. Because you never answer questions or send anything I ask for. But at least you shall know how I fare.

At this writing I am well and fine. Almost through Ride The Man Down, which I think I will risk mailing untyped.[13] Wanda is improving again, thank heaven. But scarcely up to 500 odd pages of manuscript.

The Wiborn situation grows worse. Wanda and I are now entrenched behind bulwarks of tolerance and indifference in right thinking that they cannot disrupt our lives. All the same I appreciate, and so does Wanda that he is extremely dangerous. I'll do my best to avoid a quarrel, a break. He won't stick here, that's sure. And when he goes home, no matter with what plans of returning, or going on the cruise, he will never do either.

We must get somewhere. If there is sense in my writing on, harder and better (I hope) than ever, there is sense in keeping me from cracking. I laugh at the thought. But, if my writing was ended, as is the case of Kipling, and many of our American writers, and if I have to come home to stay, never to fish anymore in this big and wonderful way I have created, I'm afraid I would crack. What would there be for me? Of course, I'm no quitter. I'd take my medicine. I love my family. I'd try to show it. But the youth, the driving force, the inspiration might leave me. Wouldn't that be natural?

To be sure I can't stay here forever and wait for better times. A year would be the most, and that d— hard. I get homesick. Since it's good for me to stay here a while longer and work then the relations to it can be considered.

I told you before that I—myself—my creative power has not been hurt by all this trouble. My idea had been to write as always, better if possible. It made me sick to read of Sinclair Lewis's new novel already gone all over the world and translated into 16 languages—a novel according to the newspaper critics, that is dull, slow, dirty—just a reportorial account of Mr. Lewis's personal hate. It does seem, sometimes, that ideals, beauty, virtue, love and romance have perished from the earth. But of course that could not be true. I refuse to be shelved by a modern materialistic callous world of writers. I'll go on trusting to my public, until I find out one way or another.

This year Harper's will have published 5 of the 10 novels contracted for. If you can get them to publish two next year we will soon be approaching a third contract. And by that time I'll be going strong again, as strong in bookstores as in the libraries.

Dolly, dear, am I sensible, clear, right?

Much love,

Doc

It was probably a good thing that distance insulated him from the crisis. Had he been at home, constant worrying would surely have made it impossible to write. But for Dolly, the worst was now reality.

MAY 6, 1933

Dearest Doc,

The last month has been the worst, financially, in our existence. All the money gave out and we were overdrawn when the bank examiner showed up! It's a queer sort of feeling to know that in another week or two there might not be enough to buy food! Of course, there was still that $1250 of yours in the bank, but outside of keeping the children on just enough to prevent starvation I would not have touched that. Our sole hope was in Paramount and the daily talk was that Paramount would fold. But a few days ago, we got another check from them, and now I suppose it is up to us to pray that they'll stay open for a couple of months until we can get something more out of them. "Give us this day our daily bread, O Paramount!" I put another $500 of what came in to your account. Now you must make that hold out as long as possible. I believe that things will improve. I believe that we will be able to develop something big in a motion picture way. I believe that sooner or later we will again be able to sell a serial. But these things take time, and meanwhile we must keep going on the very little that is available. You mention a $1000 a month budget. You might just as well have said $1,000,000 at the present state of affairs. We try to make magic, but these conditions nowadays are too cold. We had to take Bob and Romer off the payroll and whomever else we could spare, or couldn't spare, for that matter. However, Bob and

Romer will always get their food and shelter as long as I have it to provide, and perhaps they can find something else.

For the past two weeks we have been preparing our case on the 1930 income tax case—that is, intensively. It has been going on for months. Our accountant, Mr. Doyle, worked up a very good case, and Milligan went with us before the local board. There was a disallowance of something over $100,000 involving the payment of at least $15,000 in tax. This was mostly your expenses. We persuaded them that all those should be allowed and also a lot of other things. The only thing they would not permit was the taking of my losses on securities that year on the partnership deduction, which was how we had turned it in, hoping to get away with it. Anyway, we got a lot of concessions we did not even hope for. That cut the tax down to $4000, which at the present sitting is just as far away as $14,000. However, we may be able to get some kind of extension. They know how hard up we are.

There was a rather peculiar incident about the case. The question of M.K. Smith's salary came under discussion. Milligan thought it was a man. Then one of the tax men, a little sharp faced fellow, said, "By the way, how is Miss Smith? I used to know her quite well in Arizona, and I have heard all about your husband's travels there." My heart went clear down into my boots, but I explained sweetly that Miss Smith was married or about to be, etc. He looked kind of funny at that, and said he knew Jess and Lil very well and had been in the war with Lil. He also asked about that trouble you had about Arizona, but I told him that was a lot of garbled publicity. Anyway, I put it over with him, apparently, and he was the more formidable of the two. But I gleaned some experience from that. For God's sake, be polite to everyone you meet. It may be an income tax man, who may some day cost or save you thousands.

What did you want with the MS of Canyon Walls? I have sent it to you on this boat. Be careful not to repeat too much on your stories. Try to get some new ideas and situations, something different in the way of plot. And have plenty of plot and action to meet the demand of the serials. Think over all your stories. You will find that they fall into certain classes, and your heroes often repeat themselves. Thunder Mountain was different, so was The Trail Driver and Shepherd Of Guadaloupe.

Will you please send me the other manuscript of Twin Sombreros? It is perfectly safe to do so now, especially as you have the original. I have more work
now than I can possibly do for years to come, and I can't go over a manuscript
twice to correct it, nor can I afford to take the time to mark down every cor-
rection on a piece of paper. We have had to cut down to two girls in the office
and they are too busy to type manuscripts. And money is too scarce just now
to hire anyone else. Besides, I don't want to let this one manuscript out of my
hands until I get another.

Did I tell you that Ken resigned from the bank? It was getting him to the
point where he could not sleep at night. He is not constitutionally a banker. I
haven't seen him in weeks. He has been trying to get a job, and meanwhile is
still living with Ed. Ed has, among other things, taken up the bank situation,
and I have had to do so too. As soon as it is feasible, we will probably close it.
However, you must not even breathe this to anyone, as it might cause a lot of
trouble.

I have been taking up driving again and this time I intend to keep on with it.
For several weeks now I have driven down to the office in the morning and
through considerable traffic at that. I traded in the Stutz, repairs on which were
running over thirty dollars a month, and which consumed enough gasoline
for three cars, for a little Chrysler Sedan which is very easy for me to drive. I get
from 16 to 20 miles to the gallon and the Stutz never got more than eight.

Monday morning and a quantity of mail from you which has taken me
more than an hour to read. And it's my same old Doc, now on the Elysian
heights, again in the Stygian depths. But on the whole the depths seem to be
getting shallower and the heights more lofty. I can see where the Science is
gaining ground. It is not more than to be expected that you will have an occasional slump. It requires constant and painstaking application to change the
mental habits of a lifetime. And although some of your misery tore my soul, I
yet got a sense of stimulation and hope and a new influx of fighting spirit from
you. Funny, you always have that power to stimulate me. I feel now as if I
could lick the world. Neither of us is in any sense licked or ruined or finished.
Don't you think it, darling. We must just readjust to present conditions, perhaps only temporarily, and then you will be doing everything your heart
desires again. Just think of it as a period when we must work harder than ever,

be as careful as possible and hold the fort until we are out of the woods. Mixed metaphors, but you know what I mean.

Romer and Dot are not divorced, nor is there at present any discussion of that. The news of their separation merely finally got to the newspapers. And though they did not mention divorce that was the interpretation almost everyone seemed to put on it. As far as you and I go, you know that periodically they are having us divorced. The only way that could happen is for you to want it—and maybe not then!

I beg of you to be patient with the Wiborns. Perhaps your ways are as strange to them as theirs are to you. Remember the highly individualized lives they have led for so many years. And Wanda should exercise her Science to the point where they can have no effect on her. Fear has gotten her too, principally through her association with you, I am convinced, although you need not tell her that. She should be her old lovely serene self. You must help her to it. It is your own constant fluctuation that disturbs her. She has always led such a quiet sheltered existence from all the life of turbulent emotions that are a part of your very being, that it is no wonder that the poor girl is warped from her orbit. You must seek to help her by doing the right thinking and living yourself. You have easily the strongest and most dynamic personality of anyone I have ever come in contact with. You are like some tremendous magnet. You must use that power to draw people in the right direction, not have them veering like weathervanes with every random turn you take. Power like yours should be used to the end of the greatest good. In your work it has done that. Then there will be harmony and tremendous power all making to the same end, and not tearing yourself and everyone else to pieces.

I should think it would be the best thing in the world for Wanda to have some steady occupation like typing. It would be soothing and would occupy her mind. There is nothing more debilitating than idleness, no specific occupation and work.

Goodbye, once more, my dearest. Feel sure and safe about us here and about our unquestioned loyalty to you. And keep up that wonderful spirit of yours. It is essentially the thing that keeps us all going.

Love as always

Dolly

A wonderful admission that the "stenographers," as they were described, actually didn't do any typing!

Early in May they seemed to have turned a corner. *The Country Gentleman* requested a serial, the first break in over a year.[14]

MAY 12, 1933

Dearest Dolly,

Yesterday I finished Ride The Man Down. 500 pages, 105,000 words. It is too soon for me to say how good it is. I think I'll begin another very soon. It's hard to work here, that is very long at a sitting, but I am better, I think, with a novel in my mind. I have less time to worry. This time I finished strong and without the usual reaction. I shall not have any reaction. I just wrote all day and completed the story and shut off my valves, carburetors, exhausts, etc., and said, "Well, here's another one. Now let's see." This makes two long novels in 5 months.

As I wrote you before, the only thing I really fear is an end to the demand for my work. That is foolish. I should think that I'll make it in demand. We don't know for sure that it is lack of money that keeps the editors from buying Z.G.

Captain Urich wrote Wiborn that he read in some magazine that Zane Grey did not write his novels. The Smith woman has been writing that poison. It is sickening. It might influence some people and some editors. But since it is a lie—a damned falsehood—it cannot—it simply cannot—hurt me vitally. And a proof of this will be that the next novel I write is planned to be the biggest and most powerful I ever wrote in all my life. Dolly, I repeat, don't worry about my power to write. I've got it and I'll employ it.

But the other things I can't advise against—that is the worrying about them, though. I hope you won't lay awake at night worrying.

Where are you going to get the little money needed to carry me on here? Couldn't you sell a story to a magazine or a movie company—sacrifice it for a few thousand and send that money to me? Then you'd have me off your mind for a few months. It does not follow that you would have to do it again. And you would not have to allow that to establish a precedent. I must have money a few days after you receive this. God, how I do writhe when in a case like this, when I think of what I wasted on worthless people! Never again in this world, Dolly dear!

The facts are simple to chronicle.

1. I can write better here at this period and be happier.

2. If I am forced to come home it would take considerable money to pay off and get there.

3. I can't raise any money on my property and I wouldn't borrow if I could.

So it resolves itself into a question whether or not you should keep me here or have me come home. If, as Ed's letter implied, we are almost to crash as sure as the Lord made little apples I will go to jail here. But I won't, I can't believe that.

But what are you going to do about me? Here I am, President of Zane Grey, Inc, and shunted off without salary or expense money, yet my product is supposed to carry on a lot of profitless concerns. That's an infernal paradox. You must keep that ranch, if possible. But I'd advise getting rid of the bank, and the rest of those encumbrances as soon as you can do so without total loss.

Well, this will do for today. I am terribly homesick, otherwise fine. On May 19 I will have been gone five months. And life so short! I want to see you and Lorry and Romer and Betty and R.C., Ide and Bob. Not so crazy about those grandchildren!!

Love and kisses
Zane

Her good news cheered him.

Tahiti

MAY 21, 1933

Dolly dearest,

Bless you for your good letters! They have cheered me immeasurably—the first little encouragement you have sent me since I got here. From the wireless paper from the Makura, and newspapers sent to W—we have gathered that conditions at home are still critical, but promising. So many different assurances must mean that a definite return to normal has begun.

Editor Rose.[15] That was good news indeed. His query about a story. I will write it. You can promise it to him for this fall. I may write it earlier. But I hate to lay aside the wonderful piece of work I am on. I'll consider it. Anyway, you make the deal. I'll deliver the goods. I forget what Rose had for Avalanche. But it was nothing like Schuler paid for Canyon Walls, etc. Get all you can without blunting his eagerness for more Z.G. stuff.

I wanted Canyon Walls to inculcate in Ride The Man Down. But I finished the novel so will not need the MS.

Knights Of The Range. It is something that Burton was pleased with this story. My idea is that any editor who had money on hand would buy it. By all means keep it, lay it aside and wait for him, and let him know it. You have Hole In The Wall, Twin Sombreros, Ride The Man Down, all stories, different (except Hole in Wall has the isolated robber rendezvous emphasized. But it's damn good!) and any one of them Colliers should buy if they have any money. Don't forget that we slipped up on McCall's, the best of that bunch, by monkeying with Pictorial. It galls me. You must be clever and tactful and shrewd enough to win them back. Colliers and McCall's and Country Gentleman would be enough yearly to handle without conflicting.

Financial. The $1750 on hand you mentioned looked like a fortune to me. My word, what a relief, a Godsend! I will make that do until end of June, perhaps longer.

I have cut and cut expenses here. I don't like to reduce Martin. He's valuable. I have paid Pete and Charley practically nothing. The natives get half what they used to. My Chinese cost 800 francs a month. They are the best cooks and helper we've had.

Wanda has not had any salary since we arrived here. She doesn't seem to mind the lack of money. She very much wants a porch on her cottage, and a roof that doesn't leak, and I hope to be able to have them done. It will cost about 4000 francs.

She is not at all well. It is mental and as you said mostly my fault. I must and shall so control myself henceforth so as not to distress her, keep her involved in a maelstrom.

If the Vanderbilt deal goes through—fine! We'll do it next year. But I'm afraid that was a flash in the pan. Moreover, I think, and Romer told R.C. the same, without knowing my angle, that a short, far less expensive yet productive trip, should be planned. This should be South America. It would be productive of an outdoor book, and a novel of the Argentine or Pampas—a great idea!—a fine motion-picture and some shorts, and wonderful still pictures. It should not cost a great deal.

I would consider this very seriously. My dearest, if I have to come home and can't go anywhere it will cost you more for insanity, destruction of property, and funeral expenses than the whole trip! Dolly, don't discourage this. Romer says and R.C. says that motion-pictures like this are wanted and will go big. I might get a good enough one to appear and talk before regular release. That would be the way to make the money for the big cruise.

My love, my whole insides went cold when I read that you were driving a car. My God! I respect and admire your nerve. And I suppose it is all right if you have a competent driver with you. But please, Dolly, don't take any risk.[16]

I'm sorry Ken buckled under the press of bad times and uncongenial labors. He sure stuck it out long and loyally. But I wish he had done it long ago. I approve of closing that bank as soon as possible without loss.

Dolly, I admit the Elysian Heights but deny the Stygian depths. I'll be damned if I have been really deep and down black since I left N.Z. If you don't believe it read the manuscripts I'm sending.

It sure does my soul good to read that we are not licked. I didn't think so. But I've been scared at times. That one long paragraph in your letter about me, and my infernal personality, and what I should and shouldn't do—that is as good as Science to me. I'll grab it to my soul.

I love you a lot, Dolly. This terrible ordeal has brought us closer together. There seems to be more strength in you now, and an absence of that frantic helplessness.

I will plan to come home, say, in August or September, unless the big cruise materializes. So look forward to that, honey.

Love and kisses,

Zane

Only to plummet to the bottom a few weeks later.

Flower Point, Tahiti

JUNE 18, 1933

Dearest Dolly,

I am coming home on the July ship, arriving in S.F. on July 27 or 28. I had planned to stay until August but that would mean all of $1500 more of debt, which I do not dare incur here. By all means I must come home on this next ship. This decision was compelled by the financial situation. But there are other reasons why it is wise and best for me to come home now. I would not stay longer even if I had plenty of money.

Wanda would like to stay until Jan. 1, provided I could have her sister down. She has given me to understand that she will quit me upon our return home. Her reason will amaze you. She made up her mind a month ago, and since then has been improving slowly. I had hoped all would be well. But I cannot stay longer.

Wanda has been a wonderful help and comfort these trying months. I cannot express my gratitude to her, and my sorrow that I have been the cause of her distress, her physical let down. I don't delude myself that I can remedy the trouble, but I hope and pray that a definite break does not come.

It will cost $2000 or $2500 to get me out of here. And that money will have to be deposited by August 1 or thereabouts. I have no idea where in the world you can get so much money, now that money has vanished off the face of the earth. But you must raise it somehow, or leave me in the sorest straits I have ever been in. Tahiti is not friendly to Americans now. The French have fired a lot of beachcombers and turned cold shoulder to the crowd who have come here to out-ride the depression.

The novel I am on now progresses in a way to make me vastly hopeful. It is a new kind of story for me to tackle. But it is Arizona, simple, elemental—the "terrific truth of what the pioneer endured." That is my theme.[17]

From your letter and Bowen's I gather that there is a complete stagnation. That if any money comes in it must come from selling a serial or movie rights. This is a disastrous situation. If you have placed me in a position where I cannot do anything—in fact be powerless to change the situation—that is more than disastrous.

I appreciate Bowen's pluck, acumen, and loyalty. I am dreadfully sorry I have imposed all this upon you and I will do my utmost to help. But I am afraid the corporation idea was never clear to me. Even if it does save me in the end I would be little better off with a lot of real estate, ranches, taxes, insurance, salaries, etc. to pay out of what I earn with my pen.

That has been done for ten years. I never got any benefit from your deals. Somebody did. You have been spending money all these ten years to keep things up, and to become involved in more. Worse than that, which seems to me a rank futile business failure, the injury to you, the distress and toil, surely loom larger than financial loss.

I cannot help but hold all this against Ken and Ed. Not a single investment they persuaded you to undertake ever resulted in any profit. I always was against this. You remember. But while I was making such vast sums of money I was game enough, and had faith enough in you, to stand for it. But if we ever get out of this I certainly will not stand for that again. . . .

. . . . Well, this ought to do for my last letter this trip. I sure am homesick to see you.

With love ever
Zane

Communicating by mail was difficult, especially so when Zane was in the remote South Seas. Dolly wrote frequently, saving the letters up to mail on the steamer, and on the same steamer she received a bundle of letters from Zane. Thus, there was usually a lag of at least a month and sometimes six weeks between the time one sent a letter and received a reply. It seemed as if letters went into some deep chasm, never to be found again, much less answered. But even under these conditions, Zane and Dolly were able to talk over details. Dolly's letters particularly reflect her day-to-day existence.

JUNE 20, 1933

Dearest Doc:

This month has been such a busy one that it has flown fast; yet with the crowding of events, it seems a long while since I last wrote you. One of the high spots, and one of the pleasant ones was Loren's graduation from high school on June 16. They had a very beautiful and impressive exercise in the Rose Bowl in Pasadena, and I felt very proud and thrilled that my baby was graduating from high school. Of course, it is sort of a wrench too, to think he is growing so fast. He is already by far the tallest one in the family, and the improvement in him this last year has been rather remarkable. . . . He has been very much of a comfort for me this winter and since he left for Catalina about a week ago, I have felt rather lost. And yet I would rather have him over there for he is keeping busy with his fishing. I think he has landed the contract to supply the fishing barge with bait and that will bring in something to him.

Meanwhile I have been busier than ever. I go to the University Extension course on Monday and Wednesday nights. You will laugh when you hear what I am taking. It is public speaking. Don't be alarmed. It is not my intention to get up on a platform and orate to the general public, but I feel that it is a very good way to gain the confidence that I have always lacked in the sound of my own voice. I could always write things, as you know, and I could think them, but it has been very difficult for me to put my thoughts into speech. This is a handicap even in dictating letters. That the whole thing is merely an inferiority complex and a fear, I have discovered, and I am systematically running my fears into the ground. It has become a matter of survival. In the same way I tackled the driving job, and I feel it has done me a great deal of good already. I get along pretty well and run around considerably alone, even late at night. I have not yet tackled downtown Los Angeles traffic but I get into some pretty thick jams now and then as I travel back and forth from the office every day and to various other places. It is a great relief too, not to be dependent upon anyone else. Yesterday morning, for instance, I got a great kick out of going to the voting place all by myself and voting. On other occasions I always had to hang around until someone was willing to take me. . . .

Last night we had a Directors meeting of Zane Grey, Inc. at Loyd Wright's office, and we threshed out matters very thoroughly. The corporation commissioner has finally given us a permit to incorporate, which, in a way, is another triumph, for they are extremely careful to whom they give permits. That means that we are now free to sell some of the preferred stock. Lloyd Wright, our attorney, who, as you know, is one of the foremost attorneys in the city, expressed the opinion that within the next six months with governmental conditions as they are, we would have a very good chance of selling some stock and thus raise some money. We are going after that now to see what can be done. Personally I wish we would not have to do that because it really means that we are again borrowing money which eventually will have to be paid back, but things are bound to improve, and we will probably, with all the developments that we can institute here, be in a much better position to pay back what we borrow some years hence, than we are to let things ride as they are now with creditors still camping on our trail, and capable of making a good deal of trouble for us. We have them all pretty well in hand now and satisfied to receive a small proportion of what we owe them whenever we can let them have it. I feel sure that our organization in this matter has kept us from disaster. If we can sell this stock it naturally means the financing of your trip. . . .

My love to the Wiborns and to Wanda, and to you, of course, as much as always.

Dolly

Dolly cautioned him to budget every step. She advised him to make *Twin Sombreros* a sequel to *Knights of the Range,* then write a third story to finish up the Pecos Smith line. More encouragingly, she wrote that *The Country Gentleman* had agreed to pay fourteen thousand dollars for a three-part serial, only a thousand dollars less than they had paid for "Avalanche" a few years ago. And finally, she mentioned that at the Director's meeting they all urged her to go to New York to try to sell some manuscripts. She was there in November of 1931 to address the income-tax situation and sold the last series that was sold on that visit. But when Zane's letters came, she addressed the points he had raised.

Avalon
JULY 3, 1933

Dearest Doc,

Two letters of yours came over by plane. The first one is dated May 30th and I wonder if it was meant to catch the last boat. . . . My dear, there is just one thing I have thoroughly had impregnated into me during this period and that is to live from day to day. I'll leave the planning of the future up to you, my dear, but I insist that the sort of thing that again cropped up in your last letter about my investments and Ken and Ed and their culpability in the matter be taboo between us and everyone else, for that matter. You do not yet seem to have grasped the fact that my investments were a great deal better than most and in normal times would have brought us big profits, that billionaires have lost everything, that there were thousands of suicides from losses and not being able to stand the gaff. I am thrilled to pieces at your return, for you can pep me up better than anyone else, but there are certain understandings we must have. You must take my word that we have all done our utmost to save the whole situation, that there was no separation possible whereby you could be let to go on, on your own, that the whole thing hung together, that if we had not incorporated, there would have been a complete smash long ago. My dear, I concede that Zane Grey is a very great man, but when the greatest men and nations and cities of the world don't know whether they will be in existence from day to day . . . even our own U.S.A. . . . how can even Zane Grey hope to escape unsinged. We're all lucky we're alive and eating. God, how people have starved and suffered. I don't believe you have ever grasped this whole thing except vaguely, except where it has touched you. You say, "If you have placed me in a position where I cannot do anything—in fact powerless to change the situation—that is more than disastrous." That is manifestly unfair. Supposing we had not struggled day and night to avert disaster, to stave off creditors, suppose we had been forced into bankruptcy, then everything would have been taken, all your book rights, all the income from your work, past and future, until such time as all your debts had been paid. A receiver would have been appointed at an exorbitant salary, and he would not have cared what happened to you, believe me. As it is, the corporation is now taking care of that, holding off creditors, paying them off as the money comes in, conserving, holding on to whatever we can that means future security, sacrificing where we have to, selling when there is a possibility of doing so.

You must remember that I cannot go with a gun and force an editor to accept your stories. Perhaps some cheap magazine might pay a cent a word, but I'd die rather than cheapen your product. Once you cheapen your product in any of these media, you will never again get back into the first class or the big money. However, let us suppose that you yourself went ahead and sold a story for $10,000, kept the money for your own purposes and spent it. Inevitably one of your creditors would find out. Would he be sore? He'd say, "Here I've been playing along fairly, taking a small amount every month and a big sum comes in and it's spent for Zane Grey's pleasure."

On the whole, it looks to me like clearing skies for us, provided we do what is right, and that is, stick together, consider the picture in its entirely, and act accordingly. You cannot say as you did in this last letter, "Do not let finances keep you from taking this trip. It will be worth more than it costs." But darling, if the finances are not there, how can they be used? Or if they have to be used to keep us from some crisis, how can we use them for our pleasure?

That's all now. I cannot realize that ten days after you get this, I shall be seeing you. Don't fail me, my dear. My love to you.

Dolly

Zane was home in July and spent a few days in Altadena before going to the Umpqua. He returned to Altadena and remained there through November, taking occasional short trips. In late November he visited Las Vegas and the construction site of Boulder Dam, gathering material for a book set there.[18]

Dolly left for New York in October, again driving across the continent, and stayed in New York for several weeks. The strain of the past year told. Zane's resistance to the corporation and her decisions, his reproaches and accusations, and his relationship with Wanda had hurt Dolly, and when she left she wrote of that.[19] A change of locale was as necessary for her as it was for him, and she left him in charge—a good lesson for him. He responded with a rare frank discussion of his feelings for Dolly and for other women and of his management of the business and plans for another trip.

OCTOBER 14, 1933

Dearest,

I did not finish reading your letter until tonight. There was no use before because I was too wretched. But tonight I reread it—even the hateful part—and I will add this to alleviate the pangs my letter no doubt gave you. To my eternal shame and regret I admit part of your letter to be true and just. But you are morbid, unwell still, and you make mountains out of molehills. I am not ruined, and I am not going to be. No woman ever could take your place with me. To imagine that is insane. No woman ever got, or could ever get from me the same things I have given you. This is solemnly true, Dolly. You are the one indispensable person in my life, and the children follow.

It's hard for me to understand the terrific pressure of things you must unburden to me. But I believe you. Perhaps if I had had a few days to get over my hurt I'd have left out some of the things in my letter. Nevertheless I'll send it anyhow. I couldn't rewrite it. Please believe me. I am not forgetting you or your needs. But it's terrible that I alone am the person whom you must deluge. I wish I were Atlas.

You horrified me by stating that you had stood by me for 28 years. My God, but that seems true. On the other hand I have steadily loved you more and more all those years.

I'm exhausted now, Dolly darling. In spite of my agonies today I wrote 13 pages on Burton's stuff. Forgive me for everything and stick to your realization that we belong to the children.

Love and kisses

Doc

Two weeks later,

Altadena

NOV. 1, 1933

Dearest Dolly,

Your letters at hand, and the marked improvement in your mental state was very joyful news. I am fine—okay again—except for a bitter sadness when I think of WW. Three days absolutely alone here, and three awful nights, not only about ended me but gave me a realization of how you must feel when you are alone. It was good for me.

Betty came home from S.F. all in. She enjoyed the game, but said the trip up and down was hell. What she had to say about Miss B. pleased me very much.[20]

It was a relief to hear that Rose would take the Horse-thief story, but d—

disappointing that changes must be made. He has not sent the MS or instructions and that means another delay, perhaps a long one, in getting that
money. Maybe it is a stall just to delay payment. We need that money most
——————bad! Believe me, very little left in the corp. account, and I am
almost broke. It cost $39.60 for the football tickets for all of us, 12 in number.
And Loren's wages, and Betty take up so much. I have not spent much on
myself since you left.

I absolutely must begin to get busy on the trip. This is Nov. 1. Much more
delay will make it too late. By the way, after long pondering and worrying, and
laying awake at night, I have decided to give up the Australia trip and go direct
to Tahiti. My reasons are—first, expense so great that I'm afraid the money
could not be raised. I can spend five months at Tahiti and the Paumotos for what
the Australian trip would cost. Secondly, I have all along thought it was hardly
the thing for Betty. I am not at all sure of conditions in Australia, and I might get
up against a bad situation where I'd have to leave the girls on the mainland.
Betty wants mostly to go to Tahiti and so does Dot. Miss B. will be happy in any
event. Loren will like the Tahitian idea best because I can take Johnnie. I miss the
prestige of opening up that Australian fishing to the world. That I can sacrifice.
But always I stand to catch a greater fish round Tahiti, and especially at the Paumotos. So the Australian trip is off. The sailing date for the Union Line is Dec. 20.
I will proceed at once to do all I can do without cash on hand. But darling, what
in the world will I do if we don't get any?

Your report about Schuler just helped me wonderfully. It changed the
thing—that is to say, my state of mind. I am hoping the other editors will be as
nice. You have a remarkable personality, Dolly dear.

I have been able to keep Lois busy.[21] She is priceless, and I want to hang on
to her. But she has dealt my vanity a blow from which it will never recover.

A check for 50 odd dollars came from the Bell Syndicate for a newspaper
second serial sale, I imagine. What shall I do with it? By the end of the week
I'll need it terrible! Gosh, I wish some more would come in while you're away.
If it does I'll let you know. This will do for today.

Much love,

Doc

Zane sailed again for Tahiti in December, taking a pregnant Betty and baby Michele, Dorothy (Romer's wife) and baby Romer, Loren, Ken, and Brownella Baker.

Vairoo

JANUARY 9, 1934

Dearest,

I've been away now about long enough to begin to miss you and home like hell, to be haunted by your sad face, and by my rotten spells of despair, and all that I remember so recently. Sometimes I have a feeling that I might die far away from you, before you ever know how I cared, and how remorse ate at my heart. It's a bad kind of feeling.

We are all well. Started fishing two days ago. I think Ken and Loren will be fine. Loren is careless about eating, etc. He's now sure burned to beat hell. Ken is funny about mosquitos, spiders, etc. The problem is how to satisfy Betty. I had to build a new Aunt Jane [outhouse] and a porch and a fence-pen for the kids. Now I have to hire a horse and buggy. Betty is nice so long as she does what she wants. In fact, all is O.K. except the expense is more than I calculated upon with a 15 percent overlap. It can't be helped. I've done my best.

I took them all over to Tautiri on Sunday. They had a grand time. I think they all eat twice as much as they ought. We have dandy meals. But I'm afraid to look at the bills. They have to have meat. Oh, well.

Brownella has the nicest disposition of any girl I ever had with me. I am on the 5th chapter of Boulder Dam. It's coming along.

I tried to read Anthony Adverse. It is a tremendous book, a marvelous achievement. What that fellow must know! If I wrote 1000 pages of detail about Arizona desert and people I suppose he would marvel at my knowledge. But I wouldn't have my name on that book. The hero is a bastard. He is seduced when he's a kid by a 30 year old woman, and he has illicit relations with a lot of women. I don't like such passages as, "A young naked Negro was not at all embarrassed by a hearty morning erection." The book is full of vulgarity.

Well, so long for tonight. I hope you are O.K. and not so lonely, and that
there is a little hope to spur you on. Write me any news.

Love

Doc

Dolly worked on Zane's latest manuscript, *30,000 on the Hoof.* Bob
(Betty's husband), Ed Bowen, and Romer were her chief assistants.

Zane's trip was as expensive as the former one but not as contentious.
Perhaps the companionship of family was the difference. At any rate he was
home in April and stayed a few weeks in Altadena then returned to the
Umpqua for the summer. Dolly joined him for a few weeks in late June,
returning to Altadena early in July.[22]

The worst of the financial crisis seemed over. Creditors still hounded
them, but enough money dribbled in to keep them at bay. Late in July Paramount took up the rights to *Fighting Caravans,* which helped temporarily.[23]
And in August RKO began negotiations for *West of the Pecos.*[24] But Zane's
habit of faulty accounting and his negligence in telling Dolly exactly what
checks he had written created difficult situations she had to solve. For example, he told her he had written checks for bills in Tahiti in the amount of
$175.00, but when the checks came in they amounted to over $400.00.[25]
Most annoying were his periodic attempts to take control of the corporation, bouts Dolly met with increasing ire.

AUGUST 21, 1934

Dearest Doc,

I received your letter yesterday. I am perfectly delighted that you have
decided to be boss of the corporation and I hope you get busy pretty quick. I
am going to shove all the responsibility right square up to you hereafter. But
don't go off half cocked before you know all sides of a situation. It is rather
difficult to meet the various emergencies that arise so far away as you are.
And, please, when you make critical comments as to the way I do things, be
sure that you are thoroughly conversant with the conditions that gave rise
to them. For instance, on telegrams and Romer's criticism of me on that point:
I have never yet let a deal grow cold for lack of a telegram when it was

needed. The specific circumstance which led to Romer's criticism was one on which I objected to sending a telegram to New York on a Friday afternoon when there is not an office open until Monday. Saturdays everything is closed up tight, and an air mail letter much more fully explaining the circumstances would have reached the people it was supposed to just as soon as a telegram could. Even the telegraph company, when we phoned in the message, made that comment, saying that there was no one to whom to deliver a message on Saturday. However, it was sent.

For the last thirty years, I ran all the business and communication with New York, and I don't think I missed many tricks. Even with the change in conditions, I did relatively better than you will ever do again.

When Romer wrote you, he was in an extremely bad frame of mind.[26] When males are in a bad frame of mind, I always know that it is not due to existent conditions, but it is some personal reason that they hide from you. It is either women, drink, or physical condition that is complicating their existence, and casting such a lurid hue around them that they cannot see normally. They then take out their ire or disgruntlement on whoever comes in contact with them.

We are doing our best here, in every way to keep things going—and by things I mean you. I get pretty damned tired of it some times, particularly when Romer writes you and then you write back to me and censure me about a lot of things you know nothing about. In all my letters, I have purposely restrained from telling you how desperate things were at times, because you have a habit of running around and telling people what terrible letters I write you. But you are the boss, as you say in your letter, and a boss cannot function on half truths. I don't wish to go into horrid details, but you have no idea in what a precarious condition you were as regards the government and the income tax collector, and Bowen had to do some very tall talking and explaining to keep you from serious trouble. You are still far from out of the woods on that score, and I am sure that your actions will be kept very close tabs upon.

With lots of love, despite this, that, and the other, I am

As ever,

Dolly

After awhile she wrote again, mentioning recent changes in state, national, and international conditions.

AUGUST 31, 1934

Dearest Doc,

   To some extent, I have gotten over my "mad" at you. After all, it doesn't pay, I suppose, but you surely got my goat with that last letter. It seems such a thankless job to struggle along and do everything that can be done, and then to have criticism such as you. However, big things have been stirring lately, and our own little personal grievances seem rather small in the light of events that are taking place.

   This overwhelming victory of our friend, Upton Sinclair, was to me a perfectly astounding thing. At first, I had a very keen resentment about it, but now I am trying to look at it from a wider angle. There is an alarming possibility that he may be elected governor, and in that case, we surely would see some changes. According to a great many people, he would absolutely ruin California. But, after all, what is ruin? There is a trend of events against which it is useless to fight. The election of Roosevelt was almost a revolutionary thing and his actions since he has been in office have been revolutionary. Nevertheless, I think what he has done has shunted the country away from a bloody revolution, from war and disaster of that sort, and no matter what his failings have been, he has at least given the people a sense of feeling that things were getting better instead of worse. We were on the edge of a very great catastrophe, and just the overwhelming number of people that voted for Roosevelt and put him in, indicated that he was the man that should be in at that particular time. No matter what you think, and no matter what a lot of capitalists think and a lot of conservative people that have run their businesses in certain ways for years, Roosevelt has done an infinite amount of good. Of course, he has made his mistakes, his blunders and no slight ones at that, but how can a mere human being help from that? It's history. You know what Tennyson said—"The old order changeth." That is history also. Old orders change periodically and if we don't change with them, we might as well give up. I cannot feel that an accession of Upton Sinclair to the governorship of this state is going to help matters any at the present time, but if the people do put him in, what can we do about it? And then there is always the sense of humor; having met Upton Sinclair several times, I always have to laugh when I think of him as governor of California. He did strike me as a considerable nut, visionary, etc. Hitler also always arouses my sensibilities. To me he has always been a comic character. I cannot take him seriously, and yet, God knows he is serious enough for Germany and the world.

I know that I am forgetting to tell you a lot of things that I want to, but the time is getting short and we will have to get lunch and start for the boat pretty soon, so I will close this for today.

With lots of love.

As ever,

Dolly

She took her own advice and looked for new ways to make, and save, money. Ed Bowen was dispatched to the East Coast to explore business opportunities such as radio programs, games, books for children, and other ways to capitalize on the Zane Grey name. He was also to look into selling the Lackawaxen property, as the taxes on it were eating away at them.[27] Dolly had introduced him to book publishers and magazine editors the previous year, and because conditions in the publishing industry had changed, she felt it necessary to change their own methods as well. Bowen, she felt, would be able to negotiate with the editors better than she would. Her friendly relations with them precluded the tough, shrewd bargaining that Ed could do.

Zane looked forward to a productive California autumn, but his peace was shattered when R.C. suddenly died. Dolly described the tragedy in her diary.

I got home to a very upset household. Betty was sketchily getting the dinner served assisted by Brownie. They all said Doc would not eat but I went upstairs and persuaded him to come down. He still was more stunned, amazed and confused than grief stricken. I had a great fear for Doc because I knew his wonderful love for Rome. I have never seen two brothers who were as close as those two, and all his life Doc could never do enough for his brother.

After dinner, we drove up there again to find a house full of people, most of them sitting around the living room. When Doc saw the crowd, he shied and asked Ida to come into the dining room so he could talk to her for a few minutes.

After we got home, Doc talked some and the burden of his trouble was that he had not spent enough time with Rome recently and that he had let things go that he should have done. I tried to tell him that nobody could have done any more than he had and that Rome had been living a life that suited him, that he was not able to continue on the strenuous trips with Doc, etc. He would talk and then he would break down but finally I got him to bed and the most saving habit that he has, namely the ability to lose himself in sleep, came to his rescue.[28]

The next day was filled with the business of dying—visiting the mortuary, selecting a casket, choosing a plot, and so forth.

That night Doc had a very bad spell. He broke down completely and said he felt as if he were going out of his mind. I finally got him to bed and sat down beside him and talked to him for a long while and presently he calmed down. The most pathetic thing he said was that when he and Rome were little fellows they used to have to go to bed in the dark and cold and they would crawl into bed together to keep each other warm. Rome was really the only real friend of his own sex that Doc ever had, and they have never been separated for any length of time. Doc always tried so hard to make an author of Rome and to have him share in everything that he had and did.[29]

The funeral was on Saturday, November 10. After some equivocation Zane attended, but he sat in the back of the funeral parlor on a couch rather than in the front with the family. The service was a simple Christian Science one. That evening Dolly protested that she was too tired to cook, so the family all went out to dinner at Melody Lane then went to see Joe E. Brown in *Six Day Bicycle Race,* which Zane had selected.

R.C.'s death forced Zane to confront the rapid passing of time. The blow was not one from which he could easily recover. He was unenthusiastic about another adventure and stayed home for the rest of 1934 and on into 1935, perhaps the longest time he had remained at home for over ten years.

In fact he did not leave again until the middle of June, when he returned to the Umpqua, and even there his enthusiasm was absent.[30]

Dolly drove east again in early summer but was back by July. She and Betty, with Betty's two daughters, Michele and Carol, met Zane at the Umpqua in mid-August. Loren and Ida were already there with a host of helpers, including Brownella. Ed Bowen and his wife, Marjorie, were expected to come also. Dolly stayed until August 26, and Zane slowly recovered. He and Dolly returned to Altadena in September, staying until early December, when he left for a new destination—Australia.

1935–1937

CHAPTER 16

You, Who Make Home

T HE AUSTRALIAN GOVERNMENT wanted Zane to publicize Australia as he had New Zealand and Tahiti. On his part he was anxious to explore thirteen thousand miles of coast line and was sure the Australian waters, especially on the Indian Ocean side, offered some of the greatest big-game fishing in the world. Tales of man-eating sharks aroused his curiosity. He also wanted Australian backing for two motion pictures: one a fiction about Australia, the other a fishing picture featuring a man-eating shark. He sailed December 11 on the Oceanic line for Pago Pago, where he would board the SS *Monterey* for Australia. Ed Bowen accompanied him to negotiate motion-picture financing. Ed's wife, Marjorie, several cameramen, and a secretary accompanied him, and Brownie was to join them later. As usual Dolly wrote before he left, so that he would have a letter to read from her just after departing.

DECEMBER 1935

Dearest Doc,

It's always difficult for me to write this kind of a letter before you depart. I usually feel so sort of miserable that you are going, and as a defense against breaking down, I have to don a sort of mental armor. However, I want you to know that I think you will have a most successful trip—I don't see how you can help it under the circumstances. So make the most of it, and keep yourself adaptable.

There is no question that mentally and philosophically you have gone forward a great deal in the last year; that your fund of understanding of humanity has increased; and that this will manifest itself in increased richness and depth in your work. Unquestionably times and circumstances have brought misery and discouragement, but you were never the person to lie down under adversity. Remember what old John Wanamaker said to you, "Zane Grey, never lay down your pen!" Perhaps that is superfluous advice to you, for you never will.

I have never lost my faith in you and in your work; but I knew that adjustment might be a long and painful process. Now I am sure that you are ready to gird on your armor again and leap into the battle. My love and hope and faith go with you, and in this spirit I say to you, "Merry Christmas and the best that the New Year can bring you."

Your wife,

Dolly

He wrote several days later from on board ship.

Friday, 9:30 am

DECEMBER 16, 1935

Dolly dearest,

I am up this morning, very much better, but weak as a cat. Did you ever see me with that gray color on my face?

Wednesday night was awful. I thought I couldn't stand it. The wait seemed endless. I don't want any more ordeals like that. Of course, I was ill and horribly depressed. Still somehow it wasn't right.

The ribbon you held stood for a long while. Romer's lasted until the ship began to move. When they snapped it felt like my heartstrings. The last view I had of you was when you were huddled against that iron pillar, wiping your eyes with a handkerchief. Your face became indistinct after I still saw you. I went to bed, and did not sleep a wink.

I suppose you have adjusted yourself already. It'll be better for you to be rid of me for awhile. I got off the track, and couldn't get back. There appears to be a very ordinary crowd on board. Gus and Marge and Miss D—all were splendid.

Love,

Doc

He arrived at Sydney on December 31 to welcome the New Year, 1936.

DECEMBER 31, 1935

Dearest Dolly,

Well, I got here, pretty wobbly, but I am better. Once on Terra Firma I'll be O.K. You should have seen the welcome I got. Believe me it was swell. The Australians are doing all they can. Next to the Prince of Wales and Duke of York, I came third in the limiting of restrictions.

This is a great city. Ed is working like a beaver. But we still find prices high and few discounts with the exception of what the gov't. can do. All the Shell people offered for 5 radio appearances or talk was $1000. I suppose I ought to take anything.

Last night I met my Australian poetess of two years correspondence.[1] She is about 25, lovely, an aristocrat, a strange creature, a genius if I ever met one, another Charlotte Bronte. Darling, here's one lady your Don Juan (So you say!) will never wake. She said the only woman I ever really loved was you. And I'll be d— if she isn't right! I am glad to know this woman.

There isn't much more news, and I am rushed, rushed, rushed. I lost my voice yesterday. Today I've gone easier. Tomorrow I'll try to leave for Bermagui to camp.

I'm far away, Dol, but I'll come out on top. My bad spell seems to have gone.

Lots of love,

Doc

Bermagui was three hundred miles south of Sydney in the neighborhood of Montague Island, where swordfish had been observed and caught. The camp was nestled in a grove of eucalyptus trees, or gum trees as they were called. There was only one problem.

JANUARY 11, 1936

Z.G. Camp

Dearest Dolly,

This place is beautiful—a high wooded bluff overlooking the sea. But it is open to the public. And do they come! They have driven me screwy these last few days. Hundreds of visitors! Autographs, pictures, talk! But it is nevertheless flattering. I took in my horns when I found out what a hero I was in Australia. It will not be bad when I start fishing.

The Kookaburra, or laughing jackasses, visit us morning and night. Wonderful but ludicrous birds! There are other birds, all new and strange, and the view, any direction, is inspiring. Ed is in Sydney working on deals. I had calls yesterday from Cook from L.A. and I believe he is coming out on the Maungarui. That means finance, and it will solve my problem.

I'll begin writing today.

Darling, I'm so glad to write you good news, and that my black mood is gone. I'm fine. Underweight and weak! But I'll get that back. Mrs. Roy, the cook, is just splendid.

There are seagulls parading in front of my office tent now! Impressed by the great Z.G., no doubt! It seems incredible that I left home a month ago, Dec. 11.

Love to Ide and Betty and

Yourself,

Doc

Dolly continued her normal routine and wrote long, chatty letters to him in the form of diary accounts.

JANUARY 27, 1936

Dearest Doc,

This is our first mail from Australia. Accompanying it was the last letter that was written on the boat. Naturally, I opened the boat letter first and was considerably alarmed at the account of your condition. However, the land letter counteracted that, and although there was not a great deal of news, at least it was comforting to find out that you had arrived safely and that prospects were fair. I wondered from where you had been doing your broadcasting.

I was greatly intrigued by your poetess' pronouncement that I was the only woman that you had ever really loved, and your agreement with that. She must be deeply psychic to have discovered anything like that. God knows it doesn't show on the surface. Of course, your statement led to many speculations as to your conversation with her. Don't forget, darling, that I, too, am psychic.

Much love,

Dolly

JANUARY 29, 1936

Dearest Doc,

Our long hoped for rain is finally descending upon us and all we can pray for is that it continues for awhile. But the outlook is very depressing on such a day and gives me a tendency towards blueness.

Yesterday after stopping by at the doctor's, I went out to Paramount to have lunch with Romer. I always enjoy that for I meet numbers of people I know and there are always motion picture individuals to look at.

Yesterday the two most interesting were Boyer, who sat facing me, and later Marlene Dietrich, who came in a Russian peasant costume looking very fascinating. She sat down at the big table where the heads of the industry gather. When she saw Boyer, she beckoned to him, whereat he quickly jumped up and went over and kissed her hand. She ogled at him with a look that was enough to twist any man's head. However, later, I noticed her passing out the same kind of a look to various other men, meanwhile always keeping a weather eye peeled to see who was watching her.

Brownie phoned in just now that she did not have any money to pay for the trip to Australia. I told her that we were down to bedrock ourselves and that she had better cable you. I looked up a code word for her—"Sloop."[2] She needs about five hundred and there is not that much here. I might possibly be able to borrow that amount, but would be afraid to do so as we are low and on my borrowing ability might depend a great deal more than sending Brownie to Australia on the March boat.

Love, as always,

Dolly

All went exceptionally well in Australia. The camp was beautiful, his reception by the Australian government and the people was overwhelming, even more so than that accorded to him by New Zealand some years before, and the fishing was promising. There was only one worry.

JANUARY 31, 1936

Dearest Dolly,

I just cabled you that I was well, happy,—that I had caught the Australian record swordfish.

Your two lovely letters received yesterday. They made me so d— homesick that I wanted to die. I shall read them again and again.

Dolly, I was very ill on the way down here. No one knows how ill! It has taken all this time for me to get well. I just stopped coughing the last few days. All that morbid haunting terror of dying away from home is gone.

I am amazed and dumfounded at the reception given me in Australia. I found myself a favorite author, a hero fisherman, a famous celebrity come to do well by their country. And have they responded! My talks on the radio are going ever bigger and bigger. Sunday night I talked 28 minutes. But all Ed could chisel out of the Shell Co. was $1000, not pounds.

I have from 250 to 500 visitors daily. Come to see me, for autograph and photos, to buy books, to visit the famous Zee Gee Camp. They call me Zee Gee. This little town of Bermagui has become notorious overnight. Other towns are jealous. It is a most amazing tribute. So far I have been tactful, friendly, and responsive. But I cannot begin to answer my mail. Marge and Miss I. have their hands full.

Ed has three picture companies on edge to back our fishing picture and make our fiction picture.[3] The prospects are bright. They have money, but are d— close with it. And we will have to go mostly on expenses and percentage. But Ed thinks well of them.

I am almost broke! I had a little over $5000, you know. Everything here is awfully high, and so many expenses I didn't account for. I wanted Ed to give up while I had money to pay the boatmen and buy second class tickets home. But he wouldn't do it. He's a gambler and smart! We have a great opportunity here, if we can fulfill it. Ed has been offered a big job as director. In the event that we don't put it over here we will be in a hell of a fix. I'm supposed to be a millionaire American sportsman! But I warned and begged Ed. He says he can do it. And I believe him.

By the way I sent for Brownie six weeks ago. She is coming in March. I paid 25 pounds for an opal necklace for you. Gee, it is swell! I had to do it. So don't rail at me. Australian opals.

The fishermen are punk. They think they know it all. But I am being as careful as possible. All the same I have caught all the fish so far, and they have none. If I know fishermen they will murder me.

Our camp is beautiful, ideal, except open to the public. The newspapers are full of it—what I do—where I go—how I fish—and Lord knows what else. The birds are strange, lovely. The trees gorgeous. The bush (forest) magnificent. If it wasn't for the fear about money I'd be having my greatest trip. I wrote the story for the fiction picture.

Do I remember when I stood on deck and watched you wiping your eyes? Do I? Dolly, darling, my heart cracked when that ribbon broke. I never was so sick, never so sad at leaving you. And Oh! That voyage!—But let's forget it.

Dolly, I mustn't forget that I have wished you here often, just to see the people, the kids who come to see me. You'd love it. That has touched me deeply. They come from hundreds of miles away.

They gave a party here in camp for me tonight. But I donated a bottle of champagne given me because I caught the big fish. The gang made merry. I didn't drink, but I felt better than at any time since I've been away.

Goodnight. Much love to you and love to all. Write often. I'll cable any good news.

Doc

Early in February he caught a green thresher and the Australian record black marlin, but not without controversy. The Australian Society for the Prevention of Cruelty to Animals objected to big-game fishing and wanted to stop it. Australian sporting officials and businesses alike were up in arms in defense of Zane Grey and big-game fishing. Even the premier got involved.

Finally, the crowds at the camp overwhelmed him, making writing impossible, and he moved to Bateman's Bay. Despite another glorious setting, worries, doubts, and fear tortured him.

Z.G. Camp

Bateman's Bay

FEBRUARY 27, 1936

Dearest Dolly,

We got our home mail here yesterday, but I couldn't read mine till today. For me it was a thin mail except for your four letters. Nothing from any of the girls I've been so good to! Damn their souls!

Your diary notes made me so homesick I nearly died. Dolly, please write a letter to me when you send all that stuff. I don't know what has come over me this trip. I've never recovered from that illness and the agony I suffered while lying alone in bed on the ship. At night I think terrible things about you—and how time is flying and what in God's name can I do? I think I must find some real girl friend or sweetheart before it's too late! I don't neglect you, my darling, in all this torturing morbid thought. I worry myself till my breast aches. I must not take space to tell you these things when there is so much otherwise to tell. But I'd like to be home, and that means, of course a failure of this trip, and perhaps never another trip—and only to die ahead!

This camp is the loveliest I ever had. It's on a curve of white beach. With magnificent spotted gum trees, royal and stately—lovely to be under. Islands out in the bay, dark forest beyond, and dark mountain ranges. Birds of new songs and colors. I saw a black snake today, one of Australia's terrible snakes. But I saw him first. You know me! Oh but he was beautiful. Blue black and long and thick—he came sliding through the woods. When I yelled for the gang he shot into some grass to hide. Then they came, and I poked him out, and broke his back as he made for me. I wanted to scare the girls and all of them, because we are in snake country.

We broke camp at Bermagui yesterday. I couldn't stand the crowds any longer. The people of that burg are terribly sorry to have me leave. I fished all the way up here, 72 miles, in a rough sea, and caught a dandy swordfish off the Toll Gates just outside the Bay. And fetched him to camp which was all ready for me. Then I gave the fish to the men who came to meet me. They took it to town, 3 miles inland, and created a sensation. No one there had ever seen one! All of Batemen's Bay, a fine little town, are most violently grateful to me. I am a hero. The news went out over the wires. I've started another fishing resort, and perhaps the best yet. It is certainly magnificent.

News of my popularity grows apace. But Dolly, we are almost broke! I will be by the time this reaches you. I've got enough money to keep us and pay the help for about a month. Ed has an offer of 1000 pounds for the story. That is $4000, and it will take $3000 for my tickets home. At that Ed will have to stay and produce the picture. This is for the fiction movie. The fishing movie is going to fail to materialize, I am sure. With the best of changes, and incredible publicity, their movie people have not the guts to back a Z.G. sport picture. Ed says they will. But I don't believe it. He got me here. Now let him get me home. Still, it is a shame. We could clean up on that picture, make $2000, surely. I'm sorry, dear. I wanted to stay home, you remember. I had $10,000. But Bowen persuaded me. I let $5000 go for film and tickets, and here we are.

My Australian friend's an English gentlewoman, intellectual, fine, very lovely and frail! With genius in her if I ever recognized it. She is lovely, and well, honey, she thinks I am some kind of a god. But I can't deceive her. She knows, just as you always knew. If I had the nerve I'd cable Brownie to stay home. I hated to hurt her the second time.

Darling, all you wrote about home and yourself and the children damn near killed me. I can't answer any of that. You have never been stranded this way, far from home. You don't know what it's like. This is the third time! Only a miracle can save me from a most pitiful situation. Well, I hope Ed can work one. I'll try to write again for this ship.

Love and kisses

Doc

P.S. The Trail Driver made us weep so I couldn't read long at a time. What a book! It tortures me to know I can't ever write another so good! But you had it right. It's a wonderful story.

Dolly wrote in lengthy diary entries about her daily activities despite his pleas for a more personal touch. Perhaps she did this because his affairs, even at his age of sixty-four, or perhaps especially now, tortured her. At the bottom of one of these letters she pens,

> Darling—you asked me to write you personally, rather than in this form—but I cannot—at length at least. A crust of lava has hardened over the turmoil beneath and I don't want to melt it. Too much would erupt that now is held in check. Perhaps when I am less tired and more in control of myself, I will attempt it. Suffice it to say that love for and faith in you do not falter.
>
> Dolly

His casual references to other women did not help.

> Z.G. Camp
> Bateman Bay
> MARCH 28, 1936
>
> Dolly Darling,
>
> Brownie arrived safely and well. She had a grand trip. Made some nice Sydney friends, a young honeymoon couple and likes the camps very much indeed. She had to ask you for that $100, for I told her to. I sent her $400, which was all I had in the bank. I should have cabled her not to come, but I hadn't the heart to do it.
>
> My last letter should have told you what we are up against. If not, this one will. The two best movie companies here kept Ed dangling after them—working him, I surmise, then turned him down in the end. There is one more, and this one has accepted my story, and if their backer will put up the money they will pay 1500 pounds, that is $6000, enough to pay our debts and get tickets home.[4] If they don't buy it our predicament will be tragic.
>
> Some of my Australian friends have agreed to finance our Great Barrier Trip. I think that will go through. And I promoted it. However, I hope the former goes through and the latter doesn't, because I want to come home.
>
> My popularity grows. It is astonishing. It is incredible. But it is true! If we only had some money we could make a picture that would clean up.
>
> The fishing is great. We have caught 57 big fish. I have Australian records for both Black and Striped Marlin. I have caught some other outstanding fish.
>
> This marks the end of my trips—my cherished hope to do something big and wonderful. In fact, I've done it this time. However, I can't stand this sort

of life any more—this hell of trying to do things without money. In other words, I can no longer keep up this false pretense. I am well and in fine physical trim. But I have had almost continual black spells.

Love,

Doc

Even the old Mildred Smith business returned to haunt them. Briggs, the editor at Harper's, asked about Mildred's claim that she ghostwrote his work.[5] While they said they did not believe it, still they inquired. He was sure that this rumor had influenced magazine editors, making them unwilling to buy his stories. He was beginning to soften toward Mildred, he told Dolly, until this latest innuendo reached him, and he finally conceded that Dolly had her pegged all along.

Toward the end of April financing came through for the Great Barrier Reef trip, so he could stay longer.

Sydney

APRIL 21, 1936

Dearest Dolly,

Your March 11th letter, or diary, was very interesting. In fact, both your batches of mail were fine, as was all the rest of my mail. And as a result I feel happy and grateful. It's the first time I remember a lot of letters that had no miserable touch whatever. Gee! Am I glad. I did not, however, hear from one or two lady friends who might have written me. But to hell with them.

Ed put over the deal for the Barrier Reef Trip and picture, on the strength of my friend backing the deal for 10,000 pounds, $40,000. Isn't that fine! After all it was I who did it. This job is big. I can't come home till July. Ed and Marge will stay longer. This is a lot of money which unfortunately cannot be drawn upon for the expenses I have already incurred. But it will help, because the film and lab bill, Andy's expense, and some of Peter's expense, can be worked in.

There is also a good chance of my fiction story, "Rangle River" being accepted. In fact, it is accepted. But the hitch is a director from Hollywood. If they can get one the deal is on. In that case I will be able to pay my debts, and buy the tickets home, a big outlay above $2800.

We leave for the Great Barrier on May 5. The journey takes 5 days. We will have 20 people. Guess I'd better write old wiseguy Romer about it.

Love,

Doc

He and the entourage sailed north on the M.V. *Manunda*, and he was besieged on board with requests for autographs.[6] Invitations flooded in, including one to speak at the prestigious University Club; the only American to receive this honor, he decided to do it. The ship stopped at Brisbane, and he feared a mob by newspaper reporters and more. He had already received hundreds of letters from fans.

Camp

Hayman Island

Great Barrier Reef

MAY 15, 1936

Dolly darling,

Here we are on the Great Barrier, and it is glorious. A lovely, beautiful island, with mountains all around and coral beaches and reef between, colors galore, birds of strange hue and music, fish and fish and fish. It took us 5 days to get here, and the big steamer put us off right in front of the island. We had to come ashore in small boats. The passengers nearly mobbed me.

Ed will be here Sunday with the Company and we will go to work. I'll send some photos soon.

The shells and coral here are marvelous. I am crazy about them, and I don't see how I can pack home all I want to.

I am pretty homesick, as I've told you before. But what with the work to do here, and the fishing and the shell gathering the time will fly.

Love,

Doc

Negotiations continued regarding *Rangle River.* Victor Jory was signed to go to Australia to star in it, and arrangements were made with Columbia Pictures for Clarence Badger to direct the film.[7]

Z.G. Camp

Hayman Island

JUNE 7, 1936

Dearest Dolly,

We have been here 4 weeks today. It is a lovely island. The birds and bird songs, so new and strange to me, the shells and the fish keep me endlessly intrigued.

We are progressing well with our picture. Have over a 100 sequences shot already. But I don't believe we can catch the July 22 ship for home. I hope so, but I don't believe we can. Time flies here. I hardly know where the days go. The cockatoos, the Kookaburras, the ravens and magpies awaken me before dawn every morning. There are other wonderful birds, too, with glorious songs. The gulls have a regular long wailing piercing note that wakes me at night. I grow cold all over. I think things.

The tide, too, fascinates me with its different notes at different stages. The reefs are marvelous. You can walk miles and hunt shells every day, after every tide, and always find something.

The Cinema Picture Co. finally wired they are sending 1000 pounds and a contract for my story. I guess that definitely settles it. Well, it's sure swell news. I can just about pay debts and get the tickets home. If I can shove some of these bills upon Ed and the company, well and good, I'll have a little dough upon my return. I still owe $500 at Tahiti for boat repairs, camp repairs, labor, etc. But I can stretch that out a couple of months. It looks now that after all I have made an incredible success here, altogether. Romer will show you some clippings about the picture to be made from my Australian fiction story, which I wrote on the way down, ill and morbid. They think it is swell.

Columbia will make it. Clarence Badger will direct. They are trying hard to get Nola Warren, the girl I picked for my White Death picture. She is young, lovely, has talent and may go far. Oh, she'll look grand in westerns. She'd make Gail look pale by comparison.

Dolly, Hemingway's book "Green Hills Of Africa" is a fine African hunting story. But it stunned me. I didn't count the sons-of-bitches and bastards, but there must have been hundreds. Then a lot more profanity and dirty. He puts into his wife's speech; "Sonsabitches!" And there are things I wouldn't put on paper even in a letter to you. I lost my respect and admiration for Hemingway in one fell swoop. When I come home I want you to read the book and tell me what it means, what has changed, why Scribner published it, and other puzzling things.

I am well again, slim and black, almost happy, full of work and plans, but homesick. Give my love to everybody.

Ever yours,

Doc

Hemingway's work was the least of his worries. Despite his fame in Australia, the literary success and popularity of his competitors, especially Ernest Hemingway and John O'Hara, annoyed him, and the antics of his girlfriends, especially when they spoke favorably of these authors in his presence, angered him. Underneath was the nagging thought that his approach and style were out of date.

Z.G. Camp

Hayman Island

Great Barrier Reef

JUNE 21, 1936

Darling Dolly,

All mail in last night from home. You, who make home, do not understand that. Heard from everybody I care for except Connie Keating, at whom I am sore. I liked her heaps last winter. But she made me sore at her. She wrote me about getting drunk with some bullfighter. Then she denied it.

Your letters were the nicest you have ever written me since you were trying to hook me and marry me a few years ago. I read all of that typed MS three times. My love, you have not lost any of your charm for Z.G. I think I feel really happy. It's a strange sensation for me.[8]

JUNE 22, MORNING

I got flagged last night, and what with upset, quarrels, fights with the three girls I couldn't get back to your letter. Well, night before last I had picked up a book—that new novel by O'Hara, Butterfield 8, or some name like that. I had heard them talking about it. It was filthy. His first novel had a far better story.

Shorter. Less detail. And a hero you could feel sorry for, and a heroine who was swell. A fine girl tied to a cad! But these people, I don't believe such lousy people live. At least I never met any. I don't know that you have read the novel. But if you have and if you don't say it's rotten, I'll be ashamed of you. Not only has it all the obscenity and profanity that characterizes Hemingway's book, but it has dirt, just plain dirt, lugged in to cause evil-minded women to whisper: "Have you read O'hara's latest? Hot!" Etc., etc. That's why that stuff is in his book. I don't know what has happened in N.Y. In the realm of books. But I do know what is good and bad, what is literature and what is tripe, what will last and what will not, what will make people love a book and what not. And you taught me, Dolly Grey.

Well, I burned this book up. And last night when Brownie and Maia came down to see me I told B.⁹ Did she fly up? I'll say she did. I think she must have been pretty nervous. Anyway she said some caustic things, and practically ridiculed my opinion of the book. She praised it. She praised O'Hara. She said she liked him. In fact some of the things she said were hard for me to over-look. But I kept my temper. All I did was stoutly maintain my stand. Neverthe-less, I thought that if it were true that she thought that about a cheap, dirty, lousy novel and its writer, that she shouldn't be a secretary of mine. A rather strong and significant deduction for me to make!

The girls went back to their tents, and then Nola came. She was spitting fire, and when she got insulting, because of something Emil said I said, I called her good and hard. So, my love, that all was what interfered with my happy response to your letters.

Your letters were just fine, Dolly. I have read them twice, all that yellow paper stuff, too. I never complained about them. All I wanted was something written to and for me. As you used to! Well, these letters had that, and I was just thrilled and elated. Your daily diary reads like extracts from John Gals-worthy, only infinitely more human and interesting. After all what you chronicled is life—everyday life. Dolly, I'll have to sit in with you all oftener when I come home. I have missed a lot. I'll have to do a lot of nice things. I shall stay home and work all fall and winter, up to March. But, angel darling, the house must be heated. Dolly, I wake at night a lot. I don't have the morbid thoughts anymore. But I ache for you and the children and home. I dream of

Rome and I wake to grieve. The years fly so swiftly. And I have done nothing—nothing! I am still the same, whatever they say. These are bad hours for
me, or maybe good. With daylight they go away. I do not lie on my left side,
for then my heart throbs in my ear. A steady, slow, strong, muffled drum. And
it makes me think of Ellsworth, all the trouble he had with his heart, and that
night when Ethel found him, and he said: "Oh, it is the end!" And then all
Rome's trouble with his heart, because of that long run to catch the train in
Toledo—that hurt his heart—and then the way he smiled at Ida and whis-
pered, "Tough luck, Ide!" Did he know—did he realize? If so why, why didn't
he mention me? My heart, so far as strength and vitality are concerned is
sound. But it makes me wonder—will it never grow tired?

I remember when Berenice said to me: "I should think you'd have had
enough!" That always haunted me. I should have had enough and to spare.
But I haven't, Dolly. I haven't. Not enough of life and love! Of home! Of you
especially! Of work! Of achievement! Of fishing! Forgive me, honey. I got
off the track.

Did I tell you in my last that I'd heard from Evelyn? Well, she didn't say so,
but I gathered that she must be through with the Greys. I'm sorry. I liked her.
Maybe more. Just to look at her was good for me. I don't suppose I'll have a
single friend when I get back.

You needn't write any more, if you don't especially want to. Of course, I'd
like letters clear up to August 10 when the Mariposa gets to Sydney. I'll write
you again.

Love and kisses

Doc

Rain delayed filming for a week, putting them behind schedule. Zane
played a part in *White Death*, enjoyed the experience immensely, and considered doing another film. By the end of August, however, he was on his way
home. Brownie and Maia had left earlier, in July, with Maia remaining in
Auckland.

Zane longed for home and Dolly more on this trip than any other, and
when he did get home, he stayed there for some time. Throughout the fall,
winter, and spring he was in Altadena, writing, resting, but still planning

ambitious trips, most of which never materialized. He hoped to go to Florida in the spring with Romer, but Dolly and Romer balked at the expense, and even he finally admitted he was trying to do too much. He had, however, made plans to explore Wyoming for the fishing and to get material and then to return to Oregon to fish, and he would not be deterred from this.

In June he camped in Wyoming near Jackson Hole, a dramatic change from the tropical environment. Brownie was with him as well as Romer and Billye.[10]

Pinedale, Wyoming

JUNE 2, 1937

Dolly Dearest,

We're up here almost in Jackson's Hole. It is over 7000 feet, cold as hell, except when the sun shines. Wind River range is one side and the Tetons on the other. Wonderful white jagged peaks as far as you can see. Lots of range, atmosphere, and a magnificent setting for either a fur or cattle story. Guess I'll try to develop both. But the many streams and rivers are high, and fishing is punk. The girls are having a swell time, and Romer is fine. I don't rest well at night, and have been depressed. But the weather has been bad. It's sunny today, and I'll probably revert to my Calif.—South Sea temperament.

I'll let you know presently when we'll start home. It won't be a hell of a long while, darling. Hope you are O.K.

Love,

Doc[11]

It is 6:30 a.m. and nippy.

A new setting and a better market for his writing than had been seen in years failed to bring back the old exhilaration.

Pinedale, Wyoming

Sunday

JUNE 6, 1937

Dearest Dolly,

It snowed like hell yesterday, then the sun came out warm, then at night it froze. I damn near froze in bed. There was a dance hall opened, and a crowd was there. I looked in for a moment. Left Romer playing stud poker with some hard-faced gazabos. Billy was in the dance hall. I could have copped out a peach, a girl I've seen several times. But I didn't. I came back here. Brownie, who has been ill, was in bed. I went to bed. In the morning I woke up stiff. I piled all my coats on the bed, and finally warmed up again.

I have one story, an unusual one with a woman cattle rustler queen who got hanged![12] The background is magnificent, and new to me. Next I am getting closer to the fur trader story.

But Dolly, something is wrong with me. I don't care a damn. I don't have a thrill. I am not excited over the extraordinary scenery. I have gone about the business as always, except I haven't the old something. It makes me sick to realize it. I'm afraid I know why.

Now I want to start back home, and am afraid to mention it to Romer. He's fine. He's enjoying every moment, and employing it, believe me. He has not appeared dark browed, or cold, or thick—you know the way he gets—once on this trip. He loves to take pictures. And he has really wonderful ideas. Here is a wide open town and I've not seen him want a drink! Of course, all that is wonderfully precious to me. I guess it will be the same, and more so, with Loren.

But I—well I am sort of stultified. I am well of my cold, and that's damn good. I have had terrible indigestion, but that is better. My great trouble is that I can't get to sleep, or if I do, I awaken, and have morbid thoughts. I know all about it. All the same it is hell to be in this fix. It's a sort of trap. I find that my only remedy is to think of the past. This may be dangerous—to live over the past, but it seems better than the other. Perhaps you are the one and only person who could possibly understand me. I wouldn't dare confess this to any one else.

I do get a thrill out of the possibility of Harper's contract for my westerns and other stories, too. There is something tremendous and saving about it. But how am I to create the stories—and write them, without that something? You tell me, Dolly. This is the inevitable result of the years. I can't escape them, or the habit fastened on me. But I do feel young, and even if that is an illusion, I know I can write better than I ever could. That is the hell of it. I can write and fish better than I ever could. And ought I not do it?

This is rather a sad letter, Dolly. But I thought I'd better tell you. Really, I didn't get wise to what ailed me until on this trip. Now in spite of Romer, and the incentive his companionship gives me, I want to come home. Then I'll go to the Umpqua. If this damned thing crowds upon me up there, I'll be at my wit's end. But I will not go unless I know I can beat it. What's the sense of spending all the money unless merely for Loren and Romer. I know positively that that is better for them than Avalon and Hollywood.

I'm going right on seeing scenery, and acquiring atmosphere and material. Perhaps when I do get back to the Umpqua, it, the something, will come back. But I don't want to fish here any more. Yesterday Romer fished in the snow!

In about two weeks I ought to be home. But I'll keep you posted. Hope you are fine.

Ever,

Doc[13]

In July he was at the Umpqua with Loren. Ida, his sister, came with him, but Romer and Billye joined them later. Dolly and Romer had decided to close the corporate office and move it to Altadena, saving around three thousand dollars per year in rent as well as the expenses of traveling to and from it.[14] Romer stayed behind to help with moving but was soon chasing steelhead with his father and brother. Brownie did not come on this trip.

One afternoon in August, Zane fell asleep in the sun.[15] He was barefoot, and when he awakened he went into the tent to put on some sneakers. Suddenly he couldn't pick up the lace to tie it with his right hand. Thinking it was his imagination, he finally got the shoe tied, whereupon he went out and lay down in a hammock. Presently he noticed that his right leg had no feeling and that he experienced difficulty in moving it. Alarmed, he started toward Ida's tent and fell down a couple of times on the way. When he got there, he was unable to talk for two minutes.

The next morning, Lyle and Gus took him to the CCC doctors.[16] He had thought it was sunstroke or heat prostration, but the doctor said it was a slight paralytic stroke caused by hardening of the arteries. A prescription was ordered that was supposed to dissolve the small blood clot causing the trouble. Zane remained quiet, as it was only when he exercised or talked too much that he lost control of his arm and leg and his speech. The doctor was optimistic that the symptoms would diminish. Upon the advice of their physician, ten days were allowed for him to rest in a hotel in Roseburg before the trip home, after which they returned by train rather than automobile, as the car trip would have fatigued him. There was no immediate worry, at least according to the doctor, as the stroke had been slight.

Dolly did not rush to his side. By the time she was notified several days had passed, and with travel time there, she might miss them. But she immediately wrote a cheerful, practical, bracing letter.

AUGUST 1937

Dearest Doc,

Romer wrote me of your trouble and I was deeply grieved. But in thinking it over, I became convinced that a thing like that could not be serious with you. You have always been such a splendid physical specimen and have always had such control over both your mind and body, that this can be nothing that you cannot overcome. You must rest and be quiet so that nature can help you. Then you must use your mind—and you know what the mind can do. Would you like me to contact Wanda's mother?[17] You always had more faith in her than anyone, and to have a strong mental faith like that exercising should help.

Things like this can happen to anyone. When Betty was born, I had this phlebitis, which is a blood clot. But I got over it and it's never bothered me since. But at the time I had to lie very still for a long time.

You must rest now for awhile and use that wonderful spirit and mind of yours to help you. Don't be discouraged. I am not. I am sure everything will be all right with you in short order.

With all my love.

As ever,
Dolly

1937-1939

CHAPTER 17

I Never Before Loved You So Well

F OUR MONTHS LATER Zane sailed for Tahiti, taking Loren, several of Loren's friends, and Brownella Baker as his companions. He could barely walk and his arm was weak, making writing difficult, but he scribbled a note to Dolly on his arrival.

DECEMBER 15, 1937

Mom, darling,

We arrived O.K., but with me about all in. The nights were awful. I slept last night so am better today. I feel that I will get stronger here.

I have thought many, many times of the way you looked and spoke when you said goodbye to me. I think that sustained me in the dark hours. I never before loved you so well.

Always,

Doc

He did not yet have the strength to fish. Recovery was the primary purpose of the trip and a constant theme in his letters. It was all he could do to write his name three times, but he doggedly worked at it.[1] Letters were dictated to Brownie, and she typed them. Each day he walked from camp to the dock, requiring tremendous effort, but each day he was stronger.[2]

Dolly continued her chatty correspondence with him as if all was normal, writing the details of home life and world affairs. But first the shock, then the ordeal of his recuperation, were not easily forgotten.

Dearest Doc,

Your New Year's telegram reached me just as 1938 was hitting New York City—that is, nine p.m. here. It has become a custom with me to accompany the New Year across the continent on the radio. Naturally, the N.Y. New Year celebration is the most thrilling to me, as I have heard it so many times. I have always maintained that the birth of a year in New York is accompanied by the most stupendous sound I have ever heard. That is, not stupendous so much in the way of noise as in the terrific heart rending harmony it carries. To me it always sounded like the birth of all creation, especially if one was high up over it in some tall building where the individual noises were blended into the great whole.

I was happy at the content of your radiogram, the fact that you said "Improved," and now that you are settled in your beautiful paradise, I expect to hear that you are entirely well again.

While we are on the subject of the family, I want to tell you that Reba is much better. She is as round as a butterball and has a new automobile and new clothes. Pauline told me that Reba had come over to see her and that all she could talk about was "honey" that is, Mrs. Gray, her companion. She seems simply obsessed with the woman, and is gradually separating herself from everyone she ever had any contact with.

I don't know how much news you get of the world in general. The war is still going on in China and also in Spain. After a while one gets rather used to the idea and it becomes an old story without any extraordinary interest.

When I was talking about Reba, I forgot to tell you the main thing which made me mention her, and that was that she sold the house for eight thousand dollars. As I remember it, you paid ten thousand dollars for the lot alone that you gave to them. Of course, that property was in the estate and subject to the debts of the estate.

I have been out very little since you left. It is a peculiar thing how habits fix upon one, and I achieved this one during the time when I stayed home with

you so much. One sort of loses the desire to do a lot of things. Movies rarely
get me these days. Evenings I sit in front of the fire and read, or at my desk
and work. I go down to Los Angeles once or twice a week, depending upon
the demand or the business I have to attend to. I should take a trip down
to the ranch, but somehow I don't get up the incentive to do it. I hate the fact
that desire has left me to do so many of the things that I used to enjoy. It is
quite disgusting not to have the right kind of anticipation. The only thing to
which I remember looking forward with any great anticipation was the trip
to Honolulu, but that didn't pan out. And the queer thing about that was that
after it was given up, I really did not feel any intense disappointment. I think
I was so glad that you were going to Tahiti instead of Australia, that it counteracted the other.

Please, with all this, do not let me give you the impression that I feel mar-
tyred, or that I am whining. I am just trying to explain a phase—the present
phase—of my life. I have no doubt that I will get over all this and enter
another period presently. Perhaps I have just been sort of resting all this time,
somewhat readjusting from a difficult experience. In other words, to refer to
one of your favorite stories, I may be picking the shot out of the bluejay, etc.,
etc. Just what the next one will be in this case, I am not ready to say. However,
I shall try very hard to make something constructive.

With all my love,

Dolly

Zane worked on a new novel, dictated this time to Brownie, a new experience for him, yet it seemed to progress satisfactorily, proving that his imagination had not suffered.[3]

Papeete, Tahiti

JANUARY 23, 1938

Dearest Dolly,

I'm certainly wanting to hear from you soon. I will enclose some of my
specimens of the handwriting I am doing, and there will be a bit of news in
that about my condition. There isn't any particular news other than what I sent
you last letter. That was written three weeks ago, and I am glad to say in that

time I have improved. We are trying to get reservations on the March 15th
Panama boat, and we hope to spend a little time fishing at the Perlas. However, that is not sure by any means yet. Not very much that I hoped for in
the way of things here has materialized yet. I am disappointed that I am not
able to fish. But Loren is doing fine with the fishing, and he is so very well
and having such a wonderful time that I have no regrets. I'm pretty sure that
during February they will catch a big fish, and, of course, that will make everything jake for me. The serious thing, though, is that no matter what is the
cost, the trip here for me is the best thing we could have done. I was worse off
than we had any idea. That nervousness and sleeplessness has left me almost
entirely, and you know how awful that was. It is so beautiful here and so
lonely with the reef singing all day long, the rain pattering on the roof every
hour, the fragrance of the flowers, and the hot sun, all of which are fine for
me and especially the hot sun. It seems a long time since I left home. By the
time you get this it will be over two months. I'm dictating on my book everyday, and have not decided what I will take up when I am through with it. But I
want to plan a big novel to be done between now and New Years.

Much love from

Zane

He was also more patient.

Papeete, Tahiti
FEBRUARY 2, 1938

Dearest Dolly,

I received your volume of happenings and what have you and was very
pleased to get it. I still hope to do a little fishing at Panama. We leave here
March 18th and get there about April 6th—some ride on a punk little ship!

If I could permit myself anymore to get furious, what you told me about
Reba would certainly have done it. But I just laughed. I think she sacrificed
Rome's property and gave away all those pictures and things which if she had
been decent she would have returned to me. If we can find out for sure
whether she has any of those films left, projecture and so forth, I will contrive
some way to get hold of them. But Reba was always one of those stumbling
stones, one of those feet tangling weeds that Ruskin writes about. All my life

I marveled at Rome and I still do when I think of his attitude towards this woman.

You were mistaken when you took my little letter to have been done by my right hand. If I remember rightly I only wrote you a few words with my right hand. At this date I can do a little better but it exhausts me to write my name across a page of manuscript. However, it doesn't hurt anymore. In many ways I have made a marked improvement. Some of the distressing things have vanished. But my mending has been much slower than anybody figured. It seems pretty sure now that I will get the use of my arm back so that I can fish and if I knew the writing was coming back I should be happy.

We are due in Panama about April 6th and can be addressed at the Washington Hotel in Cristobal. We will stay there a couple of days and then go to Panama. If it is possible I want to fish a few weeks out of Panama. That will get us home the first of May which is time enough. I am feeling better today and am sending much love and kisses.

Ever,

Doc

P.S. I have about decided that the next novel will be The Fur Trader. But the plan will be on a big scale, the same as The Wilderness Trek. So I am going ahead with that in the way of research and will probably have to start it by dictation.

I have gotten fifty thousand words done on my new fishing book The Illiad of Ocean Monsters. Now you can laugh about that title if you want to. One of the letters you mailed me from Australia acquainted me with the fact that Western Australia, the Northern Territory, and Queensland were going to get me to exploit the fishing in their waters at absolutely no cost to myself. I hope that will hold good for 1939.

Arriving in Cristobal in the Canal Zone April 6 as planned, Zane and companions fished off the coast of Panama in the Perlas Islands for about a month then caught the *Sofia Baake,* a new Scandinavian vessel, for Los Angeles.[4] The ship was late arriving, and there was some confusion about its actual arrival day, but Dolly was there at pier 230A in plenty of time to see it dock.[5]

A lot of very brown people waving violently from the deck, and later we saw that every one of them was adorned with a mustache, even Loren and Doc. Doc looked thin, but brown as a berry and with the adornment, appeared for all the world like some Cuban planter. . . . Great quantities of baggage, freight, etc., all belonging to our outfit, came overboard and was dumped into a shed where the customs officers examined it. That is, they were very nice about it and simply pasted a lot of labels all over, without bothering to go through the stuff. The reporters were also in evidence and the cameramen, and they all climbed up and got all the information they could from Loren and Doc, also photographs. Presently the four of us, Loren, Doc, Romer, and myself were homeward bound in my Lincoln and it seemed awfully nice for us all to be together that way. About half way up we stopped at a drive-in restaurant and had something to eat, as Romer hadn't had any breakfast and I only a cup of coffee and a piece of toast about five-thirty. Then I stopped at one of the little wayside markets and loaded the car with all sorts of fresh vegetables.

We arrived home about eleven o'clock and there was the usual activity of unloading. . . . The truck came in presently loaded as usual, and Doc had a great lot of stuff that he had bought both at Tahiti and Panama.

The first thing Doc discovered missing was all his newest Australian fishing rods and he swore by heaven that he had left them on the top of one of his cabinets and that they must have been stolen. He was perfectly infuriated about it, and as usual, I got the blame, although I don't see why I should. The only time the rooms have been opened have been since they have been cleaned and that was recently, and I did that upon Doc's special orders. Whether the rods show up remains to be seen, but if they were taken, it was probably before he left for Tahiti. Anyway, they were insured. If this thing did not happen so often, I might be more inclined to fall in with Doc's views. . . . A number of other things were missing from exactly where they had been put, but managed to show up somewhere else later.[6]

He appeared to be completely healed and his usual cranky self.

From May to December he remained in California but was not idle. He worked on his book and carried on a massive correspondence with people in Oregon, on the East Coast, in England, and with numerous friends and fishing companions in Australia, gathering information and planning for another trip. They wanted him to further publicize their fishing attractions, this time on the north and west coasts. In December he sailed to San Francisco, then he boarded the *Mariposa* in early January en route to the South Seas.

At Sea

December 7, 1938

9:30 A.M.

Dearest Dolly,

I was desperately ill Wed. night and Thursday—we ran into a terrible sea right away. Ship had to hove to. I never saw such waves, and I was never so seasick! Yesterday I began to recover and today I am O.K. again, but weak.

I am terribly ashamed of my upset the last week or so, and want to forget them. I still feel that I should not have come. But it was good to get away from the cold. My hand is still stiff.

We have only a few hours at Honolulu, and that at night. Gus and Lyle are disconsolate because there are no girls on board.[7]

I am going to put in my time getting well and fit. Already I feel different.

See that you cheer up now and have a good time. I am sorry you have been down for so long, and feel that I am to blame.

Love,

Doc

They were in Honolulu only three hours, long enough for the *Star Bulletin* to send a reporter on board ship for an interview. Heralded as "the world's foremost game fisherman," Zane stated that he intended to return to Hawaii and fish its waters.[8] The rest of the passage was difficult, and he was seasick most of the way, especially the last three days across the Tasman Sea. His reception in Australia, however, was all anyone could wish for, though standing on his feet and talking all day exhausted him and he lost his voice. His book about his earlier trip, *An American Angler in Australia*, had been published in 1937 and was quite popular, making him even more of an attraction than before, and he was invited everywhere.

Watson's Bay Hotel

Watson's Bay, Australia

JANUARY 30, 1939

Dearest Dolly,

I suppose you have forgotten what tomorrow commemorates.

I wrote you about how seasick I was outside of San Francisco. From Hono-lulu to Samoa it was very rough, and in fact we had very few smooth days. At Suva it was hot, and I foolishly walked all the way from town and back to the ship, and for several hours I felt very queer. That scared me a little. At Auck-land I met my former secretary, Maia, and it was nice to see her again, but she stayed too long and in my nervous condition I got upset again. Then we had a rough passage across the Tasman. I was seasick all the way.

My reception at Sydney left nothing to be desired. They treated me won-derfully. Never looked at my baggage! Then for two days I met people and talked and talked and talked and stood on my feet until I was exhausted, and lost my voice, and on top of that caught cold. We have been here for five days, and I am glad to say that yesterday was a break in my condition, and this morning I am very much better. My secretary got me a practitioner who gave me one absent treatment and I think that helped. By the way, the young lady is very nice.

There are a lot of bits of news that I would like to remember to tell you. One of them is the fun the reporters poke at us for our colored suits and bright ties. That wonderful tie and scarf I had are considered a riot. These you know are very conservative. Wait till I have courage to take out something bright.

Ever

Doc

Fishing began fortuitously, as Zane landed a 320-pound tiger shark on February 6 and later an 800-pound white death shark. Even better, Dolly's news on business was optimistic. His most recent novel, *Western Union,* received favorable comments from editors, and both Paramount and MGM were anxious to acquire it.[9] Both *Wilderness Trek* and *The Lost Wagon Train* were being considered for Gary Cooper by MGM, and Republic was inter-ested in *The Lost Wagon Train* as well.[10] Life seemed to go on as usual. Dolly handled publishers, film companies, and even negotiations on a radio deal, while Zane began research on a new novel about George Washington. Romer and Stephen Slesinger, his agent, gathered material for him, and Hollywood had already begun promoting it, complete with book dummy, before it was even written.[11]

Watson's Bay Hotel

FEBRUARY 21, 1939

Dearest Mom,

Your letter was a lifesaver. When no mail came on the "Aorangi," and then yesterday when the mail from the "Monterey" was supposed to have come over here to Watson's Bay and we were told we could not get it till this morning, and then none, I could have died of despair. But I am not allowed to indulge in any more blue spells. After I had made up my mind to take it, there came a telephone message from the Sydney P.O. asking me what to do with the load of mail for the Zee Gee outfit, I would have raged if I had not been so happy. I hurried over and got that load of mail and believe me I am happy tonight. Just think, Dolly, no word from home for 47 days! Why, honestly I was darned near screwy, and it has been no easy time for me here. I over strained myself at home with that damned novel, and I was seasick all the way down here. Caught cold and lost my voice when I did get here, and on top of that fished too hard.

Next to the assurance that you still love me and don't forget me was the grand news that my Western Union novel is so well spoken of. I had despaired. This gives me new hope. I dictated that novel under the most trying circumstances, and I was new to that sort of thing. Imagine what I can do next time. I gather hope again from your letter and believe now that Western Union will be a big thing for me.

I have not been able to write much in long hand but am sure that if I found the time I would improve at that. However, it is not such a distressing thing now, because even at my best I can dictate more than I can write.

All the news I had from home was fine, and I am not ashamed to say to you that there were times when I had to stop reading because my eyes were blinded by tears.

I am taking it rather easy at present. We expect to go up on the Great Barrier Sunday for a few weeks and then come back to go to South Australia for
about the same time. My address will be the same, and this time I will see that
all mail is forwarded to me.

This is written in a hurry to tell you how happy your letter made me and
how much I love you, and how I am about well again, and everything is fine.

Ever yours,

Doc

After a triumphant stay and leisurely, pleasant fishing, he sailed home in
May, arriving in California in June. Summer and early fall were enjoyed in
Altadena, with some fishing off Catalina occasionally. In October *Western
Union* hit the book stands, and on October 21 he cheerfully braved the
crowds at a Pasadena bookstore to autograph copies. The next two days
were spent quietly at home with his family. Then, at 7:30 A.M. on the morning of October 23, he suffered a massive heart attack.[12] Doctors were called,
but it was too late. He had departed on his last great adventure.

Epilogue

T HE FUNERAL WAS HELD at the Altadena Mausoleum and was private, with only family and close friends in attendance. Tommy Deforrest officiated at a simple Christian Science ceremony.[1] The body was cremated, and Dolly kept the ashes in her home in a square box wrapped in paper for the rest of her life.

Dolly's work was far from over. The corporation needed her guidance and management. Twenty manuscripts were at Harper's awaiting publication. She proofed the galleys and handled all the other miscellaneous arrangements concerning them. There were still motion-picture deals to be made. Twenty-three films were made of his books between 1940 and 1956, many of them remakes of earlier films but several new to film. *Western Union,* the book he was autographing shortly before he died, was purchased by Twentieth Century Fox and released in 1941, starring Randolph Scott, Robert Young, Dean Jagger, Chill Wills, and John Carradine.[2] *The Maverick Queen* was the last of the Zane Grey films, released in 1956 by Republic and starring Barbara Stanwyck. Zane Grey's name and work continued to make money.

But the family business was not without its shake-ups. Romer collected a salary from the corporation, the only one of the children to do so, but in 1948 Loren forced a confrontation with his mother and insisted that he and his sister be included in the business. As a result, Dolly named Romer vice president, Betty treasurer, and Loren secretary, with the foreign rights to promote. Dolly remained as president. Eventually she divided the corporation stock equally among the four of them. Originally Romer had been paid 50 percent of the movie income, but that was cut to 25 percent, and Loren received 25 percent of the foreign income.

Dolly was the watchdog over her husband's name and work, as public curiosity about Zane Grey did not abate. A great many people traveled to Altadena to see the home where he had lived, even though it was still inhabited by his family. At times they were annoying, as they made all sorts of inquiries about him. In 1949 Alvah James wrote Dolly that he had received a prepublication copy of a biography about Zane Grey.[3] Dolly knew nothing about it and was justifiably upset. The author had not contacted her, and she wondered where the material had been acquired. When she saw the book, however, she decided it did no particular harm.[4] She wrote Alvah, "there is still five times as much as that which can be written about him, if ever we get to it."[5] Another letter to Alvah shows the length to which some would go in using Zane's name.[6]

MARCH 22, 1953

Dear Alvah,

The morning your first letter came, I took it with me to the doctor's in order to read it when I had a spare moment. That came when I was eating my breakfast at a drugstore lunch counter. When I read about the spiritualist, I guffawed out loud so that everyone looked at me. That Zane would be a spiritual guide to anyone, and especially a minister, struck me as exceedingly funny. If he had been haunting some beautiful girl, it would have been more in character. As for anything dogmatic to my mind that would be out. Zane had a very decided religion of his own, a beautiful one I thought it, for it was a religion of nature and more like that of the Indians. However, after awhile the humor of the situation sort of died out. After all, there are so many strange things that are part of our universe that I have taught myself to try not to doubt anything, and that there should be enough of Zane's spirit and philosophy to obsess someone, I would not question. But in this case, that anything in connection with Mr. Hirsch would be a voluntary thing on Zane's part, I cannot believe. I do not question that man's sincerity in the least, but I think it must be some kind of an obsession.

Yes, I expect to be going East this spring, possibly a little earlier than usual because the boys will have to go with me to attend to some business back there. And I do hope I shall be able to get to Lackawaxen. You must have a good memory to recall the date of our meeting some forty-nine years ago— or did you keep a diary? November 21st of this year will be Zane's and my golden anniversary!

Dolly

When business allowed, she traveled. Every summer Dolly visited New York, often stopping at Lackawaxen for awhile. In the late 1940s she went again to Europe, accompanied by her granddaughter, Carol, who had just finished high school. They visited England, France, and Germany. Always a penny pincher, Dolly insisted on wearing almost everything she owned when she went through customs, including clothes and jewelry, all under her bulging fur coat, as one did not have to declare what one wore. In 1950 she traveled again to Europe with the International Women Attorneys as an honorary member of the American Lawyers' Guild, sailing on the luxurious *Queen Elizabeth* on June 15.

When she was home she kept a daily diary, attended concerts or listened to them on the radio, entertained her wide circle of friends and used her gift for conversation, enjoyed her grandchildren, and, of course, worried about her children. Romer's temper and his alcoholism made his life and that of everyone around him miserable. His marriage to Dorothy Chasen had fizzled, as did his subsequent marriage to Billye. Eventually he married a third and then a fourth time. Betty's marriage to Bob Carney soured in the Depression years, and she filed for divorce in 1939.[7] Later she married George Grosso and remained happily married to him until his death. Loren joined the navy in 1940 and was at Pearl Harbor on that fateful December 7, 1941, eventually serving fifteen months in the South Pacific. After the war he held a number of positions at Douglas Aircraft then later as a veterans' representative for the UAW-CIO. He married Marcella Robinson in 1945, but they later divorced. He then married Bonnie McDermott, a descendant of Mary, Queen of Scots. He completed his education, the only one of Zane and Dolly's children to do so, with a doctoral degree in psychology and became a professor at California State University, Northridge. Loren visited his mother weekly when she was home; they would have dinner and go to a movie.

Time caught up with Dolly eventually, and her health began to deteriorate. She developed diabetes in the early 1940s, becoming very thin. The diabetes also caused eye problems that forced her to quit driving. In 1953 she suffered a mild heart attack while traveling in New York. The doctor wrongfully diagnosed her condition as lung cancer, and for forty-six days she lay in the hospital. When her doctor went on vacation, another one correctly diagnosed her and drained the fluid from her lungs, after which she recovered quickly. The stay in the hospital had weakened her so much that she was never really well after that. She endured several small strokes, which slowed her down more, and in 1957 a massive stroke left her in a coma. She died four days later. Dolly's ashes and those of Zane were buried together in the cemetery in Lackawaxen.

NOTES

All letters and diary and journal entries are the property of Zane Grey, Inc., unless otherwise specified.

INTRODUCTION

1. Alice Payne Hackett, *80 Years of Best Sellers, 1895–1965.*
2. Dolly Grey to Zane Grey, 13 February 1933.
3. Dolly Grey to Robert Hobart Davis, 1 January 1935, Robert Hobart Davis Papers, Manuscripts and Archives Division, The New York Public Library. Astor, Lenox, Tilden Foundations.
4. Dolly Grey's diary, 24 March 1911.
5. Dolly Grey's diary, 31 January 1936.
6. Dolly Grey's diary, 21 November 1934.
7. Dolly Grey's diary, 17 August 1935.
8. Zane Grey to Alvah James, 26 October 1936, G. M. Farley Collection.
9. Zane Grey to Dolly Grey, 21 June 1936.
10. According to Loren Grey, he and his mother burned those letters the day after his father's death.
11. Dolly Grey's diary, 11 January 1918.

CHAPTER 1 ■ THE BROWN-EYED ROSE AND THE BLACK-EYED DEVIL

1. Randy Kraft, "Delaware River's Scenic Sights, Historic Sites," *Allentown Morning Call,* reprinted in *Las Vegas Review Journal,* September 20, 1992.
2. R.C. stood for Romer Carl; however, he was most often called R.C., and I continue that usage as it differentiates him from Zane Grey's son Romer.
3. Zane and Dolly always celebrated August 28 as the anniversary of the day they met. Tom Pauly writes, however, on page 43 of *Zane Grey,* that they had actually met at the Westcolong Railroad station.
4. Lina Roth to Zane Grey, August 1900.
5. George Reiger, "Preface," *The Undiscovered Zane Grey Fishing Stories,* xxii.

6. Pauly (*Zane Grey*, 48) asserts that the printing was financed by Reba Smith, who was romantically involved with Zane's brother, R.C.

7. Patricia H. Christian, "Once Upon A Memory," 1–7. See also G. M. Farley, "Lackawaxen," 1–4; Pauly, *Zane Grey*, 54.

CHAPTER 2 ■ THE ETERNAL FEMININE

1. Dolly's upstairs neighbor.

2. Ellsworth was Zane's older brother; Romer Carl, or R.C., was Zane's younger brother; Ida was Zane's sister.

3. Information regarding R.C. and Rebecca's wedding plans and the housing is from Loren Grey, pers. comm.

4. A former girlfriend of R.C.'s.

5. The date was November 21, 1905.

6. Details of the wedding are found in Dolly's diary, 21 November 1934.

7. Dolly's younger brother Julius was sometimes called Jack, sometimes Julie.

CHAPTER 3 ■ THE HERMITS OF COTTAGE POINT

1. This quote from Dolly's diary in Frank Gruber, *Zane Grey* (Cleveland: World Publishing, 1970), 59.

2. In 1937 Dolly reread her 1906 diary and added this comment to the entry for Monday, 29 January 1906.

3. Dan Murphy, an agent for the United Literary Press, met Zane when *Betty Zane* was published.

4. George Reiger, *Undiscovered Zane Grey Fishing Stories*, xix.

5. Zane Grey to Dan Murphy, 2 June 1907, Edwin Markham Collection, Horrmann Library, Wagner College.

6. This was stated in a letter written by Dolly to Zane Grey, 23 January 1927, giving an interesting insight into the relationship at that time.

7. This is the first mention of Surprise Canyon, which Grey used in his romances *Riders of the Purple Sage* and *The Rainbow Trail*. Dolly never accompanied Zane there, and the exact location of this canyon is still not known. Possibly it is a fictional creation of Grey's. Here he begins a pattern of offering her plans of trips together when she is particularly upset and when he feels guilty. These plans rarely materialized.

8. For more about this expedition, as well as Grey's other trips to Arizona, see Candace Kant, *Zane Grey's Arizona* (Flagstaff: Northland Press, 1984).

9. Zane Grey to Lina Elise Grey, (1907), Chamberlain Collection, Special Collections Library, Northern Arizona University, Flagstaff.

10. Lina Elise Grey to Daniel Murphy, 28 December 1907, Edwin Markham Collection, Horrmann Library, Wagner College.

11. The following paragraph is taken from Zane Grey's diary, 14 February 1908.

The rest of the several pages of the entry is an account of the flooding of the Delaware River.

12. Zane Grey's diary, 14 February 1908.

13. "Lassoing Lions in the Siwash" was being considered by *Everybody's,* and "Tige's Lion" had been purchased by *Field and Stream;* there were some complications, however. According to a letter from Zane to Dolly dated 6 March 1908, Zane signed over to *Everybody's* the right to the photographs for the article that were also used in *Last of the Plainsmen.* Outing could not publish *Last of the Plainsmen* until *Everybody's* released their rights, as Zane had agreed not to use the photographs anywhere else until *Everybody's* ran the article. Before he left on his second Arizona trip, he learned that A. L. Burt and Company had acquired *The Last Trail.*

14. For more information on this second Arizona expedition, see Kant, *Zane Grey's Arizona,* 16–17.

15. First he wrote a lengthy nonfiction piece on the lion hunt that could either be serialized in a sports magazine or stand alone as a book. *Field and Stream* bought it to serialize beginning January 1909. He also wrote a novel for young adults, *The Short Stop,* using his knowledge of baseball.

16. Pauly, *Zane Grey,* 87.

17. Zane Grey's diary, 24 March 1909.

18. The complete story of this journey is told in "Down an Unknown Jungle River" by Zane Grey, published in *Tales of Southern Rivers* (New York: Harpers, 1924), reprinted by Derrydale Press (Lyon, Miss., 1951).

19. Zane Grey, "The Bonefish Brigade," *Zane Grey: Outdoorsman* (Englewood Cliffs, N.J.: Prentice-Hall, 1972), 136.

20. *The Short Stop* was sold to A. C. McClurg on May 1 for 10 percent royalty, a retail cost of between $1.25 and $1.50 per book, and thirty copies for him, according to a letter to A. C. McClurg from Zane Grey, 1 May 1909. "The Lord of Lackawaxen Creek" was in the May 1909 issue of *Outing,* "In Defense of Live Bait" was in June's *Field and Stream,* and in September *Everybody's* printed "Rabihorcados and the Boobies," which, despite the title, was about fishing. He also accepted a commission from the New York and Cuba Mail Steamship Company to write advertising copy for their pamphlets, a task he completed in October.

21. Zane Grey's diary, 31 October 1909.

22. According to his diary, by November 16 he had written 152 pages, thirty thousand words, and six chapters. By December 13 he had finished page 333, and he finished the novel January 22, 1910. Since November 1 he had written 508 pages, averaging seven hours straight each day at first, then nine to even twelve hours a day on the last four or five chapters.

23. Zane Grey's diary, 29 January 1910.

24. His account of the voyage up the Santa Rosa River was purchased by *Field And Stream,* "Lightning" was in the March edition of *Outing,* and "A Trout Fisherman's Inferno" highlighted April's *Field and Stream. Heritage of the Desert,* originally

titled *Mescal,* was sold as a serial to Street and Smith by February 10, and even Ripley Hitchcock of Harper's asked for a juvenile, which Zane began in March, calling it *The Young Forester.*

25. Zane Grey's diary, 2 March 1910.

CHAPTER 4 ■ MARRIAGE IS FOR CHILDREN

1. Zane Grey's diary, 10 April 1910.
2. The address was 103 Albion Place.
3. Dolly Grey's diary, 31 March 1911.
4. Zane Grey to David Dexter Rust, 5 March 1911, David Dexter Rust Collection, Church of Jesus Christ of Latter Day Saints Historical Department, Salt Lake City, Utah.
5. Mormon polygamy ran counter to the traditions of Western Europe and the United States and encountered opposition. Penalties were established by the federal government in the late nineteenth century, and in 1890 the church officially ended the practice of polygamy. Reaction was varied among the Mormons. Some abolished existing marriages, divesting property among their several wives, while others applied the restriction only to new marriages. In 1904 the church fathers issued a second Manifesto that provided penalties for contracting new plural unions, and in 1910 even stricter penalties were set. Those who had entered polygamous unions after 1904 were to be excommunicated. Those married after the first Manifesto in 1890 but before 1904 incurred slight penalties but might maintain their families. Marriages formed prior to 1890 were to remain intact. When Zane visited Arizona and Utah in 1907 and 1908 the social fabric of the Mormon communities was in the midst of change. Jim Emmett was a practicing polygamist, and the man called Woolley whom he had visited was also. *Heritage of the Desert* incorporated the theme of polygamy into its plot: August Naab was a polygamist, and Mescal was intended as the second wife for Naab's son Snap (the villain). The protagonist expresses repugnance at this institution.
6. Dolly Grey's diary, 24 March 1911.
7. Dolly Grey's diary, 11 April 1911.
8. Dolly Grey's diary, 21 April 1911.
9. Dolly Grey's diary, 6 May 1911.
10. Dolly Grey's diary, 19 March 1912.
11. Zane Grey to Dolly Grey, 13 October 1911, Chamberlain Collection.
12. Most likely Lillian Wilhelm.
13. Lew was Ellsworth, Zane's older brother.
14. Dolly Grey's diary, 19 March 1912.
15. Zane Grey, "My Own Life," *Zane Grey: The Man and His Work* (New York: Harper and Brothers, 1928), 18–19. According to Pauly (*Zane Grey,* 111), Grey appealed to Hitchcock's superior, Frederick Duneka, through his agent, Dan Mur-

phy, who got Duneka's wife to read the manuscript. She was impressed and told her husband so, and he then urged Hitchcock to accept the book.

16. Betty Zane was born April 22, 1912. *The Light of Western Stars* was finished April 23, 1912, according to Dolly's diary, April 1912.

17. Zane Grey to Robert Hobart Davis, 17 August 1912, G. M. Farley Collection.

18. Zane Grey to Ripley Hitchcock, 25 September 1912, Fales Library, Elmer Holmes Bobst Library, New York University.

19. Dolly Grey's diary, 18 October 1912.

20. This passage in Dolly Grey's diary entry for 31 December 1913 is a reminiscence about the preceding year.

CHAPTER 5 ■ THE GREAT BITTERNESS

1. A description of the house is found in Dolly Grey's diary entry for 28 November 1934.

2. Dolly Grey's diary, 31 December 1913.

3. Zane Grey to Dolly Grey, 20 March 1906.

4. In a letter to Dolly from Long Key dated early 1912, Grey writes, "I am sorry about the hair pins. But honey, as a matter of fact you have lost as many, if not more than any one else. I hope you didn't scatter a handful of hairpins round just to make me feel sheepish."

5. Zane Grey's diary, 15 July 1910.

6. Grey writes of this journey and his impressions upon viewing Rainbow Bridge for the first time in "Nonnezosche," *Tales of Lonely Trails* (New York: Harper and Brothers, 1922), 1–17.

7. Zane Grey to Robert Hobart Davis, 5 June 1914, Robert Hobart Davis Papers.

8. Zane Grey to Robert Hobart Davis, 19 March 1912, Robert Hobart Davis Papers.

9. Retitled *The Rainbow Trail*.

10. Zane Grey to Dolly Grey, 31 August 1915.

11. Dolly Grey's diary, 23 October 1915.

12. Dolly Grey's diary, 20 November 1934.

CHAPTER 6 ■ TEMPESTS AND STORMS

1. Zane Grey to Robert Hobart Davis, 26 March 1916, Robert Hobart Davis Papers, Manuscripts and Archives Division, The New York Public Library. Astor, Lenox, and Tilden Foundations.

2. Robert Hobart Davis to Zane Grey, 28 March 1916, Robert Hobart Davis Papers, Manuscripts and Archives Division, The New York Public Library. Astor, Lenox, and Tilden Foundations.

3. Davis to Grey, 28 March 1916, Robert Hobart Davis Papers, Manuscripts and Archives Division, The New York Public Library. Astor, Lenox, Tilden Foundations.

4. Fox Studios eventually picked up both *Riders of the Purple Sage* and *The Rainbow Trail.*

5. Lillian Wilhelm was Dolly's cousin, as was her younger sister, Claire. Elma was a cousin of Lillian's, making her distantly related to Dolly.

6. Dolly Grey's diary, 1 June 1916.

7. Mildred Fergerson was a part of Zane Grey's entourage for at least a decade. Tom Pauly remarks on page 156 of *Zane Grey: His Life, His Adventures, His Women,* that she was a trained secretary whom Zane had hired to help Dolly. It seems odd that she would accompany Zane on his trips if her purpose was to help his wife.

8. Attached to Dolly's letter of 16 August 1916.

CHAPTER 7 ■ A HYENA LYING IN AMBUSH

1. In a letter dated 24 January 1917, Dolly describes the apartment at 545 N. 111th St. "It is an enormous fireproof apartment house run on a very sanitary plan and the apartment I took has all large light sunny rooms. Some of the furniture is very good (esthetically) and some indifferent, but it's far ahead of anything I saw, and I looked at lots of Riverside Drive places. The woman finally came down to $240 a month and after my experiences, I considered myself fortunate to get it. We move there next Tuesday—and any time you want to come home, you'll find a nice comfortable place waiting for you. The manager said the walls were sound proof."

2. Later titled *The U.P. Trail.*

3. Zane Grey's diary, 3 April 1917.

4. Zane Grey's diary, 14 April 1917.

5. Zane Grey's diary, 23 April 1917.

6. Zane Grey's diary, 30 April 1917.

7. Dolly Grey's diary, 7 July 1917.

8. Dolly Grey's journal of the trip, 10 July 1917.

9. Zane Grey's diary, 25 December 1917.

CHAPTER 8 ■ YOUR ONLY, WIFE

1. Dolly Grey's diary, called the Wanamaker diary, 7 January 1918.

2. From the Wanamaker diary, 1917–18.

3. Dolly's brother's wife and daughter.

4. Dolly Grey to Zane Grey, 17 February 1918.

5. Information on the titles, dates of release, characters, and actors, unless otherwise stated, is from Kenneth W. Scott, *Zane Grey: Born to the West* (Boston: G. K. Hall, 1979).

6. The film industry migrated from New Jersey to Southern California in 1911 to take advantage of the better weather for filming.

7. Most likely a reference to Freud.

8. Zane Grey to Dolly Grey, 28 February 1918; Dolly Grey to Zane Grey, 5 March 1918; Zane Grey to Dolly Grey, 7 March 1918.

9. Dolly Grey's diary, 17 August 1935. Here she reminisces about the move to California and Ellsworth's marriage.

10. See her letter dated 14 March 1917, in the previous chapter and his letter dated 17 March 1917.

11. Zane Grey to Dolly Grey, 13 August 1918, Chamberlain Collection.

12. Dolly Grey's diary, 17 August 1935.

CHAPTER 9 ■ PENELOPE HAS TAKEN A WANDERING STREAK

1. Zane Grey's diary, 19 January 1919.

2. Zane Grey's diary, 11 May 1919.

3. Zane Grey's diary, 20 January 1919.

4. The following two excerpts are from Zane Grey's diary.

5. Zane Grey's diary, 12 March 1919.

6. Zane Grey's diary, 19 March 1919.

7. An account of the trip is found in Zane Grey, "Death Valley," *Tales of Lonely Trails,* vol. 2 (New York: Charter Books), 169–86.

8. Zane Grey's diary, 29 May 1919.

9. Zane Grey to Dolly Grey, 13 November 1919, Chamberlain Collection.

10. Gruber, *Zane Grey,* 171.

11. Zane Grey's diary, 23 November 1919.

12. Dolly Grey to Zane Grey, 26 January 1920. Postmarked New York City, to Zane Grey at Long Key, Florida.

13. Telegram from Zane Grey to Dolly Grey, 30 January 1920.

14. Mrs. Koch ("Cookie") to Zane Grey, February 1920.

15. Dolly did not learn how to drive until 1933.

16. Reprinted in Gruber, *Zane Grey,* 169–70.

17. Descriptions of the house are contained in Zane Grey's diary entries for 15 November 1920 and 19 November 1920.

18. Dolly Grey to Zane Grey, 5 October 1920, Chamberlain Collection.

19. "Part of Zane Grey Party Returns to Flagstaff," *Coconino Sun,* November 12, 1920.

20. "Zane Grey Will Hunt Bears Again Next Year," *Coconino Sun,* November 26, 1920.

21. Gruber, *Zane Grey,* 131; John Tuska, *The Filming of the West* (Garden City, N.Y.: Doubleday, 1976), 124, 131.

22. Story related by Loren Grey, pers. comm.

23. Zane Grey's diary, 23 November 1920.

24. Zane Grey's diary, 31 December 1920.

CHAPTER 10 ■ THE FROTH OF ENTHUSIASM

1. This sentence is written in code.

2. Zane Grey's diary, 3 February 1921.

3. Ibid.

4. Ibid.

5. Zane Grey's diary, 9 February 1921.

6. The latter part of this sentence is written in code.

7. Zane Grey's diary, 28 February 1921.

8. Zane Grey's diary, 12 March–5 April 1921.

9. Ibid.

10. Ibid. The last sentence of this portion of the entry is written in code.

11. Ibid. The last sentence is written in code.

12. Dolly was now thirty-eight.

13. Gruber, *Zane Grey,* 173–74. According to a telephone interview with Marjorie Bowen, August 1998, Ed Bowen was a young man, a teenager, who worked for the film studios where Dolly had met him. She was impressed with his potential, and he became a protégé of hers. Ken Robertson was Ed's friend.

14. Zane Grey's diary, 20 April 1921.

15. Zane Grey's diary, 5 May 1921. The first sentence is written in code.

16. Reiger, "Preface," *Undiscovered Zane Grey Fishing Stories,* xxix.

17. Incident recounted in Reiger, Preface," *Undiscovered Zane Grey Fishing Stories,* xxix–xxx.

18. Zane Grey's diary, 28 November 1921.

19. Zane Grey's diary entry for 28 November 1921 establishes that he took Louise with him, as does the article in the *Coconino Sun,* "Zane Grey Got Only One Bear," November 4, 1921.

20. "Zane Grey Got Only One Bear," *Coconino Sun,* November 4, 1921.

21. Zane Grey's diary, 28 November 1921. The last three words are written in code.

22. Ibid. The last four words are written in code.

23. Zane Grey's diary, 4 December 1921. Portions of this entry are written in code.

24. Zane Grey's diary, 24 December 1921. Portions of this entry are written in code.

25. Gruber, *Zane Grey,* 172–73.

26. Zane Grey's diary, 3 May 1922.

27. Lillian Wilhelm married Jess Smith, brother of Mildred, in May of 1924, and they lived in Arizona.

28. Grey formed a partnership with Benjamin Hampton to produce motion pictures in 1919. The company, called Zane Grey Pictures, filmed *Desert Gold* (1919);

The U.P. Trail (1920); *Man of the Forest* (1921); *When Romance Rides,* retitled from *Wildfire* (1922); *Riders of the Dawn,* based on *Desert of Wheat* (1920); *The Mysterious Rider* (1921); and *Golden Dreams,* based on a short story (1922). In 1922 Grey bought Hampton's share of the company then sold the entire business to Jesse L. Lasky. The deal included an agreement that films made from Grey's work would be shot in the actual setting, a ploy that he hoped would insure the fidelity of the film to the story. He was to be consulted on locations and other matters.

29. Zane Grey's diary, 7 August 1922.

30. "Zane Grey Got Three Bears in Tonto Basin," *Coconino Sun,* November 10, 1922.

31. Zane Grey's diary, 2 December 1922.

32. Zane Grey's diary, 25 December 1922.

33. Zane Grey to Dolly Grey, 7 January 1923.

34. Zane Grey's diary, 29 April 1923.

35. Zane Grey's diary, 30 April 1923.

36. Zane Grey's diary, 13 May 1923.

37. Zane Grey to Dolly Grey, 23 August 1923; Zane Grey to Dolly Grey, 31 August 1923; Zane Grey to Dolly Grey, 2 September 1923. The weights were, in order, 262 lbs., 298 lbs., 360 lbs., and 360 lbs.

38. "Filming of Famous Grey Novels to Carry Fame of Our Scenery over World," *Coconino Sun,* September 14, 1923. For more information on this trip, see Kant, *Zane Grey's Arizona,* 27.

CHAPTER 11 ■ THE FEMALE OF THE SPECIES

1. Mildred and Zane evidently collaborated on several plays. The Library of Congress lists *Amber's Mirage,* unpublished play recorded 1929; *The Courting of Stephen,* unpublished play; *Port of Call,* unpublished play, recorded 1930; and *Three Tight Lines,* recorded in 1927. All are listed as authored by Zane Grey and Millicent Smith. In addition, in an article titled "A Special Friendship: Zane Grey and Mildred Smith" by Jim Vickers and Ed Myers (*Zane Grey Quarterly* 1, no. 4 [Winter 1992]: 1, 3, 4), the authors assert that Mildred Smith was the original author of "Captives of the Desert" but could not get it published. According to Vickers and Myers, she had collected the material in 1923 and 1924 on trips to Arizona in connection with Zane Grey movies. Grey worked over the story, and it was published under his name in *McCall's* in December 1925 with the title *Desert Bound.* Vickers and Myers also say that one play, *The Critic and the Hearth,* was produced under Mildred's name in 1936 and got good reviews. It is believed this play was written in collaboration with Zane Grey. Millicent was a nickname Mildred sometimes used.

2. Zane Grey to Dolly Grey, 3 January 1924.

3. Zane Grey to Dolly Grey, 14 March 1924.

4. Dolly Grey to Zane Grey, 8 March 1924; Dolly Grey to Zane Grey, 28 January 1924; Zane Grey to Dolly Grey, 25 February 1924.

5. Zane Grey to Dolly Grey, 16 March 1924.

6. Gruber, *Zane Grey,* 127.

7. Ibid., 184.

8. Loren Grey, *Zane Grey: A Photographic Odyssey* (Dallas: Taylor Publishing, 1985), 116.

9. Ibid.

10. Zane Grey, *Tales of Fishing Virgin Seas* (Lyon, Miss.: Derrydale Press: 1990), 1–2.

11. "Evident Deer Hunt Will Soon Resume and That McCormick's Deer Drive Will Get Lasky Money," *Coconino Sun,* November 28, 1924.

12. "Last Bar Removed: Small Army Now Is Bivouaced North of Grand Canyon to Begin Big Deer Drive," *Coconino Sun,* December 12, 1924.

13. "Zane Grey Tells Why Drive Failed," *Coconino Sun,* December 19, 1924.

14. Zane Grey, *Tales of Fishing Virgin Seas,* 3–4.

15. Ibid., 2.

16. Lillian was married in May 1924 to Mildred's brother, Jess Smith. They now lived in Arizona.

17. Zane Grey, *Tales of Fishing Virgin Seas,* 182.

18. Zane Grey to Dolly Grey, 16 April 1925.

19. See this chapter, note 1, regarding *Desert Bound* or *Captives of the Desert.*

20. Loren Grey, *Zane Grey,* 124.

CHAPTER 12 ■ TO KNOW ALL IS TO FORGIVE ALL

1. Zane Grey to Dolly Grey, January 1926.

2. This record was not broken until 1984. See also George Reiger's introduction to "The Dreadnaught Pool," *Zane Grey, Outdoorsman* (Englewood Cliffs, N.J.: Prentice Hall, 1972), 194.

3. Loren Grey, *Zane Grey,* 124.

4. Ibid., 52.

5. Zane Grey to Dolly Grey, 4 May 1927; Zane Grey to Dolly Grey, 9 May 1927; Zane Grey to Dolly Grey, 22 May 1927.

6. The Delaware House was a hotel/resort in Lackawaxen.

7. This is the first direct reference to physical infidelity in any of the letters.

8. The second reference to physical infidelity in the letters.

9. The third reference to physical infidelity in the letters.

10. This was *Tales of Swordfish and Tuna,* which was published in 1927 in one book, not two.

11. "Grey's Secretary Here," *Coconino Sun,* August 26, 1927.

12. "Zane Grey Here to Hunt and Film Latest Story Says We've Sure Grown," *Coconino Sun*, September 30, 1927.

13. "Zane Grey Classifies Hollywood Movies," *Coconino Sun*, October 29, 1927.

CHAPTER 13 ■ DEAR OLD COMRADE OF THE YEARS

1. Zane Grey to Dolly Grey, 5 February 1928, from the collection of Ken Booth.

2. Ibid.

3. Dolly had a hysterectomy.

4. Zane Grey's diary, quoted in Gruber, *Zane Grey*, 198–99.

5. Zane Grey never drank alcohol himself, having pledged to his mother he would not do so, and he disapproved of others' drinking it.

6. Zane Grey, *Tales of the Angler's Eldorado: New Zealand* (Lyon, Miss.: Derrydale Press, 1926), 14–15.

7. Zane Grey, *Tales of Tahitian Waters* (Lyon, Miss.: Derrydale Press, 1990), 6.

8. The study was built by Ed Bowen.

9. Ed Bowen built this house, and he had designed and built the house on Catalina Island as well. See also Dolly's letter of 21 June 1928, this chapter.

10. Ellsworth, Zane's older brother, was an alcoholic.

11. Mildred Smith.

12. Dolly Grey to Zane Grey, 19 June 1929.

13. "Zane Grey Party Is Touring the North," *Coconino Sun*, August 30, 1929.

14. Ibid.

15. Dolly Grey to Robert Hobart Davis, 28 August 1929, Robert Hobart Davis Papers.

CHAPTER 14 ■ I LOVE YOU TILL IT CHOKES ME

1. Zane Grey to Romer Grey, 24 February 1930.

2. Mr. and Mrs. Eastham Guild, who lived near Papeete. Grey spent considerable time with them on this trip and incorporated them into *Tales of Tahitian Waters* as Ham-Fish and Carrie-Fin. They were, according to page 214 of *Tales*, novice fishermen.

3. Written 1929–30; serialized in the fall of 1930 in *Collier's*; published in book form in 1932.

4. Zane Grey, *Tales of Tahitian Waters*, 232.

5. Ibid., 297.

6. Ibid., 235.

7. Ibid., 272.

8. Zane Grey's journal, 26 August 1930.

9. Gruber, *Zane Grey*, 225.

10. Ibid., 227.

11. Information on the breakup comes from Pauly, *Zane Grey*, 283.

12. Berenice Campbell.

13. Written fall/winter of 1930; serialized in the fall of 1931 in *McCall's*; published in book form in 1936.

14. Gruber, *Zane Grey*, 184.

15. Information on this quarrel comes from a letter written by Berenice to Dolly Grey, 29 February 1931.

16. The worst thing Zane could say about anyone.

17. This is an interesting statement and almost an admission of physical infidelity on Zane's part.

18. Mildred Smith's expenses.

19. Berenice Campbell to Dolly Grey, 29 February 1931.

20. Romer's wife, Dorothy (Chasen), gave birth.

21. According to Gruber (*Zane Grey*, 229), the bills from the shipbuilding company, the outfitters and purveyors, and the ship's chandlers totaled over three hundred thousand dollars.

22. Zane Grey's journal, 10 July 1931.

23. Dolly Grey to Zane Grey, 9 June 1922.

24. Zane Grey to Dolly Grey, 11 August 1923.

25. Zane Grey to Dolly Grey, 14 August 1923.

26. Gruber, *Zane Grey*, 171.

27. Zane Grey to Alvah James, 3 November 1931, G. M. Farley Collection.

28. Gruber, *Zane Grey*, 171–72.

29. Zane Grey to *Harper's*, 14 December 1931.

30. Founder of the Bank of America.

31. Wanda Williams, Zane's current companion.

32. Zane Grey's journal, 30 September 1932.

CHAPTER 15 ■ GIVE US THIS DAY OUR DAILY BREAD, O PARAMOUNT!

1. Regarding Romer and Dot.

2. The reference here is to Christian Science, which he had taken up when last in California. Wanda Williams was also a practitioner of Christian Science.

3. Ed Bowen was the general manager of Zane Grey, Inc.

4. Dolly Grey to Zane Grey, 16 January 1933.

5. Dolly Grey to Zane Grey, 27 January 1933.

6. Zane Grey to Dolly Grey, 6 March 1933.

7. Franklin Delano Roosevelt was inaugurated March 4, 1933. He faced a crisis in the bank industry, with banks all over the country closing their doors. His immediate response was to declare a National Banking Holiday on March 5 and to call Congress into Special Session. On March 9 Congress passed the Emergency Banking Act, which provided for the examination of banks and the reopening of those that

were sound. On March 12 he addressed the nation in his first Fireside Chat and announced that most banks would open the following week.

8. Zane had proposed a lengthy fishing cruise to the Vanderbilts as their son, George, was interested in big-game fishing. The idea was that they would bear the costs in return for Zane's expertise in fishing. The resultant publicity would benefit both families.

9. In letters dated 9 April 1933 and 11 April 1933, Dolly clarified his bank account situation. Specifically, in the Altadena National checking account he had $729.32, and in the Security First National account he had $663.69. She had also opened a new joint checking account for them, through which she would funnel the deposits to his accounts. The joint checking account was at Farmer's and Merchant's National, and as of April 9 there was $1250.00 deposited there. His salary was credited on the books, even though there was not enough money to pay it. But he would receive the back amount when funds came in.

10. Dolly Grey to Zane Grey, 9 April 1933; Dolly Grey to Zane Grey, 11 April 1933.

11. Congress approved the Twenty-First Amendment, which repealed the Eighteenth Amendment ending prohibition in late 1932. The ratification process was not completed until December of 1932.

12. Zane Grey to Dolly Grey, 14 April 1933. He called this novel *Ride the Man Down*.

13. This became *Shadow on the Trail*.

14. Dolly Grey to Zane Grey, 9 May 1933.

15. *The Country Gentleman*.

16. Zane never learned to drive.

17. *30,000 on the Hoof*.

18. "Zane Grey Visits Boulder on Sunday," *Las Vegas Review Journal*, November 20, 1933.

19. According to a letter written 5 September 1934, Wanda got married on 1 September to Colin Smith, who Dolly says "must be the young man you met."

20. Brownella Baker, Zane's new "literary assistant."

21. This was an actual stenographer.

22. Dolly Grey to Zane Grey, 11 July 1934.

23. Dolly Grey to Zane Grey, 31 July 1934.

24. Dolly Grey to Zane Grey, 5 September 1934.

25. Dolly Grey to Zane Grey, 31 July 1934.

26. Romer was served divorce papers on August 21, 1934. This may or may not have been the source of his "bad frame of mind"; however, he had another girlfriend by this time, named Billye.

27. In a letter written by Dolly Grey to Alvah James, 17 September 1934, it was mentioned that Alvah James, who was now living in the Lackawaxen house, might be interested buying the Lackawaxen property.

28. Dolly Grey's diary, 4 November 1934.

29. Ibid.

30. Zane Grey to Dolly Grey, 5 July 1935.

CHAPTER 16 ■ YOU, WHO MAKE HOME

1. Pauly identifies her as Lola Gornall, who had corresponded with Grey since 1933, and says that their meeting lasted only three days and did not go well. See Pauly, *Zane Grey,* 301, 306.

2. If she was indeed a secretary, the need for a code word would have been unnecessary.

3. The fishing picture was *White Death;* the fiction picture was *Rangle River.*

4. CINEMA PICTURE COMPANY.

5. Zane Grey to Dolly Grey, 6 April 1936.

6. Zane Grey to Dolly Grey, 6 May 1936.

7. Dolly Grey to Zane Grey, 26 May 1936.

8. This is the one time in all of his letters that he says he is happy.

9. Maia Turnbull, who was from New Zealand.

10. Romer's girlfriend, who became his second wife.

11. Zane Grey to Dolly Grey, 2 June 1937. Chamberlain Collection.

12. This story was *The Maverick Queen,* not published until 1950.

13. Zane Grey to Dolly Grey, 6 June 1937. Chamberlain Collection.

14. Romer Grey to Zane Grey, 8 July 1937.

15. This account of the stroke is taken from Romer's letter to Dolly the day following the incident.

16. Civilian Conservation Corps.

17. Christian Science practitioner.

CHAPTER 17 ■ I NEVER BEFORE LOVED YOU SO WELL

1. According to Loren Grey, Zane practiced signing his name over twelve thousand times.

2. Zane Grey to Romer Grey, 23 January 1938.

3. The novel was *Western Union,* which was published in 1939.

4. Zane Grey to Dolly Grey, 6 April 1938.

5. Dolly Grey's diary, 30 April 1938.

6. Ibid.

7. Gus and Lyle Bagnard were cameramen Zane whom took along to get motion pictures of the fishing for possible use in sports films.

8. *Star Bulletin,* January 10, 1939.

9. Metro Goldwyn Mayer eventually optioned the film rights for five thousand dollars; however, it was filmed by Twentieth Century Fox in 1941.

10. Romer Grey to Zane Grey, 26 April 1939.

11. Dolly Grey to Zane Grey, 25 April 1939.

12. It was a massive rupture of the right ventricle.

EPILOGUE

1. Tommy Deforrest had married Dolly's friend Hildred.

2. Information on films comes from Scott, *Zane Grey*, 5–28.

3. Dolly Grey to Alvah James, 18 November 1949, G. M. Farley Collection. The original of the letter is in the Zane Grey home, Lackawaxen, Pennsylvania.

4. The book was by Jean Karr and was entitled *Zane Grey: Man of the West*. It had little original research and was essentially a rehash of already published material.

5. Dolly Grey to Alvah James, 2 March 1950, G. M. Farley Collection.

6. Dolly Grey to Alvah James, 22 March 1953, G. M. Farley Collection. The original of the letter is in the Zane Grey home, Lackawaxen, Pennsylvania.

7. Dolly Grey to Zane Grey, 25 April 1939.

FURTHER READING

Gay, Carol. *Zane Grey, Story Teller.* Columbus: State Library of Ohio, 1979.

Grey, Zane. *Zane Grey: The Man and His Work.* New York: Harper and Brothers, 1928.

Jackson, Carlton. *Zane Grey.* Boston: G. K. Hall and Company, 1973.

Kant, Candace C. *Zane Grey's Arizona.* Flagstaff, Ariz.: Northland Press, 1984.

Karr, Jean. *Zane Grey: Man of the West.* New York: Grosset and Dunlap, 1949.

Kimball, Arthur G. *Ace of Hearts: The Westerns of Zane Grey.* Fort Worth: Texas Christian University Press, 1993.

May, Stephen J. *Maverick Heart: The Further Adventures of Zane Grey.* Athens: Ohio University Press, 2000.

———. *Zane Grey: Romancing the West.* Athens: Ohio University Press, 1997.

Pauly, Thomas H. *Zane Grey: His Life, His Adventures, His Women.* Chicago: University of Illinois Press, 2005.

Pfeiffer, Charles G., *Zane Grey: A Study in Values Above and Beyond the West.* The Zane Grey's West Society, 2006.

Ronald, Ann. *Zane Grey.* Boise, Idaho: Boise State University Press, 1975.

Schneider, Norris F. *Zane Grey: The Man Whose Books Made the West Famous.* Zanesville, Ohio: Norris F. Schneider, 1967.

Scott, Kenneth William. *Zane Grey: Born to the West.* Boston: G.K.Hall, 1979.

Shoumatoff, Alex. *Legends of the American Desert: Sojourns in the Greater Southwest.* New York: HarperPerennial, 1999.

Zane Grey: The Man and His Work. New York: Harper and Brothers, 1928.

SOURCES

COLLECTIONS

Chamberlain Collection. Cline Library. Special Collections Department. Northern Arizona University, Flagstaff, Arizona.

David Dexter Rust Papers. Church of Jesus Christ of Latter-day Saints, Historical Department, Salt Lake City, Utah.

Davis, Robert Hobart. *Robert Hobart Davis Papers.* Rare Books and Manuscripts Division, New York Public Library, Astor, Lenox, and Tilden Foundations.

Fales Library. The Elmer Holmes Bobst Library. New York University, New York.

G. M. Farley Collection. Hagerstown, Maryland.

Markham, Edwin. Edwin Markham Collection. Horrman Library. Wagner College, New York.

Zane Grey, Inc. Woodland Hills, California. Letters, Dolly Grey's Diary, The Wanamaker Diary, Zane Grey's Diary.

BOOKS

Grey, Loren. *Zane Grey: A Photographic Odyssey.* Dallas: Taylor Publishing Company, 1985.

Grey, Zane. *Tales of Lonely Trails.* New York: Harper and Brothers, 1922. Reprinted by Northland Press, Flagstaff, Arizona, 1986.

———. *Tales of Southern Rivers.* New York: Harper and Brothers, 1924. Reprinted by Derrydale Press, Inc., Lyon, Mississippi, 1951.

———. *Tales of Fishing Virgin Seas.* New York: Harper and Brothers, 1925. Reprinted by Derrydale Press, Lyon, Mississippi, 1990.

———. *Tales of the Angler's Eldorado: New Zealand.* New York: Harper and Brothers, 1926. Reprinted by Derrydale Press, Lyon, Mississippi, 1991.

———. "My Own Life," *Zane Grey: The Man And His Work.* New York: Harper and Brothers, 1928.

———. *Tales of Tahitian Waters.* New York: Harper and Brothers, 1931. Reprinted by Derrydale Press, Lyon: Mississippi, 1990.

————. *Zane Grey Outdoorsman.* Englewood Cliffs, New Jersey: Prentice-Hall, Inc., 1972.

Gruber, Frank. *Zane Grey.* Cleveland: World Publishing, 1970.

Hackett, Alice Payne. *80 Years of Best Sellers, 1895–1965.* New York: R.R. Bowker Company, 1977.

Kant, Candace C. *Zane Grey's Arizona.* Flagstaff, Ariz.: Northland Press, 1984.

Karr, Jean. *Zane Grey: Man of the West.* New York: Grosset and Dunlap, 1949.

Pauly, Thomas H. *Zane Grey: His Life, His Adventures, His Women.* Chicago: University of Illinois Press, 2005.

Reiger, George, ed. *Zane Grey Outdoorsman.* Englewood Cliffs, N.J.: Prentice Hall, 1972.

————. *The Undiscovered Zane Grey Fishing Stories.* Piscataway, N.J.: Winchester Press, 1983.

Scott, Kenneth W. *Zane Grey: Born to the West.* Boston: G. K. Hall and Co., 1979.

Tuska, John. *The Filming of the West.* Garden City, N.Y.: Doubleday, 1976.

ARTICLES

Christian, Patricia H. "Once Upon a Memory: The Upper Delaware Equinunk Historical Society." Reprinted in *Zane Grey's Arizona Call* Vol. 3, no. 1 (Winter 1990): 1–7.

Farley, G. M. "Lackawaxen: Where It All Began," *Zane Grey Reporter* vol. 2, no. 2 (June 1987):1–4.

NEWSPAPER ARTICLES

"Delaware River's Scenic Sights, Historic Sites." *The Allentown Morning Call.* Reprinted in the *Las Vegas Review Journal,* 20 September 1992.

"Evident Deer Hunt Will Soon Resume and that McCormick's Deer Drive Will Get Lasky Money." *The Coconino Sun,* November 28, 1924.

"Filming Of Famous Grey Novels to Carry Fame of Our Scenery over World." *The Coconino Sun,* September 14, 1923.

"Grey's Secretary Here." *The Coconino Sun.* August 26, 1927.

"Last Bar Removed: Small Army Now Is Bivouacked North of Grand Canyon to Begin Big Deer Drive." *The Coconino Sun,* December 12, 1924.

"Part of Zane Grey Party Returns to Flagstaff." *The Coconino Sun,* November 12, 1920.

"Zane Grey Classifies Hollywood Movies." *The Coconino Sun,* October 29, 1927.

"Zane Grey Got Only One Bear." *The Coconino Sun,* November 4, 1921.

"Zane Grey Got Three Bears in Tonto Basin." *The Coconino Sun,* November 10, 1922.

"Zane Grey Here to Hunt and Film Latest Story Says We've Sure Grown." *The Coconino Sun,* September 30, 1927.

"Zane Grey Party Is Touring the North." *The Coconino Sun,* August 30, 1929.

"Zane Grey Plans to Fish Hawaii Waters." *Star (Honolulu) Bulletin,* January 10, 1939.

"Zane Grey Tells Why Drive Failed." *The Coconino Sun,* December 19, 1924.

"Zane Grey Visits Boulder on Sunday." *Las Vegas Review-Journal,* November 20, 1933.

"Zane Grey Will Hunt Bears Again Next Year." *The Coconino Sun.* November 26, 1920.

INDEX